HOW TO
TELL THE
SCHOOL STORY

CONTRIBUTORS

JOHN W. ADAMSON
*Administrative Assistant,
Stockton, California*

FLOY CAMPBELL
*Director of Public Relations, Public Schools,
Oklahoma City, Oklahoma*

BLAIR E. DANIELS
*Lecturer, Audio-visual Education, Temple University; Principal, Chestnutwold School,
Haverford, Pennsylvania*

EUGENE C. FLINN
*Director of Public Relations, Public Schools,
Jersey City, New Jersey*

ROBERT E. GITELMAN
*Coordinator, Special Information Services, Public Schools,
Montclair, New Jersey*

ROBERT N. GROVE
*Superintendent of Schools,
Midland Park, New Jersey*

GEORGIA B. HOWE
*Former Supervisor of Special Projects,
Portland, Oregon*

NED S. HUBBELL
*Director of Information Services, Public Schools,
Port Huron, Michigan*

DORA MARY MACDONALD
*Director of Public Relations, Public Schools,
Duluth, Minnesota*

DONALD L. TAYLOR
*Associate Professor of Sociology, Southern Illinois University; former Supervisor, School Community Relations, Public Schools,
Salt Lake City, Utah*

HOW TO
TELL THE
SCHOOL STORY

LESLIE W. KINDRED

Professor of Educational Administration
Teachers College, Temple University

PRENTICE-HALL, INC.
Englewood Cliffs, N.J.
1960

How to Tell the School Story
Leslie W. Kindred

© 1960
PRENTICE-HALL, INC.
ENGLEWOOD CLIFFS, N.J.

LIBRARY OF CONGRESS
CATALOG CARD NO.: 60–9175

PRINTED IN THE UNITED STATES OF AMERICA

43548-C

How to tell the school story and tell it effectively is a problem confronting school systems in all parts of the country. This problem came into existence with the beginning of free, tax-supported, educational institutions. Neglected for many years, it has now grown to a point in size and importance where it is no longer easy to manage. Its solution, in part, requires the application of specialized knowledge and technical skill in the use of mass communication media.

This book presents much of the specialized knowledge and technical skill needed for using mass media to tell the school story. All but the first chapter is given over to a consideration of methods and techniques for conveying ideas and information to different types of audiences. It is by no means a complete manual, but it is a compilation of successful practices for interpreting public education and promoting cooperation of people in school affairs.

In any well-planned public relations program the use of mass media must be supplemented with other activities. For one thing, personal contacts with pupils, parents, neighbors, friends, and members of the community are important in creating good will and developing better understanding of the instructional program. For another, avenues through which the general public can make its needs, concerns, and opinions of the schools known are necessary to the improvement of education and the support it receives from citizens and taxpayers.

The chapters of this book were written by individuals who have spent many years working with media in the field of school public relations. These people constitute a wealth of experience and a source of information that is unique in the literature on relations between the school and community. Chapters 1, 8, and 11 were prepared by Leslie W. Kindred; Chapters 2 and 3 by Dora Mary Macdonald; Chapters 4 and 5 by Robert E. Gitelman; Chapter 6 by Georgia B. Howe; Chapter 7 by Blair E. Daniels; Chapter 9 by Ned B. Hubbell; Chapters 10 and 13 by Floy Campbell; Chapter 12 by John W. Adamson; Chapter 14 by Robert N. Grove; Chapter 15 by Donald L. Taylor; and Chapter 16 by Eugene C. Flinn. The concept and outline of the book was developed by Leslie W. Kindred, who also compiled and edited the manuscript.

We hope that school public relations workers will find this book helpful in refining and strengthening their own use of communication media, and that new workers will look upon it as a ready source of information on employing mass media to best advantage. The book should be of benefit, as well, to graduate students in their preparation for administrative positions and to teachers who are interested in taking over responsibilities in the public relations program of their districts.

The writers wish to express their appreciation to everyone who assisted in the preparation of the book. They would like to extend thanks especially to superintendents, public relations directors, principals, and teachers who furnished photographs, written descriptions, and samples of their work. A note of thanks is likewise due to the authors whose writings have been quoted and to the publishers who have granted permission to use copyrighted materials.

L. W. K.

CONTENTS

PLANNING THE STORY

The school story should be told according to a detailed plan of action—a plan conceived and put into operation in and by the local school system. Such a plan of action is the best assurance possible that essential information will be spread in the community and that communication will be established with members of selected audiences. As will be shown in this chapter, the development of a plan for telling the school story involves a number of important considerations and a logical sequence of procedures that must be followed carefully.

WHY TELL THE STORY?

Several reasons may be stated for telling the school story. Some are inherent in the social character of the institution; others arise out of circumstances under which it must operate. All describe the need for informing the people fully and accurately about the educational program and the responsibility they have for determining the quality of education their money buys.

PUBLIC OWNERSHIP

Perhaps the primary reason for talking about the

school at all is that the schools belong to the people. They have a *right* to know what is being done for the education of children, how well the efforts are succeeding, and whether or not certain problems are standing in the way of further progress. This right emerged from the long and often bitter struggle over the principle that all children should receive twelve years of schooling at public expense. Once this principle won acceptance, it was written into the constitutions of the several states and progressively translated into a body of statute laws. These laws spell out clearly the power of the people to act on the selection of school board members, tax rates, bond issues, curriculum offerings, and related matters. Popular decision sets the limits within which the schools may function and influences, fundamentally, the policies and programs adopted by public representatives—state legislators, school board members, supervisors, principals, and so on.

Those who represent the people in the management and direction of local school systems have both a legal and a moral obligation to render an accounting of their stewardship. They must place the state education plan in operation, and they must supplement that plan to meet local needs; this means that they must interpret the needs and interests of people in the community and express what they find in the policies and programs of the system.

Interpreting the needs and interests of the people is a difficult task for lay boards of education; the members ordinarily do not have the necessary formal preparation. It is their right, however, to exploit the knowledge and talent of administrators and other professional staff members who are employed in the system. These people can be assigned to find out what the public wants in the schools and can prepare reports for the board of education so that the board can tell the public about the purposes, programs, problems, and accomplishments of the schools.

Unfortunately, too many boards of education are indifferent to their obligation of rendering an accounting to the people except when partisan issues arise or proposals must be made that require popular approval. As a result, citizens in the community often lose contact with the schools and become apathetic toward them. This condition is apparent in the reluctance of many parents and taxpayers to provide more than minimal financial support for education.

PUBLIC UNDERSTANDING

Inadequate reporting by boards of education and their professional workers has aggravated the need for increasing popular understanding of the schools. People generally do not know much about the instructional programs and the problems of schools in their own communities. For example, in the Michigan Communications Study,[1] a seven per cent random sample of citizens was interviewed in five separate communities. These men and women were asked ten rather simple questions about their schools. Out of the replies from a typical one hundred persons, it was found that only one *could answer all* of the questions correctly, that only one *could not answer any* of the questions correctly, and that the *average number* of correct responses was approximately five. A survey conducted in Detroit in 1954[2] produced the finding that only 25 per cent of the citizens knew that members of their board of education were elected to office by popular vote.

Even without the benefit of survey findings, it is apparent in conversations with parents and other citizens of the community that many possess a limited and superficial knowledge of such matters as provisions for slow learners, the nature and extent of guidance services, grouping in reading instruction, the quality of pupil achievement in basic subjects, activities of the student council, disciplinary policies, college success of high school graduates, remedial and corrective work in physical education, growth in pupil population, distribution of pupil intelligence, and related facets of the instructional program.

[1] "The General Public and the Public Schools," *Administrator's Notebook*, IV:1–2 (April, 1956).
[2] *Ibid.*

It is ironic that this condition should exist where public education depends for its support and advancement upon the understanding and cooperation of the people. Unless the average man on the street has a reasonable knowledge of what schools are doing and the purposes of their programs, particularly as they affect his children, he will not interest himself in their work nor approve the payment of higher taxes. The generalization is sound that the quality of public education in a community seldom rises significantly above the level of citizen understanding of and confidence in the educational program.

PUBLIC CRITICISM

The public schools have become a target of mounting criticism in recent years. Millions of written and spoken words are brought to citizens through every media of mass communication casting doubt upon, and spreading discontent about, the quality of instruction received by children. In fact, this avalanche of criticism is so great that it has taken on the characteristics of a national campaign.

The most common criticism is that children complete the elementary grades without having acquired the necessary skills in reading, writing, and arithmetic. This alleged failure to teach the fundamentals is often accompanied by the idea that helping the child adjust to life has replaced the absorption of knowledge as the major aim of the school. Along this same line, the complaint is made that secondary education has been watered down with easy courses—courses which no longer discipline the mind and provide the training which made the critics the astute scholars and successful businessmen they are today. The schools are also accused of promoting mediocrity and conformity instead of nurturing a healthy respect for excellence.

Other criticisms emphasize failure to teach moral and spiritual values; too much stress on extracurricular activities; indifference to the development of good study habits; poor preparation for college, jobs, and citizenship; retention of pupils who have neither the disposition nor the capacity to profit from a high school education; disorder in place of discipline; small enrollments in mathematics and science classes; neglect of the intellectually gifted pupils; lack of concern for the transmission of historical traditions; insufficient amounts of homework; careless use of English; textbooks that criticize free enterprise; the study of controversial issues such as those relating to housing, socialized medicine, and civil rights; useless courses in art, music, home economics, and driver education; lavish school buildings; and teachers who are overpaid for the amount of work they do.

Some of these criticisms are made by sincere and responsible citizens whose intent is that of improving the quality of education in public schools. A good many come from parents who have had unpleasant relationships with teachers and administrators with respect to the progress of their own children. A small number represent nothing more than attention-getting devices of professional cynics and blowhards. The majority, however, emanate from individuals and groups whose interests conflict with those of the public schools. They are the ones who try to influence and distort the feelings and thoughts of people.

And how valid are most of the criticisms and complaints that are heard today? The evidence shows that they are seldom supported with quantitative data and that they come from men and women who have had no contact with the schools for a long time. These people know practically nothing about modern teaching methods, the adaptation of instruction to individual differences, and procedures employed for the evaluation of pupil progress. If challenged, they are unwilling to search out the truth or even examine the facts placed before them. They prefer, instead, to rest their case on a series of disparaging labels and sweeping generalization, or else to build their own straw men and then knock them down.

Even though the bulk of criticism is unfair and misleading, still it represents a dangerous threat to the welfare of public education. Entirely too many people lack an adequate understanding of their schools, and they are unable to judge whether the complaints they hear are justified. Already the minds and feelings of some have been won over by the critics and others will follow unless something is done. In countering the current wave of propaganda, it must be remembered that the American people have always had faith in the system of public education; they have demonstrated on more than one occasion that they can think and act constructively when they understand a situation. There is every reason to believe that they will respond and stand behind the work of the schools when the facts are laid before them in a clear and understandable fashion. It would seem obvious, then, that the antidote to any misinformation is an attractively presented, well-disseminated, full and truthful report about the schools as they really are.

EDUCATIONAL PROGRESS

Progress in public education depends in large measure upon the consent of parents and other citizens in the community. While it is true that schools have been forced to adjust programs and provide new services to meet the personal and social needs of a growing pupil population, it is equally true that the basic pattern of education has remained fairly constant. This pattern is deeply rooted in the past and it has the support of the people. They have resisted consistently many excellent ideas and proposals for change because they departed from traditional beliefs and opinions.

Great stress is still laid on the memorization of bodies of subject matter found in textbooks, despite the fact that much of this material is abstract and unrelated to the lives of pupils. Pupils are expected to conform to established academic standards or fall by the wayside even though they vary tremendously in interests, cultural background, and the capacity to learn. The measure of success is principally achievement scores on teacher-made and standardized tests related to the content of instruction without much regard for citizenship behavior, skill in problem solving, use of critical thinking, application of principles, interpretation of data, social relationships, and other essential goals of a well-rounded education.

This design of education might be more acceptable in a static society, but it has no place in one where life is being altered almost daily through the contributions of science, where political problems have taken on new and different dimensions, where democracy is being challenged and threatened by the impact of other ideologies, where new skills and knowledges are necessary to keep up with technological developments, and where the individual must adapt his behavior to new conditions and apply his knowledge to the solutions of personal and social problems.

The great need for revising traditional education has not been recognized nor understood by the vast majority of the American people. They have been content to preserve and perpetuate a series of beliefs and practices that lag behind the demands of a world in which their children are living. This lack of progress will not be overcome until the public knows why change must take place and how it will benefit pupils and society.

FINANCIAL SUPPORT

In an economy with rising costs and a growing population, more money will be required to operate the schools. People must be made aware of the fact that new buildings have to be constructed and old ones replaced; that teachers must have sufficient and larger amounts of instructional supplies, equipment, and materials in order to do their work efficiently; that the curriculum must be revised and improved by trained men and women in the system with the aid of outside consultants; that salaries must be adjusted to living costs and made attractive enough to retain experienced teachers and bring new ones into the profession; that special services in guidance, health, remedial reading, transportation, and the like are essential to the education and welfare of pupils; and that clerks, custodians, and maintenance personnel must be employed and paid decent wages. These needs must be explained carefully and their relationships to rising costs pointed out clearly.

The problem, however, of securing adequate support of

schools goes beyond the understanding of need alone. For one thing, people must have confidence in the fiscal management of their schools. They must be convinced that public funds are being handled wisely before they will approve higher expenditures. They should be told of the budgetary procedures employed in the local system and the measures taken to effect economies. If evidence of good fiscal management cannot be presented to the people, then the reasons for deficiencies should be stated and proposals made for their correction. Complete integrity is basic to the development of public confidence in the school's management of public funds.

For another thing, citizens should be given information as to the sources of school revenues. Such information helps to prevent misunderstandings about the amount of money allocated to education. They should be shown how much is received from local, state, and federal governments and the proportions that come from property, sales, income, and other taxes. The future will bring much more concern over the share that should be contributed from governmental units and the tax sources from which these monies are derived.

It is also in order to compare educational costs with those of other services. These services have made heavy demands on tax funds and they have been responsible for a relative decrease in the percentage apportioned to education. For example, the amounts allocated to highway construction and maintenance, public welfare, national defense, and governmental administration should be stressed. Not only should the public be made aware of the huge sums of money going to these services, but also of the fact that the dollar invested in education yields a higher return to the individual and the social welfare.

The problem of public consent for the adequate financing of schools now and in the future is one of the strongest reasons for telling the school story. Securing this consent requires a high degree of skill in presenting information that will command attention and reach all segments of the population.

PRESSURE GROUPS

A considerable number of organized groups in the country take a definite interest in the public schools. They take an interest for varied reasons—from advertising their wares to a captive and receptive audience to performing worthwhile services for the school.

Some of the more powerful of these groups conduct campaigns to influence school officials and to build supporting public opinion. Their methods include lobbying in state legislatures; attending board of education meetings; sponsoring of contests; conducting investigations; speaking at public meetings; providing speakers for classes in school; employing all the communications media—radio, television, the press—with methods varying from distributing literature to children, parents, and instructors to lending motion pictures to teachers; conducting special drives; and establishing front organizations to carry on their work. All too frequently the public is oblivious to the methods employed by pressure groups and the motives behind their action.

As a matter of common sense—as well as of good public relations—schools should cooperate with all groups in the community that have a wholesome and sincere interest in the welfare of children and the advancement of education. They should not, however, be parties to programs for the promotion of selfish interests. This distinction is of real importance because the public school is committed by heritage to the principle of being an impartial institution that is free from prejudice in its teaching.

Sometimes it is difficult to distinguish between genuine cooperation and exploitation on the part of pressure groups. As a result, a substantial number have managed to bring their influence to bear on the organization of courses of study in selected subjects, the supply and use of instructional materials, and the policies of the institution. They have succeeded in placing members on boards of education and securing the passage of legislation inimical to good instruction and the adaptation of that instruction to changing circumstances. They have obtained school sponsorship for a wide variety of contests as a means of advertising products and services. They have done effective work in a number of localities to keep school costs down and to defeat bond and millage proposals.

Pressure groups can be a threat to the normal functioning of the school. Steps should be taken to acquaint the public with their activities. This is difficult to do without alienating the good will of people who are sympathetic to the programs of some of these less desirable groups and who do not understand the motives behind them. The answer lies in the careful and continuous presentation of facts concerning the problems these groups pose and the involvement of leading citizens in the formulation of policies for handling these problems.

WHAT THE PUBLIC WANTS TO KNOW

Before decisions are reached on what additional information should be prepared and disseminated in the community, the schools should be looked at from the viewpoint of parents and taxpayers. A good many people have questions for which they would like answers from school officials. Others harbor attitudes and convictions that need correcting before they will stand behind increased support of public education. And if the findings of opinion polls are accurate, at least half of the citizens in typical communities have no opinions at all on important issues related to their local school systems. When taken together, these segments of the population constitute a large bloc of public opinion. This bloc of opinion is a starting place for building more and better understanding of the schools.

Certainly current criticism and complaint should be taken into account in deciding what the public wants to know about the schools. However, the emphasis in dealing with criticism and complaint should never be on defending educational policies and practices but rather on an affirmative explanation of how pupils are taught and the services they receive. For example, it would be a mistake to advance arguments in defense of homemaking courses that have been labelled "a fad and a frill" by critics in the community. A better technique is that of preparing an attractive publication for wide distribution. This publication should show what is done in these courses, their place in the curriculum, and their value to students. It would offset the criticism without engaging the school in a verbal contest with the critics. If questions are raised publicly concerning the nature and cost of guidance services, the chances are good that people generally are ill-informed on this subject. A series of publications, a television program, a motion picture, or illustrated talks at parent-teacher association meetings are devices that might clear the air and prevent the spread of hostility.

Studies have been made over the years on what citizens would like to be told about the schools. Some of these studies are listed in the chapter bibliography. They show consistently that people want information on the curriculum, opportunities for vocational preparation, teaching of moral and spiritual values, success of high school graduates in college, goals of education, practices for meeting individual differences, courses of study offered in high school, preparation for family life, qualifications of teachers, handling of discipline, homework policy, extracurricular activities aside from athletics, marking and promotion policies, pupil standing on tests, health teaching, comparison of the local system with others, and additional matters that are centered around the welfare and progress of pupils.

This, of course, presents another problem: What do particular groups of citizens want to know? Interviews with a panel of leading citizens can yield reliable information on prevailing attitudes, popular misunderstandings, and topics of general interest. Such interviews, though carefully planned and executed, can be conducted with ease and informality at times and places convenient to the individuals with whom they are held.

Opinion polling is another method which offers excellent opportunities for finding out what people think and what they want to know. Even a simple questionnaire distributed at parent-teacher association meetings often produces a wealth of sound

information. Mail ballots to parents or ballots taken by pupils
to a selected sample of the population help the school to gain a
deeper insight into the thoughts and feelings of people in the
community. Better still, interviews with a stratified random
sample of the population, using a well-designed ballot, will
produce accurate findings on the status of public opinion and
suggest what to include and emphasize in telling the school story.

THE OBJECTIVES ARE CLEAR

The objectives in telling the school story to the public are
clear. First, people should understand the purposes of education
in a democracy. They should know that there is *more* to be
gained in a good educational program than a mastery of the three
R's. This understanding is best accomplished when they are
given a voice in the determination of the philosophy and objectives of the local school system. Second, the story should seek
to develop a broader and deeper understanding of the instructional program. This can be done by an attractive presentation
of information covering existing opportunities for individual
growth and development, the nature of the curriculum from
kindergarten through the senior high school, and the methods of
teaching used in directing the learning process. Third, reports
should be made periodically on the accomplishments of pupils.
People want to know how well the children in the schools are
doing, how their achievement compares with that in other school
systems, and whether the results are better today than they were
in the past.

Fourth, changes in the nature and number of the pupil population should be emphasized and repeated often. Few laymen have
any real knowledge of what compulsory attendance laws and
accelerated birth rates have meant to the public schools. They
should know, for example, that enrolments in secondary schools
went up from 32 per cent of all high school age youth in 1920
to more than 80 per cent today. They should be made aware of
the fact that every pupil who is educable must be accepted and

given a chance to learn. They should see why a single program and common standards of accomplishment are not feasible with pupils who vary greatly in interests, needs, and capacities to learn. Moreover, the problems which a large and diversified population of youngsters has created in housing, supplies, courses of study, textbooks, and the like should be described to them.

Fifth, it is highly important that explanations be made of financial management of schools in the local district. People should know how much money has been received from local and state taxes and how it has been spent. They should be apprised of the factors behind the rising cost of education—such as salaries, new buildings, larger enrolments, new equipment, and better supplies. They should be shown exactly what educational services their money buys and how additional ones could be provided with adequate funds.

Sixth, citizens should become acquainted with problems facing the local school system. They should be told about overcrowded classrooms, inadequate play space, turnover of personnel, and poorly equipped shops. Schools should not be expected to produce excellent results under difficult circumstances beyond their control.

Seventh, popular confidence in the worth and value of the educational system should be increased. Under the impact of so much criticism, people tend to forget that this system has produced more high school and college graduates than any other in the world, that it has demonstrated the ability to meet the varied interests and learning capacities of thousands upon thousands of children and youth, and that it is responsible for the preparation of leaders in all walks of life.

Eighth, citizens should understand more fully the duties and responsibilities of those who direct and carry on the work of the school system. The majority of people seem to have only vague and undefined ideas of the duties performed by teachers, principals, chief administrative officers, and members of the board of education. The duties and responsibilities of these individuals should be described in detail and the value of their services indicated in reports that are made to the public. This is more important now than in the past because of the highly specialized nature of their work and the amount of money required to keep competent and well-trained individuals in the profession.

Ninth, the special services that play a vital part in the education of children should be explained. They should be explained for the reason that some citizens regard them as an unnecessary part of the educational program. Services such as guidance, health, transportation, remedial reading, corrective speech, recreation, and lunch do not mean much to the older members of the community and to taxpayers without children in the schools.

Tenth, citizens should be induced to assume greater responsibility for the quality of education provided by the local district. This can be achieved by showing the relationship between instructional practices and the adequacy of finance, by showing how the solution to existing problems depends upon popular interest and support, by showing how the school profits from the suggestions and advice of people in the community, by pointing out opportunities for citizen participation in school affairs, and by urging that both sides of a controversial issue be examined before decisions are made. The fact should likewise be stressed that the schools belong to the people and that they have an obligation in a democracy to see that children receive a first-rate education for their own sake and that of society.

Eleventh, the final objective should be that of establishing a strong partnership between the school and community. This means that parents and others should take an active part in the daily affairs of the institution, exchange ideas with school officials on the improvement of instruction, serve as consultants on the determination of policy matters, and undertake studies for the solution of significant educational problems. Nothing else does more to develop an intelligent understanding and appreciation of the school, its purposes, program, accomplishments, and limitations, or to cement firmer bonds of good will and loyalty to the institution.

DRAFTING THE PLAN

A detailed plan of action is necessary for achieving these objectives. The plan starts by finding out what people think and feel about their schools. More specifically, information should be gathered showing (1) what citizens know about such things as homework policy, promotion, disciplinary actions, instruction about health, teaching methods, and the marking system, (2) if people are dissatisfied with some phases of the school program and how widespread these dissatisfactions are in the community, (3) the points of conflict that exist between the school and individuals as well as organized groups, (4) what misunderstandings seem prevalent concerning the policies and practices of the system, (5) what the public should know to decide intelligently proposals to be made in the future, and (6) other problems to which attention should be given.

Pertinent information may be gathered in several ways, namely, through the observations of school officials; the recording of comments made by pupils, parents, clergymen, business leaders, friends, and neighbors; clippings from local newspapers; general conferences with parents and patrons on selected questions; individual interviews with a panel of representative citizens; and opinion polling using a stratified, random sample of the population.

The data collected by these methods may indicate that the stated objectives should be modified somewhat for realistic and practical reasons. If apathy and ignorance are dominant on the part of the population, this condition will have to be overcome before a strong partnership between the school and community can be built. The findings may indicate further that it would be best to concentrate more heavily upon an interpretation of the special services provided by the system than to spend time trying to promote understanding of board and administrative responsibilities. This does not mean that the principal objectives should be pushed aside, but rather adjustments should be made until it is feasible to pursue them directly.

The next step in drafting the plan is to block out the broad lines of action that will be followed in telling the story. Perhaps more attention should be focused upon the value of personal contacts and the in-service training of personnel as interpreters of the system and as its ambassadors of good will. Perhaps a whirlwind campaign should be conducted to cut down the spread of criticism and promote a more accurate understanding of the instructional program. Perhaps effort should be limited for the time being to solving the more immediate problems which offer promise of quick success. Perhaps it is more necessary to lay a solid groundwork of understanding of needs and conditions in anticipation of a millage campaign in two years. Perhaps two or three broad lines should be followed concurrently, judging from the data on what people think and feel about the schools.

Once the broad lines of action have been determined, attention should be turned to the question of the appeals to be used in telling the story. The art and science of advertising has demonstrated unequivocally that information must be hung on a peg or theme that attracts attention and touches the thoughts and feelings of people. As examples, a booklet describing the duties of guidance personnel would have slight appeal compared with one telling how the problems of children are handled by this service branch of the school system; the human interest factor would draw readers into the publication. A radio program dramatizing the saving of tax dollars through efficient business management would be received more widely and leave a deeper impression on taxpayers whose pocket books are involved than a fine lecture on the purchase, storage, and distribution of equipment and supplies by the business office. Teaching love of country through the social studies as a theme for an all-school exhibit has an emotional appeal that brings a response in people much faster than a theme emphasizing a knowledge of national history. Unless information presented to the public is made appealing, the chances of establishing communication are reduced greatly.

The actual methods to be used in telling the story should be brought into the plan at this point. Their selection will vary with the purposes that have been formulated, the nature of the audience, funds and facilities available, and the competence of personnel. For example, if one purpose is to clear up wide-spread misunderstanding of the reading program within the shortest time possible, the methods employed would differ considerably from those used to bring about a much deeper parental understanding of the philosophy and objectives of the school. The nature of the audience often dictates the choice of method and technique more than is generally realized. For instance, an annual report in tabloid newspaper form would appeal to more people in one community than another because of differences in reading habits. Activities for spreading ideas and information are influenced strongly by the availability of funds and facilities. As an example, there may not be enough money to put out letterpress publications for wide distribution. Quite often plant facilities prohibit the staging of pupil demonstrations for large audiences or equipment is lacking with which to undertake worthwhile public relations projects. The competence of personnel may determine the extent to which mass media play a part in telling the story. It takes individuals with knowledge and experience to prepare materials and programs for reaching the public through these channels of communication. However, there are usually men and women on the instructional staff who can work successfully with mass media after receiving appropriate training.

In order to facilitate the smooth handling of work connected with the program, some form of organization must be developed. It should include a description of the relationship of one functionary to another and a definition of their respective responsibilities. Provision should likewise be made for supervision and coordination of the entire undertaking.

The last step is to place the entire program on paper so this blue print for action may be reviewed by all personnel in the system. It should be recognized that changes in the blue print are inevitable as experience is gained in working with the program and adjustments must be made to new needs and conditions.

RULES THAT COUNT

In carrying out the plan for telling the school story, certain rules should be followed. Although some of these were implied in the discussion of planning, nevertheless they are worth repeating. Experience has proven that they must be observed if the plan is to be successful. First, a skilful use of media is necessary to establish communication with the public. People will not take the time or trouble to acquaint themselves with facts and figures unless they are interpreted and presented in an attractive setting. Second, information should be presented in terms that appeal to the interest of the audience for whom it is intended. Individuals are drawn to ideas and concepts that line up with their own patterns of thought and action. Third, all information presented to the public must be truthful—it has to be truthful to win the sympathetic understanding and confidence of citizens. Fourth, the story must be told simply, patiently, and persistently. Ease of comprehension and repetition for fixing recall are essential ingredients of good communication. Fifth, the story must be kept in balance so that all aspects of the school program are presented and interpreted to parents and others in the community. And sixth, the fact must be accepted that all persons who hear the story will not take a constructive interest in the school. The attitudes and opinions of some will not be changed in the slightest, and others will remain fairly neutral in their reactions to the school. It is the large middle group whose cooperation and support are wanted in raising the sights of education in the community.

BIBLIOGRAPHY

Bortner, Doyle M., "A Study of Published Lay Opinion on Educational Programs and Problems," *Education*, 71:641–50 (June, 1951). A summary of findings and conclusions drawn about the attitudes and opinions of laymen concerning elementary and secondary education. Useful in checking judgments made in planning local school public relations programs.

Boss, Henry T., "What Earlier Polls Have Shown," *The Phi Delta Kappan*, 27:66–74 (November, 1955). This study was made to find out what effect on public opinion resulted from the recent heavy criticism of schools. The results of this poll were compared with those of earlier polls on similar items.

Crosby, Otis and Philip J. Proud, "What Citizens Really Think About Their Schools," *The Nation's Schools*, 52:61063 (November, 1953). This article reports the findings of an opinion measurement study conducted in Michigan.

Hines, Vynce A. and Hulda Grobman, "What Parents Think of Their Schools and What They Know About Them," *The Bulletin* of the National Association of Secondary School Principals, 41:15–25 (February, 1957). Data are reported from a study covering the points contained in the title of the article.

Kindred, Leslie W., *School Public Relations*. Englewood Cliffs, N.J.: Prentice-Hall, Inc., 1957. Chapters 1, 2, 4, 5. These chapters discuss the public character of the school and the preparation that should go into the development of a school public relations program.

Lovelace, Walter B., "Surveying the Survey," *The Phi Delta Kappan*, 27:61–66 (November, 1955). The results of two surveys are reported here. The findings indicate that citizens have confidence in their schools despite the wave of criticism.

McCloskey, Gordon, *Education and Public Understanding*. New York: Harper and Brothers, 1959. Chapters 1, 2, 3, 4, 6. These chapters deal with the context of public understanding of schools and the process of communication.

Merrill, Edward C., Jr., "A School Board Should Know How the Word Gets Around," *School Board Journal*, 130:29–31 (February, 1955). A helpful analysis of how opinion is formed on school issues.

The public is interested as never before in public school education, but the public, unfortunately, tends to be either misinformed or uninformed about the schools. This is the problem that faces us. Educators must accept this situation and attempt to reshape the popular picture of the schools. Perhaps the most vital—and immediately available—means of communicating with the public is the press. As a result, most educators must wear two hats, one as an educator and the other as a newspaper reporter.

While newscasts on radio and television may have a stronger impact at the moment, they are of necessity brief and fleeting, while a newspaper story with its details is a tangible thing to which the reader can refer. When he "sees it in print" in a reputable newspaper, the reader can believe a story and, with a chance to reread it, is less apt to be left with a confused idea. A national magazine has conducted a campaign on the slogan "It is the written word that lives."

IMPORTANCE OF GIVING SCHOOL INFORMATION

Most school people agree that one of their responsibilities is to inform the public about the schools. They realize that taxpayers have a big investment in the schools and have a right to know what they are getting for their money and effort. The public, taxpaying and non-taxpaying—if there are any such animals left—has more than a financial interest; it has the future of its children at stake.

Schools are not altogether altruistic in supplying information. They are looking for support, financial or other, and they know that an informed public is more likely to support its schools; nobody wants to "buy a pig in a poke." The report from the White House Conference on Education stated: "It is our firm conviction that when the people have all the facts, they will make the right decisions."

Although publicity is only a part of a public relations program, it is a vital part. However, mere reporting is not enough; school activities frequently need interpretation. This interpretation can sometimes be better accomplished through a story than by any other means. For instance, when Mrs. M——— visited her son in the fifth grade, she came away from school bemoaning to any person who would listen that, "There's just no discipline. The kids were all around the room, sitting in groups and talking, and the teacher didn't even care." It took a newspaper story about the committee work in that class to interpret school discipline to Mrs. M———.

PURPOSE OF GIVING SCHOOL INFORMATION

The purpose of giving school information is neither publicity nor interpretation alone. The purpose is to shape an attitude favorable to the schools. Moffitt states it: "Interpreting the schools is the art of influencing and channeling the emotions, actions, and minds of men."

This concept of publicity to mold public opinion is not an idea conceived in the space era. Over a hundred years ago, Abraham Lincoln said: "Public sentiment is everything. With public sentiment nothing can fail; without it, nothing can succeed. Consequently, he who molds public opinion goes deeper than he who enacts statutes or pronounces decisions. He makes statutes or decisions possible or impossible to execute."

The purpose of school publicity is not entirely a bid for support; it is also a means of encouraging progress in education. "The schools reflect the community" is an axiom. If members of the community know only the type of education they experienced twenty years ago, a Model T curriculum will satisfy them, even in this jet age. No one wants an automobile with swivel seats or a stereophonic phonograph if he has not heard of them; advertisers know this. A community must be informed about modern educational opportunities if it is to demand or even acquiesce to quality in its local schools.

Giving information about the schools serves still another purpose. The public reads articles in magazines about national school problems and conditions. When Dad reads in his favorite magazine that children are not taught to read in today's school or that Russia's schools offer a better education than America's, he believes it—and spreads the information.

PEOPLE READ ABOUT SCHOOLS

Schools are news; in fact, they have become page one news. Newspapers realize this, as is obvious from the increased amount of space given to stories on public education.

Joy J. Taylor, former newspaper woman, now editor of publications for schools in San Bernardino, California, comments:

Time was when the only school news hitting the newspaper pages with nods of approval from seasoned editors was on the occasion of a rampant board of education session, a superintendent absconding with the system's funds or teachers wailing for higher pay.

Today some newspapers and school systems in California are learning together that well-written, honest, and interpretive news stories on school curriculum and activities and problems of the district can fall in the "news story" classification instead of "publicity."[1]

[1] Joy J. Taylor, *Partners in Public Relations*, California Teachers Association Journal, 53:9, October, 1957.

From 1955–56 through 1956–57, the total number of column inches of school news in the San Bernardino *Sun* increased from 16,591 to 23,728. Moreover, a readership survey of the 64,000 subscribers showed that 30,000 people had an interest in reading about the schools, and 19,780 read the weekly Sunday column on schools.

A similar readership survey of the Sunday *News Tribune* of Duluth, Minnesota, with approximately 70,000 circulation, determined that about 15,000 women and 10,000 men in Duluth alone read the education page in a single issue. In the trade area, about 49,000 readers indicated they had read the text in whole or in part.

Comments Orville Lomoe, executive editor of the Duluth *Herald* and the *News-Tribune*: "We feel that in giving the community information on the schools, the press has helped signally in obtaining passage of two school bond issues to finance a building program and in developing schools with an educational program that meets the standards of the community and the educators."

The *Herald* (a daily evening newspaper) and the *News-Tribune* (a daily and Sunday newspaper) devoted about 4,000 inches to school stories in 1957–58, including, during the school year, a weekly page for students and a weekly page in the Sunday magazine section.

WHAT PEOPLE WANT TO READ ABOUT THEIR SCHOOLS

It is not enough for schools to supply information they feel the public should have; they also have to give information the public wants to read. The public has definite ideas of what it wants to know about schools.

Back in 1929, Belmont Farley, former chief of press and radio for the National Education Association, made a study to determine what people wanted to know and how much space newspapers devote to these areas. He found the percentage of news space devoted to 13 topics to be:

Topic	Per cent
1. Extracurricular activities	47.1
2. Teachers and school officers	9.2
3. Parent-Teacher Association	8.2
4. Pupil progress and achievement	5.6
5. Board of education and administration	5.2
6. Course of study	5.0
7. Business management and finance	4.8
8. Buildings	4.1
9. Health	3.3
10. Methods of instruction	2.9
11. Discipline	1.7
12. Value of education	1.5
13. Attendance	1.3
Total	99.9

In contrast, the study found that 5608 patrons in 13 cities rated their interest thus:

1. Pupil progress and achievement
2. Method of instruction
3. Health of pupils
4. Courses of study
5. Value of education
6. Discipline and behavior of pupils
7. Teachers and school officers
8. Attendance
9. Buildings and building program
10. Business management and finance
11. Board of education and administration
12. Parent-Teacher Association
13. Extracurricular activities

A comparison of these two ratings shows clearly that at the time the study was made, newspapers were giving nearly half of the school space to extracurricular activities, which rated lowest in reader interest.

In American Education Week, 1958, the public schools in Duluth, Minnesota, conducted an opinion poll of visitors to an open house at the schools. The poll had one question based on Farley's study. Parents—5761 of them—were asked to check the first three topics about which they wanted more information. Results of the poll were:

		Per cent
1. Pupil progress and achievement	3742	25
2. Methods of teaching	3092	21
3. What pupils study	2810	19
4. Special services (reading clinic, classes for the handicapped, program for pupils with superior ability, audio-visual aids, health program, guidance and counseling, driver training)	1815	12
5. Discipline	1276	8
6. The activity program (games, sports, programs, clubs)	802	3
7. Buildings	444	3
8. Board of education proceedings	371	2.5
9. Textbooks	357	2.3
10. School costs	328	2.1

Although there are deviations in the two questionnaires, the ratings do not differ greatly. The items ranked first and second are the same; Duluth's third in interest is ranked fourth in Farley's study, but that one has an intervening item not included in the Duluth questionnaire. A difference in administering the latter questionnaire was that, instead of ranking all subjects in order, parents were asked to rate the three in which they were most interested.

It would seem, however, that schools and newspapers now recognize what patrons want to know and are making an effort to give them what they want. In the San Bernardino *Sun*, referred to earlier, during the school year 1955–56 through 1956–57, curriculum stories increased 50 per cent; professional growth stories increased 62.7 per cent; Science Fair, 57.8 per cent; and special programs, including the "more capable learner program," 79.2 per cent.

A PUBLIC INFORMATION PROGRAM

Grinnell and Young give these characteristics of a good information program:

It is planned; it is continuous; it is intrinsic; it is dynamic and interesting, it is well balanced; it is designed to reach everyone in the community; it uses all media available; it should be flexible.[2]

That about covers it. However, one item especially might be enlarged upon—*designed to reach everyone in the community*. The schools have varied publics: their own professional group, the pupils, the parents, and the rest of the community—management and labor, Democrats and Republicans, the mentally retarded and the geniuses—with indiscriminate overlapping among these groups. The public information program is designed to reach each of these publics in a way that it can easily understand.

BASIC PRINCIPLES OF THE PROGRAM

Integrity is the basis of any sound public information program. One teacher assigned to the work was given only one bit of direction by her superintendent: "Be honest in everything you write, even though it might not be complimentary to the schools. Just tell the truth—that's all." That was good advice—but it does not mean that one need go out of one's way to hunt up weaknesses in the system. Once a school story is published that is biased, or a half-truth, or an exaggeration, or a whitewash job, both the public and the newspaper editor lose faith in information coming from the schools. A news story that tells what young people are doing in a program for academically superior pupils when the program is only on paper is worse than no story at all. Failure to give the true context of a statement is a particularly dangerous error—especially when working with statistics. Consider the previously mentioned public opinion poll taken in Duluth. Every time its results are cited, it must be explained that it was answered only by parents visiting schools—in other words, by people especially interested in the schools. If the school should intimate that the results are the thinking of the entire community, the whole thing is dishonest.

The positive approach is another important ingredient of a

[2] J. E. Grinnell and Raymond J. Young, *The School and the Community* (New York: The Ronald Press, 1955), pp. 200–205.

good school information program. It is wasted energy to try to defend the schools against adverse criticisms. Schools *should* need no defense; they should need only to have the true story told. As an example, in one city there was a swelling undercurrent of criticism among sports enthusiasts about the rental price for use of the public school stadium. "The stadium is paid for by the community, and teams shouldn't have to pay a percentage of their gross receipts from a game to use it." The school news director wrote a feature on the maintenance department of the schools. It began:

> It's fourth down and one yard to go for a touchdown for the home team. The crowds at Public School Stadium are screaming in excitement —all but one man, who paces the sidelines muttering to himself, "They're getting the field all cut up." He is Henry Campbell, foreman of general maintenance for the board of education.
>
> Campbell has respect for each blade of grass on that gridiron, and he flinches when he sees a chunk of turf plopped into the air by a brisk scrimmage.

The story went on to tell about the time, materials, and cost of maintaining the football field and the stadium seats. Then, in order to turn the obvious reaction to good use, the story explained that "The taxpayers don't pay for all of this" and told exactly what percentage of the receipts each team paid in rental for the field. While the story may not have mollified the drugstore quarterbacks, it had its effect on a large number of other taxpayers.

The present-day criticisms of schools as "soft"—as not giving a sound academic program, as being devoted to fads and frills— all were met by at least one superintendent in a story which mentioned no criticisms, but merely enlarged on the philosophy of the local schools: Education for All. It explained the course of study in terms of the needs and abilities of *all* the pupils— from the extremely bright to the dullards.

Perhaps one of the biggest mistakes educators have made in

COURTESY *Duluth News-Tribune.*

The community serves the schools. Material from the local dairy council.

public information programs in the past has been to work with the press only when there is a crisis or a special activity. A good program is built upon a continuous flow of news, not upon sporadic attempts at publicity. A good information program ties in the schools and the community. It reports on field trips into the community, on members of the community who have unique contacts with the schools—persons of special interest to the students who appear before the class—it tells what community organizations are doing for the schools, and it carefully reports classroom study of the community, from the work of "community helpers" in the first grade to the survey of local needs, problems, progress, institutions, and government made by a senior high school group. An information program seeks to place stories in all departments of the newspaper—news, women's page, feature section, sports, and even in the advertising section. The women's editor will take a feature on an art class making

Christmas decorations or a home economics class making cookies —with recipes, as a final touch.

ORGANIZATION OF A NEWS SERVICE

The organization for maintaining a news service differs in various communities. The one constant factor is that some, one person should have the responsibility of directing the public information program. Reporting activities cannot be left to chance.

As the chief administrative officer, the superintendent of schools has the responsibility of interpreting the school program. However, it is unrealistic to think that a superintendent can act as something of a press officer and still solve the problems of finance, building programs, curriculum changes, and bus service for the fourteen-year-old who lives a half-block off the line. While he is always available to the press, he frequently assigns someone to the news service—a teacher, who is given a lighter teaching load; a committee; or a full-time director, responsible directly to him.

Such a director may hold any one of a number of titles—anything except publicity director or press agent. He is frequently called a public relations director, director of school-community relations, assistant to the superintendent. With such titles, news service is only a part of the program; consequently, he may be called a director of information services or of news services. The title is unimportant, but the job is clearly defined—to work with the press to help give honest, unbiased information to the public about the schools. He cannot do the job alone; he needs the cooperation of the entire school staff. Generally, he is a teacher with some journalistic training or experience, or he may be a journalist who devotes his skills to the interpretation of education.

Directors distribute their activities among different organizations, but from the central publications office come the assignments, and in the office is kept the "future book," a calendar of events, and a scrapbook of all clippings from newspapers. A general plan of operation may be summarized somewhat like that following:

Responsibility for the release of school publicity to local news outlets should be centralized in one or more offices, depending upon the size of the school system.

The school's publicity office should maintain a calendar of school publicity on a year-long basis, with stories spaced throughout the twelve months.

The superintendent in every district should maintain his own news notebook, such as a desk calendar, in which pertinent news items can be noted.

Flow of news from the school staff can be facilitated by using news-story forms, which are in the hands of all the teachers.

A file should be maintained for recording publicity ideas and materials.

A second working file should be maintained for articles produced by the school.

Valuable help and information will be gained from exchanging publications and other materials with school systems throughout the state and nation.

Superintendents should plan some form of regular contact with the press.

The plan of operation—which should be a definite part of administrative policy—should be discussed at faculty meetings early in each school year.

Every relationship of the school to the press should be on a professional basis.[3]

TYPES OF NEWS SERVICES

Joy Taylor tells how the San Bernardino school news organization began:

A meeting of school administrators, the school public information person and newspaper editors was called. Several policies were adopted. . . .

1. All news except that developing from journalism and public relations of the two high schools would be channelled through the school's publication office, with the newspaper reserving the right to make contacts with the schools.

[3] *Public Relations for America's Schools*, Twenty-eighth Yearbook, American Association of School Administrators, 1950, pp. 277–279.

2. Special feature picture on holidays, and the closing and opening of school would rotate from school to school.

3. Workshops would be presented by the newspaper for school personnel (one for elementary and another for secondary schools) at which time newspaper techniques and headaches in covering schools would be presented.

4. Picture pages from the schools were authorized, if the pages had reader interest and could be developed into top newspaper material.[4]

Some school systems have an advisory council or committee of staff members; this is true of Wilmington, Delaware, and Urbana, Illinois. In Wilmington, however, an administrative assistant is responsible for releases from administration and a coordinator for system-wide stories, while each school and department sends in its own news releases. In Urbana, news releases are channelled through the committee. In other systems, the program varies from clearing everything through a central news desk to the almost complete autonomy of each school in regard to the release of its own news.

CHECKING WITH THE CENTRAL OFFICE

In most systems where the representatives of individual schools send stories directly to the newspaper, they are asked to send a carbon copy of releases simultaneously to the central office. This is important, not for checking or censorship, but for record purposes. If, however, stories *are* handled through one office, there will be no repetition. A story about merit award winners should be sent to the paper, not from one high school, but from all in one story. The news director can establish control here by watching the copy channelled through his office.

WHO GATHERS THE SCHOOL NEWS

In the organizations previously mentioned, teacher-reporters and directors of information services gather the news. However, there are others who perform the service.

[4] Joy J. Taylor, "Curriculum is News," *American School Board Journal,* 138:27–28 (February, 1959).

THE NEWSPAPER COVERS THE SCHOOL BEAT

Big newspapers include education editors and writers on their staffs. Benjamin Fine, Fred Hechinger, Tony Ferrar, Millicent Taylor are only a few of those whose names are synonymous with good education writing, particularly on the national level. For the local story, however, newspapers generally assign a reporter to cover the schools. He is apt also to cover sundry spots, including, perhaps, night clubs and other entertainment places. He may or may not see public school education as the hope of the future; he may feel he has done his job if he merely asks the superintendent, "What's new?" or attends monthly

COURTESY *Duluth Herald.*

"For this I pay taxes?" Schools need interpretation.

board of education meetings. Usually, he does not have the background for interpretation of the schools; he has not been exposed to courses in "Education, history of" or "Methods of teaching." He can spend a half-day in a kindergarten, give an honest report of activities and at the same time create among taxpayers the reaction: "For *this* I pay my taxes? Why can't the kids play at home?"

To interpret the schools, the reporter must know the educational principles behind activities. He must know that children learn through play. He must know that the little girl working at a pegboard is developing small muscles that will later be used in writing; that the youngster engrossed in doing a jigsaw puzzle is learning to differentiate shapes and sizes, to help him to identify letters by configuration when he begins to read. The average reporter cannot be expected to know these things; he needs help if he is to realize not only *what* is going on, but the *why* of the activity. Teachers are the ones who can give him the greatest help. The reporter cannot spend all his time in all the schools. Without the cooperation of educators, he is bound to slip up on some of the good stories the readers want. Teachers can give him tips on such stories.

STUDENTS COVER THE NEWS

In some school systems students help to gather the news and write copy. The Abington Township School District in Abington, Pennsylvania, channels news through a senior high school press group under the director of public relations. A teacher-adviser and the principal edit the copy. Senior high school students take an intensive training program given by the PR director, visit a city newspaper office, attend an instruction clinic conducted by a local newspaper editor, and participate in the Columbia Scholastic Press Association convention. Then they hold a clinic to instruct teacher-advisers and young reporters.[5]

[5] *Let's Go to Press* (Washington, D.C.: National Public Relations Association, 1954), p. 43.

COURTESY *Duluth Herald*

Student-written pages are a weekly feature of the Duluth, Minnesota, Herald.

The Duluth *Herald* also runs a school page once a week. A publications adviser in each high school appoints one student to write one or two big stories of the week for each issue. Student-reporters request a press photographer for pictures. A newspaper staff man is editor of the school page. He holds a dinner for the advisers early in the year for preliminary planning, and conducts the students through the newspaper office, with a box lunch provided in a lunch room. At the close of the year, the paper gives a dinner and gifts to the advisers and students. The *Herald* also gives a "working scholarship" to the outstanding reporter. He works with a salary on the paper during the summer.

HOW-TO-DO-IT PUBLICATIONS

Just as newspaper reporters have had no courses in education, most teachers have had no training in journalism. To help them, various directors of news services have prepared booklets which set forth their duties, procedures in reporting, types of stories, and techniques of journalism style. Indianapolis, Indiana, and Champaign, Illinois, have each sent out a "primer in public relations" which includes information on getting and writing school news. *News and Views* is a booklet from the publications office in San Bernardino, California, issued to help teachers tell the school story.

It is rather common practice to send blank forms to teachers, which make reporting easier. Here is a simple news reporting form:[6]

DATE ....

WHO ....
WHAT ....
WHEN ....
WHERE ....
HOW ....
STORY GIVEN BY................
REMARKS ....

PHONE ....

[6] *Ibid.*, p. 45.

WHAT IS NEWS?

"News is a report of a recent event," states Webster's dictionary. It then gives a second definition that should be ingrained in the mind of every individual submitting material to a newspaper: "A matter of interest to newspaper readers." The definition of news used in many journalism classes is Bleyer's: "News is anything timely that interests a number of people; and the best news is that which has the greatest interest for the greatest number."

Newspapers are not interested in "giving publicity" to the schools; but they are vitally interested in publishing good stories. They receive a wealth of such stories every day—local stories, syndicated stories, and news service stories through press associations. A story on the schools has to compete with satellites, murders, disasters, which movie people are getting divorced or married, the lovelorn column, and what the President ate for breakfast. To meet this competition educators must submit newsworthy stories.

TESTING NEWS STORIES

Several criteria can be used to test the worth of a news story:

News must be timely. The old saying is that "news a day old is history." Editors want a story about an event *before* it happens, if possible. School reporters must remember this and not try to turn in a story about something that happened a week before.

A story has news value if it is connected with an event of national or general interest. The fact that high school pupils are studying political parties is of more interest at election time than at any other time. Introduction of Russian into the curriculum is of more interest now than it would have been ten years ago.

The unusual is of interest. When the teacher gives a report card to a child, that is routine. When she gives a card to the child's dog that has accompanied him to school every day, that's news. In fact, there are two elements there besides the unusual that appeal to a reader, a child and a pet.

"Names make news" is a cliché that is not entirely true; if it were, a newspaper would publish a list of the names in a telephone directory. However, big names do make news. When the superintendent of schools states that high school pupils are more serious about their work than in former years, the story is more newsworthy than if an unknown person made the statement. Of course, if the superintendent were caught in a gambling raid that would be *real* news, including the element of the unusual.

Stories of struggle and success have news value—the Negro boy who lives in the country, finances his way through high school by working at a drive-in, and receives a scholarship to Harvard; the deaf boy who is graduated from high school.

"People are essentially provincial," says Gunnar Horn. "To most of us incidents are newsworthy in relation to their proximity. The ten-dollar prize won by the girl next door is more interesting than the $10,000 prize awarded some author for the best first novel of the year—simply because *the girl* is next door."[7]

Events that will affect the reader have news interest. A proposed school bond issue is always good for the front page.

Stories about the schools and the curriculum can be tested by one or more of these elements.

HOW TO RECOGNIZE NEWS

Many a good school news story is lost to the public because it was not recognized as news by the only person who knew about it—the teacher.

DEVELOP A "NOSE FOR NEWS"

A "nose for news" is the natural attribute of some people. Consider, for example, the self-constituted news woman on the party line. Others have to develop their ability to smell out news. This is especially true of educators, whose study and experience have been far from the journalistic world. A nose for news is

[7] Gunnar Horn, *Public-School Publicity* (New York: Inor Publishing Co., 1948), p. 9.

just pure curiosity. What's going on in class? Why is that kid lugging a stuffed owl to school? Why is Miss J———so dressed up today? How come there seem to be so many more men teachers around this school? Herman A. Allen, education editor, Associated Press, has said, "How do you know when you have a story? Just ask one question: 'Who cares?' "

News is all around a school—it is bound to be, with so many human beings and fresh, new activities all in one building. Never can a good teacher truthfully say, "Nothing's happening. I don't have any news." She has only to take off the hat of the educator and put on the hat of the reporter, and then look around her classroom. A school story seldom appears that a teacher cannot say, "I could have written that." She can determine if she has a story by asking herself: *What's interesting in my class? Will it interest others?*

TYPES OF STORIES

The newspaper story is written to inform, to educate, or to entertain. To cover this field, there are two types of stories, the straight news and the feature. Not under consideration here are photographic stories, editorials, and "letters to the editor."

THE NEWS STORY

The straight news story is a straightforward account of a happening. It gives the facts, and that's that.

There are the advance story, which tells as much as possible about a coming event, the cover story (frequently telephoned), which reports happenings on the day they take place, and the follow-up story, which comes not more than a day after the happening. It is a summary, more complete than the cover story, which frequently contains interviews.

Besides stories of events that will take place at a specified time—meetings, programs, workshops—there is news of events that happen unexpectedly. Here are found stories of an award received, an accident, actions taken by the board of education.

THE FEATURE STORY

The feature story does not need to be so timely. It gives leeway to the creative ability of the writer, since it is not so formalized as the news story. Its basic element is *human interest.* Although it is considered the most difficult type to write, it is also the most fun to write, since it allows the writer to give perspective and emotional content to the story.

The schools abound in feature stories that could not get into the news. For instance, there is no earth-shaking news value in the fact that a first grade goes on a train ride to the next town; but a feature plays up the fact that while all these youngsters have ridden in automobiles and nearly all in planes, few have ever been on a train before; it gives their reactions in their own words. Many stories that do not qualify as news make good features. They can be more interpretive than news stories, but should be neither promotional nor propaganda.

Some features are a single shot; others are in series. The Duluth *News-Tribune* has perhaps one of the longest run series of education stories; it is now in its twelfth year. The story, with pictures taken by the press photographer, is a full page of the magazine section of the Sunday newspaper. The director of public relations gets ideas for these stories in five ways: (1) a teacher or a principal telephones that he thinks he has a story; (2) a reader or a parent telephones a suggestion (it's a happy day when a parent calls to say his little girl's class is doing something interesting); (3) a national story of wide-spread interest suggests a local angle; (4) the writer hears a rumor that needs the light of truth; (5) the editor suggests a story.

The first paragraphs of three of these stories show the wide range of subjects that can be covered:

Every evening at the dinner table, the first week of school, a father asked his small daughter, "What did you learn in kindergarten today?" The question brought only silence until the fourth day, when the youngster, bursting with pride, said triumphantly, "I learned two friends."

COURTESY *Duluth News-Tribune.*

"Brown and white go good together." A study in human relations fostered by the public schools, Duluth, Minnesota.

The little girl had learned one of the basic lessons in living in a democracy.

*   *   *

This is a story for those readers who are sick 'n tired of hearing about juvenile delinquents, hot rodders and the leather jacket boys. It is a story about the ninety-and-nine—the approximately 99 per cent of junior and senior high school pupils who measure up pretty well to standards for responsible citizens.

*   *   *

In a "country on wheels," safe driving is fundamental to life, liberty, and the pursuit of happiness; therefore, driver education is a part of the public school curriculum.

*   *   *

Perhaps nothing is more deadly to read than a list of school subjects. The Duluth *Herald*, however, ran a series of five stories during American Education Week, 1957, on "Mr. Smith Goes To School"—a series that began on the front page. The series tried to catch classroom atmosphere as well as interpret education. For instance, in the kindergarten:

> A small boy stood at the teacher's side, digging deep into his pockets.
> "I know I had it," he muttered, and then grinned happily as he handed something to the teacher. "Here it is. It's a present for you. It's the biggest ladybug I ever saw!"
> The teacher thanked him and put the gift with others from the children—a huge sack of dead leaves, a collection of rusty paper clips and an apple with small tooth marks in it.

The Duluth daily newspapers have run other stories of features: a reporter revisited his junior high school, attending classes; a reporter interviewed people in the community on *The teacher who did the most for me;* teachers wrote on *I Remember Teacher;* and 25 teachers wrote 25 articles on such subjects as *Literature vs. Comics; Problems Turn Out to be Privileges; Marks Don't Always Hit Mark; Pupils' Problems; Why I Like to Teach; Parents Can Help; Students, Teachers, and Homework.*

NEWS WRITING

The straight news story is fairly well confined to a format. It has two parts, a lead and a body. The lead, which is the first paragraph, tells the gist of the story. In the rest of the story, the body, details diminish in importance as the story progresses. There is a good reason for this organization; if the story has to be shortened, the copy reader can just chop off the last paragraphs, knowing that they are the least important.

The lead gives the essence of the story, in approximately 40 words or less. It answers the questions *who, when, where, what* and *why* (commonly called the Five *W's*) and sometimes *how*.

Here is an example of a conventional lead:

Local high school students (who) will meet with the Mayor (what) at 3 P.M. Monday (when) in the Council Chambers (where) to plan a workshop on city government (why).

The first sentence contains the most important fact of the story. The important element may be any one of the *W's* or *how*. What is important is determined to some extent by the public for which the story is written. For instance, a junior high school boy, well-instructed in this phase of leads, had an assignment for his school paper to write about the death of a member of the board of education. He began his story: "Students will have a holiday Monday afternoon because of the death of ———."

VARIETY IN LEADS

A newspaper would be monotonous reading if every lead were the same. The reporter can work for variety.

The *summary lead* gives the *Five W's* as in the above paragraph.

A clause or phrase may contain the *feature:*

If there is a way to learn about their city government, local high school students have found it.

A *crowded lead* packs a number of items:

Local high school students will meet . . . to plan a workshop on city government, to schedule a series of future meetings, and to organize a program of speakers from the City Council and departments, as preparation for Student Government Day.

A *1–2–3 lead* gives a numerical listing of items:

Local high school students and the Mayor are agreed that:

1. Students should know more about their city government.
2. A series of workshops could help them to learn about government.
3. City commissioners and department heads are the ones who can best conduct the workshops.

In a *contrast lead,* there is a change of thought:

High school students may dig rock 'n roll the most—but they're also interested in their city government.

The *question lead* is simple:

What do high school students know about their government?

A *descriptive lead* is seldom used, but is possible:

In the cold dignity of the City Council Chambers, teen-agers will meet. . . .

A *staccato lead* uses short sentences:

They want to know about their city government. They mean to find out. So they go to the Mayor. Local high school students . . .

An *epigram lead* uses a familiar quotation or phrase:

Curiosity killed a cat—but it leads local high school students to the Mayor to find out. . . .

A *quotation lead* might be:

"We want to know about our city government," says John Doe, president of the Student Council, "so we are meeting with the Mayor to plan. . . ."

HOW TO DO IT

The news story tells accurately—above all, accurately—and objectively about a happening. Editorializing, expression of opinion, or interpretation is taboo. The writer cannot say, "The new home economics laboratory is the equal of that in any school"—but he can quote the supervisor or the superintendent as making the statement. Whenever a writer gives a quotation, he must state its source.

Because the news story is objective, it is written in the third person. Only stories with a by-line may use the first person pronouns.

Sometimes a schoolman, not understanding the meaning of *news*, asks the school reporter to run an article on his pet philosophies. No self-respecting paper will use such a story, unless there is a news peg to hang it on. The reporter may have the man give this little masterpiece as a talk at some meeting. Then it (or part of it) can be reported in a story of the meeting. The city editor appreciates a copy of a talk before it is given, so that it can be condensed. A newspaper seldom gives the full text.

News stories are not fancy writing with beautifully constructed, complex sentences. Sentence structure is on a basis of subject, verb, object, but with an occasional phrase or clause to avoid monotony. The average length of a sentence is about 15 to 25 words; and the average length of paragraphs is 75 words.

The vocabulary is simple Anglo-Saxon words. The professional terms of the educator—pedaguese, baffle-gab, gobbledegook, or what have you—are carefully translated for the doctor, business man, housewife, mechanic and milkman. Such phrases as *maturation level* and *enriched learning experiences* are for the educator, not the public. One of the prize examples of pedaguese is quoted in *It Starts in the Classroom:*

The integrated curriculum, adapted to the maturation level of each child, includes geographical concepts coincident to the occurrence of proper interest stimuli.[8]

In a newspaper story, *curriculum* becomes *subjects*, and the whole thing could be written something like this:

Subjects are related to each other and suit the mental age of the

[8] *It Starts in the Classroom* (Washington, D.C.: National School Public Relations Association, 1951), p. 11.

child. They include ideas of geography in which the child becomes interested.

One education writer says that the highest compliment she ever received was from a taxi driver, who said, "I can understand every word you write in the paper."

A news style is streamlined. *Print It Right* says to beware of such wooly words as *problem, project,* and *question* unless the meaning is clear; time-markers such as *concerned, involved,* and *respectively;* and such shilly-shally phrases as *without question, it is the opinion of this writer,* and *eminent authorities assume.*[9]

A news story, like a conversation, should studiously avoid clichés, those tired, time-worn phrases such as: *each and every one, in every manner, shape and form, fads and frills, enemies of the public school.*

Picture nouns and vivid verbs replace the adjectives and adverbs that can clutter up a sentence. Instead of using the verb *said* with an adverb, one of the more than 100 verbs can be used: *whispered, shouted, explained, hooted.*

A verb in the active voice is more vivid and uses fewer words than one in the passive voice. "John Brown received a scholarship" has more impact than "A scholarship was received by John Brown."

Names must be spelled correctly and given in full. Mr. Smythe is incensed if he is referred to as Smith; that is not his name. The title *Mr.* is not used when the initials or the first name is given. In referring to women, *Miss* or *Mrs.* is used with the first and last names. The second time a name is used, *Miss* or *Mrs.* is used with the last name only. Some newspapers use the man's last name, the second time, without the title. A single initial is not used; the general style is two initials or the first name.

Newspapers vary in rules of style. The writer should ask for a style sheet or study the paper to determine the preferred capitalization, punctuation, abbreviations, and spelling.

[9] *Print It Right* (Washington, D.C.: National School Public Relations Association, 1953), p. 27.

PREPARING THE COPY

Newspaper copy is prepared according to certain rules. The reporter should:

1. use 8½ by 11 inch paper;
2. type *on one side of the paper only;*
3. double-space;
4. keep a carbon copy for reference;
5. type in the top left corner of the first page his name, the name and address of the school, and both the school and his home telephone number; type his name on each page;
6. in the top right corner, write *RELEASE* followed by the release date or the words *any time;*
7. number each page, on the top-center;
8. leave about a third of the first page blank, so the copy desk can write the headline there; leave a one-half inch margin on the *left* side of the page, and one inch at the *right* and *bottom;*
9. avoid hyphenation of words at the end of lines;
10. if possible, do not split a sentence or a paragraph at the bottom of a page;
11. if the story runs more than one page, type *MORE* at the bottom of each page except the last;
12. at the bottom of the last page, type the newspaper term *30* or # # # or *end.*

"A PICTURE IS WORTH 1000 WORDS"

The Chinese proverb may be a bit exaggerated, but the worth of a good picture in a newspaper story is not devaluated even in an era of inflation. This is an eye-minded period, as can be seen by motion pictures, television, and photojournalism.

WHAT MAKES A GOOD PICTURE?

A picture can be judged on its content or subject matter, its composition, and its photographic quality. *School Photojournalism* says: "To achieve maximum impact in our photograph—symbol—to make it as vivid and eye-catching as possible—we must achieve drama and emotion, action, sharp characterization, composition and strong play of light and shadow."[10] These

---

[16] *School Photojournalism* (Washington, D.C.: National School Public Relations Association, 1958), p. 19.

elements abide around school, because children are ideal subjects if not formally posed. Editors avoid like a plague any picture that looks posed. They call the pictures of people lined up looking as though they were facing a firing squad, "mug shots." The subjects in a picture should look natural. The little boy with the tousled hair and a sweat shirt makes a more natural picture than the lad with slicked down hair, shirt, necktie, and coat. It is better not to let children know that pictures are going to be taken. One little girl with pigtails and pinafore knew that she would have her picture taken playing her violin; her mother sent her to school next day with her hair in stiff formal curls and in a dark velvet dress with a lace collar. The picture was not typical of school. In contrast, a teacher should always know if

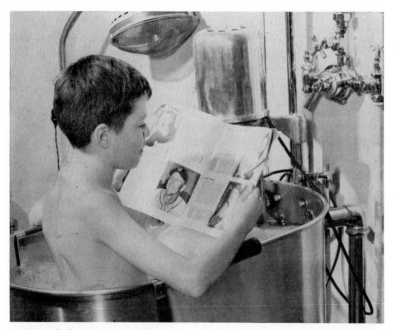

COURTESY *Duluth News-Tribune.*

Get human interest. In a whirlpool bath, a physically handicapped boy reads batting averages.

her picture is to be taken. Adults need the fortification of wearing the clothes in which they feel they appear best.

Pictures should report as honestly as a story with words. They should truthfully give classroom situations. At a time when schools are presenting Christmas pageants that are productions attesting the hard work of a teacher, it is refreshing to see The Christmas Story as youngsters present it in their classroom, with cut-out cardboard sheep and crude costumes. It is the simple rather than the showy classroom work that is appealing and that truly pictures the school.

According to press photographers, more than five people in a picture make a mob scene; three are better; and one is perfect. The idea gets across better. For instance, there is nothing appealing about a formal picture of a school orchestra; in the news-

COURTESY *Duluth News-Tribune.*

Get action into pictures.

paper, the heads are merely dots. However, a small section of the orchestra gives the same idea and is attractive.

Subjects should not stare at the camera. They should be in action, intent upon their work. Action is important in school pictures.

The choice of a subject sometimes poses a problem. Teachers universally want to have their best students in pictures, whether they are photogenic or not—or else they want the prettiest girls and the handsomest boys. A press photographer, however, does

COURTESY *Duluth News-Tribune.*

Go into the community for pictures on field trips.

not care a hoot if the freckled-faced, pigtailed girl with the mobile expression gets an *A* or an *F* in geography; he wants her because she photographs well. The *Duluth News Tribune* photographer selects his own subjects, but checks with the teacher to find if there is any reason not to use that particular pupil. No high school wants to be represented by a boy who is a fugitive from a reform school.

In general, only attractive teachers are included in pictures. They may be young or old, men or women, but they are chosen as good representatives of the profession. The male non-conformist who shuns a necktie is never included in a school picture unless he is conducting a physical education class or a rehearsal.

It is a good idea to include "outsiders" in pictures, if possible, to tie up the school and the community—and to get more people interested in school stories. When a class goes to a bakery for a field trip, the guide or one of the workers can be in the picture.

COURTESY *Duluth News-Tribune.*

Get a new angle. A pupil introduces dog to his new doghouse made in class.

A picture should have one center of interest. It loses impact if it tries to show one child in a reading corner, another working on a science project, and still another at an easel.

Backgrounds should be simple, not "busy." Bulletin boards and blackboards are too static to have appeal. If the bulletin board *is* the story, it should be not quite complete, and a child can be working on it.

There is a *must* for all school pictures. They must include pupils. The human element makes the picture. A swimming pool with no one in it, a scene for a play with no characters—these are lifeless, and school is no place for lifelessness.

COURTESY *Duluth News-Tribune.*

Have pupils in the pictures, even when showing a new swimming pool.

PICTURES TELL THE STORY

In general, school pictures will give an idea rather than a spot news story. They interpret what is being done in school. Sometimes the story is told in a series of pictures. To help make the story clear, each picture needs a brief caption as well as careful identification of people.

WHAT TO WRITE ABOUT

While stories are all around the school, perhaps these suggestions will help to pinpoint them:

Curriculum

Every subject, so that the whole program is presented
Studies in international relations
Units of work
Field trips
Projects

Textbooks and their selections
Debates
Speech contests
Test results
Libraries
Discipline

Activities

Student publications
Athletics
Student Council

School plays, pageants, music programs

Special Services

Speech correction
How we teach the deaf; the blind
Classes for the mentally and physically handicapped
Classes for the gifted
Home instruction

Guidance
Audio-visual aids
School cafeteria
Health
School bus driver
Test results

Students' Achievements in or out of School

Scholarships
Honor roll
Published stories; poems
Officers of clubs; class

Human interest stories
Representatives of school to meetings
Conferences
Winners in contests

Teachers

Outside activities
Service in the community
Published articles
Human interest stories

Unusual hobbies
Advanced education
Travel

Administration

Finance
Building program

School board activities

BIBLIOGRAPHY

Barlow, Alice Townsend, *Public Relations Primer*. Champaign, Illinois: Public schools, 1958. This is another mimeographed handbook for teacher-reporter.

Ciernick, Sylvia, *How to Wiggle Your Nose for News*. Dearborn,

Michigan: Public Schools, 1952. This is a mimeographed "how-to-do-it" guide for teacher-reporters.

Grinnell, J. E. and Raymond J. Young, *The School and the Community.* New York: The Ronald Press, 1955. Chapters 11 and 12. These chapters describe a public information program and discuss news services, news values, and preparation of news stories.

Horn, Gunnar, *Public-School Publicity.* New York: Inor Publishing Co., Inc., 1948. Chapters 1, 2, 3. These chapters discuss where to find school news, how to write school news, and how to get stories published. A manual of style is included in an Appendix.

Kindred, Leslie W., *School Public Relations.* Englewood Cliffs, N.J.: Prentice-Hall, Inc., 1957. Chapter 16. This chapter discusses news, news coverage, types of news stories, and news sources.

Let's Go to Press. Washington, D.C.: National School Public Relations Association, 1954. This guide to better school news reporting gets down to grass roots on spotting and writing school news and describes systems that work.

Parker, Jack, *A Primer in Public Relations.* Indianapolis, Indiana: Public Schools, 1957. Chapter 4. The director of school-community relations gives practical advice to his teacher-reporters in this mimeographed booklet.

Print It Right. Washington, D.C.: National School Public Relations Association, 1953. Pp. 24–29. This chapter deals with "putting it into words," giving practical advice on writing school stories.

Public Relations for America's Schools. Washington, D.C.: American Association of School Administrators, 1950. Chapter 12. This chapter describes a plan of operation of a public relations organization, pp. 277–279; the newspaper, p. 283; and school photographs, p. 290.

School Photojournalism. Washington, D.C.: National School Public Relations Association, 1958. This book, by the editors of *Look* Magazine, who published the picture stories "What is a Teacher" and "What is a School," tells what makes a good picture, suggests ideas for school pictures, and gives many excellent photographs.

A "good press" comes from a good product *and* good press relations—and press relations are really only good human relations. Feuding with the press will get the schools nowhere—except behind the eight-ball.

Frederick J. Moffitt, in a talk on school public relations, contrasts the techniques of two school men, Ichabod Crane and Mr. Chips:

> Because Ichabod regarded himself as the storm center of all activities, he aroused resentments which are all too common in the public relations business, and he was unseated with some force. As a result, he became victim of a bad press, and his program was seriously impaired.
>
> On the other hand, consider Mr. Chips, who wasn't half so good a school administrator as Ichabod. But, note well, Chips walked circumspectly and ran a good school. He genuinely liked people and enjoyed working with them—real prerequisites for any successful public relations program. As a result, Chips secured a good press, an increase in salary and a charitable biographer.[1]

In building school-press relations, the educator begins by deleting the word *publicity* from his vocabulary. He

[1] Frederick J. Moffitt, editor of professional publications, Silver Burdett Company, Morristown, New Jersey.

knows that it is the business of newspapers to give news, not publicity; and that newspapermen are as allergic to the word *publicity* as educators are to the phrase *fads and frills*.

EVERYBODY'S GOT PROBLEMS

Before going into school-press relationships, one might consider the different areas of agreement and disagreement between the schools and the press. In 1955, the New England School Development Council made a study of the points of strength and weakness in the relationships between about 113 newspaper men and 100 school administrators in New England. A part of the study deals with grievances. The following table lists the major grievances of superintendents, along with the percentage reporting each grievance and the percentage of the press who say that each grievance is justified.

SUPERINTENDENTS' GRIEVANCES AND PRESS AGREEMENT[2]

Grievance	Per cent of super-intendents reporting grievances	Per cent of editors in agreement
Press overemphasizes bad or sensational news	35	11
Reporters assigned to school news spend only small per cent of time on educational news	34	33
Press does not work to make significant facts about education interesting	25	16
Insufficient space allotted to school news	13	9
Reporters assigned to school news are inexperienced	10	4
Press indulges in criticism for its own sake	7	1
Misquotes and statements out of context are excessive	7	3
The press always ignores the strengths of the schools	6	1

[2] *The Schools and the Press* (Cambridge, Mass.: New England School Development Council, 1956), pp 20, 32.

THE PRESS HAS GRIEVANCES TOO

The same study includes major grievances of editors and superintendents' agreement or disagreement to these.

PRESS GRIEVANCES AND SUPERINTENDENTS' AGREEMENT[3]

Grievance	Per cent of press reporting grievance	Per cent of superintendents in agreement
School people are often evasive in interviews	38	25
Educators have no idea of what news is	34	17
School press releases are poorly written	27	26
Principals and teachers not allowed to make statements to press	14	10
Educators always complain about press coverage and never commend a good story	11	11
Educators speak an uninterpretable jargon	8	15
Schools give preferential treatment to some papers	5	8
No one in schools to whom we can go for factual information	4	0

GROUND RULES

The press and the superintendents disagree somewhat on the "ground rules" in this study. For instance, in statements covering the superintendents' rights and duties in their relationship: 85 per cent of the press and only 13 per cent of the superintendents agree that "it is legitimate for individual school board members to make statements to the press without being specifically authorized to do so by the board"; and 58 per cent of the press and 95 per cent of the superintendents agree that "it is legitimate for a superintendent to refuse to release certain kinds of information to the press." In general, of the eleven items of the ground rules, the greatest disagreement is on items implying a restriction of the press's access to information. On five out of ten items of the ground rules—in addition to the disagreement

[3] *Ibid.*, pp. 22, 30.

cited in the paragraph above—a *majority* of superintendents hold a view opposite from that of the press:

AGREEMENT ON THE GROUND RULES

Statement	Per cent of press in agreement	Per cent of superintendents in agreement
A reporter should always clear with the superintendent's office before contacting a teacher or principal with a story	16	64
An editor should honor a request from the schools to withhold a story	29	73
It is legitimate for the press to take an editorial stand on the hiring of school personnel	80	44
A reporter should submit a story to a school superintendent for approval if the superintendent requests it	31	66
A paper should print any newsworthy item about the school regardless of its effect on the school	74	40

On only one item is there practical unanimity (98 per cent of both groups): that "a reporter should take time to become acquainted with general school problems in order to facilitate his writing specific school stories." On the remaining five, there were varying degrees of majority agreement.[4]

GOOD RELATIONS BUILT ON UNDERSTANDING

Educators need to know and understand the workings of the press if they are to have good relations with this medium of communication. A horrible lack of knowledge was seen at a convention banquet where the two speakers were an educator and the executive editor of a newspaper. The educator, a brilliant man and a leader in school affairs, spoke first and denounced newspapers in general for their "attitude against the schools." As an example, he told of a story he had personally written for

[4] *Ibid.* Information taken from pp. 36, 38.

a paper in which he first informed the public that school taxes would have to be increased because the budget was the highest in history and then how he had given the reasons for the large budget. He contended that anyone could see that the important thing in the story was that school progress required the increased budget. However, he said, "The reporter wrote the head about the increase in taxes, just to bait the public."

The editor's retort was scathing as he took the educator apart, telling him forcefully that he was an ignoramus where newspapers were concerned. The editor pointed out that the most important items should have been in the lead; that the heads are written from the lead; that a reporter does not write headlines; and that, finally, newspapers are not against the schools. Here was evidence of criticism based on ignorance—the very thing educators are fighting in criticism of the schools.

LEARN THE FACTS OF LIFE

Although newspaper organizations differ to some degree, they are essentially the same. The publisher is the top brass, the man who owns—or at least, controls—the paper and formulates its policies. The editor sees that these policies are carried out in the columns of the paper. The managing editor is in charge of general news and the reportorial set-up. The city editor is in charge of local news. There are also department editors for sports, women's activities, features, and other areas, the number depending on the size of the organization.

The reporter gets the news on assignment from his editor and on his own initiative. He is assigned regular "beats" or areas to cover, such as schools, city hall, financial district. He writes the story, after which it will go to the editor, to a headline writer, to a copy reader to be checked for accuracy, and to the composing room, where the paper is made up. A proofreader and the editors go over the story again in the proofs to check for mistakes.

On a small paper, men double-up on these jobs; a publisher

may do almost the entire office procedure, including the writing of editorials and the procuring of ads.

Any person writing school news must know whom to contact and the deadline for each issue of the paper. If he is contributing to weekly papers (these are important), he must know the publication days. He should also know when editors and reporters—the school news director will deal with both—are least busy, and get in touch with them at those times. Editors of a morning paper are available in the late afternoon; of an evening paper, after 12 noon; and of a weekly, the day after publication.

Besides becoming familiar with the general organization of the newspaper, the schoolman should know what keeps it going. He realizes that about 60 per cent of a newspaper is devoted to advertising and 40 per cent to news; and that the size of the paper fluctuates from day to day, depending upon the amount of advertising sold. Fewer ads mean fewer pages, less space for news, and, therefore, a greater chance for a story to be thrown away or drastically cut. The newspaper lives on its advertising, not its subscriptions. Subscriptions are important in that the more readers there are, the easier it is for the paper to get ads— and the higher the ad rates that can be charged.

MEET THE PRESS

School people who work with the press should become acquainted with the editors and reporters to the extent of a first name friendship, if possible. It must, however, be an honest friendship built on mutual respect and understanding, not one of expediency. Bill and Fred can work together on what is best for the community, where Mr. Devereaux and Dr. Merrick may look with a bit of suspicion at each other.

The schoolman does not presume upon his acquaintanceship. He knows that freedom of the press is a vital democratic principle jealously guarded by the press of this country. Any intimation of censorship of news on the part of a school system is suspect and wrecks all good working relations between the school and the press. The educator cannot conscientiously disregard the responsibilities of the press to give the public information about its schools.

Superintendents who have the most trouble are usually those who discourage an editor from going directly to the original school source for his information. This type of censorship can be imposed in two ways. Each is deadly. (1) Issue an administrative notice that all school personnel should refer editors to the superintendent rather than answer questions. (2) Tell the newspapers that they must go to the superintendent for all information.

When formal restrictions are not made and the superintendent has worked at building up good personal relations, the following practices will usually develop over a short period of time: Editors, or their reporters, will go first to the superintendent because he usually has the most information and is willing to take the time to see the editor, even during his busiest days. Staff members, once they realize that they are also responsible for what the newspapers write about the schools, soon learn how to meet the editor. If they are helped to recognize the normal limits of their authority, they will not attempt to speak for the entire school system, but only for those areas for which they are responsible.

Editors should not be kept out of classrooms or away from teachers. . . . Once all the doors are open, most editors will be satisfied.[5]

A good relationship cannot survive if built on sporadic contacts made only when the schoolman needs the paper in a crisis. When a school bond issue arises or American Education Week suddenly appears on the desk calendar, some schools suddenly rediscover the long-lost bond between education and the press. The rest of the year, they are unaware that the press exists unless the paper publishes a letter from some disgruntled soul complaining that his secretary can't spell because "the schools don't teach spelling any more." Time was when the situation was such that when a superintendent went to a newspaper office, the editor's immediate reaction was, "What does he want now?" Now, administrators have taken a lesson from business and industry; they have learned that continuous contacts build up confidence and understanding.

[5] *Schools Are News* (East Lansing, Mich.: Bureau of Educational Research, College of Education, Michigan State University), p. 2.

Another strain on friendship is the schoolman's occupational habit of speaking "off the record." While most editors will honor such statements, some refuse to listen and none likes them. The educator and the editor should come to some agreement on "off the record" statements before irrevocable damage is done. A demand for immunity from the press can be fatal. Probably no friendship between schoolman and editor can survive the educator saying, "Don't print that." Those are fighting words, intimating that the newsman does not know his business. The editor's reaction is the same as the educator's would be if the newsman were to say, "Don't teach anything about communism in the schools"—a directive in conflict with the school's policy of "freedom to learn." An editor is an educator to the thousands of people who read his newspaper. He has definite policies for running his paper and these must be respected, if there is to be mutual understanding.

When a schoolman and an editor can talk over school problems with understanding, the community benefits. One superintendent always consults the editor to discuss a proposed bond issue before the project is definitely decided upon. The editor can help; he is aware of the public pulse.

SOME EDITORS ARE DIFFERENT

Let's face it—some editors are naturally unfriendly to the school system. The reason for this attitude must be discovered if the problem is to be solved. Perhaps the editor had unfortunate experiences with teachers in his school days (don't think this won't carry over into adult life); perhaps his son has failed in mathematics and has been dropped from the football team; it may be that he is nearing retirement and fears any progress that will raise his taxes when he is on a pension; it may be that he is a "gifted adult" and arrogant to the point that he disagrees that schools should be for everybody; he may not like the superintendent or anything about him and "his school"; and perhaps he has ulcers. No matter what the reason is, if he allows his personal feelings to develop an "antagonistic press," he poses a problem to the school system. Knowing what his mental block is gives the superintendent something to work on.

Working on the principle that schools need constructive criticism, the superintendent might confer with the editor, asking frankly for his evaluation of the schools.

If relations are strained between the superintendent and editor, the former might call in shock troops to confer with the editor—a mutual friend, a committee from the PTA. The latter must be carefully selected. In one such committee, a woman threatened the editor: "My husband advertises in your paper, and if you don't change your attitude toward the schools, he'll take out his advertising." She could have said nothing more tactless.

If there is soundness in the idea that people who understand the schools stand up for them, then the superintendent—or some other member of the staff if there is a personality conflict between the superintendent and the editor—might invite the editor to take part in school activities. This might involve nothing more at first than coming to lunch in the school cafeteria. From this beginning he could be asked to serve as a member of a working committee, a speaker, a judge for a contest, a consultant in planning a course in journalism, or as a guest at a worthwhile learning activity.

Whatever else he does, the superintendent neither argues with the local editor nor vacillates from his policy to supply newsworthy stories on the educational program.

REPORTERS ARE PEOPLE

Good relations with the newspapers start with the reporter.

The old-time stereotype of the reporter as an irresponsible fellow who sits in the newsroom with his feet on the desk and his hat on the back of his head and who covers his beat from a telephone in the corner saloon is as untrue today as is the cartoon of the spinster schoolteacher with her dowdy clothes, stern expression, and switch in hand.

The average reporter—if there is an average one—is a college graduate, married, who is vitally interested in schools and taxes because they affect him. He has children in school, and he attends PTA, at least on Dad's Night. He attempts to get his wife's club notices in the paper, sheepishly turning them into the society or women's activities editor after the deadline. If the school his children attend gets more space in the papers than other schools do, it is because he sees the news value in what his kids say about their school day at dinner.

Another exploded fable is that you get a good press by buying drinks for reporters. The coffee break, however, provides a convenient time to discuss matters. A reporter appreciates *help* on a school story as long as you don't try to tell him what to say or how to write it, and he will eternally love the person who gives him tips on other stories. The teacher who happens to hear about a housewife who was in aviation or the Ziegfeld Follies thirty years ago, or who has just had a book published, can do a good turn by calling a reporter or editor.

Newspapermen also have affection for the one who digs up information for him when he needs it, who gives him advance notice of a big story, and who gets his own stories in before the deadline. It is a mystery that a teacher, who insists that his pupils get their work in "on time," will cheerfully disregard a newspaper deadline.

Newsmen work odd hours and have extremely tight schedules, and the teacher or news director who refuses to cooperate in a hunt for a picture of an old alumnus or for human interest material about a child who has been hurt—and refuses merely because it is before eight or after five—is running the risk of being branded indifferent to the press—and the inevitable consequence that the press will be indifferent, even hostile, toward the school.

School people can also help to develop good press relations by practicing common courtesies: welcoming reporters to classrooms and complimenting them on the way they have written a story. One does not, however, thank anyone on the paper for running a story; it is understood that stories are run on their merit, not as a courtesy to the school.

There are a few sure ways to alienate the affections of reporters. One of these is to play favorites among rival newspapers or among newspapers, radio, and television, either by controlling news releases or by time. Where one reporter will be happy over an exclusive story, the others will be standoffish when you approach them with another story.

The different media of communication pose a problem in timing. For instance, if you release all copy in late afternoon, radio and television will always have the news before the morning newspapers. Some thought should go into scheduling releases in turn, giving all media, and weeklies as well as daily newspapers, an opportunity for the first release. This procedure applies only to copy on which the timing is not important to the school.

Another means of making enemies instead of friends is to divulge a reporter's idea to another reporter. If a newsman gets an idea for a story—maybe a feature about hoola hoops, or rockets, or a science quiz—that is his exclusive story. Even though he asks for help on it, no one has a right to give the idea to another reporter. The schoolman will also carefully avoid telling a reporter how to write his story, complaining about a headline, a cut or rewrite of a story, the omission of a story, or the position of a story in the paper. For one thing, the reporter has no control over these; and for another thing, they are the business of the newspaper.

IT'S THE STYLE

One way to make friends with the press is to contribute workmanlike copy that saves time in the news room, that is, "clean copy" that follows the style used by the paper. Every newspaper uses a certain *style* in the mechanics of writing. The school reporter should ask for a copy of the style book, and if none is available, study each newspaper to determine the style it uses. *Style includes*

1. Spelling, when there is a choice: adviser, advisor; vice president, vice-president; per cent, percent.

2. Abbreviations.
3. Capitalization: P.M. p.m.; Central High School, Central high school; Board of Education, board of education.
4. Punctuation.
5. Use of figures: some papers use numerals for all numbers over 10; some, for numbers over 100.
6. Titles.
7. Designation of time.

THE PRESS PHOTOGRAPHER

The press photographer is both artist and reporter. He gives the school story through pictures. As an artist, the photographer knows what makes the best picture. The teacher can tell him what she wants the picture to tell—and then she's wise if she stands back and lets him go about his work. This does not mean that she should allow a picture that is not truth; for instance, if a lad is typewriting, she insists upon proper posture and position of the hands. However, she does not demand that more pupils be in the picture than the photographer wants; nor does she insist upon a certain background or angle. The photographer knows his business and is apt to be intolerant of advice.

The press photographer works on a close schedule. He has no time to wait until pupils are rounded up for a picture. He likes to go to a school where everything and everyone are ready for him. He may be late because of an unexpected assignment, but he expects that the school assignment will be set up for him. There is sometimes a problem in having a photographer come to take a picture of an event. In an assembly program, for example, it is difficult to estimate the exact time the Queen of Athletics will be crowned. In such cases, the picture can be posed before or after the assembly program. If a photographer is asked to take pictures *during* a program, he should expect courtesy, not glares. He does his best to be unobtrusive, but he has a job to do, and he has to move about and use a flash to do it.

It is helpful to a photographer to know the number of the room where he is to go. Wearing an overcoat and galoshes and carrying heavy equipment, he does not relish having to go to the principal's office on the second floor, only to find that the

picture is to be taken in the basement. That principal is thoughtful who has someone meet the photographer at the school
entrance and accompany him to the room or rooms where he is
to go. Another courtesy, if he is taking pictures in different parts
of the building, is to appoint one of the larger boys to help him
carry his coat and his equipment.

Gracious cooperation with the press photographer pays off
in better school pictures.

BAD NEWS IS STILL NEWS

Even when news is bad, the editor still feels his responsibility
to publish "all the news that's fit to print." The worst possible
thing to do is to try to suppress a story, bad or good; it cannot
be done, anyway. Knowing an unfavorable incident is approaching, a superintendent can talk to the reporter or editor, giving
all the facts to be sure the story is accurate. He can be ready to
answer all possible questions. If the newspaper asks for information, there is only one thing to do—give it; and be thankful
the press goes to the schools for accurate reporting.

If the bad news break is caused by an inaccurate or half-true
story, little is gained by a denial or a request for retraction. The
damage is done, and more discussion simply keeps the story
alive. It is better to offer a constructive story to the press. For
instance, part of a ceiling falls in the corridor of a new school
building; the resulting story leads the public to think that its
money is being wasted in inferior construction in all new buildings. A subsequent story about the swimming program in the
school may describe the pool and explain that the humidity has
seeped into the corridor ceiling, loosening it; or the story can tell
of repairs to the ceiling, giving the reason for the need of repairs.

There is disagreement between school and press people on the
printing of bad news. At a seminar of the National School
Public Relations Association, the subject was brought up in a
discussion group. School people and lay citizens were indignant

about front page stories dealing with the dismissal of a teacher who was a former "call girl" and present mistress of the school physician. They thought the papers should not identify her as a teacher. Newspaper people tried to explain that that was the crux of the story. As one editor said, "You don't very often find a teacher who is a former call girl. That's news." Members of the press felt that a story about one wayward schoolteacher could not greatly affect a good school system.

COVERAGE OF SPECIAL EVENTS

Few newspapers have a staff large enough to send reporters to cover thoroughly every meeting, lecture, workshop, convention, and other special events. The school news reporter should discuss and plan coverage with the city editor ahead of time, to know who will cover what, and how much material the paper will use. Whether the newspaper or the school news service does the job, arrangements must be made prior to the event. If the newspaper sends a man, the school news director should give him every assistance possible.

LECTURES

The most satisfactory way to get the best coverage of a lecture is for the director to get a copy or a summary of the lecture before it takes place. The speaker frequently appreciates this, for he can then point out the highlights. The copy is given, with a time release, to be run after the lecture. This procedure gives the reporter more time to prepare the copy. It is especially convenient for a lecture at night when there would be a rush to meet the deadline, or at a noon luncheon when the report would probably have to wait till the morning paper.

If a reporter covers the lecture in person, the director should arrange for him to sit at a table near the speaker—if he wishes to; some reporters prefer to sit with the audience near an exit.

A school news director covering a lecture should ask the editor if he should telephone the story in or write it immediately after the meeting. The city editor must know if the story is coming, especially if it is an evening lecture, so that he can leave space in the morning paper.

MEETINGS, WORKSHOPS, SEMINARS, CLINICS

The school news director generally covers local teachers' and pupils' meetings, workshops, seminars, and clinics. If several groups meet at the same time, as in a workshop, he needs to appoint a staff to report to him. He will consult with the editor about pictures and will have the people for pictures ready in the place and at the time designated for the press photographer.

One of the hardest jobs for a school person, in covering such meetings, is to remember that while a spirited discussion is intensely interesting to him, it may have little reader appeal to the average newspaper subscriber. The paper is more interested in what was done than in what was said, unless the latter was radical.

When the subject of a workshop has popular appeal, the newspaper is apt to cover it. For instance, at an all-day Youth Traffic Clinic, a photographer was present for the inevitable picture of registration in the morning, so that the afternoon paper carried the picture with a story of the program. A reporter listened in on discussion groups and then got individual students' opinions on the discussion subjects. The story in the morning paper ran the interviews with a picture of each student and a summary of the meeting. Even though the newspaper covers the story, advance copy, which includes the full program, should be given to the editor.

CONVENTIONS AND CONFERENCES

A news director is a busy man—or woman—during a convention; he should have *no other duties*, such as committee work. As in other meetings, coverage of a convention should be planned with the city editor ahead of time. If the paper assigns reporters, the news director still has responsibilities that will keep him from serving on committees or from going on an extracurricular fishing or shopping trip. If the school is to cover the convention, the news director organizes and instructs a press staff to be sure that every angle is covered.

Benjamin Fine gives good advice on the work of a news director:

Unless the publicity director prepares for the conference, he will find himself swamped with detail that may cause him endless woe and ill-will. . . .

You cannot neglect publicity details, ignore the reporters and editors, and expect the event to be a success. Yet, many publicity directors proceed on the principle that everything will get along somehow. It is the muddling-through process that causes the hardboiled reporter to scoff at publicity men.

Reporters will cooperate if you provide them with the kind of help they need and have a right to expect. If you feel that reporters and photographers should be kept in the balcony, locked away so that they will not disturb the orderly functioning of your celebration, you are headed for trouble.[6]

This preparation for a convention includes procuring pictures, biographies, and advance copies of speeches of each of the major speakers. It means digesting their biographies and talks, condensing them, and sending copies to all newspapers, with the release time given prominence. It means procuring pictures and biographies of officers, and submitting copies of these to the press. It also means advance copy on the convention itself—history, plans, local committees (with pictures), and program. Not only the local press is given service but also the press in areas from which people are coming to the convention. In connection with out-of-town newspapers, stories should include mention of any people from these towns who are taking part in the convention as speakers or committee members.

For the convention itself, a press headquarters should be set up in a room easily accessible to both the press and convention participants. The room is equipped with tables and chairs, one

[6] Benjamin Fine, *Educational Publicity* (New York: Harper & Brothers, 1943), p. 181.

or more telephones (depending upon how many press people are expected), typewriters, paper, pencils, and ashtrays. An added convenience is a mimeograph or veri-fax machine, with someone assigned to it to run off copies of day-by-day news releases as they come in. (A warning goes along with this part of the work: you will find that delegates will want these copies to facilitate writing up their reports). One or two school people should be on duty in the press room to help reporters throughout the convention; in addition, students assigned as messengers can save teachers much legwork.

The press room is generally headquarters for photographers. They will want action shots, such as someone receiving an award or the president taking over the gavel, but they will also take informal shots of officials and speakers. It is not always possible for the photographers to be present at the exact moment for action shots, so these are frequently posed before or immediately after the event. One of the school staff helps the photographer by getting people together for his pictures. He consults with the photographer on places to pose the "unposed" pictures of officials, speakers, and committee members; some of the convention spirit can be included when these informal pictures are taken at various exhibits. He rounds up groups of delegates from areas served by each paper.

The news director arranges for interviews requested by reporters; he points out major speeches and activities; he arranges good seats at convention luncheon and dinner meetings. He is helpful, but not dictatorial.

If the newspapers leave convention coverage to the publicity director, he assigns his staff to definite meetings, speeches, and photographs and sends the copy to the papers, telephoning late copy. He takes his orders from the city editor as if he were on the staff of the paper.

THE PRESS CONFERENCE

"Good morning, ladies and gentlemen—the Superintendent of Schools," impressively announces Lee Demeter, administrative assistant, school-community relations, Great Neck, New York, at the opening of each press conference.

This is a community press conference, modeled after the President's press conference, with the superintendent of schools taking on all comers. Besides the press, anyone is invited who wants to ask a question on any aspect of education issues, local or national. The conferences are announced in the newspaper; they are 35 minutes in length and may be held in the morning, afternoon, or night, once a month or oftener.

Addressing the National School Public Relations Association in 1957, Demeter said

> This conference gives the superintendent a cross section of what the community thinks and gives the community a better understanding of the superintendent. . . . Not every superintendent is suited to this type of thing. He must have a conviction that every citizen has a right to know about his schools. . . .
>
> We like to anticipate questions. Principals may discuss some of the questions. The superintendent needs some staff members present to refer to.
>
> We hold the conference in a small room. The superintendent is careful not to discriminate among those with questions; he recognizes people as their hands go up from every part of the room. Every questioner must give his name and address—that gives him a sense of responsibility for what he says. We insist on *questions*, not *statements*. Answers are brief. We make sure there is some kind of follow-up in newspapers and on radio and television. We're enthusiastic about future conferences.

This is a novel type of press conference in that it involves persons other than reporters. It serves a double purpose, providing community contacts as well as grist for the press.

Press conferences are gaining in popularity. Robert Casey, in his delightful reminiscences of newspaper life, *Other Interesting People*, says that everybody will flock to a press conference no matter who is holding it.

The run-of-the-mill school press conference is called by the superintendent or news director when he has an important announcement to make or when he wants to discuss some matter with the press—an annual report, the budget, a building program, a bond issue, a change in curriculum, dedication of a school. Sometimes the superintendent calls a press conference when he wants advice. The San Bernardino, California, schools did that when they were establishing a news service.

The press conference is an efficient and time-saving way for the superintendent to get material to all press representatives; it assures that all will get the same information in the same way; it gives reporters an opportunity to get a more thorough background, as they hear each other's questions; and it provides personal contacts, which are vital in developing school-press relationships.

Benjamin Fine tells about a new junior college which established good press relations as well as a good publicity program when the college president called in newspaper editors and publishers within a radius of fifty miles to help establish a publicity program. Weekly conferences were held over a period of two months.[7]

BOARD OF EDUCATION MEETINGS

Both the schools and the press generally agree that board of education meetings should be open to the public. However, there is definite disagreement on executive sessions from which the press is excluded.

In the survey made by the New England School Development Council, only 14 per cent of the school systems held no executive sessions; 17 per cent of the superintendents said that the press was invited to all school board meetings, including non-public sessions; and 26 per cent indicated that newspapermen were *sometimes* invited to such sessions. A large majority of both superintendents (77 per cent) and newspapermen (71 per cent) felt that "little of a school board's business should be transacted in private sessions."[8] So-called executive sessions give members

---

[7] *Ibid.*, pp. 265, 266.
[8] *The Schools and the Press* (Cambridge, Mass.: New England School Development Council, 1955), pp. 7, 8, 39.

of the board an opportunity to talk things over and to discuss touchy subjects. They can also wreck a beautiful friendship between the editor and the superintendent.

In one school system, the board members have dinner together once a month for discussion only. The superintendent meticulously invites the editor to come or to send a reporter to the dinner, so that the paper can be assured that no secret action is being taken. So far, the newsman has not reported the discussions, which sometimes become quite personal.

According to the survey mentioned above, in answer to the question, "Does your paper have a reporter present at the school board meetings in your community?" 59 per cent of the press (including 97 per cent of the large dailies) answered "always." Only 20 per cent answered "sometimes" or "never."

Education reporter Wilma Morrison, of *The Portland Oregonian*, states:

> To get a responsible press you have to have a responsible and, above all, an open school administration. . . .
>
> Your only safeguard against a bad press is knowledge of school operations and problems by the reporter and his editor. And the only way for them to get that knowledge is to sit in on the schools, day-by-day, pressure-by-pressure, deficit-by-deficit, personnel-controversy-by-personnel-controversy.
>
> First step toward that responsible school press is a school board and administration truly open to the press—not just paying lip service to an "open policy." Second, is to convince the editor that he should keep *one person* on the education beat and permit him really to cover the schools, not just catch up with them when a crisis occurs. Chief objection of schoolmen to opening their meetings to newspaper coverage is that editors send an assortment of uninformed reporters and they frequently go off half-cocked on headline falsehoods or half-truths that do grievous harm.[9]

An example of the uninformed reporter was seen after a board meeting in which members took action to spend more than $100,000 in tax money. They also voted to pay a principal's

[9] *No News Is Bad News* (Washington, D.C.: National School Public Relations Association, 1955), pp. 23, 24.

expenses to attend a meeting of a national honorary education group to which he had been elected. One member of the board asked why the expenses would be paid and was told that such a membership was a rare honor which reflected upon the schools. The motion was passed. The next morning, the newspaper story played up "the controversy over paying principal's expenses" and passed over the $100,000. This, definitely, was irresponsible reporting; and it did not help friendly relations between the principal and the board.

A newspaper that accepts its responsibility to inform the public of board of education proceedings generally assigns one of its own reporters to cover the meetings, rather than a school news director. This does not relieve the superintendent and news director of a responsibility to help the reporter.

They should make the reporter feel that he is welcome and should see that he has a good seat from which to listen. To help eliminate poor reporting, an administrator should go over the agenda with the reporter.

Newspapermen in an Eastern city, asked by a superintendent how he could improve the school system's press relations, requested:

Advance briefing on the problems, issues, and proposals to be placed before the board.

All meetings to be open.

Opportunity to meet with the superintendent after board meetings to discuss the significance of actions taken by the board.[10]

A board meeting can be used for more than transacting business. It can also supply board members and the community, through the reporter, with information on specific areas of the education program. Some superintendents devote part of the meeting to the teachers, who give demonstrations or exposition of their work.

[10] *The Superintendent, the Board, and the Press* (Washington, D.C.: American Association of School Administrators, National School Boards Association, and National School Public Relations Association, 1951), p. 10.

SPORTS EVENTS

The sports reporter covering a game has difficulty in doing a good job if he has to sit among the exuberant, shouting, jumping-up-and-down young people.

Better press relations will be developed if he is assigned a "press box," even if it is only a table and chair set aside for him in a spot where he can easily observe the game. The reporter will also appreciate having someone with a thorough knowledge of the teams assigned to help him in identifying players and in giving background information.

PUBLICITY CAMPAIGNS

Even though a school keeps up a continuous flow of news to a paper, it may still need to carry out an occasional publicity campaign for a bond issue, a change in curriculum, or what have you. While the successful campaign is based on years of informing the public about the schools, it still needs special attention.

Before the campaign starts, before ideas are completely formed, the editor is asked to join in the planning. Joint conferences will help to develop press relations as well as the campaign. The superintendent or news director—whoever is in charge of the campaign—asks the editor for one man on the staff to handle copy and works with him. He conducts the campaign vigorously according to plan, constantly providing good, fresh copy, with new ideas to the newsman. The story has to be kept alive—and the school people are the ones who must keep it living.

Leone Baxter of Whitaker and Baxter's *Campaigns, Inc.*, consultants for local, state, and national campaigns, gives some excellent advice on writing for campaigns:

Use clear, dramatic, picture-building, honest language. Language is the instrument that can give pulsing life to a campaign or can murder it in cold blood. Dramatic, stirring picture-making words bring a campaign to life—words that clarify, not confuse; dramatize, not deceive—words that dent the mind. Copy should be thoroughly readable, thoroughly interesting, and equally effective in securing action from a truckdriver, banker, college professor, clubwoman or her husband.[11]

Newspapers may be as interested in getting the campaign across as are the schools; but they need the help of the schools for information, charts and graphs, and news of action being taken.

SPECIALIZED STORIES

For certain types of school stories the reporter needs help if he is to give an honest account. These are stories which might be dynamite if handled without adequate interpretation. And they are stories that only the schools can give to the papers.

THE SURVEY

A survey, based on a questionnaire answered by either pupils or adults, usually makes an interesting story. It can be made more interesting if it is well handled. Results alone without any interpretation may be misleading.

The reporter must know who made the survey, who and how many people participated in it, how it was administered, how results were obtained, and what the purpose was.

In the recent survey made of parents by the school system in Duluth, Minnesota, Alvin T. Stolen, superintendent, stated the purpose clearly: "We are asking for frank opinions on the Duluth public schools, to help us to serve the community better."

If the newspaper prefers to handle the story rather than have the schools do it, the public relations director will go over the results with a reporter. He will point out that the questionnaire was not weighted scientifically, but was an honest attempt to gather opinions on schools by patrons who had a personal interest in the schools. He will comment that the question, "How do you feel about the schools in regard to buildings?" was answered "excellent" by parents of children attending a new building, and "poor" by parents of children going to school in an old school.

---

[11] Address to National School Public Relations Association seminar, July, 1956.

Along with answers to the question, "Do you think the schools are not spending enough time on certain subjects?" he will point out that the "yes" answers usually gave as examples, science and mathematics, even in elementary schools where children have ranked high above the national norm in science. He will refer to subjects given as those on which schools spend too much time. He will correlate the answers on "too much homework" with the amount of time parents said their children spent on homework. He will make no excuses for results that may be unfavorable, but will make clear that these results show problems that the schools must work on.

If the questionnaire brings out conditions that need remedying, the schools will work on these in the future and the reporter will be given stories on what is being done, always referring to results of the questionnaire, to show patrons that their opinions are respected. If, on the other hand, criticisms did not follow accepted standards, this fact will be explained.

TESTS

Parents want to know, first, how their own children do in school, and, second, how the local school children rank when compared to others in the nation. They are interested in results of standardized tests, if they understand them. However, if the results are given in such terms as *norm, variability* and *percentile,* they are meaningless. The newspaper will appreciate the story written in words readers can understand without a dictionary.

Test results can sometimes be embarrassing to the schools. If they are low, they may require explanations of *why* or of *what is being done.* These must be part of the story. However, there is no law that says the story has to be given to the press—unless the paper asks for it—and then not law but honesty dictates the proper course.

The schools can give the press a good story on academic tests, by giving some of the questions in the tests. Tests themselves, like student-written paragraphs, bring the public close to the schools.

THE ANNUAL REPORT AND BUDGET

Both the annual report and the budget can be such dull reading that they are no competition to the story about a TV star's income. Faced with the columns of figures, the reporter feels the lack of human interest. Rather than let him struggle along, the superintendent should help him to write a creditable story by going over the important points with him.

TEAMWORK

DEDICATION OF A SCHOOL

An example of this teamwork is the advertising section, used in connection with dedication of a new school building. One school gives the advertising manager of the paper a list of firms working on the building and their contract prices. The advertising department gets ads from these firms, to be used in connection with pictures and text, and the school supplies an announcement of the dedication, describing the building, and explaining its educational program.

AMERICAN EDUCATION WEEK

Many newspapers have one advertising page, contributed by merchants, as a public service in promoting their communities. This is a natural for American Education Week. The schoolman and the advertising man work together to provide an attractive page containing worthwhile information.

BACK TO SCHOOL

In August, many papers issue a back-to-school supplement, which they subscribe to from the Associated Press. Other papers plan a back-to-school issue of their own. Either way, they use the issue in connection with advertising for back-to-school clothes.

The schools can help by printing school stories of immediate, local interest. In such an issue, the Duluth *Herald* ran stories on such things as "standards for teachers constantly rising here"; "early college preparation urged"; "education not luxury in competitive world"; "$8,214,080 spent in operating, building Duluth schools last year"; "West grade school set for opening"; "do's and don'ts for parents"; "meetings social events set for new teachers"; and so on.

BUSINESS-EDUCATION DAY

Schools work with the newspaper as well as with other business and industrial firms in planning and carrying out Business-Education Day. Either the newspaper or the schools act as host, giving the guests a chance to learn what makes the other's business tick. Each comes to the end of the day with renewed respect for the other's work. Good relations are developed throughout the day.

TEACHERS' WORKSHOP

At a teachers' workshop on public relations, one section is devoted to the press. Here, again, is an opportunity to work together, as editors and reporters act as leaders. Teachers state their problems with the press to the press, and newsmen reciprocate—and both come to a better understanding.

THE NEWSPAPER AS A TEXTBOOK

When a newspaper in one city wanted a brief unit in reading newspapers inserted into a high school course, the schools agreed. Although some educators thought the project had a slight taint of a promotion angle, it still offered young people an opportunity to study what has been called a "living textbook." There are sound educational principles back of such a unit. Gordon A. Sabine, Dean of the School of Journalism, University of Oregon, has said:

I wish there could be a guarantee that every graduate would get, somewhere during his years in high school, just that one hour of instruction on how to read a newspaper intelligently, on how it gets its news, on how to find the useful facts and not get lost at the bargain basement counter which serves only froth and frosting.[12]

TOGETHERNESS

Building a good press is a simple matter, requiring no fancy techniques nor mysterious power. The basic ingredient is a good product, a good school. No amount of skilfully contrived and written publicity can gain favor for a poor educational program; it can only cause newsmen to lose confidence in educators. A good press is built on a common understanding, a sense of responsibility, and hard work. A good press is the result of school men and newspapermen working together—good human relations.

BIBLIOGRAPHY

Fine, Benjamin, *Educational Publicity*. New York: Harper & Brothers, 1943, pp. 181, 265, 266. A practical guide written by a top education writer.

No News Is Bad News. Washington, D.C.: National School Public Relations Association, 1955, pp. 10, 21, 23, 24. Sections of this booklet are written by a superintendent, a board member, an editor, and an education writer; each gives his viewpoints on schools and the press.

Schools Are News. East Lansing, Michigan: Bureau of Educational Research, College of Education, Michigan State University, pp. 2, 5. There are two sections on school-press problems, one dealing with educators and the other with editors.

The Schools and the Press. Cambridge, Mass.: New England School Development Council, 1955, pp. 7, 8, 20, 22, 30, 32, 36, 38, 39. Results of a survey of superintendents and editors to try to develop a good working relationship.

The Superintendent, the Board, and the Press. Washington, D.C.: American Association of School Administrators, National School Boards Association, National School Public Relations Association, 1951, p. 10. A booklet which summarizes school-press relationships.

[12] *No News Is Bad News* (Washington, D.C.: National School Public Relations Association, 1955), p. 10.

4

Speaking before a national meeting of educators several years ago, the superintendent of schools of a small community defended the drab appearance of his system's publications with the statement: "We don't have much money, and besides, we're not in competition with *Life* and *Look*."

The fact is, all school system publications are in competition with national media. Besides the attractive national magazines, school publications compete with local newspapers, the avalanche of direct mail advertising which reaches every American home, television, the movies, golf, bowling, and the great do-it-yourself movement. The American worker has never had more free time and has never had more ways to occupy his leisure hours.

Finding readers for a school publication, or any other unsolicited publication, boils down to getting the man who receives it to say "Now this looks pretty interesting." It should be noted that the amount of money spent on a publication isn't necessarily decisive in evoking this reaction, although as in every other undertaking, it can help.

Unless Mr. Average Taxpayer thinks your publication

looks "pretty interesting," it may be that the only people who will read your school material are those folks with what might best be called a compulsive interest in school affairs. Any superintendent of schools will testify this represents a pitifully small percentage of the community. The job, then, is to reach the others, the great majority of people whose heart is in the right place, if you know where to look.

HOW TO GET STARTED

The school system with a public relations person on its staff, whether he's called a PR Director or one of the numerous euphemisms employed to cover the same function, will undoubtedly include responsibility for the school publications among the many duties of the PR office.

The school system which doesn't have a PR person, and most don't, is well advised to give responsibility for *all* school printing to a single individual, whether it be the superintendent, a teacher, or even a secretary. The word *all* is italicized because it is the key to successful school publications. Assignment of a new person to each new publication minimizes the likelihood of efficient printing methods and procedures and severely limits the system's opportunity to develop publications which reflect the spirit and character of the system. The basic starting point, then, in good printing, is to fix responsibility. The next step is to determine what you want to accomplish with your publications.

WHY PRINT ANYTHING?

School publications give the system an opportunity to say what it wants to say, *the way it wants to say it*. The school system whose local media print its news releases without editing is blessed. If the newspaper, TV, and radio people review with you stories they originated themselves, the system is twice blessed. Most school systems are not quite so fortunate. Even those whose releases are skilfully written and who enjoy the most cooperative relationship with local media find that space or time limitations often do not permit the system to develop fully what it has to say. The school publication suffers no such binding restrictions, although the closer it hews to the swift style of the popular press, the better its message will come through.

The basic purpose, then, behind any school publication, is to convey information and to convey it directly, by-passing the media middlemen. The information may be about the entire system or about a specific phase of it; it may be aimed at the entire community or a specific segment of the town. A publication may be designed to cultivate thoughtful evaluation of the school's efforts, to point up problems or, more often, accomplishments, or it may attempt to move citizens to action. Whatever the publication's purpose, it will succeed only if it is read, and it will be read only if it seems to be worth reading. Determination of what the public in a given school district will consider worth reading conforms to no known set of guides. What the sophisticated executive in Grosse Point considers worth his time might end up discarded and unread in the home of a Detroit assembly-line worker.

In its excellent booklet *Print it Right* the NSPRA suggests the following ways to make your reader pay attention:

By tying your message to his interests.
By telling your story in a lively, simple, sincere way.
By pictures and type and layout that catch and hold his eyes.

KNOWING YOUR AUDIENCE

When the Montclair, New Jersey, schools developed a new method of reporting to parents and pupils in 1958, *The New York Times* heralded the event on the front page of the second section, devoting five columns from the masthead to the center fold to pictures of the new cards. Below the centerfold a 13-inch story explained the dual reporting system under which students are evaluated in a personal report in relation to their own ability, and, in a second report issued to parents, in relation to other students in the same grade.

The story made *The Times* because the Montclair reporting method combines what was best in traditional methods of reporting with what is best in current reporting procedures. Two lines from the story explain the extravagant (for *The Times*) space provided for the cards themselves: "The result of several years of study and experimentation, the reports are a far cry in both appearance and content from the A-B-C-D-E type of cards most parents received when they went to school. In fact, the new reports are not cards, but folders, which are printed in color and contain cover illustrations."

The attractive format of the Montclair report cards did not result by chance; they are, in fact, the result of knowing the audience. Montclair, a prosperous, suburban community, with a large number of New York executive-commuters, has a population which responds to good taste and good design. When the new cards were planned it was decided to present them in a format which would be attractive to both pupils and parents. The predecessors of these cards were dull, drab, and forbidding. Whether the same approach to printing would be successful in nearby industrial towns is not certain. The Montclair cards were designed for Montclair parents alone, successfully so, because school officials knew what parents in their community like and expect.

Something else was known about this community—its reading interests. Fully 50 per cent of the population reads either *The New York Times* or *The New York Herald Tribune*, choosing these newspapers in preference to the local *Newark Star-Ledger*, *The New York Daily News*, or *The New York Daily Mirror*. The first two publications rely most heavily on the printed word, using pictures sparingly. The other three present the news in somewhat less detail and rely heavily on photographs.

Cued by this information, Montclair school publications attempt to strike the same balance between copy and art. One of the most successful publications is a 12-page pamphlet which explains in great detail the curriculum in grades 1–3 to parents of such students. Illustrated by only a handful of professional line drawings, the booklet has been tremendously successful, as letters in the school files indicate. Favorably mentioned in several educational publications, copies of the booklet have been requested by more than 300 school systems in some 30 states.

What is successful in Montclair may not be successful in another community. Each system must decide for itself what will be most effective in its own community.

WHAT TO LOOK FOR

To determine the reading interests of a community, the school system has many avenues. The best place to begin is the office of the local news and magazine distributor to find out how many copies of which newspapers and magazines are sold locally. One Montclair principal, dissatisfied with a merely general overview of the town's reading habits, checked every stationery store in his school area to find out what newspapers and magazines were read most heavily by the parents of *his* students.

It is possible to learn from some publishers the circulation of their magazine in a given community. If this approach is unproductive, the local postmaster can provide the same information. Another excellent source of information about reading habits is, of course, the local library. If your town has a successful library, and it can only be successful if it knows its community, much information can be gathered which will help you determine your own approach to printed matter.

PLANNING

The production of any publication begins with careful planning. While the final decisions, the actual job of getting a publication into print, should rest with a single person, the planning, for maximum efficiency, should involve a group of people who may be expected to contribute to the quality of the work.

Who will sit on such a committee depends on the nature of

the publication planned. The publication supervisor must ask *who is this publication being prepared for* and *what do we expect it to accomplish?* These two questions are not only a major topic for the committee to consider, but a major consideration in determining who will be involved in planning. The committee's effectiveness can be increased if laymen, as well as professionals, are included. Removed from the immediate problems and projects of the schools, the lay person can offer objective contributions. He can be helpful in providing answers to such questions as "What do parents really want to know about this subject? Are we talking over the heads of parents?"

The committee's first job is to decide on a main theme and to determine the detail and depth of the publication. This, in turn, is dependent on the audience the publication is aimed at. A booklet for parents of incoming kindergarten pupils will be quite different from one which will be distributed to local industry to describe the business training program at the high school.

The publications' committee will often find it helpful to examine publications of other school systems and of business and industry. An examination of the kind of material which comes across the desk of local personnel managers may determine, without further discussion, the format, the quality, and the editorial treatment of a publication intended for personnel people.

Although distribution is the final phase of any printing job, the various methods which may be employed must be considered before the format is arranged or the copy written. Will it be a self-mailer? Will it be mailed in envelopes? Will it be distributed by the children? Will it be an enclosure to be distributed with report cards? Will it be used only for distribution at various public meetings or speaking engagements of school personnel?

The problem of which comes first, the copy, the format, or the illustrations, is usually settled by the material on hand. Usually, in school publications, copy comes first and pictures are

It is helpful to examine publications of other school systems.

selected to illustrate specific points. However, occasionally (very occasionally) a picture so vividly demonstrates the message that copy is built around art.

Whichever comes first, pictures or art, eventually the copy must be prepared, and at this point the committee of many is best reduced to a committee of one. One member should be charged with the responsibility for producing a first draft which will be submitted for approval, suggestions, and changes by the rest of the group. For the person who has not spent many years having his copy read and approved by superiors, this can be the most trying, nerve-wracking and demoralizing of experiences. He may find solace in two thoughts: It is much easier to edit someone else's copy than to write it in the first place. If someone else had been given the initial writing assignment, you'd probably be doing to his copy what he is doing to yours.

Copy completed, you are ready to lay out the publication and search for illustrations. Design and layout are best learned by practice after reading reliable books and observing the numerous publications every school person receives during the year. When you reach this stage, you'll find local printers capable of assisting you to produce a publication which meets the high hopes you've set for it.

HOW TO PRESENT THE MESSAGE

The handiest thing for a publication supervisor to keep in mind is that you can't please everyone in a single printed piece. Thoroughly understood, both emotionally and intellectually, this thought will serve as effective armor against the inevitable potshots from those who think the publication is too small or too big, too detailed or too cursory, too expensive or too cheap.

An annual report which has been praised in many quarters will invariably draw criticism along the following lines: it wasn't an annual report at all; it was too expensive; it covered too much territory; it didn't cover enough.

A printed piece which is all things to all men is virtually impossible to produce and an expensive way of doing business. On the matter of size, most school systems will find it more expedient to publish small reports which are quickly read and easily understood—making certain, however, that the public knows that fuller information, complete statistical matter, and so forth are available for examination at the offices of the Board of Education. The number of people who will take advantage of this opportunity to dig deeply is an indication of the interest with which a thick report would have been received.

Many ways to present your message are available whether the publication is an annual report, a one-shot campaign piece, a handbook, or a regular monthly report to the public. Here are some of them:

Annual report. The annual report may have a specific theme or may use the entire school system as its theme. Generally, better results come from concentration on a single theme, on two or three major ideas. The annual report which gives a little information about a lot of subjects is probably less useful than one which gives a good deal of information about a few subjects. The theme should be a phase of the curriculum, not the whole curriculum. Best advice: Find a theme and stick to it.

One picture is worth a thousand words. The pure picture report is the lazy man's approach to communications. The man who first ventured the opinion that one picture is worth a thousand words was probably a camera or film manufacturer. More likely, one interesting picture is an exceptionally effective way to attract attention to a 1,000 word story. Reports which rely almost entirely on pictures with brief captions are a perversion of the sound ideal of keeping your message brief and to the point. Another shortcoming of the picture report is that most school systems cannot afford the services of a truly creative photographer. The result is clearly evident in most school publications which rely heavily on photographs. Too often they are a dismal collection of unimaginatively posed people seen in pictures made from poorly exposed film. The best advice is to use pictures to support *good copy*.

Statistics, charts and dollar signs. This is the problem that tries a publication man's soul. The statistics your public either should have or you are required to provide can be presented in the annual report or as part of a larger report dealing with a number of matters. The former course has the virtue of allowing your other material to be published uncluttered by tedious tables and statistics. Since the demand for such figures is exceptionally small, such a special report can be printed in small quantity. The inclusion of a financial report within the pages of the annual report is less expensive and may provide a wider audience. Use graphs, tables, line charts, pictographs, and color to make figures readable. A list of books and commercial sources of graphic aids is given at the end of Chapter 5. After using ingenuity, courage, and daring in liberal amounts, follow the example of the elaborate

corporative reports which consign statistics and tables to the
back pages.

	Current Expenses*	Debt Service and Capital Outlay	Total Expenses
BRONXVILLE	954	47	1001
MANHASSET	891	110	1001
ROSLYN	846	145	991
BEDFORD CENTER	835	142	977
GREAT NECK	795	180	975
SCARSDALE	812	151	963
TUCKAHOE	747	125	872
GARDEN CITY	727	142	869
WHITE PLAINS	665	145	810
TARRYTOWN	666	132	798
EASTCHESTER	684	108	792
MAMARONECK	672	115	787
PELHAM	657	101	758

COURTESY PUBLIC SCHOOLS, GREAT NECK, NEW YORK.

Statistical information can be presented clearly and understandably.

House publication. Formerly known as the *house organ,* a
term which has fallen into disfavor, this publication provides an
excellent way for the school system to maintain a continuing
channel of communication with the public. Published monthly,
bi-monthly, or quarterly, it can provide up-to-the-minute information about the schools. An established school publication
issued on a regular basis builds an interested audience and provides a handy method of dealing with important issues which
might otherwise require a special publication which has no
ready-made audience. A study of industrial publications of this

type will show that business management finds them an effective way to reach people. A monthly newsletter or newspaper will cover many subjects with no direct relationship to each other, except that they are all school matters. Even in this type of report, however, it is worthwhile to occasionally feature a particular subject in a given issue—such as, the system's testing programs, the role of the junior high schools, reading instruction, or guidance.

Leaflets, handbooks and pamphlets. Here are the real work-horses of your publications program. Usually keyed to one audience and one subject, they are invaluable in keeping your public informed. They answer specific questions about specific matters which the public is interested in—or ought to be. Brief, and therefore relatively inexpensive to print, they can be used to deal with such matters as how your school system is teaching the fundamentals, the effectiveness of reading instruction, the curriculum in the elementary grades, enrolment problems—in short, anything. Assume for a moment that, working with the P-T-A Councils, the school system plans an information-packed two hour program on the three R's in grades 1–3. Out of 5,000 parents in the community, an unusually large number turns out, some 350 mothers and fathers. If the program is worth giving, isn't it worth reducing it to printed form to reach the vast majority of parents who did not attend the public meeting?

SIZE AND STYLE OF PRINTED PUBLICATIONS

Standard-size publications are the least expensive and fastest way to print, whether your publication will be a large or a relatively small printing. Any rush job will be printed sooner if its size is standard. Paper stock used by the printer comes in standard sizes from which your publication size will be cut. The basic sizes which can be cut economically from standard paper stock are 8½ x 11, 8½ x 5½, 9 x 12, or any size which results from dividing these dimensions by two. If you choose a size which is not standard, expect to pay more.

Several things must be considered when a page size is chosen:

Is the publication for future reference? How will it be distributed? Who will use it? What is its purpose?

If a publication is to be distributed personally by a teacher to a parent, perhaps it should fit easily into a woman's handbag or

MONTAGE BY ROBERT E. GITELMAN.

In choosing a size for your publication, you must consider several factors.

the inside breast pocket of a man's coat. A publication for internal use, one which will be filed, indicates an 8½ x 11 or 9 x 12 size. If the publication is to be mailed in envelopes, be sure its size corresponds to standard envelope sizes or an added expense of special envelopes will be incurred.

The style of your annual report is determined both by content and audience. This is a highly subjective area for which there are no standard guides. Whether you choose a formal approach or a relaxed style will depend on what the people who make such decisions think best suits the publication and its planned audience.

A formal publication is characterized by few pictures and a standard (but not static) layout. It gives the impression of substance and permanence and has an authoritative and responsible air. The informal publication will use more pictures, possibly a more imaginative layout, or at least a layout which is not likely to be seen anywhere else in just the same way. It will use more color. While it is possibly more attractive to look at, the informal publication runs the risk of being regarded as superficial. One authoritative educational publication defines a pictorial report as one with just enough text to carry the message. You would be better advised to give your reports just enough pictures to carry the text.

School systems in increasing numbers are turning to a newspaper format for their annual reports in preference to booklet publications. The chief recommendation of the news format is that it is comfortably familiar to everyone. The format itself suggests that this will be worth reading because it will be filled with news.

The newspaper format has the additional virtue of flexibility. What you have to say can be written in straight news style as a feature, and a great deal of information can be served up in a small amount of space. It also serves as a checkrein against the ponderous stuffiness that characterizes educational writing in the eyes of the layman. Since newspaper articles should be short and to the point, there is no room for learned treatises. Such essays are unlikely to be read by anyone but the professional staff, and even this audience is by no means certain.

Newspapers lack the permanence of a magazine or booklet but, before considering this a disadvantage, one would have to determine how many members of the general public keep and preserve the more elaborate annual reports from year to year. Printed in tabloid size, the report is as easy to file as any other.

school facts

A REPORT FROM YOUR SCHOOLS

report no. 11

finances
information
statistics

BOARD
OF
DIRECTORS
ROLAND E. HEWITT
President
HARRY C. CLARK
Vice-President
MRS. ELLSWORTH K. ILAAS
WENTWORTH E. GRIFFIN
MRS. TOM J. STUBBS
HOMER C. WADSWORTH
JAMES A. HAZLETT
Superintendent

school district
KANSAS CITY
MISSOURI

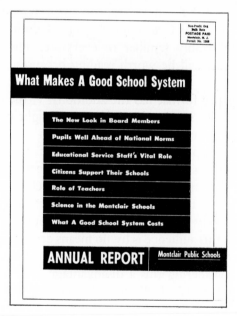

What Makes A Good School System

The New Look in Board Members

Pupils Well Ahead of National Norms

Educational Service Staff's Vital Role

Citizens Support Their Schools

Role of Teachers

Science in the Montclair Schools

What A Good School System Costs

ANNUAL REPORT | Montclair Public Schools

ANNUAL
REPORT

New Orleans
Public
Schools

A report cover should provoke interest.

Although newsprint is an acceptable choice of paper because it is familiar and possibly desirable for economy's sake, the total edition of an annual report is seldom so large as to preclude the use of a brighter, whiter paper. The slightly higher cost of a little better paper will result in substantially better picture reproductions, more attractive appearance, and much easier reading.

An outstanding virtue of the newspaper format is that it looks (and is) inexpensive. In an annual report, or any other school publication, the system is well advised to avoid the flossy publication which may elicit the reaction: "Look at this, will you. No wonder our school taxes are so high."

If a newspaper format seems attractive to you, consider the possibility of enlisting the help of a local editor or reporter. He may not know much about education, but he knows how to write so that he'll be read. What he doesn't know about education you can tell him.

Whatever format you choose, your annual report will require a compelling title and an appealing cover. *The Blankville Schools* (substitute the name of any community) is an excellent title insofar as it leaves no doubt as to what lies between the covers. As a means of *interesting* readers into investigating just what does lie within, it leaves a good deal to be desired. Compare it with *What Makes a Good School System.*

The title should first provoke interest. Identification of the publication can follow in a subtitle. For example, *What Your Children Learn in Grades 1–3* (main title), *A Report to the Public by the Blankville Board of Education* (subtitle).

If your report will follow a newspaper format and, consequently, have no distinguishing title, be certain the lead article and its headline are eye-catchers. "Will Blankville H.S. Graduates be Crowded Out of College?" will draw more readers than "The College Situation."

The cover of a magazine or booklet serves the same purpose as the title; it should interest the reader in the rest of the publication. Color is helpful, but not necessary. Good design and attractive type can be satisfactory substitutes for color. Your printer can be helpful here. If you can afford only one color but would like two or more, investigate the possibility of screens which render a single color in different degrees of intensity. Against the added cost of an engraving needed for the screen effect, there is the much greater saving which results from the printer being able to run the page through the press just once to get as many different screenings as there are engravings. For each distinctly different color, as against shading of one color, a separate press run is required. This is considerably more expensive than the engravings which will make screening possible. Ask your local photoengraver or printer for illustrations of screens.

TABLE OF CONTENTS

A table of contents can be included in the report either for the reader's convenience or because the various subject titles will further interest the reader in the report. Where titles of articles have been chosen with care and ingenuity, it is sometimes profitable to place the table of contents on the cover itself. Be certain your articles have headlines or titles that insure favorable reader reaction. "High School Students Improve Reading" may draw a yawn from the busy reader. "High School Students Read Better Than Their Parents" is more likely to slow down the reader hastily skimming through your report.

SUMMING UP

Pinpoint your objectives for the annual report. It's a better idea to give the complete story about some phases of the system than to be sketchy about many things. Use pictures to support text. Avoid cliché poses; keep the number of people in each picture down to a manageable few. Write simply and succinctly. A good test for your copy is your next door neighbor's reaction to it. Don't assume that because you understand it everyone will. You are writing for readers of the *Blankville Times,* not of an educational journal. It's questionable whether statistics can ever be completely absorbing to the reader, but some of the sting can be removed by effective use of numerous graphic ways to present figures.

PRINTING PROCESSES

After deciding what is to be printed, the next step is to determine how it will be printed. Should the job be handled in the office on the system's mimeograph or multilith machine? Would it be better to use a professional printer? If so, should the job be letterpress or offset?

Your decision should be based on two factors: cost and appearance. Without highly skilled personnel you are not likely to achieve professional results in the office, even if office machines were capable of producing the same quality work as professional equipment. As for cost, do-it-yourself printing is cheaper, but probably less so than it appears to be. A true analysis of office printing costs includes not only the price of materials used, but the wages of the personnel doing the work. Some jobs, such as those which require a great amount of collating, can become expensive indeed if wages are included in the cost picture.

The following sections will serve as a guide in selecting the kind of printing process which can best meet your requirements.

MIMEOGRAPHING

In terms of cost and ease of production, the mimeograph has no equal. However, its use is limited in printing the kinds of publications that have been considered. It can be used for posters, handbills, programs, and small folders. A method of preparing stencils by an electronic process has greatly increased the scope of the mimeograph. These machines may be purchased outright, or a machine owned by a local dealer can be used at modest cost per stencil.

Despite this advance, for annual reports, pamphlets, handbooks, and house publications, printing processes other than mimeographing are more suitable.

MULTILITH

Recent years have seen the small, office-type offset duplicators in schools in ever-increasing numbers, and they have proved to be even more talented than their older-brother mimeographs. Offset duplication, compared to mimeographing, offers cleaner reproductions of typewriting and sharper renderings of line drawings. Photographs can be reproduced on an offset duplicator.

Copy for offset duplication is prepared on a typewriter in the same way as mimeograph copy. In place of the mimeograph stencil the offset duplicating machine uses a hard-surfaced paper master. Corrections can be made easily with a soft eraser.

Another advantage of the offset duplicator is the ease with which complete layouts, including pictures, may be transferred in reduced, same size, or enlarged forms to metal plates which are locked in the machine and run in the same manner as the paper masters. Thus, the machine can furnish reasonably good facsimiles of previously printed material such as newspaper extracts, magazine reprints, ruled forms, and the like. Metal plates are produced by a photomechanical process which requires expensive extra equipment not practical for installation in a school office. However, within easy reach of mail or messenger you will find one or more firms that specialize in converting copy (typing, photos and art) into metal plates suitable for running on your offset duplicator. The cost of these plates is usually quite reasonable.

OFFSET LITHOGRAPHY (SOMETIMES CALLED PHOTO OFFSET)

The basic process of offset lithography was in daily use in thousands of commercial shops across the country long before it became available on a "do-it-yourself" basis in school offices. Even today there is no question that any good commercial shop will produce better printing by offset than you can hope to put

DEARBORN SCHOOLS

REPORT CARD

. . . to the community

January, 1959   DEARBORN PUBLIC SCHOOLS   Dearborn, Michigan

Students Taking More Math, Science

Report Card Explains High School
Purposes, Program and Achievements

REPORT CARD breaks its pattern this issue to present a special edition on the Senior High Schools.

We think it is important that every parent understand what the senior high schools are attempting to do for our local youth.

The current national spotlight on secondary education has created a frenzy of questions in everyone's mind. Everyone—from submarine specialists to erudite college professors who probably have never seen the inside of high school since graduation—are telling the schools what they should be doing.

Newspaper and magazine stories leave the reader wondering, "What is the academic standing of our high schools?"

Fortunately, we are beginning to realize that the generalities and isolated incidents quoted in the general press cannot be applied to any one high school.

The following pages will tell about Dearborn and its high school program for local youth. We hope it will answer many questions and give you a guideline as you read and talk about education.

We have attempted to present a factual report on the schools. It is important that you know what is good about the high schools. On these points we will honestly brag. It is also important that you know of some of the major tasks and problems facing the high schools. On these points we will be very specific.

Students in Dearborn High Schools this year are taking more mathematics, more science, and more basic academic subjects than the students of just three years ago.

Much of this increase is due to stiffer graduation requirements adopted last year. Credit also can go to a stepped up counseling and guidance program which attempts to see that each student is taking those classes that match his ability and interests.

MORE!
MORE!
MORE!

Equally important, is a new seriousness in education on the part of students and their parents who have recognized the challenge of Sputnik and see entrance into college and technical and semi-skilled jobs becoming increasingly difficult.

See The Program on Page 2

Planning the Next Three Years

Planning a student's high school program is the concern of the student, the counselor, and the student's parents. A Board of Education ruling requires that the parents sign the student's program of courses for the three years and that they are consulted on any major changes made later on. It is only possible occasionally for the parents to be present when the student and counselor work on the student's program. However, students are urged to consult closely with their parents. To insure the schools that the parents have been involved, the signature on the program card is required.

Discussing a change in career plans for Mark Grambau at Edsel Ford are the counselor Ford Haskins and Mr. and Mrs. Herman Grambau.

Our Aims

THE DEARBORN SENIOR high school curriculum is based on a set of objectives and philosophical premises that insures each student a well-balanced and complete high school education.

The philosophy and objectives have been prepared by the high school teachers through long and earnest hours of work and are available to anyone upon request, however, they have been summarized in the following four points.

Our high schools are constantly striving to provide:

1. A program of classes that gives all youth the opportunity to attend high school and to learn to the top of his or her own abilities.

2. A firm foundation of fundamental subjects that every person needs no matter what he plans to do in the future.

3. An opportunity for each student to develop to his maximum potential and to meet his personal goals and interests.

4. Each student with a feeling of responsibility to others and to the democratic principles that keep America great.

This statement serves as the foundation for all knowledge and skills each student must acquire and for the interests and appreciations each student must develop.

SPECIAL EDITION— OUR SENIOR HIGH SCHOOLS!

COURTESY PUBLIC SCHOOLS, DEARBORN, MICHIGAN.

Copy of a page done in offset lithography.

out unless (and this is unlikely) you have as good equipment and as much experience. "Offset" in its simplest definition means that you are printing from a plate bearing a chemically reactive

image of type, typewriting, lines, pictures, scribbling, or whatever, which is transfered to a rubber "blanket" that, in its turn,
transfers the image to sheets of paper.

Whether to offset print a given job in the school's office or
contract to have it done in a commercial offset shop is usually
dictated by the requirements of quality, quantity, and speed. The
commercial offset operator has a world of know-how that your
operator will probably never even glimpse. *And* he is not subject to interruptions and the pressure of other duties, as your
part-time operator is likely to be. If a large number of copies are
needed in a short time, the commercial shop may help you meet
a deadline that you could not otherwise meet without costly
and unpopular office overtime.

Commercial offset shops have equipment capable of handling
sheets much larger than your office duplicator will take. They
also have facilities for preparing your copy (linecasting and
proving machines, special typewriters, photoengraving cameras,
and so forth) and, often, one or more artists to help with your
layout, illustrations, and over-all planning.

LETTERPRESS PRINTING

When a raised, inked surface (type, plates) is lightly pressed
against paper, letterpress printing results. Practically all daily
and weekly newspapers, all but a handful of national magazines,
most trade books, and many textbooks are produced by letterpress.

Copy for letterpress printing is set on linecasting machines or
by hand, drawings and photographs are made into plates by a
photomechanical process, and the potpourri of type and plates
is locked into metal frames in a layout determined by the editor
or author. Letterpress is the basic printing process; it usually
produces the best visual results, and is almost always the most
economical except where the number of copies is small and the
proportion of pictures to text is very high. When pictures are
being used in quantity, it is a good idea to get quotations from
letterpress printers as well as offset lithographers.

Another factor to be considered in choosing between letter-press and offset is that the cheaper the offset job the worse its appearance is likely to be. A bad offset job, which tends toward a gray appearance rather than black, makes the cheapest letter-press job look good. Good offset work, however, can be very good indeed—and just as expensive as letterpress.

DISTRIBUTION—METHODS AND TIMING

Distribution should be a part of your original planning for the obvious reason that your publication can only be effective if it reaches readers. The basic choice is between mail distribution or hand delivery; if the latter, by whose hands. At first thought (and it is usually the first thought), students would seem to be excellent postmen. Before deciding to use students, however, it might be wise to check with teachers on whether printed notices seem to get into the home. The trip between school and home is fraught with many perils for the printed piece which you have so carefully developed. This peril can be minimized by enclosing your publication in something else which must be brought home and generally is—the report card. A safer method than student distribution is teacher distribution, if your system employs parent-teacher conferences during the course of the school year.

Mailing is undeniably the safest, most efficient method of dis-tributing printed materials. While it involves an expense, it is a worthwhile cost which should be included in the publication budget. One of the chief values of mailing, compared to student distribution, is that you can reach non-parents as well as parents. Although students can also be used to distribute school material to neighbors, there will very likely be repercussions to using children in this fashion—not to mention the tremendously in-creased likelihood that a great percentage of your material will never reach the audience for which it was intended.

Mailed material can be sent in envelopes or merely folded or stapled. Savings can be recorded through bulk mailings and by taking advantage of the special rates for non-profit organizations. Your postmaster can give you accurate information on the ways available to you to mail your publications.

The key to successful mailing is a good mailing list. For a townwide mailing, it may be easiest to use the facilities of a commercial mailer such as the weekly newspaper or "shopper," many of which maintain a mailing plate for every residence in the community. For a relatively modest fee, the publisher will either turn over his plates to you or have his staff stencil your publication or the envelope in which it will be mailed so that one copy reaches every residence in town.

Generally, your publication will go to a more limited audience, and, for these people, selective mailing lists can be kept by the school system itself. Include in these lists club and organization presidents, civic leaders, town officials, church groups, labor unions, veterans' groups, women's organizations, ministers, and doctors and dentists (who will usually leave it on their waiting room tables). If possible also prepare special lists based on special interests. Certain publications may go to almost everyone on your lists, but some publications may go only to particular groups. A pamphlet on homemaking in the high school is something that every father should read, probably, but a more practical distribution would provide for mailing to women's organizations and similar groups.

Your message can also be distributed at meetings; it can be used as a stuffer with your own regular mailings or with those of commercial organizations, or distributed through local stores. There are numerous ways to distribute your printing, but none as certain as the mails.

Timing is the art of getting your printed matter before the reader when it will do you the most good. Accordingly, don't send out material which explains, however convincingly, your need for new or extra funds around the first of the month, when your reader also receives his bills—or around April 15, for obvious reasons. The middle of the week is also to be preferred to Monday when the mail volume may be heavy and the competition for the reader's time is acute.

A popular song of some years back asserted that "it ain't what you say, it's the way how you say it." While no educator can subscribe to this advice *in toto* without being morally delinquent, there is a great deal of truth in the thought "it's the way how you say it."

The economic importance of writing style is demonstrated every day in cities which have more than one newspaper competing for the reader's nickel. Essentially they cover the same news, but they cover it differently. More often than not, that difference lies in the writing style. Even if he is less than enthusiastic about the contents of a given edition, the newspaper purchaser is likely to read a good part of the paper, if for no other reason than to get his nickel's worth. Beyond his economic commitment, he wants to know something about the day's news developments. Not so the reader of a school publication. He's received unsolicited material. It may be disposed of as summarily as the day's accumulation of direct mail advertising, unless it is interesting. It *must* be worth reading, otherwise the time, effort, and expense that have gone into it are lost.

WRITING WORTH READING

If you would write well, be brief. Only slightly less important than brevity—but equally vital—are simplicity, clarity, and directness. If you ignore these rules, you will simply not be read.

Brevity is the skill of saying what you want to say in the fewest possible words. It is achieved by a careful selection of facts based on a thorough knowledge of both subject and reader interest.

Clarity is the skill of saying what you want to say in words your reader will understand. It is the precept of good writing most violated in educational publications intended for a lay audience. The key to clarity is the substitution of common words for professional jargon. It is worth doing even if there is some loss of exactness; there is little point in achieving the precision of professional language if the reader doesn't know what you are talking about.

Directness is the skill of saying what you want to say without the use of superfluous words, elaborate grammatical structure, or fanciful writing.

These are the elements of good writing. They make a reader aware of what you are saying without being aware of how you are saying it.

SELECTING AN AUTHOR

Most of your publications will be prepared by a committee; none of your writing should be. The committee's function should be to decide what ought to be published, what it should include, the format it will take, at whom it will be directed, and how it will be distributed. Writing must be the responsibility of one person whose work can and ought to be checked and edited by the committee.

Every system includes a number of people who write well. Most of them will be able to write only certain things well. A teacher whose messages to parents are a model of clarity and conciseness is a good choice for most school publications. For a pamphlet explaining the critical need for school construction funds, the best writer might be found in the city room of your local newspaper rather than in a classroom.

GETTING COPY GOING

The writer must know the subject and the audience. What he will say about his subject will be shaped by how much he knows about his audience.

There is a great deal of space in writing manuals devoted to the art of keying copy to selected audiences. For the most part, lay audiences of school publications do not know a great deal about school matters. An exception might be a leaflet for local bankers in which your school banking program is described. In this case, talk his language not yours.

To reach a broad audience (and that's what most school publications generally do) the writer must relate the school message to the interest of the people who comprise that audience. Appeal to security, pride, parenthood, sense of civic responsibility. Make the reader believe that what you have to say is important to him. That, in the final analysis, is what really matters to him.

GETTING OFF TO A GOOD START

A television critic once remarked that he gives a TV drama 60 seconds to interest him. At the end of a minute he either stays with the show, switches to another channel, or turns off the set. While the average reader probably sets no mental limits on how long he will give the writer to interest him, in one minute he might read some 300 words, and if you haven't snared him then you may have lost him.

The key to reader interest lies in your opening paragraphs. You don't have to shock or jar the reader, but sometimes it's not a bad idea to try. It is easier to say what is not interesting than what is. Rambling, irrelevant openings deaden the reader's will to continue as effectively as any of the more sophisticated opiates. Leaden openings, paying obeisance to the Board of Education, Funk & Wagnalls, or the Superintendent of Schools, may make

your publication second only to the late late show as a soporific.
A few examples may clarify things:

Bad: The Blankville Schools today issued a list of 12 ways in which
parents can help teachers do a better job of educating their children.

Good: Even if Dad's science education did end when he learned how
to wire a doorbell, educators agree that he still exerts a lot of influence
on how well his youngsters fare in school. And Mom may not be able
to help in diagramming ionic and covalent compounds, but she still has
a big hand in the next generation's school progress.

Bad: The fourth grade class at Forest Grove School presented a play
with a patriotic theme last week before an audience of 150 parents.

Good: Patriotism isn't listed as an official subject in the course guides
by which Forest Grove teachers plan their programs, but in every
classroom patriotism is as important as the three R's.

Teaching patriotism as such is relatively easy since children are pre-
disposed to be patriotic. But teaching a rational love of America, rather
than encouraging empty flag waving is another matter. Reading about
the Pilgrims, the Revolutionary War, the westward expansion, and
other great events which have shaped the United States, helps to
develop patriotism, but children can also learn much by "experiencing"
these events through such means as musicals.

Last week a program at the Forest Grove School did just that.

PUTTING MUSCLES ON THE BODY OF YOUR STORY

Once you've gained reader interest go on and tell your story.
Keep it interesting by using words the reader will understand,
concrete words rather than abstractions, by writing about people
rather than things or situations. Use quotes liberally. Here is an
example:

It is no longer possible to shoehorn all the classes students want to
take, need to take, and should have an opportunity to take into the
existing school day.

The urgency today for increased educational opportunity, coupled
with greater excellence in the quality of a student's total education, is
causing the Dearborn Schools to consider two major changes in the
existing educational program.

These changes would (1) extend the school day to include more class
periods and (2) extend the school year to include an expanded summer
school program.

A story on how reading is taught in the first grade will interest the reader more if it is told in terms of a real class with a real teacher. A pupil in the class may be socially immature, but for the sake of reader interest and clarity you'd better say he doesn't get along with the other children.

Depend on verbs to carry your story. "Johnny hurt himself badly" is an opinion. "Johnny lay on the ground, his fists clenched, his teeth biting into his upper lip as the doctor examined his twisted leg" helps the reader visualize what the former phrase asked him to accept on faith.

Try to avoid the passive voice; it takes too much space, is cumbersome and slows the pace of your writing to a dead crawl. Don't write: Howard was spoken to by the principal. Do say: The principal spoke to Howard.

In an attempt to write in understandable language, don't go to the other extreme of using words which make you sound like a country bumpkin rather than a school person. Try to avoid time-worn phrases. Invent your own and let others use them often enough to make them clichés.

LAYOUT

Layout is the interior decorating of publications. It is the art of assembling text and illustrations into an agreeable unity which will interest the reader.

It is probably harder to master than good writing. Most school people should be able to express themselves well, but, without formal training, most will think themselves incapable of original and interesting publication design. You can always turn to your art teacher, but unless she's a commercial artist, which isn't likely, she won't be much help.

TEXT OR LAYOUT—WHICH COMES FIRST?

There is no single answer for all publications, but there are guides which usually, but not always, apply to specific kinds of publications. In most cases, text and layout develop simultaneously, each shaping the other.

The layout for a leaflet or small brochure may come before the text because you know just how much space you will have and copy must be written to fit a specific space. An informal, picture-type annual report may be easier to prepare if the illustrations and layout are prepared first and copy is written to fill the space that is left. If money is a consideration (and isn't it always?), it would be prudent to get estimates on the cost of a particular publication based on the anticipated number of pages. If your budget will permit only an eight-page publication, copy and layout can be completed with that in mind. It is frustrating indeed to prepare copy and layout and then discover your funds won't cover the kind of publication you had planned.

Layouts result from shuffling copy and illustrations until you come up with a design you like. This can be done literally—that is, by working with printers' proofs and colored paper cut into various sizes and shapes to represent pictures, or by sketching on layout paper. Whatever method you use, scissors or pencil, what you are doing is weighing the importance of your materials—your copy and art work—to achieve a desirable effect.

Make your layouts on a plain sheet of paper the same size as your publication. Indicate the margins, and, if the publication will be folded for distribution, lightly draw a line where the fold will be—you won't be as likely to find your key pictures and headlines ruined by a heavy crease through them.

Think of layout not only as establishing a good relationship between text and pictures, but as establishing a proper balance between light and dark masses. In drawing your roughs, which is just what it sounds like, use thin, straight, horizontal lines to indicate copy; thick, closely spaced, diagonal lines to indicate pictures. An imbalance of tones will be clearly visible; you'll be able to see whether your layout is top heavy, bottom heavy, whether there are too many unrelieved areas of grays, whether your page is so crowded that nothing stands out, or whether the wrong things are prominent.

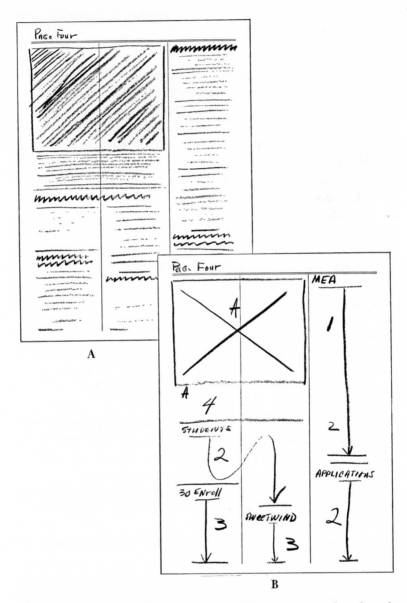

From rough to printed page. A rough (A) serves you rather than the printer. Its purpose is to give you an idea of what the printed page will look like. The dummy (B) is for the printer. The dummy identifies each story which will be used (MEA, Students, and so forth), gives the number

Teachers learn from pupils at a system-wide art workshop conducted by Sarita Rainey, consultant in elementary art. Observing two Grove Street pupils creating unusual effects with forms made from old inner tubes are Beulah H. Johnson, Helen S. Blomstrom, Elizabeth L. Young, and Mamie S. Schmidt, all of Bradford School. Workshop provided an opportunity for teachers throughout the system to share teaching techniques by observing children engaged in numerous art activities.

M.E.A. Honors Teachers

Ten Montclair teachers who have retired this year or will retire at the end of June were guests of honor at a tea given by the Montclair Education Association at the Women's Club of Upper Montclair.

Besides the teachers, the system loses three members of the custodial and maintenance force because of retirement. Leaving in June will be Clarence Benson, a carpenter with the Montclair schools since 1919; Claude Miller, head custodian at George Inness, 18 years in Montclair; and James Stanco, custodian of George Washington, a 16-year veteran.

The retiring teachers, who have practiced their profession an average of 39 years each, of which 34.5 years were spent in Montclair, are: David Bean, Harry W. Burdick, and Miss Lucile Chamberlain of Hillside; Mrs. Margaret C. Hansen and Miss Ann R. Reynolds of Glenfield; Edgar Leach of the high school; Miss Louise S. Roe of Edgemont; Miss J. Isabel Stalker and Mrs. Mabel C. Taylor of Mt. Hebron, and W. Stewart Taylor of George Inness.

Dean of the group in point of service is Burdick who completes 44 years of teaching in June, 40 of which were in Montclair.

Each of the teachers was introduced to the assemblage—estimated at 300 people—by a close associate who expressed the appreciation of the community and the school system for the retiring teacher's service to Montclair. Miss Wilma Angelbeck, vice president of the MEA, presided at the ceremonies.

Students See Problems in Historical Perspective

To relate current American problems to history and to develop writing skills and reasoning ability, Betty Specht, social studies teacher at Mt. Hebron, has eighth grade pupils maintain a book of newspaper clippings related to the previous week's reading in history.

Alongside each clipping the student tells the gist of the article, why it is related to classroom studies, and comments on or interprets the relationship between the current situation and similar historical concerns.

In practice it works out this way: Reading about the tariffs of 1824, 1828 and 1832, and their impact on sectionalism in the pre-Civil War period, a student may select a current news story or editorial on tariffs for his clip book. In his commentary he discusses who favors tariffs now, the reasons tariff proponents offer, and the similarity or lack of it to the reasons advanced in the early 19th century, and finally, the student offers his own opinions on tariffs.

30 Enroll in Summer Reading Workshop

Thirty teachers have enrolled in the reading workshop to be given by the school system June 22 - July 3. The workshop will meet for 60 hours over the two week period under the direction of staff reading consultants Dr. Charles T. Letson and Dr. Elizabeth Speidel.

Registrants will meet in general sessions to study methods, practices and problems common to all teachers and in small group sessions will discuss specific problems faced in the classroom at a given instructional level.

Fifth Grade Uses Sweetwind

A simple instrument called a sweetwind is used by Margaret K. Hanwell to foster the enjoyment and interest of her Glenfield fifth graders in music. Somewhat like a recorder and easily mastered, the sweetwind can be used for solos, in groups, or for accompanying singers.

Job "Applications" Help Students Develop Letter Writing Skills

To help pupils write better business letters, Ann Kapulsky divides her seventh and eighth grade English classes at Hillside into two corporations, each with an elected president and staff.

Using help wanted ads clipped from newspaper classified sections, students write letters of application for one position with each corporation. The secretarial staff screens the letters, selecting for job interviews applicants whose letters are most persuasive, clearly written, and properly typed. The students discuss what should be covered in the interview which is then conducted by the president. After the interviews, the class votes on who shall get the "jobs."

C

of the galley where the story can be found (1, 2, 3, 4) and shows the exact placement of each story and picture. If a paste-up dummy is used, the number of the galley on which each story can be found should be written on the proofs. The printed page (C) is the result of this careful planning.

Roughs are approximations of what you want to end up with. Visuals are layouts designed to show, with fairly close accuracy, the space assigned to copy, pictures, headlines, captions, and margins. A paste-up dummy, which isn't necessary for most jobs, is a layout in which proofs of art work and copy are pasted into the exact position they'll have in the finished job.

If you don't give your printer a paste-up, your visual must be carefully marked so that he can set up your publication properly. Usually letters are used to key pictures and numbers to key copy. To show which picture goes where place a letter in the area on the layout reserved for a particular photo. The same letter should be written on the back of the picture. Use a china or grease pencil to avoid having the letter show through the front of the picture. On your visual, show the exact amount of space each caption will require and key the caption to its picture. In the margin of the layout state the type size and spacing required for copy. The same instructions are used on the manuscript.

A FINAL WORD

If your publication is attractive and interesting, it will be filed by many business organizations, art directors, advertising people, and the like, for future reference. To be blunt, it will be used as an inspiration and guide by other publications people. This information is offered not as an example of the artistic heights you may reach if you work hard enough, but to suggest that before you sit down to design your publication, you peruse some of the better ones which have come across your desk. There probably isn't a professional who doesn't file worthwhile publications and who doesn't adapt treatments from his file for his own use. Try it. It's particularly useful when you've got a ream of copy and a batch of photos littering your desk and you're muttering that back in teachers college they didn't tell you anything about assignments like this.

CHOOSING PAPER AND INK

All you really need to know about paper is that it comes in a variety of weights, textures, and colors, that you can get from your printer samples of every kind of paper stock that is made, and that your printer's experience is your best possible guide to correct paper selection.

Coated papers (the "slick" papers seen largely in magazines) are used for best results in reproducing photographs by letterpress. However, some people object to the glare of coated paper when used for extensive reading matter. Another school of thought identifies coated papers with high cost, and this type of paper may indeed have a built-in criticism factor. Letterpress reproductions of good photographs show up almost as well on English finish and dull coated papers, and these papers offer a good answer to the objection of glare; they are often a bit lower in price, too.

Ink is rarely a problem. Don't worry about it. Ask your printer to show you an ink book so that you can specify colors correctly. But let him use the *kind* of ink he likes and you will get the best job from him.

TYPE FACES

With hundreds of type faces to choose from it is possible to select one which will be completely harmonious with your publication. This abundance also increases the possibility of a poor choice. Fortunately most printers have only a relatively few of the many faces available. This minimizes the possibility that you will choose the wrong type and does not materially affect your opportunity to choose the type which will do most for your book. This seeming contradiction stems from the fact that the type faces found in most small printing establishments are the workhorses of the business, those which are most commonly required. Persons responsible for publications, unless they are type experts who know a great deal about the readability and suitability of many types, are well advised to rely on the standard faces. If you do wander from the beaten path on the basis of a few lines of type seen in a type face book, consult with your printer on possible limitations. If at all possible see the type set in a paragraph. It may look entirely different.

For body type, stick to faces such as Bodoni Book or Baskerville in a roman face. Italic versions of these faces and sans serif type faces are hard reading over a long pull. Use a lightface type for text matter and boldface to emphasize certain words, chapter headings, or subheads. The monotony of a printed page without pictures can be relieved by using boldface alternately with lightface paragraphs or by breaking up the story with subheadings between paragraphs.

The danger is particularly strong in grades 4–6 when reading habits and interests are being formed into a pattern which may shape a child's interests in books throughout his school years and beyond.

To determine the achievements of high school students the colleges rely heavily, although by no means exclusively, on the student's performance in the annual College Board examinations.

The College Boards, taken by hundreds of thousands of students in both public and private secondary schools, rate each youngster in comparison with other would-be college students. In a sense they also measure the standards of the school, testing whether a grade of A means the same

The danger is particularly strong in grades 4-6 when reading habits and interests are being formed into a pattern which may shape a child's interest in books throughout his school years and beyond.

To determine the achievements of high school students the colleges rely heavily, although by no means exclusively, on the student's performance in the annual College Board examinations.

The College Boards, taken by hundreds of thousands of students in both public and private secondary schools, rate each youngster in comparison with other would-be college students. In a sense they also measure the standards of the school, testing

How Montclair Teachers Help Pupils Build Vocabulary

The number of ways elementary school children add to their vocabulary is limited only by the ingenuity of their teachers which seems to be unlimited, judging from the number and variety of teaching practices used in just three schools.

On the advice of elementary education consultant Evelyn Foote, many teachers have their pupils make their own dictionaries. When an unfamiliar word crops up in a classroom discussion, during "show and tell," or in a book, the children are encouraged to enter them in their dictionary for reference.

Mabel M. Hudson, who teaches a fifth and sixth grade class at Glenfield, believes that words are more often "caught than taught." Accordingly she tailors her own vocabulary to include new words which she wants the class to learn. In spelling contests Mrs. Hudson will often ask the children to spell a word and then to give a synonym, homonym, and antonym. In this way they incorporate words from their dormant vocabulary into their active vocabulary and at the same time others in the class learn new words.

Charles C. Anello, sixth grade teacher at Glenfield, has his pupils select new or important words from their reading and use them in a different context

Having children substitute a single word for a descriptive phrase is a technique used by Glenfield's Anthony S. Lolacono to increase his students' vocabulary. For example, a pupil who reports that someone doesn't know how to read or write will be asked if he can say the same thing using only one word.

Many teachers use holidays as a peg on which to hang vocabulary lessons. Second graders in Mary Scott's class at Nishuane learn new words in this fashion. Miss Scott also places captions below bulletin board pictures relating to the holiday, providing a good visual approach to vocabulary building.

Most teachers help pupils build their vocabulary by employing games which make learning fun. Reta Dietrichson's fourth graders at Nishuane close their eyes when they come across a new word and try to visualize the varied meanings it may have. They then write stories utilizing the new words and illustrate them.

The daily newspaper is a fertile source of new words for children in Kay Healy's fifth grade class at Nishuane where current events are used to build vocabulary. Miss Healy injects fun into vocabulary building by having the class play on words. They'll start with a statement such as: If you are smart, and you know you are smart, you are not half as smart as you would be if you were smart and didn't know you were smart. Appropriate words are substituted for the word smart.

Third grade pupils in Jean Barclay's class at Watchung are given individual language assignments. Each child receives an index card which gives directions for an assignment; the ability of the pupil to handle the assignment indicates areas in which special help or additional practice may be needed. A typical card, in reference to a picture in the room, might include these questions: "Tell about this picture. What do you see in the picture? How does the picture make you feel? Did you ever see or do anything like this? Tell about it."

Thomas Randazzo's sixth grade pupils at Watchung keep a list of unfamiliar words gleaned from stories they've read in class or from spelling lists. Each week, after dividing the words on the list into syllables and finding the correct meanings, they hold a contest in which each child must write a story using as many of the new words as possible. The winner is the pupil who uses the most words correctly in a coherent story.

In Katherine F Garnar's first grade class at Watchung the children compete for balloons in learning new words. Mrs. Garnar draws balloons on the blackboard and inserts new words in each. The children "catch" a balloon by pronouncing the new words whose meanings are then given by Mrs. Garnar

These are just a few of the methods used by Montclair teachers to help students build their vocabulary. Each teacher uses techniques which he or she has found to be most productive. Besides these individual practices, Montclair teachers use in vocabulary building a basic reader, spelling lessons, a special text book which teaches reading skills, dictionary drill and any other text books or reading matter the children may use.

Back in the United States after a year in Costa Rica, Mrs. Donald Knowlton recently shared her experience with a fourth grade class at Edgemont School. She showed slides, discussed life in Costa Rica and displayed examples of the country's handicrafts. The wife of a Glenfield School teacher who was granted a sabbatical leave last year to study in Costa Rica, Mrs. Knowlton is pictured here with Janie Walling and Ricky Wood. Teachers who would like Mrs. Knowlton to speak to their class may make the necessary arrangements through the office of the Director of Instruction.

COURTESY PUBLIC SCHOOLS, MONTCLAIR, NEW JERSEY.

The monotony of a printed page can be broken by using bold face alternately with lightface paragraphs.

thing in one school as it does in another.

whether a grade of A means the same thing in one school as it does in another.

10 pt. Baskerville, leaded 2 points.

10 pt. Intertype Bodoni, leaded 2 points.

It is false economy to save pages by using small type. Except for newspapers, don't use less than a 10-pt type. Newspapers can be read fairly comfortably despite the fact that they are printed in 7 pt or 8 pt type because they use narrow columns. For wider columns, 10 or 12 pt is recommended. Even 10 pt may be somewhat difficult to read unless space is created between the lines (this is called *leading*).

In determining line length, a handy rule of thumb is to make the line a length which will take between 39 to 65 characters of the type face which will be used. For easier reading, it is necessary to have more space between long lines than between short ones. A page with long lines, therefore, requires wider margins, or else the text will look disjointed because of the heavy leading.

If the type is to be used in a reverse plate (white letters against a dark background) boldface is necessary. The thinner faces will be obscured in such a treatment. Some papers affect the appearance of type, too. Check with your printer to determine whether the type face and paper you've selected are harmonious.

For contrast with body text, use sans serif and other modern faces for your display or headline type. A word of caution: Don't mix too many different faces in one publication. Be creative, but avoid a circus appearance. For most publications, one display face is sufficient. Where more than one is used, be sure they are compatible. Where there are many headlines, use italics in the same face, and different sizes.

It is not necessary to know technical terms to deal with a printer, but it helps. Keep in mind that while you deal in inches, the printer deals in picas. Unfortunately, many engravers measure in inches, and the two are not precisely the same, which is important to know when ordering engravings.

A pica is ⅙ of an inch and just a hair more. For practical purposes 6 picas equal 1 inch, but the hairline difference builds up in a long measurement so that 72 picas is about ⅛ of an inch longer than 12 inches. The printer measures length of type lines, width of margins and dimensions of cuts in picas. He measures the height or depth of a page in inches.

Type is measured in points, a point being 1⁄12 of a pica. Theoretically, then, a 12-pt type should be 1 pica high. Sometimes it is, sometimes it isn't. This comes about because the *body* of the type (the piece of metal that supports the individual letter) rather than the *face* (the actual printing surface) determines the size of the type, and the ratio between the sizes of these parts varies from one type face to another.

When space is created between lines artificially, the lines have been leaded. This can be done by hand or by having the type set on a slightly larger slug (a line of type). A 12 pt line can be set on a 12 pt slug or it can be set on a slightly larger slug, perhaps a 13 pt slug, to increase the space between lines without doing the job by hand.

ILLUSTRATIONS

Illustrations are to a publication what a good story is to a speech: they help prove or demonstrate a point and make the presentation more interesting.

PHOTOGRAPHS

Photographs are the principal illustrations used in school publications, probably because they are cheaper than good drawings and because it is easier to illustrate a specific situation with a photo. In selecting photo-illustrations, keep in mind these points:

Give the picture a center of interest.
Keep the number of people in it down to a manageable few. It is far more effective to show three children working on a science project than

Note the center of interest and sense of action in this picture.

to have your photographer stand in the doorway and attempt to photograph the entire class working on the same project.

The elements of the picture should be arranged attractively. Good composition in photos directs the reader's eye to the center of interest. In using a profile of a person be sure he is facing toward the center of the page rather than looking out into the margin.

Backgrounds should be unobtrusive. This is a problem in classroom photography where unrelated chalkboard work, pictures, drawings, and other displays may distract from the point of the picture. If a suitable background cannot be found, the intruding areas can be either airbrushed out of the picture, masked, or the negative can be retouched.

The most effective pictures have action. The situation which tries a photographer's soul is the presentation ceremony. The shot of two men shaking hands while one holds a plaque, scroll, or what have you, is a cliché, but it is decidedly better than a picture of the same men staring into the camera as rigid as the guards at Buckingham Palace.

Be sure the print is clear, sharp, and a crisp black and white. A washed out photo or one in poor focus is better not used at all.

FINGERPRINTS, PENCIL MARKS, AND PAPER CLIPS

Photographs are easily damaged, and, once the damage is done, a new print must be used. Try to hold it along the edges; fingerprints and scratches will sometimes show on the engraving. If you write on the print to identify it or crop it, use a blue china marking or grease pencil. Such markings can be wiped off with a soft facial tissue without harming the photo. Never write on the back of a photograph with anything but a china marking pencil. Even the slightest pressure will result in the impression being visible on the face side of the photo. Photos are often marred by paper clips. If you must use a clip, place the photo between two sheets of cardboard.

CROPPING

Most pictures used in publications are only a portion of a larger photograph. They are the result of careful cropping, which is to photography what editing is to writing. Prudent cropping can make a commonplace photo into a prize winner. Cropping may also be required to change the proportions of the picture so that it will fit a given space. Crop marks should be made in grease pencil in the margins of the photograph. They may be placed on the photograph itself, but sometimes they are hard to see, and in any case, should not be placed within the area to be engraved.

The easiest way to determine what part of the picture you want to engrave is to use two L-shaped cardboard strips marked in inches. By moving the strips around, you can determine, simultaneously, the part of the picture to be used and its size. If the art work does not have to fit a specific space, the picture can be cropped with only one consideration in mind, to make it more interesting and effective. Sometimes, however, a picture must be cropped so that it can be reproduced in a given size to meet layout requirements. If this will make the picture less effective, or in the case of a full face photo which cannot be cropped, it may be necessary to change the layout or, if possible and desirable, to have the picture reduced.

How to Crop and Scale a Picture at the Same Time. The solid lines enclose the original art. The dotted lines represent an overlay of tracing or onion skin paper on which the actual size the art will be reduced to is drawn in the upper right hand corner. The diagonal of the proposed reduction is drawn to the end of the paper.

In this illustration the boy at the right is eliminated by not including him in the area covered by the overlay. Much of the space above the children is also eliminated by the position of the overlay. A little space between the girl at the left and the edge of the picture being desirable, a line is drawn from the top of the overlay to the diagonal (AB). Where this line meets the diagonal, a line (BC) is drawn to the right edge of the overlay. The area enclosed in the rectangle ABCD will reduce to the size of the rectangle in the upper right hand corner of the overlay.

To eliminate more of the table at the bottom of the picture a line would be drawn from the right side to the diagonal, perhaps just below the cake. From the point where this line met the diagonal a line would be drawn to the top of the overlay. In this case part of the girl with the horn would be eliminated. It would be possible to eliminate the bottom of the table and retain the girl in the picture by moving the overlay up to the top of the picture.

This illustrates how to reduce along the diagonal of a given area set aside in a layout. If the layout is flexible, that is, if the art can be of any size, the editor would then crop his picture and reduce along the diagonal of the picture, making it any size he wished to.

In this illustration Fototype letters were used; the dotted and solid lines were made by using Chart Pak tape, and the picture itself came from the Volk Corporation.

SCALING

Art work is reduced or enlarged along its diagonal. The formula is *Width* : *Depth* :: *Reduced Width* : *Reduced Depth*. For example, a photograph is 10 inches wide by 8 inches deep. The new width must be 7 inches. What will be the new depth? The formula, then, is $10:8::7:X$. The depth would be 5.6 inches or roughly $5\frac{1}{2}$ inches.

The formula can be expressed mechanically. Place a piece of onion skin or tracing paper over the photograph so that its top and right edge are flush with the top and right side of the photograph or with that area of the photo which is to be reproduced. Since the paper will have to be removed so that lines may be drawn on it, fold under that part of the paper which goes beyond any edge of the photo. This insures the paper will be replaced accurately. Place a light mark on the tracing paper on the lower left corner of the area to be reproduced. Remove the paper from the photograph and draw a diagonal from this point to the upper right corner, then replace the paper over the photo.

If the picture is to be reduced to 7 inches wide, measure 7 inches from the top end of the diagonal across the top of the tissue. Either remove the paper or lightly with a grease pencil draw a line from this point, parallel to the sides of the photo, down to the diagonal. The length of this line will be the depth of your reduced photo when it is engraved.

If, on the other hand, you want the art reduced to $5\frac{1}{2}$ inches deep and want to determine its new width, mark off $5\frac{1}{2}$ inches on the right edge of the tissue from the top. Draw a line from this point to the diagonal. The length of this line will be the width of your reduced photo.

Where you have a piece of art which must conform to a given space in your layout, the dimensions of the art which will be reproduced are governed by the diagonal of the space provided in the layout. Place your tracing paper over the photograph in the same manner as before with the top and right sides of the area to be reproduced flush. From the top right corner draw the space allotted in the layout to the photograph. From the top right corner draw the diagonal of this space right to the end of the tracing paper. Any set of lines drawn from the top of the tracing paper to the diagonal and then to the right side of the tracing paper will show exactly what part of the art work will reduce to the size allotted in the layout. If you are not satisfied with the result, start over again by adjusting the size of the area to be reproduced. This is easily done by moving the tracing paper up or down, right or left until you find the right spot.

ART

The pitfall of the school publication is the student artist or art teacher. The former is usually amateurish; the latter is generally not a commercial artist. Art work of the quality produced by eleventh grade students should appear only in publications prepared by eleventh grade students. The services of a good commercial artist are expensive, much more so than a photographer. However, organizations such as the Volk Corporation of Pleasantville, New Jersey, supply booklets of professional art work arranged by subjects at a cost of pennies per illustration.

Typical illustrations available from A. R. Meeker Co. for use with mimeograph stencils.

Line drawings have the virtue of being simple and sharp. To make them more interesting, line drawings can be given highlights, shading, or other special effects by the artist or the engraver. It is less expensive to have the artist do it in the first place. For mimeograph use, various effects can be obtained by using the shading plates available in any art supply store or from the manufacturer of your machine. Numerous patterns of shading sheets, also available in art supply stores, are easily affixed to drawings to provide emphasis, dimension, shading, or highlights; these can give the effect of several colors, just as an engraver's screen does.

Determining whether to use art or photos begins with the consideration of whether your budget permits buying good art work. On a limited budget you can buy better photos than art. The purpose and content of the booklet governs, to a great extent, whether art or photos will be used. A general booklet describing the curriculum in the system's elementary grades in which no reference is made to specific classes, students, or teachers, may very well be suitable for art work. A booklet about a given class for the gifted cries out for specific illustrations of actual situations. Finally, the decision is a matter of aesthetic judgment. Which will look best? Only you can decide.

PROOFREADING

The responsibility for errors in your text is yours. When your copy has been set in type, the printer will provide a galley proof, which is a long strip of paper with wide margins on which corrections and changes are noted. Usually the printer will have checked the proofs and made corrections before sending them on to you. However, the ultimate responsibility is yours.

Special symbols are used to make corrections. Your printer should be able to furnish you with a proofreading chart listing these symbols and their meanings. Changes which are not made necessary by the printer's errors are known as author's alterations. Most printers charge for them. The surest way to avoid errors from appearing in your printed piece is to proofread out loud. One person should read the original copy to another who makes corrections on the proof. It is a job best done slowly and meticulously. The eye sees words in printed matter that aren't really there. It seems they ought to be, and the eye and brain oblige. The famous last words of the proofreader who spots a missing verb or article are "I could have sworn it was there." A good practice is to ask the printer for proofs before the job goes to press and after the galleys have been broken up into pages. From these, previously unnoticed errors can be caught and a better idea of how the completed job will look can be arrived at. Changes at this point will cost more money, but the expense may be well worth it.

FOLDING, STITCHING, AND BINDING

There are many ways to fold a printed piece. Any printer worth his salt can show you dozens. The decision on folding should be made at the beginning in terms of utility, size of envelope, and similar practical considerations. Avoid the temptation to pioneer new folding territory. The result is apt to be cute, unworkable, and pointless.

A newspaper type of publication consisting of two or more single-folded sheets need not be bound at all. Booklets usually are saddle-stitched, unless they run to 100 or more pages when side-wire stitching and a glued-on cover may be indicated. Plastic bindings are colorful, add novelty, and permit a booklet to open flat. New adhesives make possible the so-called *perfect* binding, which means that the sheets are trimmed square along the binding edge and glued under pressure to the wrap-around cover. A perfect bound booklet opens flat, and sheets pull out or fall out only after considerable usage.

For permanence, nothing has yet replaced *case binding*, in which the printed *signatures* (a sheet of paper folded into pages) are sewed together and covered with a binding of cloth over boards, as in most textbooks and trade books. Your printer knows quite a lot about binding. He will be glad to give you comparisons to show what various types of bindings will cost when related to a particular publication.

BIBLIOGRAPHY

Butler, Kenneth B., George C. Likeness, and Stanley A. Kordek, *101 Usable Publication Layouts*. Mendota, Ill.: Butler Type-Design Research Center, 1954. One-page layouts are shown and discussed. Covers layouts with and without art.

_____, *Practical Handbook on Effective Illustration*. Mendota, Ill.; Butler Type-Design Research Center, 1952. This book provides inspiration for eye-catching illustrations.

_____, *Practical Handbook on Effective Illustration in Publication Lay-Out*. Mendota, Ill.: Butler Type-Design Research Center, 1954. Actual headlines and page layouts which may be adapted for the reader's own use are provided in this handy work.

East, Marjorie, *Display for Learning*. New York: Dryden Press, 1952. Explains use of charts and pictures in teaching; gives pointers which may be applied for exhibits and publications.

Flesch, Rudolf, *The Art of Readable Writing*. New York: Harper & Brothers, 1949. This well-known book explains the art of being understood and how to test and measure the readability of copy and key it to the grade level of your readers.

Langdon, Grace E. and Bryon C. Jorns, *Proportions for Bulletin-Booklet Layout and Illustrations*. Madison, Wis.: University of Wisconsin, Department of Agricultural Journalism, 1950. A useful and easy-to-understand treatment of page size, margins, spots of interest, and cropping pictures.

McCullough, Wava, *Practical Layout; From Ideas to Printed Page*. New York: Art Books for All, 1950. This book is concerned with advertising planning, illustration, and layout, but the principles should be helpful in any field.

Modley, Rudolf *et al.*, *Pictographs and Graphs*. New York: Harper & Brothers, 1952. This book tells how to make and use pictographs to make charts and statistical material more meaningful and interesting.

More for Your Printing Dollar. Neenah, Wis.: Kimberly-Clark Corporation, 1951. Helpful pointers on type, layout, and paper.

Petrill, Thomas, *Photo-Offset Production of School Publications.* Irvington, N.J.: American Graphic, Inc., 1952. A worthwhile booklet for beginners. Covers copy, illustrations, and layout for offset printing.

Postage Economies. St. Louis, Mo.: Cupples Hesse Corporation, 1952. A handy reference work for systems which use direct mail.

Stevens, W. J. and J. McKinven, *How to Prepare Art and Copy for Offset Lithography.* Maywood, N.J.: Dorval Publishing Company, 1949. A practical guide to art and copy for offset lithography.

AIDS

Pictographs. Chart Pak, Inc., Leeds, Massachusetts.

Shading and tinting sheets. Ben Day Press Sheets and Shading Sheets. Ben Day, Inc., Summit, New Jersey. Contak Shading Film. Transograph Company, 30 W. 15 Street, New York. Zip-A Tone. Para-Tone, Inc., LaGrange, Illinois.

Lettering. Presto Paper Type. Presto Process Company, 240 N. Water Street, Rochester 4, N.Y. Fototype. Fototype Company, 1414 W. Roscoe Street, Chicago 13, Illinois.

6

Good understanding and satisfactory rapport between the public schools and the community is, of course, the result of a spirit which permeates the whole school system. Nevertheless, there are a variety of avenues open to us which give us a direct method of appeal to the community's understanding. We have considered the press and various ways of reaching the reading public. Just as powerful as the printed word is the auditory and visual appeal of radio and television.

Radio and television have this tremendous advantage— they reach many people, who otherwise would not be reached at all. These uninterested persons are as important on election day as those most vitally concerned. If we can foster interest and understanding in this group, we will have accomplished much. Radio and television offer one of the surest ways to make contact with those who have no special interest in school affairs.

In considering the use of radio and television in this chapter, we are referring to programs aimed directly at creating an understanding of the school program and of school problems by the community. This is quite different from what is meant by "educational television." This latter has a limited appeal and is often carried on special channels with not too wide a coverage. The ideas suggested in this chapter can best be carried out over commercial stations and by using many of the psychological principles found in advertising.

VALUES TO BE SECURED

Let us consider what values we should expect from the use of radio and television programs. First of all, we get a chance to tell our story to many people—those concerned with schools and so already interested, as well as countless others whom we could reach in no other way. The appeal of sight and sound affords an opportunity to help people to visualize the work and problems of the school.

Business spends vast sums on simply familiarizing the public with its wares. Repetition is very telling in its effect, and modern advertising makes one wonder about the old adage, "Familiarity breeds contempt." It is to the advantage of the schools to be heard and seen under many circumstances and through a variety of programs that come before the public week after week.

Besides telling your story, such programs give an excellent opportunity to enlist the cooperation of leaders within the community. Nothing wins understanding more effectively than participation. When important members of the community are asked to join in a panel discussion, to help get the props for a television show, or to appear as a resource person in a classroom, their interest is vitally awakened and, from that time on, they will be more alive to the whole school situation.

Radio and television programs are valuable outlets for the talents of teachers and students. It is quite possible to use some programs as a part of the enrichment needed by especially gifted young people.

The production of programs forces effective self-evaluation upon all who take part and thus may become a vital factor in in-service training. Furthermore, it forces evaluation of educational procedures and problems on the listeners and the viewer.

As a general rule, an informed public will support a good school system. It is the community where the schools have failed to publicize what is being done that loses school tax measures on election day.

SOME FACTORS TO BE CONSIDERED

The whole field of public relations, as far as education is concerned, is relatively new. The idea that it is an obligation of a tax-supported school system to make the public aware of its activities, its problems, and its underlying philosophy is one that only recently has been accepted by schools. Even yet, many school systems fail entirely to accept this point of view.

Even after a school system becomes convinced that it has need of a good public relations program, it must find out how this program may be inaugurated and carried forward. The use of radio and television is one aspect to consider, even though it is foreign to any experience which most educational systems have had. The question then is, how does one go about taking advantage of the air waves?

There are many factors to be considered. We shall list a few of them and later consider each in turn:

1. How may time on commercial stations be secured?
2. What types of programs should be planned?
3. What facets of the school program should be emphasized?
4. How can we secure effective cooperation within the school system?
5. How can we foster interest and cooperation on the part of the community leaders?
6. How does one put on a radio or television program? What techniques are to be used? How much competence in radio and television production is required of the school person in charge?
7. Should we make a direct or indirect appeal to the thoughts and feelings of people in the community?
8. How should the whole program be coordinated?
9. How can a good audience be secured?

HOW TO SECURE TIME

Commercial stations are on the air to make a profit. This is done through advertising, and success depends upon the size of the audience. Every station is required by the rulings of the Federal Communications Commission to maintain an over-all program that is in the public interest. This means that all stations devote a portion of their time to non-commercial public service programs. It is for this reason that school systems are able to secure free time.

Stations are free to decide what public service programs they will sponsor. They naturally want only programs with popular appeal which will secure a reasonably high audience rating. Furthermore, they want the production of these programs to give them the least amount of trouble possible.

PROGRAMS MUST BE WORTHY

The first requisite would be that you have something good to publicize. If your school system will not bear scrutiny, you had best keep off the air. This does not mean that unsatisfactory conditions should never be publicized. Far from it. Some years ago, a school system put out an annual report devoted to showing in pictures the lamentable condition of the whole physical plant. The report had wide circulation, the newspapers were enlisted, and a vast program of informing the public about the tragic situation resulted in dramatic response by the taxpayers.

The teaching program, however, must be as good as available resources will allow. The schools may be handicapped by certain factors, possibly oversized classes or lack of instructional materials. However, if the philosophy behind the instruction and the methods employed can be justified, a school system may safely embark upon a program to make the public aware of what the schools are doing.

Besides having a good school system upon which to report, interesting and appealing programs must be planned. You are selling something, and it is just as important that you produce audience-catching programs as it would be were you an advertiser.

ORGANIZATION AND DEPENDABILITY

Before you make a request for time on any channel, have your ideas well planned and organized. Do not ask for time and then decide what to do with it. Go to the local program director with a definite outline of what you would present. Be able to give evidence that the program would appeal to a wide audience.

Some stations have a special program director for public service programs. In that case, he is the man to approach. Otherwise put your request to the general program director.

Once you have secured an allotment of time, remember radio and television are like show business—the show must go on. Never fail to produce what you have agreed upon. Radio and television come close to being a split-second operation, and commitments for rehearsal or taping must be met on the minute. A program must be timed with absolute accuracy. Never appear at a station with a program that "you think" will take fifteen minutes. "Dead air," or having to resort to fill-in music, is a catastrophe to radio people. Never cancel a program unless some satisfactory arrangement has been arrived at with the station. Keep the studio informed in advance of each step in your activities.

START IN A SMALL WAY

If you can get time for a series of four or five fifteen-minute programs and make that series a real success, you'll have no difficulty in getting more time, not only on that channel but on others. Do something dramatic—something that will catch the public interest.

The schools of a certain community were asked to participate once a week on a daily community club program. The schools' program was so outstanding that other stations offered time and, as a result, this school system was able to develop quite a satisfactory public relations program on the air.

In 1957, the Portland, Oregon, school system had four half-hour television shows each week, as well as two half-hour, and three fifteen-minute radio programs. This very ambitious and effective schedule all grew out of a fifteen-minute radio series, inaugurated in 1948 over a minor station. For the original series the school system chose the field of special education. It presented tellingly what the schools were doing for the blind, the crippled, the deaf, the home-bound, and the maladjusted children of their city. Most people were totally ignorant about that phase of the educational program, but their sympathies were touched, and there was an astonishing response to the series. Other stations asked for school programs, and it was eventually possible to secure any amount of time that was requested.

PLAN FAR IN ADVANCE

Commercial channels are programmed months ahead, and it is futile to request time for something you want publicized next week. If you have a regular block of time, you can, of course, adjust your programs to publicize things as they occur.

Present your over-all plans for a school year in the preceding spring or early summer. It is advisable to put your plans into writing and to get a written agreement with the program director. This does not mean that each detail must be worked out in advance, but the broad outline should be agreed upon with the understanding that changes may be made. Some such letter as the following would give both the station and the schools a definite basis for a year's activity:

Program Director, Radio ....
Dear Mr. ....

As you know, the schools have agreed to produce a series of half-hour discussion programs during the 1960–61 school year. This is the "Your Schools and You" program continued from last year. We understand that these programs are to be broadcast from 8:00 to 8:30 on Sunday evenings and that the tape will be made in Studio B at 10:30 on the preceding Friday morning. All participants will be in the studio by 10:00 a.m. for a preliminary planning period.

We are suggesting the following topics for this year's series:

Oct. 28. What is the schools' responsibility for the education of the exceptional child?

Nov. 11. How should the schools meet the challenge of the gifted child?

Nov. 25. How can we meet the needs of the handicapped most satisfactorily?

Dec. 9. The cost factor in the education of the exceptional child.

Dec. 23. How satisfactory is our present-day instruction in reading?

Jan. 20. How effective is our teaching of arithmetic?

Feb. 3. What is the purpose of social studies in our schools?

Feb. 17. Should controversial subjects be dealt with in classrooms?

Mar. 3. Should a study of international affairs, the United Nations, UNESCO, etc., be a part of the high school social studies curriculum?

Mar. 17. What part does the school board play in the school system?

Apr. 7. Is a merit system advisable in deciding teachers' salaries?

Apr. 21. The school budget.

May 5. What is the present financial situation of our school system?

You will notice that there will be an hiatus between Dec. 23 and January 20, and between March 17 and April 7 owing to the Christmas and spring vacations. You remember we discussed this and you agreed to fill in with other programs.

If this schedule is satisfactory, will you please send me a letter of acceptance?

Sincerely yours,

TAKE THE BURDEN OFF THE STUDIO

Commercial stations do not expect to spend as much time in the preparation and production of community service programs as they do on regular programs bringing in revenue. You will find yourself much more popular with the station if you are responsible for as much planning and preliminary production as possible.

To do this, find out what form the station prefers for program format. Send as many copies as the station requests. Some want as many as ten copies. Have all the needed paraphernalia and props at the studio well in advance of production. The person responsible for the program might well check with the studio the day before production to be sure that everything is in order. Later in this chapter, types of format and program outlines will be presented.

Sometimes students interested in stagecraft, dramatics, or radio can be regularly assigned to help put on a television show. This increases the value of the program by giving talented young people valuable training.

Student helpers get instructions from floor director just prior to show.

RELATIVE VALUE OF TELEVISION AND RADIO

When you are considering whether to attempt to get radio or television time, it should be understood that both mediums are of great value. Each, however, has its own particular purpose. For discussion, general news, spot annoucements, repetition of an idea, interviews, and explanation, radio is even superior to television. Excellent music programs may be featured on radio. For presenting school procedures and classroom techniques, television is much more effective. It is the medium through which student talent, as a rule, can best be exhibited. Both appeal to large audiences; experience has shown that both cause gratifying responses.

Remember that television production takes infinitely more time than does radio. Certainly for the time and effort spent, radio is as rewarding as is television. Television is more striking, and, for some things, television is vastly superior and warrants the time and effort required, but both are needed if your program of creating understanding of the schools is to be really effective.

SOME IMPORTANT CONSIDERATIONS

Simply to give an actual picture of school activity is not enough. The result might be compared to the misinterpretation resulting from quoting something out of context. It is not possible to show the whole sweep of school activity, and, consequently, choices as to what to present must be made. These choices are tremendously important.

A young superintendent, faced for the first time with using television as a tool for community understanding, told his director of public relations, "I don't care what you present but I want it in every case to be an absolutely true picture of what we do."

So a program on third grade reading was presented. The classroom was attractive, the children eager and animated, the atmosphere charming. They played games about horses, they galloped like horses, they were working on a mural about horses, and some were modeling horses in clay. Not a book was seen or touched, not a word was read by anyone, but the opening caption had said, "Third Grade Reading Class of ———— School."

Now, a primary teacher of the modern brand would have

known that this was an activity period growing out of much reading about horses or else a motivation for a unit on the same subject. As such, it was an admirable presentation. However, there was no word of explanation, no interpretation. It was just what the superintendent ordered—a true picture of a school activity. This came at the height of the furor over *Why Can't Johnny Read?* What impression would the ordinary viewer get from that program? He'd say, "What do you mean—reading! They're just playing."

Radio and television are two-edged tools when used for school public relations. The first thought in planning must be, "What idea do I want to get over to the public?" After this idea is firmly determined, then choose and plan every step to lead to that end. The activities portrayed must be honest and real, never faked, but they must be a means to an end, with necessary editing and comment assuring that the viewer will get the right idea.

What could have been done to give a reassuring picture of third grade reading and at the same time have made it evident that reading today means more than going from child to child each reading a paragraph out of the same sterile book? A typical reading lesson could have been in progress with possibly two or three groups involved showing that not all students are on the same level. Some place along the way, phonics could have been employed as a means toward word recognition. The use of the classroom library could be indicated through a passing reference. At the very end of the program, the activity period could be started, and the fade-out could leave the children busy with interests growing out of the reading period.

In the section, "Techniques and Production," examples will be given of the type of explanation and comment that helps viewers to get the desired impression. In tape recording some actual class activity, the person doing the taping could, from time to time, interpolate a word or two of explanation that would make the ensuing program much more meaningful.

Everything going out over the air should be scrutinized and evaluated before it is released. The chief criterion should be,

"Will this give the kind of impression we want?" Other considerations are, "Is this a true picture?" and "Will this catch the interest of an audience?"

IMPORTANCE OF TITLES

Advertisers spend much thought on catchy titles, and school people should seek to find arresting and intriguing names for programs. The stations are impressed if you can suggest a title that will help "sell" the program. Here are a few suggestions not mentioned elsewhere in this chapter:

Your Schools and You, a discussion program between educators and representative members of the community;

Quiz 'Em, a contest program on current events;

Live and Learn, an adult education program;

Class Time, a schoolroom show;

School Workshop, a program going into many phases of school concern;

Meet the Teacher, a series of interviews with outstanding teachers;

Junior Citizens, a series of interviews with outstanding students of all age levels;

Opinion Unlimited, a discussion program for senior high school students;

See How They Learn, a television series tracing the teaching of each subject matter field from primary grades through high school;

Fifty Thousand Children, a radio program of dramatizations of typical school situations in a school system of 50,000 children.

Titles must of necessity be short and should be popular in their appeal.

CHOICE OF PARTICIPANTS

In the matter of choosing those who shall take part in radio and television programs, there are many factors to be considered. The paramount consideration, however, is the ability of the person in question to produce the desired effect.

In radio, we have simply the person's voice and manner of speaking upon which to depend. Naturally, the person must have something of value to say, but it is extremely important

how he says it. Choose persons with pleasant voices that record
well. Fluency and ease of speech are important—as is a good
vocabulary. Avoid at all costs those who are prone to make
grammatical errors in speech. The schools are particularly vul-
nerable to criticism in this regard. Some excellent teachers simply cannot project themselves through radio.

In television, we must consider, as well as voice, appearance
and the ability to withstand stage fright—which is a very real
hurdle in successful television production. Consider the person's
neatness, ease of motion, alertness to suggestion, and general appearance. Remember that the teacher who appears on the scene
will represent the concept *teacher* to a very large audience.

After this first consideration is met, we must then remember
to use as many different people as possible, to see that many
schools are represented, and to choose participants who are eager
to take part.

HIT WHILE THE IRON IS HOT

If a subject is causing unusual public interest, seize the opportunity to make the most of this concern. A few years ago it
was the reading program. Now it is the importance of science
and mathematics. If a community is stirred up about report
cards, make this an opportunity to secure a better understanding
of the whole evaluation and recording concept.

COMMERCIAL ASPECT

Inevitably, any school system that goes into radio and television will sooner or later have to meet the threat of commercial-
ism. School talent will be requested for advertising purposes.
Talent scouts for commercial programs will seek to work
through music and dramatic departments. There are two sides
to this question. By so operating with these commercial interests,
a larger audience is secured, more young persons are given an
outlet for their talents, and much good will toward the schools
is engendered in some quarters.

On the other hand, such participation presents a situation that can very easily get out of hand. If a school choir sings on a program sponsored by a department store, any other commercial establishment feels it has a right to demand such participation.

Furthermore, when any representative of the schools appears on a program other than one sponsored solely by the schools, the schools lose control of the situation and cease, therefore, to be able to determine the kind of impression that will be made upon the public.

The whole matter needs careful consideration. It might be well to have a conference between studio representatives and school officials in order to formulate a policy. After a policy decision has been reached, it is advisable to put this agreement into writing and file it with each station. Persons involved in the music and dramatic departments of the various schools should also be aware of the policy that has been adopted by the administration in this matter. The following statement is an example:

On Wednesday, April 27, a meeting was held, made up of representatives of our three television stations and the school administration. They discussed certain policies which we think should be established concerning the relationship between the television stations and the Portland Public Schools. This meeting was attended by: Mr. Samuel Herrick, of KLOR; Mr. Gene Ragle, of KPTV; Mr. Luke Roberts, of KOIN-TV; Dr. Amo DeBernardis, assistant superintendent; and Georgia B. Howe, supervisor of special projects.

The decisions reached would establish a policy as follows:

1. No program series sponsored jointly by the Portland Public Schools and a commercial television station will ever accept commercial sponsorship.

2. Whenever student talent or school personnel is used on participating programs, plans for such use must be cleared through Miss Howe's office.

3. This does not refer to talent that is recruited on the outside through means other than public school facilities. When, however, school personnel or individual student talent is used in this situation, the station will be careful not to associate the persons involved with any particular school and will make it clear that the program involved is in no sense a school program.

4. No public school equipment or facilities will be used on a television program without express permission from Miss Howe's office.

5. The management of a television station will feel a responsibility in these matters even when the participating program is a "package" program.

6. The Portland Public Schools will do everything possible to see that the quality of the programs and of the talent used is of the best.

COOPERATION WITHIN THE SYSTEM

The production of radio and television programs requires arduous work and effective cooperation on the part of many persons. No program can be carried out unless the school system as a whole is interested in and enthusiastic about the enterprise. There are many considerations that need to be taken into account in this matter of system-wide cooperation.

Naturally, the administration must be behind such a program. True, their enthusiasm will grow as the program proves its worth. As the project develops, board approval and administrative leadership will have to be evident. If the program is not too ambitious at first, there will be an opportunity to demonstrate the value of such public relations efforts. Having proved its worth, the program can develop with administrative approval and encouragement.

GETTING COOPERATION OF SCHOOLS AND SCHOOL PERSONNEL

The wider the participation, the more chance there is for effective cooperation. For this reason, every effort should be made to draw programs from as many sources as possible. Give many schools, teachers, and classes an opportunity to present programs. Guard against the temptation to fall back upon veteran performers.

See that every subject field and every phase of the school district's activity are given attention. Plan at the beginning of the year with supervisors and directors so that they will be formulating ideas.

It is desirable to have some definite organizational plan through which the director of public relations and the various supervisors and other administrators can systematically work together.

During the production of a program, give the teacher and others involved all the help, consideration, and reassurance possible. Give them suggestions about techniques, tell them what to wear, advise them about movement and voice. Give them ample time to rehearse within their own classroom.

At all times, be systematic, clear in your instructions, and considerate of those novices who are involved in a program. Interfere as little as possible with the time schedules of classes. Above everything, be generous with praise where deserved and of expressions of appreciation.

One school system followed the policy of having the superintendent write a letter of appreciation to every member of the staff who participated in such programs. A copy of the letter went into the individual's file. Since taking part in radio and television productions is time-consuming and nerve-wracking, it is only fair that participants get some recognition for their efforts.

GETTING AN AUDIENCE

The whole purpose of these programs has been defeated if they fail to have wide audience appeal. The first factor in securing an audience is the worth of the programs; if they are good, people will dial for them. They are, however, competing with costly professional programs paid for through advertising; the competition for radio and television audiences is keen and if the schools embark upon this type of effort, they must do what they can to meet that competition.

Even though programs are good, you still need to win community interest, and there are ways of doing this. People must be aware that the schools have a series of programs on various channels. Mimeograph or print each month's schedule with brief explanatory notes about each individual program; circulate these among civic groups, women's clubs, and parent-teacher circles and post them in such places as public libraries and civic recreation centers. Keep the newspapers interested and informed. If possible, get the schools' program schedule included in the daily radio and television section. (Another excellent device is to publish the schedule in school newspapers or to send the announcements home through school children.) Try to get some feature writer to do an article on a school production. Portland's *Spotlight on Youth* program was able to inspire a two-page center spread with this opening line, "Biggest live television operation in Portland, and by all odds, the most interesting to watch in production, is a public school show, *Spotlight on Youth,* which appears every other Saturday from 1:30 to 2:00 p.m." Welcome every opportunity to speak before community groups about these programs on the air. Mention of them could be made in connection with any talk by a representative of the schools at a community gathering.

There are other ways of awakening interest besides these direct methods. Every person outside the school system, who in some way is involved in a program, becomes a press agent. Enlist community leaders from a wide variety of fields in discussion programs and interviews. Sometimes you can get the attention of a whole group by requesting that the organization suggest good participants. For example, instead of simply inviting some well-known Legionnaire to take part in a discussion, write to the local commander of the Legion post and ask him for suggestions.

Where feasible, work with organizations in planning programs. The Junior Chamber of Commerce in a certain city sponsored a radio series on community affairs. It was a well produced program with a wide, established audience. They devoted eight consecutive programs in this series to school affairs. These programs were planned jointly by the school public relations representative and the radio committee of the Junior Chamber of Commerce. Do not hesitate to ask for assistance in such matters as properties for television shows. All large stores have amazing resources in the matter of "props," and they are glad to work with the schools as a part of their own public relations program. One large department store became so interested in the school shows that they gave publicity to the schools' radio and television schedule in their house organ.

No opportunity should be lost to gain publicity for these programs. They are expensive in time and effort, and this investment is lost if the programs, no matter how excellent, fail to secure a significant audience.

TYPES OF PROGRAMS

There are countless types of programs, and the choice of which to employ depends upon your purpose. Assume for the moment that the following purposes are the ones that a school system wishes to accomplish:

1. Present classroom techniques.
2. Present problems facing the school system.
3. Discuss controversial issues.
4. Familiarize the public with the philosophical principles underlying educational procedures.
5. Give an overview of the whole educational system.
6. Highlight certain poorly understood phases of the school program.
7. Familiarize the community with school personnel.
8. Explain the financial setup and problems of the district.
9. Give school news.
10. Justify some procedure.
11. Keep schools before the public in a constructive light.
12. Give an outlet to the talents of students.

What, then, are the best types of programs for satisfying these purposes? Philadelphia has an excellent schedule of public relations programs. The nature of these series changes from year to year, but in 1958–59 the schedule included the following:

Progress, a weekly colorcast put on in cooperation with the Pennsylvania Education Association and the New Jersey Education Association. This program interprets problems and services of the schools. It won a national award in 1957.

Careers Unlimited, a weekly television program featuring three high school pupils interested in engineering. They discuss career opportunities with expert professionals in the field. This is excellent for public relations purposes because it presents superior students, shows quality of school preparation, and enlists outstanding laymen in a school activity.

Stars of Tomorrow, a weekly radio program featuring teaching of music and the talents of outstanding pupils. This program won a first award at Ohio State University in 1957.

Career Forum, a weekly radio program. Gives twelve high school pupils from public, private, and parochial schools an opportunity to ask questions of an outstanding leader in business, industry, or government. Each week a different career is highlighted.

Besides these scheduled programs, regular news is supplied to all local stations. At various times, school officials send taped statements to the

COURTESY PUBLIC SCHOOLS, DULUTH, MINNESOTA.

Very simple sets are often effective. This is from Classroom Karnival, Duluth Public Schools.

various stations. Feature stories are also sent to both radio and television stations. Silent film is used for the latter, with commentary.[1]

The Duluth Public Schools, in 1954–55, had a weekly radio program called *Classroom Karnival* in which elementary pupils participated. They also maintained a weekly television show called *These Are Your Schools* which sought for better school understanding. Typical program material included a lesson in reading, an art demonstration, music appreciation, spelling, and the education of blind children.[2] The public schools of Springfield, Missouri, produce a weekly telecast called *Television Classroom*. It has been very successful and has had wide publicity. Through this program the citizens of Springfield become familiar with all phases of school activity.[3]

PRESENT CLASSROOM TECHNIQUES

To present classroom techniques, television is the best medium. Some stations are able to televise actual scenes in the classroom. However, televising scenes in the classroom is extremely costly to the station; moreover, it is not as satisfactory, on the whole, as simulated classroom programs produced at the studio. Simulated classroom programs can be done with video tape when convenient to both the school and the station and released at the scheduled time.

Quite informative classroom programs can be done by radio —tape-recording right in the school. This would serve in certain areas such as social studies, music, and some phases of language arts, but it takes real skill to make a successful radio tape. Explanatory comments as the tape proceeds are helpful.

Classroom techniques may be discussed on radio in the form of interview or discussion. When having such a discussion, pedagogic language should be avoided. Remember that, while "drill"

[1] Information supplied by Martha A. Gable, Director of Radio and Television Education for the Philadelphia Public Schools.

[2] Information supplied by Dora Mary MacDonald, Director of Public Relations of the Duluth Public Schools.

[3] Information supplied by Robert C. Glazier, Director of Public Information, Springfield (Missouri) Public Schools.

may be to the educator "purposeful repetition," to the ordinary listeners it's drill. Empathy is a fine word, but on the air some more popular expression would serve better. Use the words and expressions that will have meaning to a lay audience.

PRESENT PROBLEMS FACING THE SCHOOL SYSTEM

This may be done on radio interviews or through a discussion program. It can be done forcefully on television if sufficient visual material is available. For example, if a school system is faced with the necessity of a large building program, the super-intendent or the chairman of the board could make an effec-tive presentation. He would need much visual material—maps, graphs, and pictorial charts. Care must be taken in preparing charts and other visual materials to be sure that they are plainly visible when televised. This type of program needs rehearsal be-cause the presentation of visual material over television is not easy and requires practice.

DISCUSS CONTROVERSIAL ISSUES

Radio is the best medium for the discussion of controversial issues. It is more effective if the discussion group, which should not exceed five, is made up of persons with varying opinions. There should be at least one person who can ably uphold the point of view of the schools. Also, there should be someone who is known to hold somewhat contrary views. The other members should be chosen because of their standing in the community and their effectiveness in discussion. If, for example, a com-munity has become aroused over whether or not the school should teach students about communism, a good discussion group might include the director of social studies, a represen-tative from the Daughters of the American Revolution or the American Legion, a parent-teacher leader, a well-informed in-dustrialist, and a top-grade senior student.

It is questionable whether this type of program should be re-hearsed. Rehearsal takes the edge off spontaneity. A preliminary letter could set the stage for the discussion, and a brief planning period at the studio could precede the unrehearsed discussion.

PRESENT SCHOOLS' UNDERLYING PHILOSOPHY

The schools' underlying philosophy will be presented indirectly through practically all public relations programs; certainly it will be made evident in classroom presentations and in interviews. No opportunity should be lost in discussion, comment, interview, and explanation to voice clearly the philosophy upon which the school program rests. Of course, the same philosophical principles would make good subjects for discussion groups.

GIVE AN OVERVIEW OF THE WHOLE SCHOOL SYSTEM

Giving an overview of the whole school system must be considered in planning your over-all yearly program. See to it that every phase of the activities of your school district receives attention. The instructional program, the physical plant, the business office, the administration, school personnel, the activities of the board, all are of interest and can serve as inspiration for programs.

A series of short interviews over a radio station bringing in various people in key positions would be one means of showing the breadth of activities that are the school district's concern. Besides heads of departments and people in the administration, interview such people as a custodian, a school nurse, a secretary, a student leader, a kindergarten teacher, a teacher in special education, a football coach, or an adult education teacher. Such interviews might be used as breaks in a program of student musical talent.

A most effective program was produced featuring the person in charge of the repair of athletic equipment in a large city system. The listeners were impressed with the attention given to economy and to student safety. A radio tape recording describing a visit to the instructional materials department, calling attention to the schools' resources in the form of books, films, projectors, models, pictures, records, tape recorders, science kits, and other devices would be a revelation to most people. There is wonderful program material lurking where least expected.

HIGHLIGHT LITTLE-KNOWN ASPECT OF SCHOOL PROGRAM

Such activities as the testing program, education of the gifted and the handicapped, the handling of scholarships, guidance procedures, the choice and handling of instructional materials, all are intensely interesting but not too well understood by the ordinary citizen.

A television program called *New Tools for Schools* presented a ten week series demonstrating new instructional materials by showing a class actually using some particular tool. One program showed a class using a film with preparation and follow-up indicated. The film itself, though of necessity, very short, was excellent. Another in the series showed a class which had just returned from a field trip. Discussion indicated the nature of the trip and the reason for taking it, and activities growing out of the trip followed. Many other tools for learning were shown during the series, and, at the beginning of each program, the director of instructional materials took three or four minutes to discuss the use of the tool in question.

FAMILIARITY WITH SCHOOL PERSONNEL

As you have realized in the description of program types already considered, almost every one of them presents an opportunity to feature several school people. It is particularly important that the public be familiar with the superintendent and his chief assistants; it is effective to have these persons make a report once or twice a year. This is well done on television, if plenty of visual material in the form of graphs, charts, models, and pictures is used. An excellent way to introduce the supervisors or directors of the various subject matter fields is to plan a television series devoting three or four programs to each field and to let the supervisor in question take charge. Introductions and explanations would be given by him, with classes or small groups demonstrating and illustrating his points. In this manner, it would be possible, for example, to trace the teaching of science from kindergarten through high school.

A series such as this would serve many purposes other than that of introducing school personnel. Classroom techniques would be demonstrated, excellent teachers would be seen, and a chance to explain the basic principles underlying instruction in a certain field would be afforded.

EXPLAIN FINANCIAL SETUP AND PROBLEMS

Few citizens have an adequate understanding of the financial picture as it applies to schools. They should know where the money comes from and where it goes. They should be impressed with the extent of the planning that goes on in the financial affairs of a school system and the efforts toward economy and wise use of school money. Many devices can be used to convey this information. Short talks or interviews are good. A well-known citizen might interview the superintendent, asking just the questions in which the ordinary citizen would be interested. A telling presentation could be made over television with large charts and graphs. The use of the flannel board is effective in this connection.

SCHOOL NEWS

School news could include both student news and news concerning educational activities. The chief purpose of this type of publicity is to keep the schools before the public and to increase audience appeal.

Most radio stations would be happy to sponsor a weekly newscast for the schools. News may simply be sent to the station and handled by the studio, or a newscaster may be furnished by the schools.

Student news should be in the hands of student reporters and probably broadcast by student newscasters. This gives a fine opportunity to many talented and interested young persons. *Hi-News,* broadcast for several years by the Portland Public

Schools, was typical of this type of program. Two student reporters from each of the high schools phoned news items to the school public relations office each week on Thursday afternoon. Two student newscasters prepared a 15-minute newscast from these items and made a tape recording at the studio late the same evening. The program was broadcast Friday evening just following a local newscast. The script was in the form of a breezy conversation between the two newscasters, each from a different school. The assignments as newscasters rotated among the various schools. From time to time an outstanding student leader was interviewed on this program.

News in the form of spot announcements is most effective. Furnish a variety of short, effective news items to each radio station and let them use them at their own discretion. News items should include announcements of activities, outstanding accomplishment on the part of school personnel or students, reports of new facilities, significant statistics, and a wide range of educational matters.

A report of actions of the school board should be of interest. One city system has its public relations representative attend the weekly board meetings. He takes the news to a local television station which includes it in the regular newscast at eleven o'clock. This puts the school news on a par with other local news.

JUSTIFY SOME PROCEDURE

This is rarely advisable, but at times it is not only expedient but justifiable. In the normal course of affairs, the constant publicizing of school procedures and techniques serves as an indirect justification. However, occasions arise when some particular activity is under fire. If the school system's case rests on firm ground, the best thing to do is to face the criticism and justify the schools' stand.

A certain community faced persistent and harmful criticism by a small but very vocal minority regarding the teaching of facts concerning the activities of UNESCO. A series of radio discussions on the subject was planned and given wide publicity. On the panel were representatives of patriotic organizations, educators, and representative citizens. The whole procedure cleared the atmosphere and rendered the criticism ineffective.

KEEP THE SCHOOLS BEFORE THE PUBLIC IN A CONSTRUCTIVE LIGHT

Of course, your whole public relations program is working toward this end. However, there is one device that works particularly toward this objective. Keep all radio stations supplied with a number of interesting, significant spot announcements featuring some facet of the schools' activities. The station will run these between programs and thus keep the schools before the public. The various state and the national educational associations make use of this method as does the National Citizens Committee for Schools. It is particularly effective on the local level. The accompanying spots are examples of the type of material suggested.

```
MANY TIMES THE QUESTION IS ASKED--WHAT GOES INTO THE

EDUCATION OF YOUTH TODAY?  HERE IS A GENERAL IDEA OF

THE OBJECTIVES FOR YOUTH:  GOOD CITIZENSHIP; LEARNING

TO DO HIS OWN THINKING AND MAKE HIS OWN DECISIONS;  A

KNOWLEDGE OF THE SCIENTIFIC WORLD; DEVELOPMENT OF GOOD

CHARACTER; A SENSE OF RESPONSIBILITY; GUIDANCE AND

TRAINING IN LEARNING FOR EARNING.  ALL OF THESE FACTORS

ARE PART OF THE TRAINING YOUR SON OR DAUGHTER RECEIVES

IN THE PUBLIC SCHOOLS.
```

WHAT DO YOUR TEACHERS DO AFTER SCHOOL HOURS? WELL, FOR ONE THING, THEY ATTEND IN-SERVICE TRAINING CLASSES IN ORDER TO DO AN EVEN BETTER JOB OF TEACHING YOUR CHILDREN. LAST YEAR 500 TEACHERS WERE ENROLLED. THIS YEAR THERE WILL BE MORE. IT'S ALL PART OF THE PUBLIC SCHOOLS' CONTINUING EFFORT TO GIVE YOUR BOYS AND GIRLS THE BEST EDUCATION POSSIBLE.

YOU KNOW, THE BEST PLACE TO FIND OUT WHO RUNS THE SCHOOL DISTRICT IS AT A SCHOOL BOARD MEETING. HERE THE BOARD MEMBERS, WHO, INCIDENTALLY, ARE ELECTED BY YOU, FORMULATE THE POLICIES UNDER WHICH YOUR SCHOOLS ARE OPERATED. SESSIONS ARE HELD EVERY SECOND AND FOURTH MONDAY AT THE ADMINISTRATION BUILDING. PLAN NOW TO ATTEND AT YOUR EARLIEST CONVENIENCE.

ARE TODAY'S REPORT CARDS GOOD OR BAD? DO SCHOOLS TEACH PHONICS. WHAT SCIENCE COURSES ARE OFFERED? MAY WE SUGGEST, TO OBTAIN ANSWERS TO THESE AND MANY OTHER QUESTIONS HAVING TO DO WITH EDUCATION, THAT YOU ATTEND YOUR LOCAL PARENT-TEACHER ASSOCIATION MEETING. THE P.T.A. MEETS MONTHLY. IF YOU ARE NOT SURE OF THE DATE, CALL YOUR LOCAL SCHOOL. TAKE AN INTEREST IN SCHOOL AF-

FAIRS. JOIN THE P.T.A. IN WORKING FOR BETTER EDUCATION.

IT'S A FACT--STUDIES REVEAL THAT 56 PER CENT OF OUR LO-
CAL HIGH SCHOOL GRADUATES HAVE TAKEN EITHER PHYSICS OR
CHEMISTRY IN THEIR HIGH SCHOOL CAREERS. INCREASED EN-
ROLLMENTS TODAY TAX THE USE OF OUR SCHOOLS' SCIENCE
FACILITIES. THIS AWAKENING INTEREST IN SCIENCE IS NOT
A JOB FOR SCHOOL PERSONNEL ALONE, HOWEVER, IT'S ALSO
UP TO YOU AS PARENTS TO SPARK THAT SCIENTIFIC INTEREST
OF YOUR SON OR DAUGHTER. HELP OUR SCHOOLS TODAY TO
PRODUCE THE SCIENTISTS OF TOMORROW.

GIVE AN OUTLET TO TALENTED STUDENTS

There are innumerable opportunities to accomplish this objective. Talent programs are, naturally, the most obvious method.
Programs of student talent give an outlet to young people with
musical, dramatic, and artistic ability, but there are ways of
giving a chance to other types of talent. A series of student
discussion programs on current topics has many advantages.
In the previously mentioned radio series called *Opinion Unlimited*, senior students in the high schools of Portland, Oregon,
discussed such subjects as "Fluoridation of the City's Water
Supply," "Segregation in Schools," "Should the Voting Age Be
Changed?" "Should Portland Adopt the County Unit Plan?"
and many others. This program stimulated the participants to do
valuable research and produced an excellent impression on the
radio audience.

We have mentioned using student helpers in the production
of television programs. Where this is feasible, it gives wonderful

COURTESY PUBLIC SCHOOLS, PORTLAND, OREGON.

Rehearsal and preparation for an art class featuring the gifted-child program of the Portland Public Schools.

experience to a few students. Students can be included in discussion programs with adults when student opinion is particularly pertinent.

TYPICAL OVER-ALL PROGRAM PLANS

The Portland, Oregon, schools maintain *each week* three television and four radio programs devoted to good public understanding. These programs vary from year to year, because, in both radio and television, novelty is an important factor. Their schedule for one year was as follows:

What Your Schools Are Doing. Radio, Sunday, 7:00–7:15 p.m. Interview or discussion covering miscellaneous features of school program. Taped at studio. (This program has run for nine years.)

Hi-Time. Radio, Sunday, 8:00–8:30 p.m. High school musical program featuring music department of various high schools. Five-minute interview at midpoint of each program. Taped at a high school.

See How They Learn. Television, Wednesday, 4:30–5:00 p.m. Live program from studio. Run in series of three programs each devoted to a subject field.

The School Show. Television, Thursday, 11:30 a.m.–12:00 noon. Live program from studio. Each program features some phase of school curriculum. For example: adult Americanization class, kindergarten, vocational work in Benson Polytechnic, and so on. At the beginning and close of each show, someone from the school discusses the subject in question with a representative of the station. The class present in the studio is used to illustrate points emphasized.

60,000 Children. Radio, Friday, 7:15–7:30 p.m. Taped in classrooms or in studio depending upon nature of program. Programs concerned every phase of school activity. These are typical subjects:

Interview with supt. and school architect on building costs.
A student council meeting.
United Nations Day program.
Education of blind child (a dramatization).
An arithmetic class (taped in class).

Look-in School and *Spotlight on Youth.* Television, Saturday, 1:30–2:00 p.m. These two programs alternate. Spotlight on Youth features the finest individual and group talent within the school system. On each program one high school choir performs and the rest of the program is made up of soloists or small groups presenting vocal, instrumental, or dramatic numbers. At the midpoint on this program comes the so-called "school commercial." It is a 3-minute talk on some serious educational subject, given by the director of public relations. These "commercials" reach a wide audience and were found to be extremely

COURTESY PUBLIC SCHOOLS, PORTLAND, OREGON.

A program featuring a kindergarten class. This is from the Look-In School, Portland Public Schools.

effective. The nature of these midpoint talks is indicated by the following examples:

There was a day when you bought schooling for your children in exactly the same way as you bought them food and clothing—you paid for what you got. Of course, a great many parents paid nothing because their children didn't go to school. In those days, the child of the common man had to make his way without benefit of learning. We, here in America, have long since decided that the education of children is the responsibility of all citizens, and the cost of schooling for every child is paid for out of taxes collected from all the people. We have not, of course, gone all the way in our thinking. There are still many people who cannot see that the people of the richer areas should help to educate the children from regions where the economic level is very low.

Have you ever stopped to think what it costs to educate a child? There is no one answer. One woman may pay $2.00 for a hat, whereas another might pay $50.00. The same wide variance is found in education costs throughout this country. In 1947, there were districts in the United States where not more than $50.00 per pupil was spent on education. On the other hand, some cities spent as much as $285.00 per pupil. In Portland, in 1947, the taxpayer paid $175.00 for each child who attended our schools. If parents had had to provide individually for schooling for their children, the cost to them would have probably been very much greater, for the cost per pupil in private non-religious schools in this area ranges from three to four hundred dollars per year. Statistical studies show that good education in any region increases the productive power of that region, its economic level, and its spending potentialities. There is probably no government expenditure which pays as high returns as money spent on the education of our young people.

There was a time when, upon entering a schoolroom, you would have expected to find the children in rows of seats, each sitting very straight indeed—with the teacher standing in the front of the class, clothed with an attitude of authority. You would probably have measured the effectiveness of the situation by the quietness and decorum of all concerned.

If you entered a classroom in Portland today, you would, in all probability, see quite a different situation. You would be impressed by an air of informality, activity, and enthusiasm. Pupils would be in groups around tables, or if the room were furnished with desks, there might be a more or less informal arrangement within the room. Certainly, not all of the pupils would be doing the same thing. Some pupils might be working at a workbench in one corner of the room; others might be working on a mural illustrating some subject being studied. There would be a classroom library with many different kinds of books on many different subjects. At first glance, one might get a certain impression of confusion, but upon closer observation one would see that this was all the result of activities planned by the teacher and the pupils.

What has happened in educational thinking that would bring about this marked contrast in the last 25 years? In the first place, there has been more thinking about education in the last 25 years than in any comparable period of time. Through an understanding of the principles governing child growth, we have come to see that educational experience must be based upon those characteristics which are a part of childhood: curiosity, a desire for physical activity, a need for working with others, and the necessity of learning through experience. Then too, we have come to see that the end of education is not in the development of skills alone but rather the development of fine human beings. Skills are merely a means to a larger end. As Ernest Thompson Seton once said, "Manhood, not scholarship, is the first aim of education." We have come to see that the kind of characteristics which we wish to develop in our young people are such things as the ability to take responsibility, to solve problems, to understand one's environment, to get along with other people, and to be adaptable to change.

If those are the things that we wish to develop, then the things we do in the classroom must give experience that would lead to such development, and in a modern classroom we see just those types of activity that should lead to these characteristics.

Look-in School is a simulated classroom presentation. A full description of this program will be furnished in the next section of the chapter.

Hi-News. Radio, Saturday, 7:30-7:45 p.m. Student newscast. Student reporters and student newscasters. Taped in studio.

TECHNIQUES OF PREPARATION AND PRODUCTION

The production of television programs is a comparatively new field and one that is little understood by most public school people. Radio is a more familiar area, but in both cases there is much to learn if we are to put on a meaningful and effective production aimed at good understanding of the schools. In this section of the chapter a view of the actual production of both radio and television programs will be given and an attempt made to furnish some guides to their preparation. One way to give this information is to trace the preparation and production of an individual program from its inception to its final production.

PRODUCING A CLASSROOM-TYPE SHOW

The series referred to as *Look-in School* is such a program. It seeks to take the viewer into the classroom and give him a better understanding of what goes on in our schools. The classroom, of course, will be simulated at the studio.

As has been indicated previously, the first step is to decide on what will be demonstrated. The subject of the program to be described will be "The Education of the Blind Child in a Regular Classroom." The subject was chosen at the beginning of the year, and the supervisor of special education has been giving the problem much thought.

The date of production is to be April 28. About the first of March the school producer, usually the person in charge of public relations, would meet with the supervisor and begin to plan the program. First, they would decide upon the points to be emphasized. In this case there will be four points: First, the advantages of educating a blind child in regular classes; second, the special help received by the blind child; third, the expense involved in such a program; and last, the effect of the plan on teacher and class.

The supervisor would suggest several situations which might be utilized. After the producer has visited these classrooms, a decision would be reached as to which situation would be the most desirable. This decision would depend upon the general classroom atmosphere, the personality and appearance of both the teacher and the blind child, and their willingness to participate.

After this has been decided, the rest of the preparation is with the teacher and the class. The teacher and the producer decide just what activities will best bring out the points to be demonstrated, how the classroom will be arranged, and how the half-hour time schedule will be divided.

In April, the class will be studying the early American explorers, and for this particular lesson they will be reading about Magellan.

The first sequence, 16 minutes in length, would be something like this: Mr. Taylor, the supervisor, comes on camera and talks for a moment about the education of blind children. The camera then shifts to the classroom where the class is engaged in talking and reading about Magellan. Several pupils take part—one gives a short report, others read from a story about Magellan. Finally, Gregory, the blind child, is asked to trace the voyage of Magellan on his globe. This is a special piece of equipment, a large, revolving globe with the land masses raised. He does this, telling where Magellan went as he feels his way with his fingers. This is the end of the social studies lesson and the teacher gives an assignment for the next day. The class then goes into a short recreation period consisting of a game.

The furniture is moved back, Gregory helping, and a short game of some kind of classroom ball is played. Gregory takes part with the others.

After they have returned to their places, a child says, "Can't Gregory play for us? He promised he would." So Gregory plays a selection on the piano. As he plays, his special teacher, Miss Kennedy, stands in the doorway and when he finishes she says it is time for Gregory's lesson. Gregory leaves.

Placement, movement, and sequence are rehearsed, but *not* dialogue. There should be no attempt to memorize.

As Gregory leaves, the camera comes to Mr. Taylor, who talks briefly about the nature of the special instruction which Gregory receives.

The camera then turns to Gregory and Miss Kennedy who are busy with Gregory's world with the use of Braille reference books, the Braille typewriter, and the Brannon slate. This sequence will take 8 minutes.

At the close of the program, Mr. Taylor will discuss the situation of blind children in the school system and the cost of such a program.

All this is carefully planned—the furniture to be used determined as is the exact placement. All necessary paraphernalia is decided upon, the children are told what to wear and are given practice in moving about to keep noise and camera interference to a minimum.

This preparation may entail two or three classroom visits, but one should guard against overrehearsal. About a week before the show is to be produced, all involved should get copies of the program outline. This would include the studio, the teacher, the supervisor, and anyone else involved. A suggested outline follows:

GENERAL PLAN FOR LOOK-IN SCHOOL FOR SATURDAY, APRIL 28, 2:00 P.M.

SUBJECT TO BE DEMONSTRATED:	The teaching of a blind child in a regular classroom.
GROUP TO BE USED:	15 students from the 5th grade class of Mrs. Dorene Bryan, James John School.
WHAT WE WANT TO SHOW:	How we educate the blind child with sighted children and still give him the individual attention he needs.
ARRANGEMENTS OF STAGE:	The stage will show the classroom as we sketched on the accompanying diagram and, in addition, a corner away from the classroom with a 2-station table and 2 chairs.

TIME ALLOTMENT AND GENERAL CONTENT OF PROGRAM:

1. Mr. Taylor's introduction   1'45"
2. Classroom demonstration by the teacher and her group   16'
3. Mr. Taylor's midpoint   1'15"
4. Blind child and Miss Kennedy in special corner   8'
5. Mr. Taylor's closing.   2'30"

Mrs. Bryan will arrive at studio at 12:30 p.m. Class will arrive at studio at 1:00 p.m. Prior to the final short rehearsal, the class will be taken on a tour of the studios. Parents may accompany children but must remain in the viewers' room. Studio is located at 2nd and Main.

Mr. Taylor's opening: 1'45"

This afternoon we should like to try to give you an idea of how we approach the problem of the blind child in the Portland Public Schools. Wherever possible, we feel that the blind child should be educated with sighted children in a normal situation. For that reason, wherever possible, we start a blind child in with an ordinary class during his kindergarten year and let him continue on through the grades. This is not always possible. There are situations where, because of emotional factors, it is wise to have a child spend at least some time in a residential school for the blind. Some children will need to gain all their training in a residential school.

As part of the cooperative plan between the State and the School District, contact is made with the family of the blind child at a very early age, and the wisest possible plan is made for that individual child. Of course, a blind child attending regular class needs a great deal of special attention. He must learn Braille. He must master the use of the Brannon slate, and he must have certain accessories for his educational development that a sighted child does not need. All of this special attention he receives, but, most important of all, he learns to live in an ordinary situation and to make a satisfactory adjustment to the kind of life he will have to lead to be successful.

Now, I would like you to look in on a 5th grade class of Mrs. Dorene Bryan, of James John School. The blind child in this particular case is Gregory Robinson.

Mr. Taylor's midpoint: 1'15"

As you saw, Gregory has just left his regular class for his special work with Miss Pat Kennedy, who is a special teacher for the blind. Gregory has mastered Braille. As you saw, he reads as fluently and about as rapidly as an ordinary child. The special globe has been furnished so that he can have an adequate idea of geographical placement. Gregory was taking notes on the Braille writer, and he will later transcribe them on to a Braille typewriter.

The only thing that a blind child learns to actually write, the way we write, is his name, and this is usually a very difficult accomplishment. One of the most difficult things a blind child has to do is to master arithmetic without the use of pencil and paper. Wherever possible, he depends upon mental arithmetic, but wherever this is not possible, he makes use of the Brannon slate. Now, let's look in on Gregory and see what he is accomplishing today with Miss Kennedy.

Mr. Taylor's close: 2'30"

When a blind child is very young, and just starting to use Braille, he will have one session a day with the special teacher. As he gets older, he may have two half-hours a week. I know you have wondered how it affects an ordinary teacher to have a blind child in her room. The teacher is given certain preparation for this and is never assigned such a child unless she is quite willing to take the responsibility. Most teachers think it is an extremely rewarding experience.

As a child progresses through the grades into high school, he has very little need for the Braille teacher except as a counselor, a person who will help him solve any problems which come up. Naturally, in high school, it is not possible to furnish a blind student with the wealth of material he needs in Braille so the School District provides him with a reader who spends a certain number of hours a week to help him with his assignments. At the present time we have 13 blind children in elementary school, and 3 in high school.

Next year there will be 5 new children entering kindergarten. One boy, Claude Garvin, is graduating this year from Washington High School. He is president of the student body and has been granted a very fine scholarship to study law at Willamette University. His progress up through the grades has been watched with tremendous interest and satisfaction by all his teachers.

Now, of course, this program is very expensive. It costs several times as much to educate a blind child as it does to educate an ordinary child. We do get financial support from the State for this program; however, regardless of cost, this method of educating blind children pays off as far as society is concerned because we are developing self-supporting, independent members of society. The Portland program for the education of the blind is very well known throughout the United States and is very highly regarded.

Two weeks from today, on May 12, we are going to show you an unusual class from Cleveland High School where we attempt to teach foreign children of high school age the English language as quickly as possible so that they may enter regular classes.

Details of this production have been included because they give a concrete example of the following guides in preparing a classroom-type program:

1. Decide what is to be impressed on the audience.
2. Plan activities to give these impressions. The activities, especially in their sequence, need not be exactly as they would be in the classroom.
3. Plan far ahead of production.
4. Have your comments lead into the program and interpret it to the viewer.
5. Rehearse but do not overrehearse.
6. Put all instructions in writing.

This is an unusual program, dealing as it does with a blind child; however, the same procedures and guides would hold good for any program whether attempting to show how phonics are utilized, how spelling is taught, how self-direction is developed, or how any other phase of your school program is carried out.

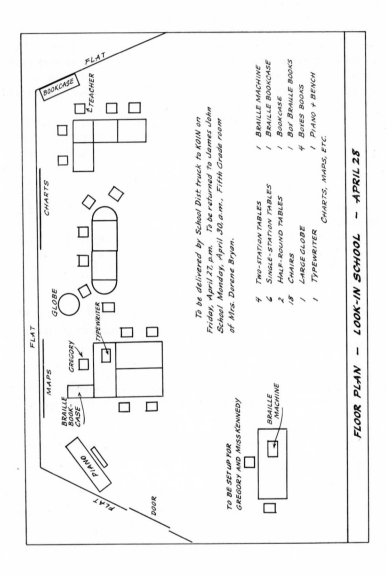

FLOOR PLAN — LOOK-IN SCHOOL — APRIL 28

To be delivered by School Dist. truck to KOIN on Friday, April 27, p.m. To be returned to James John School Monday, April 30, a.m., Fifth Grade room of Mrs. Dorene Bryan.

4   TWO-STATION TABLES
6   SINGLE-STATION TABLES
2   HALF-ROUND TABLES
18 CHAIRS
1   LARGE GLOBE
1   TYPEWRITER
1   BRAILLE MACHINE
1   BRAILLE BOOKCASE
1   BOOKCASE
1   BOX BRAILLE BOOKS
4   BOXES BOOKS
1   PIANO & BENCH
    CHARTS, MAPS, ETC.

FLAT
BOOKCASE
TEACHER
CHARTS
FLAT
MAPS
GLOBE
GREGORY
TYPEWRITER
BRAILLE BOOK-CASE
PIANO
FLAT
DOOR
TO BE SET UP FOR GREGORY AND MISS KENNEDY
BRAILLE MACHINE

164

TALENT PROGRAMS

Programs of this type have two purposes: to exhibit fine student talent and to afford an opportunity to deliver some educational message to a large audience under auspicious circumstances.

If the program is to be on television, it would in all probability be done on video tape at the studio. As a rule, a television station will go to some lengths in putting on such a show because, if well produced, it will be as appealing as many professional programs.

The staging of such a show should be as effective as possible. Wonderful scenic effects may be secured with comparatively little outlay. As has been mentioned previously, there are many sources within the community where props may be secured at no cost and to the school system's advantage.

The talent may be secured in many ways: Through a system-wide series of tryouts, through talent from a particular school or on recommendation from music and dramatic teachers. School instrumental and vocal groups can, of course, be utilized. One city maintained as part of its gifted-child program a city-wide television orchestra which supplied all instrumental background music and which presented orchestral numbers. This group, in the course of a year, became little less than professional, and the experience gained was invaluable to the students.

Rehearsal is extremely important in producing talent shows and ample time for studio rehearsal should be allowed. Without it, good effects cannot be procured.

The educational message can be in the form shown in connection with the description of *Spotlight on Youth.* Use could also be made of short interviews as midpoints.

Radio talent programs can be done in the individual schools thus obviating the necessity for transporting large numbers of pupils to the studio.

COURTESY PUBLIC SCHOOLS, PORTLAND, OREGON.

Spotlight on Youth Orchestra.

DISCUSSION-TYPE PROGRAMS

Discussion programs on an amateur level can be very ineffective. If not carefully planned and organized, they may become so discursive as to be pointless. On the other hand, if too definitely planned and rehearsed, they become lifeless and unconvincing. The answer to effective programs of this type lies in pursuing a course that will avoid both of these extremes.

The program *Your Schools and You* is an example of discussion that did have a telling effect upon public understanding of educational questions. It continued for five years and appealed to a significant audience. About ten days before each discussion, members of the group received letters stating the question, the time and place of recording, and the names of all members of the group. Included in the letter were suggested questions which might arise during the proposed discussion. It was made clear that this list of questions did not preclude others being raised. The whole group met for half an hour before the taping and decided upon the general outline of the discussion. There was no actual rehearsal. The success of discussion programs depends, in large measure, upon the skill of the leader. It is his function to keep the discussion to the point and to see that some definite results are accomplished.

FORMAT

Every station has its own requirements and preferences as to format. Before starting to plan a program, consult the program director and get specific instructions.

The format shown in connection with *Look-in School* is one type of outline. The format presented below is preferred by many stations:

KPTV
NEW TOOLS FOR SCHOOLS
SUNDAY, NOVEMBER 21
9:30 to 10:00 A. M.

VIDEO	AUDIO
CAM CARD—"NEW TOOLS FOR SCHOOLS"	ANNOUNCER: (In Announcing Booth) The Portland Public Schools, in cooperation with KPTV, present the seventh in a weekly series of public service programs devoted to a better understanding of the educational program. Today, Mrs. Hazel Karr, science teacher at Jefferson High School, will show you how she uses the film, "The Sun's Family," as a tool in her 9th gr. science class.

WITH CAMERA ON MRS. KARR, SHE INTRODUCES THE FILM, ENDING WITH THESE SENTENCES:

"These are some of the books they may wish to use as they read

FILM—"THE SUN'S FAMILY"
(10 min.)

about our universe. Now, let's look at the film." (2 min. in all) Sound Film.

WITH CAMERA ON MRS. KARR AND FOUR STUDENTS AT A TABLE, THEY DISCUSS THE FILM. THEY MAKE USE OF CHARTS HANGING BEHIND THE TABLE. NEAR THE END OF THE DISCUSSION, THE CAMERA SWITCHES TO TWO STUDENTS AT A DISPLAY TABLE, WHO DEMONSTRATE THE THINGS IN THE ASTRONOMY KIT. MRS. KARR COMES INTO THE PICTURE AND AT THE PROPER TIME, SHE CLOSES THE DISCUSSION AND ENDS WITH THIS SENTENCE:

"Thanks for coming to visit our classroom. Perhaps we'll meet again on a rocket ship as we travel through space." (17½ min.)

CLOSE:
CAM CARD—"NEW TOOLS FOR SCHOOLS"

ANNOUNCER: (In Announcing Booth)

The film used today was published by Young America Films, Inc., and has been shown with their permission.

On December 5, at this same hour, Mr. Rulon Miller, social studies teacher at Richmond School, is going to show you a variety of educational tools used in his field.

This public service series is presented by the Portland Public Schools in cooperation with KPTV.

Find out the number of copies required. Some stations require as many as ten copies, and they want all material in their hands at least 48 hours before the program is produced.

VISUAL MATERIAL

All slides, pictures, cards, charts, and other material should maintain a 3 x 4 ratio. Lettering should preferably be done on pearl gray, non-reflective cardboard with ink that is not jet black. Persons using visual material should have adequate practice beforehand so that the material will televise effectively.

DIRECT AND INDIRECT APPROACHES

Those involved in creating good relations between the school and the community are always faced with this question: Is it better to justify something, to plug for a tax measure, to uphold a procedure in the face of criticism? Or to indirectly aim at the effect you want?

Unquestionably, the latter procedure is preferable, but it requires far-sighted planning and effective strategy. The person responsible must sense areas of criticism, must be aware of the future requirements and demands of the school system, and must work toward an over-all program that will lead to an affirmative attitude toward the schools' activities and needs.

If a school system is faced with a decision at the polls concerning a special tax levy or bond issue, the task of getting voters in the frame of mind to cast the necessary vote should be a year-long activity. If the program of public relations has been good, the vote will in all probability be favorable. People resent a direct appeal to vote a certain way, and, furthermore, many radio and television stations will refuse to allow such a direct appeal over a public service program. Instead, show through a variety of ways what good work is being done, how economically the schools are being maintained, and what intelligent leadership is in charge of the running of the schools.

A few years ago, the whole country was in a critical mood concerning the teaching of reading, and the popular notion was that the whole difficulty stemmed from not teaching the ABCs first and not teaching phonics. Little or nothing would have been gained by going into an academic defense of the modern method of teaching reading. A more effective way of dealing with the subject would have been to put on a number of classroom programs devoted to reading on various levels. The programs would show how phonics are used and, if cleverly planned, could show where phonics are ineffective. They could show how widely our children read and how important meaning and understanding are as opposed to the mere calling of words. They could show efforts at remedial reading for slow students and accelerated programs for gifted children. With demonstrations of this nature interspersed in the year-long program, you might commence to hear people, when confronted with criticism of the schools' teaching of reading, say, "They *do* use phonics. I saw it on television."

The American schools are facing, at present, quite a wave of criticism concerning the teaching of mathematics, science, and foreign languages. The unfortunate part of all this is, that in most cases, the most severe critics know very little about what our schools are doing, and through ignorant criticism much that is valuable may be lost. Our first concern in the public relations field should be to see that the community is familiar with the purposes and activities of our schools.

WHO SHOULD COORDINATE THIS PROGRAM?

Certainly, the best results in a public relations program through radio and television are obtained if the program as a whole is in the hands of one person. This person should also be responsible for other phases of community understanding. It is not possible to do a coordinated piece of work unless the whole public relations program can be considered in all its phases.

Some school systems, feeling that their own personnel lack the ability to cope with television, have gone outside the field of education for a coordinator and employed an expert in television production. This may have unfortunate results. The first requisite for such a responsibility should be a wide and deep understanding of education and school problems and procedures. The ideal person would be an educator of considerable and varied experience with some knowledge of radio and television techniques. However, if a choice has to be made between a grounding in education and a familiarity with radio and television procedures, it would seem that the former is the most necessary. You are, first and foremost, presenting the school and its problems. A background for this requires an educator. The "how" in this case can be acquired much more easily than the "what." We have here the same choice of emphasis that has developed in teacher training. Is method as important as a foundation in what is to be taught?

Whoever is to head such a program must not only be completely familiar with education but must also be a person of resourcefulness, tact, intelligence, and energy. It is a comparatively new field and should prove a challenge to many ambitious young people in education.

BIBLIOGRAPHY

Abbot, Waldo and Richard L. Rider. *Handbook of Broadcasting: The Fundamentals of Radio and Television*, 4th ed. New York: McGraw-Hill, 1957. A complete revision of the book which first appeared in 1937. Original technical treatment of radio is expanded into the field of television. A book of techniques and their application to the programming of every type of show.

Bretz, Rudy. *Techniques of Television Production*. New York: McGraw-Hill, 1953. A book of production techniques developed from a study of 76 television stations. Treats large network production as well as small station programing.

Chester, Giraud and Garnet R. Garrison. *Television and Radio: An Introduction*, 2nd ed. New York: Appleton-Century-Crofts, 1956. A technical treatment of the field of broadcasting. Revised and enlarged to include new developments in radio and television in particular.

Glazier, R. C. "Springfield's Telecast Informs Adults, Teaches Student Participants," *American School Board Journal*, 136: 26-7 (April, 1958). What began as basically a public relations project is now a public relations project *and* a learning situation for students. Describes the planning and production of a half-hour weekly show that does not "sell" issues but reflects school life by focusing on different phases of the program each week.

Greene, Robert G. *Television Writing: Theory and Techniques,* rev. ed. New York: Harper & Brothers, 1956. Discusses changes in techniques brought about by recent technological developments. Discusses sound and sight as writer's tools.

Hubbell, Richard W. *Television Programing and Productions,* 3rd ed. rev. and enlarged. New York: Rinehart, 1956. Formulates in non-technical language the basic theory of television for its development as an art. Practical techniques of program production.

Levenson, William B. "School Public Relations Through Radio and T.V.," *American School Board Journal,* 135:45–6 (September, 1957). A discussion of the use of mass media in terms of audiences and programing. Summary consists of eleven "lessons" learned in the presentation of 500 radio and television programs in Cleveland.

Lindsay, Charles F. *Radio and Television Communication.* New York: McGraw-Hill, 1952. Endeavors to show the effect of radio and television upon society and to indicate type of radio performances, the skills and techniques needed, and the possibilities of radio and television as a career. Non-technical.

Mattis, Marie. "Radio Program Betters School Public Relations," *Pennsylvania School Journal,* 105:100 (November, 1956). A student school newscaster has an early morning program over the local radio station. Program is about people and events. Discusses the organization and use of personnel in preparing the program.

Merkley, Elaine. "Know Your Schools," *National Elementary Principals Bulletin,* 37:27–30 (February, 1958). The use of television to show the classroom situation, especially the everyday teaching of the skill subjects. Program televised from a classroom erected in the television studio. Describes how cameras and microphones are concealed to allow the children to react as naturally as possible.

O'Connell, E. F. "T.V. As a School Public Relations Tool," *School Executive,* 77:53–55 (February, 1958). A discussion of staff or organization for utilizing T. V. as a public relations tool. Describes how one school district approached the many ques-

tions of what, when, and how to present the school program
to the public via T.V.

O'Meava, Carroll. *Television Program Production*. New York: The
Ronald Press, 1955. A non-technical, comprehensive manual for
those who plan a career in the programing side of the television
industry.

Tarbet, Donald G. "Know Your Schools By T.V.," *American
School Board Journal*, 135:46 (September, 1951). An excellent
illustration of the use of television in one phase of a total public
relations program. Instead of interpreting the school to the
community by showing the school in action, the article deals
with the use of a forum type discussion of school problems.
Describes the use of school staff and lay personnel in the programing.

The use of slides, filmstrips, and motion pictures should be considered carefully in planning how to tell the school story. They are, without doubt, more effective than any other media for creating understanding and stimulating constructive action with reference to particular types of problems.

A brief search through the published catalogues of professional education associations and commercial firms in the audio-visual aid business discloses a wealth of materials on different phases of school policies and practices. Quite frequently these materials are easy to adapt to local needs and conditions, and they may prove to be highly effective in interpreting the life and work of the school to the community.

Besides taking advantage of commercial materials, every school system that is interested in good public relations should think about producing its own audio-visual materials. As will be shown in this chapter, school-made slides, filmstrips, and motion pictures can do much to build wholesome public opinion, and the work of producing them is not too difficult or costly.

THEIR IMPORTANCE IN PUBLIC RELATIONS

Before examining the technical details of how to make slides, filmstrips, and motion pictures, it might be well to review some of the reasons why a school system should employ these media in its community relations program.

It is obvious that a collection of appropriate audio-visual materials enables the administration to take the school to the people. Through the reproduction of information on a screen, they can acquire an accurate and realistic understanding of the system, its conditions, needs, and practices. And when reproduction is accompanied by interesting and pertinent commentary, the chances are better than even that members of an audience gain as much, if not more, from this experience than from a personal visit to the system.

Moreover, good audio-visual productions bring numerous invitations from community groups that want to see them. Not only do they regard these productions as fine entertainment but also as a means to learn something more of the schools for which their taxes pay. It takes merely a newspaper announcement of their availability or the distribution of a flyer listing their titles to bring requests from women's clubs, business associations, church societies, and other community groups.

As a rule, people generally prefer to see rather than to hear or read about a given thing, and particularly when the subject is children or taxes. Unquestionably this preference stems from the fact—no matter how complex the subject may be—that visual pictures can be understood and appreciated with a minimum of effort. Even graphs, charts, and tables take on new meaning when projected on a screen and interpreted through captions and oral commentary.

Another reason for including audio-visual media in public relations work is that they leave deep and lasting impressions on those who hear and see them. Accurate recall may continue for weeks and months after initial impressions were formed. These etchings on the mind may play a dominant role in the formation of attitudes and opinions toward the institution and its program.

Furthermore, much can be accomplished with slides, film-strips, and motion pictures that bring actual conditions, good or bad, to the attention of people in the community. The showing of favorable conditions and practices helps to develop a strong sense of local pride in the system, while the showing of un-favorable conditions and limitations awakens interest and stim-ulates the desire to effect essential changes and improvements. These outcomes are especially true when the frame of refer-ence for any audio-visual production is the welfare of children and society—a consideration that must always be kept in the foreground of all interpretative programs.

It should likewise be emphasized that audio-visual productions are not a substitute for other materials and procedures that have been effective in telling the school story. Instead, they should be used in many instances to complement and supplement other media when there is need for clarifying and strengthening ideas and information which have been presented to the public.

In preparing audio-visual materials, it will be found that slides and filmstrips can be readied for use much more rapidly than motion pictures. And in addition to this advantage, they are equally, and perhaps more, effective in dealing with static condi-tions or the kinds of data that are best treated in charts, maps, graphs, and tables. Motion pictures, on the other hand, permit the use of action, a factor that makes any presentation more appealing and dramatic. Taken together, however, they are among the most useful tools at the disposal of a school system for increasing popular understanding of the institution and its program.

APPROPRIATE SUBJECTS

There are many appropriate subjects, but, in any school dis-trict, selection will of necessity be based upon the public rela-tions needs at a particular time. In many cases the choice of a subject and details of its presentation should be determined only after careful consideration of the particular audience involved with regard to such factors as economic status, cultural and educational background, temperament, interest, and prejudices.

Slides, filmstrips, and motion pictures will be used frequently to create a sympathetic attitude and a broad understanding of the school system, its curriculum, and its objectives. Also they will be used to reach specific groups concerning a single project, program, plan, or idea requiring immediate consideration or action.

Among the subjects which can be effectively treated by these media for public relations purposes are the following:

Arithmetic in a new setting
A day in the kindergarten
A day in the library
Adult education
Audio-visual equipment and materials
Business education
Bus transportation
Career training opportunities
Citizenship education in our schools
Club activities
Guidance services
Handicrafts and hobbies
Health services for children
Highlights of assemblies
How spelling is taught
Instructional activities and techniques
Juvenile delinquency in our schools
Learning without textbooks
Modern instructional materials
Modern necessary equipment
Music instruction in the elementary schools
Music instruction in the secondary schools
Musical activities
Newly adopted ideas and programs
Opportunities for vocational preparation
Our attendance officer and his work
Our dental health program
Our medical health program
Our teacher workshops
Physical conditions of the school plant

Promoting leadership
Recent changes in the curriculum
Records and their uses
Remedial physical education
Safety education for everyday living
School-work experiences
Science teaching
Sportsmanship through athletics
Teaching reading in a modern school
The agricultural education program
The audio-visual coordinator
The luncheon program
The maintenance of school buildings
The school custodian
The school matron
Your children in school
Your tax dollar

GUIDING PRINCIPLES

A picture story to be told through the production and use of slides or filmstrips should be specific and limited to things not requiring motion for complete understanding. A story of broader scope involving motion, as an essential factor, can be told more effectively through the production and use of a motion picture film. However, no matter what medium is chosen, careful and detailed planning should be completed before beginning actual production.

The subject matter of a production should be selected and treated in such a way as to make it suitable for the kind of audience with whom it will be used. It should be kept as free as possible of extraneous and unrelated materials, and it should not be developed too rapidly. Too rapid a development makes it difficult for the inexperienced to follow the concepts presented.

Productions concentrating upon a single idea or activity are much more effective than those attempting coverage of too broad an area with numerous minute details. Crowding too much into the production will inevitably decrease its effectiveness.

The slide, filmstrip, or motion picture should not be used for propaganda or to build up personalities but should always depict the school story with complete candor, truth, and accuracy. As a result, citizens of the community will increase their knowledge, improve their understanding, and heighten their appreciation of what the schools are doing for children and society. Any attempt to conceal or misrepresent a school condition or situation would create suspicion and mistrust in the community. It is clear that these media, used properly, generate good school public relations but when improperly used can be equally effective in generating bad ones.

While it is recognized that local production of slides, filmstrips, and particularly motion pictures cannot be maintained on a basis of strictly professional quality, nevertheless all productions can reasonably be expected to meet the requirements of substantially good or excellent photography. Certainly narration, dialogue, or commentary, whether recorded or given in person, should be in a clearly audible voice and in plain, lucid English.

School district funds should be used to finance the production of these media as a necessary and efficient means of enabling a board of school directors to give a good account of their stewardship and at the same time render a vital service to the taxpayers of the community.

PLANNING THE STORY

A matter of primary importance in planning the story is to know what pictorial material to tell and to whom to tell it. Once the basic purpose or idea has been clearly stated and the audience identified, then work on the script or scenario can be started. It is essential to remember that the *pictures* must tell the story well, with the narrative, dialogue, or other sound filling in and completing it smoothly.

For the sake of clarification, a script or scenario may be compared to a book and the sequences to chapters in which a scene is a part—one or more shots—taken with the camera in one location. Regardless of the photographic medium chosen, economy and good sense dictate that the story must be carefully planned before the taking of pictures begins. It is sometimes believed that this applies only to motion pictures, but thoughtful consideration will indicate that it applies equally to slides and filmstrips.

The proper medium is the one which will *best* tell the story at a reasonable cost commensurate with the importance of the purpose to be achieved. If telling the story as accurately and effectively as possible requires motion, then the motion picture should be chosen; but if motion is not essential for thorough understanding and acceptance by the audience, the sound filmstrip or slide set will be a better choice. Generally, the motion picture should be selected when dramatic treatment is required for the most effective presentation. If sustained attention is required for understanding such things as charts, graphs, drawings, and diagrams, accompanied by verbal explanation, the use of filmstrips or slides will be advantageous.

Slides, filmstrips, and motion pictures should be used in their most effective form in a good public relations program. This requires that they be produced with recorded sound. Recorded sound will control the showing time and insure a uniform and carefully prepared presentation. The availability of good tape recorders makes this entirely practicable for local production work.

It is noteworthy that when pictures are accompanied by recorded sound, the need for captions, titles, subtitles, and labels is reduced to a minimum and audience concentration on the pictures is increased.

SOUND FILMSTRIPS AND SOUND SLIDES

These two media are considered together because they are basically the same in that either a set of slides or a filmstrip is a group of still pictures. A difference between them is that the order or organization of pictures is fixed in the filmstrip but may be varied with the slides. In the case of sound slides, this difference disappears, for the order must be fixed unless the recorded sound is changed.

The subject must be chosen after careful consideration of the purpose for which the filmstrip or set of slides is to be produced and the limitations of still pictures accepted. With the general story well in mind, a group of sequences can be selected and arranged to represent different phases of the story after which scenes must be planned to provide the details necessary for complete understanding and appreciation.

Careful scene by scene narration is required to insure a smooth and interesting presentation. Scene descriptions should be clear, meaningful, and interesting but should never drag.

The script which tells the desired story should be written, criticized, and rewritten before any pictures are taken or decisions made concerning the use of charts, drawings, diagrams, titles, captions, and legends. Once chosen, it is common commercial practice to arrange all of these materials on a story board for critical evaluation and possible revision before deciding upon the final form.

In producing a sound filmstrip or sound-slide set there need be only a main title, an end title, and such printing as is required for tables, diagrams, charts, and graphs: the recorded sound eliminates any need for other titles, subtitles, captions, and legends.

SOUND MOTION PICTURES

The preceding statements concerning selection of a subject, choice and arrangement of sequences, planning of scenes, and skilful use of narration or dialogue apply equally to motion picture production. From the angle of economy, they apply with much greater force because in this medium poor practice and needless waste may increase the cost considerably.

Sound motion picture scripts are basically the same as those for sound filmstrips and slides, but for motion pictures it may be desirable to include greater detail concerning the length or number of shots, camera direction, and lighting. The simple form following will suffice for most situations and is used here as a practical guide for beginners in this type of planning.

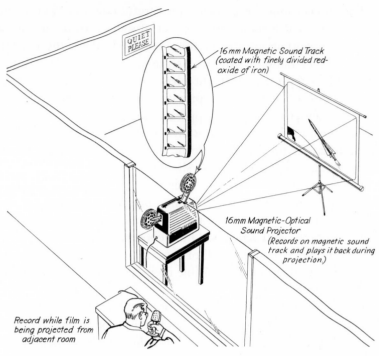

16mm Magnetic Sound Track (coated with finely divided red-oxide of iron)

16mm Magnetic-Optical Sound Projector (Records on magnetic sound track and plays it back during projection.)

Record while film is being projected from adjacent room

An arrangement for recording on 16 mm magnetic sound track should include a quiet location for the microphone and an opportunity for the speaker to view the screen as the pictures are projected.

SCENARIO: ORIENTING OUR NEW TEACHERS

Sequence	*Scene*	*Length*	*Narration*
A	1. Long shot (LS) group of teachers near school bus.	3′	Here is our bus which will take us on a tour of the township schools. There are ten elementary schools and
	2. Medium shot (MS) group Moving toward bus.	3′	two secondary schools: one junior and one senior high school.
	3. Closeup (CU) group chatting in cheerful mood enter bus.	4′	The tour will require about an hour, so let's get started in order that we may be back for lunch at 12 o'clock.

4. (MS) Group leaving in bus and arriving at first stop. *Lap dissolve.*	5' Our first stop will be at Brookline School. Here we are: Mr. Buchanan, will you as the principal tell us about your school?
5. (CU) Mr. Buchanan and some of the teachers in bus, then school building.	6' Mr. B.: Brookline is one of our older schools having an enrollment of 400 pupils and a staff of 15 teachers.
6. (MS) Building receding as bus pulls away.	3' The pupils come from excellent homes and think their school is one of the best. Of course I agree.

PRODUCTION PRACTICES

Assuming that for reasons of economy, necessity, or convenience a school or school district decides to produce certain desired filmstrips, slides, and motion pictures with or without sound, it is both possible and practical to undertake the project. Excellent results can be obtained with slides and filmstrips without excessive expenditures for equipment, but it must be recognized that a strictly professional quality with motion pictures cannot be achieved without the expenditure of considerable sums for professional equipment.

Local production costs, contrasted with commercial production costs, for producing slides and filmstrips are modest and will cause little or no financial concern in most school districts. Frequently the necessary equipment is available from a school camera or photography club. In other situations it may be available from members of the faculty or student body. In either case the expense is reduced largely to the cost of film and incidentals since school personnel can usually do the production work.

For the sake of perspective, it is interesting to note that commercial costs for production in color, involving both studio and location shots, may cost from $25 to $45 for each slide or frame of filmstrip. These figures should not be confused with the cost of having standard black-and-white slides made from copy or a negative, commonly amounting to approximately two dollars each.

Unless distribution of motion picture films is to be broader than for the local community, a strictly professional production may not be required since the cost for a single print of such quality is very high. For all but a very few wealthy school districts, it will suffice to say that a 16 mm professional camera without any of the many expensive accessories required for professional production work may well cost in the area of $5000 or $6000, and the average commercial cost of shooting a 16 mm color film—including film, sound recording, studio facilities, crew, and uncomplicated props—may range from approximately $600 to $1500 per minute, depending upon the type of film produced. Several years ago the Association of National Advertisers, 285 Madison Avenue, New York 17, New York, found that a group of institutional 16 mm color films of good professional quality had a median production cost of $9240 per 400-foot reel which usually runs for 10 to 11 minutes. The median production cost for a black and white sound filmstrip was $2840.

LOCAL PRODUCTION OF SLIDES

The most commonly used photographic slides are 2 x 2 inches and $3\frac{1}{4}$ x 4 inches in size. The smaller size may be obtained by using a 35 mm camera and the larger size by using a camera taking $3\frac{1}{4}$ x $4\frac{1}{4}$-inch pictures. Slides of both sizes may be obtained in color by exposing the proper film—Anscochrome, Ektachrome, or Kodachrome—in a conventional manner and sending it to the manufacturer or other processor. If requested, the 35 mm exposures will be returned in 2 x 2-inch cardboard mounts ready for projection, but the larger size must be mounted between $3\frac{1}{4}$ x 4-inch glass plates and properly taped. If black-and-white slides are desired, ortho- or panchromatic film is used. After it is developed, direct contact positives for projection are made in the same manner as in making paper prints. Direct positive panchromatic film is available in the 35 mm size. This size makes it possible to obtain 2 x 2-inch black-and-white slides directly from the film used in the camera at a minimum cost. If slides are to be made from typewritten or printed copy and line drawings, it is desirable to use negatives made on process film for projection. They are much more pleasing to view on a screen than positives of such copy material. Projection of positives of such material results in a glaring white

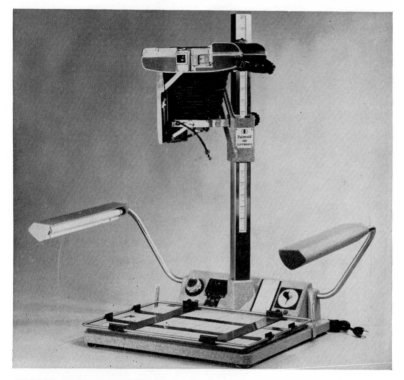

The Polaroid Copymaker, used with a Polaroid Land Camera, enables the operator to copy easily maps, charts, documents, photographs, and small objects.

light on the screen which gives inferior visibility for the black lettering or lines.

Photographic slides of excellent quality in 2¼ x 2¼-inch and 3¼ x 4-inch sizes can now be made in three minutes from the time of exposure in a camera using the new type 46 or 46L Polaroid film. This film is very fast having an ASA rating of 1000 and yields a black-and-white positive transparency rather

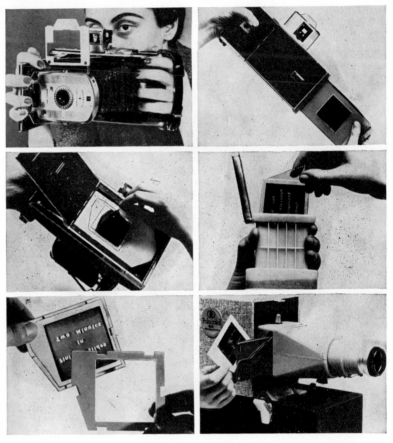

**New Polaroid Land Transparency System makes "Finished Slides
on the Spot."**

than a print. The transparency can be quickly and easily prepared for projection by placing it in a special snap-on mount. The film represents a great advance over previous types because negatives can easily be made from the positive transparencies for projection and making paper prints. The great speed—a newer film with a rating of 3000 has just been put on the market—makes it possible to take many indoor pictures without using flash or flood lighting. If such lighting is necessary, the light may be directed toward the ceiling in order to reduce or eliminate harsh shadows frequently characteristic of shots taken in this manner.

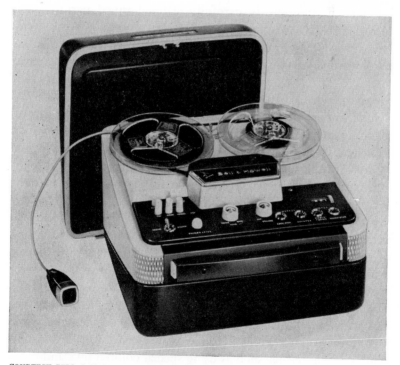

COURTESY BELL & HOWELL COMPANY.

Moderately priced tape recorders, such as this Bell & Howell 785 Tape Recorder, are suitable for recording the commentary to be used with a set of slides or a film strip.

The 2¼ x 2¼-inch transparencies can be trimmed slightly and placed between two pieces of 2 x 2-inch cover glass to make a slide which can be projected in commonly available 2 x 2-inch slide projectors. If a 3¼ x 4-inch slide projector is available, the most satisfactory course is to use the larger size 46L film. This film makes it possible to modify composition by considerable control of masking.

A fine set of photographic slides, accompanied by a carefully planned and well-recorded commentary, is an excellent public relations tool for use with large or small groups, especially when the personal appearance of a member of the school staff is not indicated or required.

Commentaries must be carefully planned, timed, narrated, and recorded to achieve a finished and effective product. A magnetic tape recorder of moderate price is suitable for making the recording—one having speeds of 3¾ and 7½ inches per second is desirable—but it should be used with a good external speaker for the playback before large groups.

It is impossible to overemphasize the importance of careful planning and skilful narration for achieving full impact upon an audience. Unless one particular person must be the narrator, the most skilful person available should be chosen for the part. Timing must be accurate, with provision for signals to the operator for changing slides, in order to avoid awkward delays. Recording should be done by the most highly trained and experienced person available to insure the best possible results. Final editing of the tape can be greatly facilitated by recording at the highest available speed, then re-recording the edited tape at a slower speed, if necessary, in order to get the complete recording on a single reel for playback. In any case, a duplicate copy of the recording should be kept as insurance against accidental erasure.

There are other kinds of slides which can be made by non-photographic means, such as using special colored inks and crayons to draw on plastic sheets or on plain and etched glass. Handmade slides of this nature are generally of poorer quality than photographic slides. For this reason they have not been considered for use in school public relations programs although they are unquestionably valuable for use in classroom instruction.

LOCAL PRODUCTION OF FILMSTRIPS

Production of filmstrips is basically the same as for 2 x 2-inch slides except that a working script must be prepared in advance, indicating the precise order in which the pictures are to be photographed, the titles, labels, captions, and any other printed material to be included in the finished product. Skilful camera work with such a script will yield good double-frame filmstrips in color when Kodachrome or Anscochrome film is used. If the final product is to be in black-and-white, a direct positive film may be used when only one print is needed. If negative film is used, prints may be made from it on positive projection stock in any number desired.

While single-frame filmstrips require more equipment, time, and skill to make, nevertheless they reduce the amount and cost of film required. For those who want the single-frame type, it will be helpful to study *Simplified Filmstrip Production* and its manual. They may be obtained from Ohio State University, Teaching Aids Laboratory, 13 Page Hall, Columbus, Ohio.

All that was said concerning the commentary for 2 x 2-inch slide sets or sound slides and the recording of it on tape applies equally to filmstrips, since the order is pre-determined in both of them.

If photographic equipment for copying and producing filmstrips and 2 x 2-inch slides is not available, and a decision has been made to produce such materials regularly for public relations purposes, the following list of equipment should be considered for immediate purchase:

1 35 mm camera (reflex type preferred)
1 Sunshade
1 Filter holder
1 Set of correction filters
1 Set of color-balancing filters

1 Quick-set elevator tripod
1 Wide angle lens
1 Telephoto lens
1 Standard photo-electric exposure meter—G.E. Guardian or Weston Master III
1 Strobe flash unit
1 Flash extension
1 Color-temperature meter
1 Folding Bounce-ray bar with adjustable ends and intensity control
2 1000-watt floodlights
2 Parabolic No. 2 photoflood reflectors with clamps
  Other lights as needed
2 Heavy-duty extension cords with double-outlet boxes
1 Tape recorder

Since the camera is of supreme importance, care should be taken to see that it is of good quality and sufficiently flexible to satisfy all production requirements. Some of the most desirable features are:

An f/2 or at least an f/2.8 normal lens
Color corrected lenses of high resolving power
Accommodation for interchangeable lenses
A focusing range extending from about 6 inches to infinity
A shutter speed of at least 1/500 second
An internally synchronized flash mechanism
A coupled range finder
Thru-the-lens focus

Although prices are constantly changing, it may be said that 35 mm cameras of acceptable design can be purchased from approximately $100 to $500 and acceptable tape recorders from approximately $225 to $350.

A Polaroid camera with Copymaker and a projector can be purchased for less than $300.

LOCAL PRODUCTION OF MOTION PICTURES

There is general agreement that school production should not be undertaken except for material that cannot be purchased. Since a good school public relations program deals largely with local situations, production is the only way to obtain vital and dynamic motion pictures which will provide efficient communication with the public concerning pertinent information and ideas.

This Kalart/Victor 5893 Projector can be converted for 16 mm magnetic recording and playback by means of a magnetic recording attachment.

The magnetic-optical sound motion picture projector makes it possible to record sound—or re-record it as desired—on 16 mm motion picture film during projection and at a reasonable cost. Magnetic striping of sound or silent film with finely divided oxide-of-iron is commonly done for about 1½ cents a foot. The necessary projector which records magnetically and plays both magnetic and optical sound tracks may be purchased for approximately $700. Since the projector can be used as any other 16 mm sound projector for projection of commercially produced instructional films, the cost seems reasonable.

After determining to produce a motion picture film, selection of a suitable subject is the first step. It should be followed by careful planning of the story and preparation of a shooting script. These steps were discussed under "Planning the School Story" and are mentioned here only for the sake of continuity in considering the over-all school production.

It is beyond the function of this chapter to go into detail concerning the technical aspects of shooting a film, such as on-stage lighting, effective use of angle shots, and specific camera techniques required for good motion picture production. Sources of information concerning technical details are given in the bibliography at the end of the chapter. Space limitation alone precludes the discussion of details which must be known and understood by one or more members of the production crew. However, it should be known that a group of high school students under the direction of a competent teacher, with the necessary production equipment and a good amateur knowledge of photography, can produce motion pictures—as well as slides and filmstrips—that will be eminently satisfactory for use in a school public relations program. It must be recognized, however, that it is practically impossible for the average school district to obtain all the equipment, facilities, and competencies of personnel necessary for strictly professional production.

Before deciding that production of sound motion pictures is feasible, costs must be considered. Most important of all is the camera with the necessary supplementary lenses and accessories. Since the quality of the production will be limited by the quality and versatility of the camera, it is recommended that a very good, sturdy, and durable one, similar to the Cine-Kodak Special II, be purchased. The cost will be in the area of $1500 if work is to be limited to outdoor filming and somewhat more if indoor filming is to be included. It will be a matter for individual judgment as to whether cheaper equipment should be considered. Over a period of years, during which films are regularly produced, the differential in average cost per year of excellent over

The Bell & Howell 70DR 16 mm Spool-loading Camera is compact and sturdy. It is made to use 100-foot spools of film.

poor to fair equipment is of little significance when the criterion for judgment is quality of production. It is clear that if a high quality camera with at least two supplementary lenses is purchased and the total cost of the magnetic-optical projector is charged to production—it might be considered more logical to charge approximately $250 in the light of other purposes for which this equipment can be used—the over-all investment for equipment may range from $2200 to $3000.

For full production, the following equipment may be considered a reasonable minimum:

COURTESY EASTMAN KODAK COMPANY.

The Cine-Kodak Special II 16 mm Camera is highly versatile and will accommodate a 200 as well as a 100-foot film chamber.

1 16 mm camera with turret such as the Cine-Kodak Special II
1 Wide angle lens
1 Telephoto lens
1 Collapsible tripod with free head
1 Pan head with precision gear drive
1 Light meter, Norwood type
1 Light meter, such as Weston Master III or G.E. Guardian
1 Set of filters
1 Colortran
1 50-foot heavy-duty extension cord with double outlet box
1 100-foot heavy-duty extension cord with double outlet box
5 Grip-mounted 150-watt bulbs in reflectors
1 1000-watt spotlight
1 Pair professional rewinds
1 90° film splicer
1 Film viewer—5" screen is desirable
1 Titling outfit—may be homemade
1 Editing bench—may be homemade

1 16 mm Magnetic-optical sound projector which *must* operate smoothly and efficiently in *reverse*, such as the Bell and Howell Filmosound 302

COURTESY BELL & HOWELL COMPANY.

This Magnetic Optical 16 mm Sound Motion Picture Projector, Model 302K, will run film forward or in reverse with equal facility.

Securing personnel is the first and most vitally important step to be taken after deciding to go into production. The crew will consist of a director, a cameraman, and a soundman, assisted by others in charge of lighting and property, with two or more handymen to handle technical adjustments and physical arrangements.

In most high schools it is possible to obtain the services of a faculty member for the position of director—a faculty member who has the necessary knowledge and competencies coupled with an essentially deep and persistent interest. He must be given sufficient time for his work during the school day if he is to function satisfactorily. The amount of time required will depend upon volume of production. In some cases, the director may function temporarily as cameraman, but, generally, it is far better for him to be free from the mechanics of operation so that his entire attention can be given to direction. The cameraman is second in importance only to the director. He should have a strong interest in photography and some background of experience in using cameras. Usually a student can be found for this position, though it may be necessary to use a teacher until a student can be trained to assume this responsibility.

All other members of the crew can easily be recruited from the student body, but special care should be exercised in the choice of the student to be placed in charge of recording sound. He should have a genuine interest in the recording and reproduction of sound, coupled with good mechanical aptitude and the ability to do things precisely.

When adults who are professionally competent in this area live in the community, it may be highly desirable to seek their assistance in whatever way seems practicable.

PROCURING THE BEST

Whenever satisfactory projection materials are available to tell the school story, it is better and cheaper to purchase them than to attempt local production. Decision should be based upon a carefully considered answer to the question: which will best serve the purpose for its use? In some cases all pictorial projection items must be produced locally, but, in others, commercially available materials may be entirely acceptable or may be used to supplement those produced locally. The decision depends entirely upon the problem at hand and the outcomes that are wanted.

There are commercially produced filmstrips which can be profitably used in many situations to render a valuable service in the community and, at the same time, promote a very fine public relations program for the school district. Those which are listed at the end of this chapter have been selected because of their potential for informing the public in a helpful way concerning numerous aspects of education, thus enabling people better to understand and evaluate the schools of their own community. They can be purchased at a small cost and made available, with locally recorded commentary, to all groups wishing to see them. Wisely used, they would help to generate and develop support for the local school program.

OPPORTUNITIES FOR USE

In any community, there are many opportunities for the use of projected public relations materials. Audiences may include, among others, PTA groups; civic associations; business, professional, service, and women's clubs; granges; and fraternal orders.

In presenting audio-visual materials to such audiences, it may be desirable to have a member of the professional staff present to answer questions that arise. However, in some instances, the material and necessary equipment can be entrusted to a member of a group who will use and return it promptly to the library or school office.

Motion pictures may be shown over television when it is essential to reach the largest possible unselected audience. Unless these pictures have been produced by the latest methods, and specifically for this purpose, their quality will be inferior to that of a video tape or studio presentation. Inferior pictures seldom hold the attention of casual viewers.

USING THEM EFFECTIVELY

To assure a reasonable return on the time and money invested in slides, filmstrips, and motion pictures, one must consider carefully the methods and techniques for using them effectively.

The person who is to handle the presentation of slides, film-strips, or motion pictures, as the case may be, should be familiar with the equipment—or have a projectionist to manage the mechanics—and have a thorough knowledge or understanding of the subject matter involved and the purpose or purposes of the story. In instances where film and equipment are requested on loan to an organization, care must be exercised to insure that a competent person is available as a projectionist in order that irreparable damage may be avoided. If it seems necessary or advisable, a member of the high school projection squad can be assigned to the job. In any case, it will be desirable to brief the member who is in charge of the program about the equipment and how to present the material and stimulate good discussion afterward.

The introduction, immediately preceding projection, should clearly state the purpose or objective of showing the material, mention items meriting special attention, give necessary background, and define technical or other terms that may be unfamiliar to the group. Skilfully done, this will whet curiosity and insure an active interest in the material that follows. A touch of humor may be desirable in the introduction, but it should be remembered that the basic purpose is to prepare the audience for a complete understanding of the material presented.

Projection equipment should be as efficient as possible, maintained in top condition, and provided with spare lamp, fuses, and extension cords of proper gauge—14 A.W.G.—and suitable length. Neglect of any one of these factors may ruin a program and cause unnecessary irritations leading to charges of inadequacy or inefficiency from people who tend to be unfavorably disposed toward the school or its personnel. Meticulous care with respect to these same factors, coupled with skilful projection techniques, inevitably creates good reactions.

Darkening the room for projection is of vital importance in achieving the best results, and particularly so when the materials are in color. The degree of darkening needed for satisfactory screen images varies with the type of material being projected.

This Graflex SVE School Master projector is manually operated and it accommodates 2 x 2 inch slides as well as filmstrips.

Generally, it will be adequate when there is just enough light to permit reading the ordinary headlines of a conservatively styled newspaper. Direct light from any source other than the projector should not be allowed to reach the screen. Since projection will occur under different conditions, it will be necessary to have a screen with a highly reflective surface—beaded or aluminum. If the room used for projection can be well darkened and a very efficient projector is used, the flat white or matte screen will prove more satisfactory. This is true because there will be no grainy quality to the pictures and the audience can be seated at a wider angle without a noticeable variation in screen image brightness. When slides are to be projected, the screen should be square to permit use of vertically positioned shots without loss of image above or below the screen.

Commonly accepted seating standards indicate that the first row should set set back from two to two-and-a-half times the width of the screen, and that the last row should not be more than approximately six times the width of the screen from the front. Seats at the outer ends of rows should be not more than thirty degrees from a line drawn perpendicular to the center of the screen, and the length of any row should not exceed the greatest distance of its outer seats from the center of the screen.

Following the projection of materials, the leader or program chairman can stimulate worthwhile discussion by asking questions or eliciting comments concerning points brought out in the presentation. It is sometimes advisable to close the presentation and discussion with a concise summary. An alternative is to use the presentation as a preface to a panel discussion. For instance *Skippy and the Three R's* might be used to spark a discussion of the methods and success of our modern American schools; or *Secure the Blessings* as a good starter for a discussion of the role of schools in a democracy.

Sometimes it is desirable to show a motion picture, filmstrip, or selected slides a second time without the recorded sound, but with an occasional comment, for emphasizing major points. A second showing frequently clarifies information and results in a better discussion afterward.

If a lecturer prefers to comment during the projection of a set of slides or a filmstrip, the results will depend, in large measure, upon how well the commentary has been prepared; the degree of success in delivering it so that every one in the audience can easily hear and understand; and the ability to project his personality in a pleasing manner.

To tell the school story effectively with locally produced slides, filmstrips, or motion pictures, one must select subjects that will be of interest and significance to adult citizens in the community. The story must be planned with great care, adapted to the most suitable medium, and produced as well as possible with available facilities and personnel.

BIBLIOGRAPHY

Alton, John, *Painting with Light*. New York: Macmillan Company, 1949. An excellent treatment of the artistic and technical aspects of motion-picture lighting, equipment, and effects.

Brobeck, Emil E., *Handbook of Basic Motion Picture Techniques*. New York: McGraw-Hill Book Company, Inc., 1950. This handbook is of great value to both beginners and experienced motion-picture producers for its discussion of mechanics and techniques of the camera, lenses, and exposure. Panning, using the tripod, shot breakdown, screen direction, matching action, build-up, composition, indoor lighting, and applied techniques are thoroughly discussed in a very practical manner.

Brown, James W., Richard B. Lewis and Fred Harcleroad, *A-V Instructional Materials and Methods*. New York: McGraw-Hill Book Company, Inc., 1959. Chapter 20. A general treatment of photography in relation to school production of still and motion pictures.

Child, Eleanor D. and Hardy R. Finch, *Producing School Movies*. Greenwich, Conn., 1941. A non-technical manual presenting a very complete picture of 16 mm silent film production in the Greenwich High School.

Curran, Charles W., *Screen Writing and Production Techniques*. New York: Hastings House, Inc., 1958. This deals with the production of filmed, taped, and live T.V. programs, professional and non-professional motion pictures. Cost information is given.

Eastman Kodak Company, Rochester, N.Y.

Better Movies in Color. 1950. An elementary booklet dealing with indoor and outdoor photogaphy.

How to Make Good Home Movies. 1958. Deals with the making of amateur motion pictures in non-technical language.

Photographic Production of Slides and Filmstrips. 1959. Deals with making slide sequences or filmstrips in black-and-white and color.

LeBel, C. J., *How to Make Good Tape Recordings*. New York:

Audio Devices, Inc., 1956. A non-technical handbook on the basic techniques of the art of tape recording.

Livingston, Don, *Film and the Director*. New York: Macmillan Company, 1953. This is a first class director's guide dealing with the basic problems and principles of film direction, as well as the skills of film production.

Offenhauser, William H., Jr., *16 mm Sound Motion Pictures: A Manual for the Professional and the Amateur*. New York: Interscience Publishers, Inc., 1949. This is an authoritative textbook on the production of 16 mm motion pictures. Particular attention is given to color, equipment, editing, and sound recording.

Rose, Jackson J., *American Cinematographer Handbook*. Hollywood: American Society of Cinematographers, 1956. This is a pocket-size reference guide for the cameraman, giving information concerning all types of cameras.

Spottiswoode, Raymond, *Film and Its Techniques*. Berkeley: University of California Press, 1951. A basic textbook for the advanced film-amateur. Presents the steps of production from the writing of the script to the final screening of the film.

Tall, Joel, *Techniques of Magnetic Recording*. New York: Macmillan Company, 1958. See Chapter 6 for an excellent treatment of the fundamentals of magnetic sound recording, and Chapter 10 for an authoritative discussion of editing tape recordings.

Wheeler, Leslie J., *Principles of Cinematography*. New York: Macmillan Company, 1959. Deals in detail with the processes and equipment used in motion picture production.

MATERIALS AND SOURCES OF SUPPLY

FILMS

Angry Boy. International Film Bureau, 1951.

Desk for Billie. National Education Association, 1956.

Education is Good Business. General Pictures Productions, 1947.

Fight for Better Schools. McGraw-Hill Book Company, 1950.

Learning to Understand Children. McGraw-Hill Book Company, 1947.

Maintaining Classroom Discipline. McGraw-Hill Book Company, 1947.

Practicing Democracy in the Classroom. United World Films, 1950.

Priceless Heritage. Superior Coach, 1953.

Quiet One. Athena, 1948.

Safety on our School Bus. Encyclopaedia Britannica, 1957.

School and the Community. McGraw-Hill Book Company, 1952.

School Board in Action. National School Boards Association, 1954.

Skippy and the Three R's. National Education Association, 1953.

Student Government at Work. Coronet, 1953.

The Search (Community Education Program). Young America, 1955.

The Search (Inadequate School Facilities). Young America, 1955.

Who's Delinquent. McGraw-Hill Book Company, 1949.

Who Will Teach Your Child. McGraw-Hill Book Company, 1949.

FILM SOURCES

American Museum of Natural History, Central Park West at 79th St., New York 24.

Bailey Films, Inc., 6509 DeLongpre Ave., Hollywood 28, Cal.

Coronet Films, Coronet Bldg., Chicago 1.

Educational Film Library Association, 345 E. 46 St., New York 17.

Encyclopaedia Britannica Films, Inc., 1150 Wilmette Ave., Wilmette, Ill.

McGraw-Hill Book Co., Inc., Text-Film Dept., 330 W. 42 St., New York 18.

Teaching Film Custodians, 25 W. 43 St., New York 36.

Young America Films, Inc., 18 E. 41 St., New York 17.

FILM GUIDES AND LISTINGS

Educational Film Guide, H. W. Wilson, 950 University Ave., New York 52.

Educator's Guide to Free Films, Educator's Progress, Randolph, Wis.

An excellent listing of producers of films and filmstrips will be found in Edgar Dale's revised edition of *Audio Visual Methods in Teaching,* pp. 399–401.

FILMSTRIPS

Centralized School. American Council on Education, 1944.
Crises in Education. Wayne University, 1953.
Education in America. Museum Extension Service, 1953. Color.
Functional Arithmetic in the Elementary School. Ohio State
    University, 1953.
How a Textbook Was Selected. California University, 1956.
    Color.
Learning to Read. Bomar, 1954. Color.
Objectives of Education. Erle Press, 1952.
Oral and Written Expression (Series of 4). Jam Handy, 1955.
    Color-sound.
Reading (Series of 13). Jam Handy, 1955. Color-sound.
Report Card Comes Home. Wayne University, 1951.
Responsibility Can Be Taught. New York Metropolitan Study,
    1954. Color.
School and the Community. McGraw-Hill Book Company,
    1952.
School Buildings and Equipment. American Council on Educa-
    tion, 1952.
School Looks at the Community. Wayne University, 1956.
Teacher and Public Relations. National Education Association,
    1952.
Unit Method of Teaching. Long Filmslide Service, 1955.
Your School and Community Relations. Museum Extension
    Service, 1955. Color.

FILMSTRIP SOURCES

American Council on Education, 1785 Massachusetts Ave.,
    N.W., Washington 6, D.C.
Jam Handy Organization, 2821 E. Grand Blvd., Detroit 11,
    Mich.
McGraw-Hill Book Company, Text-Film Department, 330 W.
    42 St., New York 18.
New York Times, School Service Department, 229 W. 43 St.,
    New York 18.
Ohio State University, Teaching Aids Laboratory, Columbus
    10, Ohio.
Society for Visual Education, Inc., 1345 W. Diversey Parkway,
    Chicago 14.
United Nations, Films and Visual Information Division, New
    York.

Wayne University, Audio-Visual Consultation Bureau, Detroit
1, Mich.

Young America Films, Inc., 18 E. 41 St., New York 17.

FILMSTRIP GUIDES AND LISTINGS

Educational Filmstrip Guide, H. W. Wilson, 950 University
Avenue, New York 52.

Educator's Guide to Free Filmstrips, Educator's Progress Service, Randolph, Wis.

Where to Buy 2"x2" Slides, Enoch Pratt Free Library, Baltimore, Md.

SLIDE SOURCES

American Museum of Natural History, Slide Division, Central
Park West at 79th St., New York 24.

Keystone View Company, Meadville, Pa.

Paul W. Nesbit, 711 Columbia Road, Colorado Springs, Colo.

Philadelphia Museum of Art, Division of Education, Philadelphia 30.

Radio-Mat Slide Company, 222 Oakridge Blvd., Daytona Beach,
Fla.

Society for Visual Education, 1345 Diversey Parkway, Chicago
14.

8

It has been pointed out that pictures, both still and action, are effective means of telling the school story. Like pictures, displays of work done by pupils and exhibits of information related to the educational program are another important channel for reaching the public.

Exhibits should be used whenever it seems apparent that better results may be obtained through this medium than through oral and written presentations. Experience has shown that carefully prepared and skilfully arranged exhibits make deep impressions on viewers and lead to many helpful forms of action.

The emphasis in this chapter will be placed upon details that must be considered in the planning and organizing of various types of exhibits. These details will answer many questions that are bound to arise when a school begins to work with this medium of communication.

WHY HOLD EXHIBITS?

There are a number of reasons why the school should hold exhibits to which the public is invited. Among these reasons are the following:

1. Exhibits are a quick and convincing method of disseminating information that will stimulate popular interest in a particular subject or problem. Whether other means will achieve these outcomes just as well depends upon the nature of the subject or the problem being presented.

2. In many instances, ideas and information may be brought to public attention more concretely and dramatically through exhibits than through any other medium of communication.

3. A well-arranged exhibit enables the viewer to grasp the central idea with a minimum of time and to take away impressions that may have a strong influence on his attitudes and actions toward the school.

4. Exhibits offer the possibility of telling an old story in a new setting so that it takes on a new appeal.

5. Not infrequently, people become aware for the first time of the amount of specialized knowledge which pupils receive in the course of their regular instruction. They inevitably conclude that pupils are receiving far more in school today than when *they*, the parents or neighbors, attended a public elementary or secondary school.

6. After viewing an exhibit, many parents and other taxpayers have a new sense of respect for the institution and its instructional personnel. In fact, the result with some patrons is a stronger sense of pride in the local system and a desire to work for its further advancement.

7. Because exhibits normally attract adults out of curiosity, if for no other reason, a considerable number are drawn to the school who would not ordinarily read a pamphlet, listen to a lecture, or otherwise become informed on the subject exhibited.

8. At the same time, an exhibit that attracts a wide range of adults may also do much to stimulate a continuing interest on the part of many who were previously indifferent to the work, needs, and accomplishments of the system.

9. If teacher and pupil attendants are present, they can talk with visitors and give detailed explanations of the work behind the things on display. Not only do they help visitors to acquire a better understanding of the educational program but also to feel more friendly toward the institution because of the courteous and intelligent manner in which their questions are answered.

10. Sometimes an exhibit may be prepared jointly with some community group or organization. Such an exhibit attracts many more people and brings about better relationships with the group or organization than existed before.

11. It must always be remembered that a showing of things done by pupils invariably draws mothers and fathers to the school, including those who for one reason or another seldom take part in its affairs.

While additional advantages could be cited, those just enumerated are strong enough to emphasize the benefits that come

COURTESY PUBLIC SCHOOLS, DAYTON, OHIO.

Visitors are usually surprised at the knowledge and skill demonstrated by pupils in school today.

from exhibits when they are used effectively in the work of interpreting the school to the public.

TYPES OF EXHIBITS

Exhibits may be classified by types for convenience of identification. The types are suggested usually by factors of size and location.

CLASSROOM EXHIBITS

The most common type of exhibit found in public schools is the classroom exhibit. Here materials are displayed to show the accomplishments and progress of pupils. The materials may include individual and class progress charts, attractively covered booklets, portfolios of pupil work, maps, graphs, pictures, and other student-made objects. The displays may be placed on bulletin boards, chairs, desks, tables, and window sills. In a few of the newer school buildings, show cases are recessed in classroom walls and three dimensional bulletin boards have been constructed to make displays more interesting and attractive.

Classroom exhibits, aside from regular instructional purposes, are prepared for occasional visits by small groups of parents and meetings of room mothers in elementary schools. Generally, they are prepared in connection with open house, parent-night, and building dedications, or they may be the main feature of an annual all-school exhibit. More or less representative of practice is the use made of classroom exhibits in the Nyack, New York, Public Schools:

Perhaps our greatest number of exhibits and demonstrations occur during two meetings that we have for our parents in each school during the year. One is what we call a Parent Orientation in which the parents actually have a copy of their child's program and follow it through in a limited fashion during the evening with teachers explaining and demonstrating the work which would ordinarily be carried on during the regular class period during the day. The other opportunity for exhibits and demonstrations occurs during our spring open house in which parents and friends of the school are welcome to come in and visit for an evening, talking to teachers and seeing the work of the various youngsters. During these sessions we have, for example, an audio visual demonstration which takes place usually in the projection room. Here all of the equipment is set up and members of the Projection Club are on hand to explain their use and operation. One of the projectors is usually loaded with film, and a slide projector has certain slides which are of educational interest, covering different subjects for parents who stop in to view the display. Also on hand in the projection room is a tape recorder, and parents are quite amazed at their ability to record their own voice and learn the various uses of this machine. Displays are also made during this evening of the science department conducting certain basic experiments in the three fields of science, and the vocational and industrial arts departments have on display exhibits of the craftsmanship of the youngsters enrolled in those courses. We find this experience uniformly rewarding for all concerned, and the parents usually turn out in vast numbers to view these exhibits and demonstrations at this time.[1]

CORRIDOR EXHIBITS

Placed in cases with glass fronts and illuminated indirectly with artificial light, corridor exhibits help to acquaint the school visitor with samples of classwork done by pupils. It is natural

COURTESY PUBLIC SCHOOLS, PHILADELPHIA, PA.

Corridors may be used for all-school exhibits.

[1] Description furnished by Robert J. Schild, Director, Research and Curriculum.

for people who walk through the corridors to look at materials on display and to give them more than a casual glance if they are well arranged and have brief, explanatory placards. Among other locations in corridors, some of the exhibits should be placed near the main entrance of the building where they may be seen by every visitor who has business in the school.

In Detroit, Michigan, a corridor exhibit is maintained in the Board of Education Building:

> This consists of large photographs, about 20 x 24 inches, or other flat material depicting the work of the Detroit Public Schools in the various instructional areas. The exhibit area, in this case, consists of two large (6 feet by 12 feet) bulletin boards facing each other from opposite sides of the corridor. Each exhibit remains on display for a period of about six weeks, and each instructional department is offered an opportunity to present their story. We feel that this corridor display is a particularly useful public relations device, for it reaches people from all walks of life who come to the Board of Education Building. The corridor serves as a kind of waiting room, and chairs are located at the base of each display.
>
> No special budget is allocated to this display. The photographs for it are selected from our own photo files, and materials used come from our photographic department stock. Even this expense is reduced when children's or teacher's work is displayed.[2]

Other desirable locations are near doors leading to the facilities that are used by adults in the evening, such as the auditorium, gymnasium, and cafeteria.

MUSEUM EXHIBITS

Any display of materials for long periods of time are known as museum exhibits. Schools that have been experimenting with this type of exhibit find that some of the material becomes out-of-date and must be changed unless it is rich in historical significance. A good museum exhibit, located preferably near a waiting room connected with central administrative offices, is valuable for reminding the public of past achievements and for stimulat-

[2] Description furnished by Peter Golej, Supervisor, Audio-Visual Education, Detroit Public Schools.

ing pride in the work of the local system. The objective of a museum exhibit is realized more fully when the collection of items on display is small in number and closely related to a single topic.

ALL-SCHOOL EXHIBITS

This type of exhibit is undertaken by the individual elementary or secondary school for the purpose of acquainting parents

COURTESY PUBLIC SCHOOLS, OMAHA, NEBRASKA.

Exhibits of pupil work invariably bring adults into the school.

and others with the educational program carried on in grades and various subject matter departments respectively. Display materials may represent all grades or subject-matter departments of the school, or they may be limited to a single instructional area, such as language arts, science, and homemaking, with a different area being featured each time the exhibit is held. Without doubt, the all-school exhibit is one of the best means available for bringing people into the individual school, no matter whether it is held independently or in connection with some special event like American Education Week.

SYSTEM-WIDE EXHIBITS

A system-wide exhibit is one that brings together materials from various instructional units and divisions of the district. Located at a central place which is convenient to the public, this type of exhibit may feature the work of all schools in the system, those at a particular level in the educational ladder, including adult, or it may concentrate upon achievements in selected fields of subject matter. An example of the latter is seen in Carlsbad, New Mexico. Entitled, *School Arts Exhibit*, it is described as follows:

> The Exhibit displays all creatively outstanding art work pupils in grades pre-first through twelve created during the year. The work includes drawings and paintings in all media as well as three-dimensional experiences in such materials as clay, leather, metals, and native materials. Joining us in the Exhibit, the Industrial Arts Department displays the fine wood and metal products turned out in the junior and senior high school shops. We also use this means to display the very professional graphic arts turned out by students in the high school printing classes.
>
> A committee selects from this Exhibit items to make up the schools' booth at the State Fair the following fall. In keeping with our philosophy of art education, we try to avoid the idea of prize winners or an identification of "best" articles. The articles selected are merely the ones considered typical of those turned out during the year and ones that would best present the Carlsbad art program in the State Fair Exhibit. Since the public is accustomed to "prize winners" in an exhibit of this type, it has been difficult to avoid this interpretation of the selections.[3]

STORE WINDOW EXHIBITS

Increasingly, school systems are taking advantage of opportunities to hold exhibits in the display windows of downtown stores where the exhibits may be seen by large numbers of people. The general purpose behind them is to enlarge public knowledge on the subject being shown. Examples of store win-

[3] Description furnished by Richard Miller, Chairman, Arts Department.

Store window exhibits are seen by large numbers of people.

dow exhibits sponsored by the public schools of Duluth, Minnesota, suggest a wide range of possibilities:

1. A replica of a stockade built by two fourth graders with the help of one father. The class was studying Booneville, Kentucky.
2. A projector revolving to show colored slides of school activities.

3. Displays of work done in different departments—industrial arts, art, home economics, and English composition (showing themes from kindergarten through the senior high school).
4. A display of textbooks, organized under identifying cards giving the areas of learning.
5. The old and the new classroom—one with the oldest desks available, a dunce stool, and a switch in a prominent place; the other, with the newest furnishings and equipment.
6. A display of audio-visual equipment used in the schools.
7. A display of articles made or contributed to the Junior Red Cross.
8. The articles used in class for teaching safe driving.[4]

In addition to exhibits of objects, photographs, drawings, and the like, the tendency is growing to give demonstrations of modern teaching methods with live classes in store windows. More will be said about these demonstrations in the chapter that takes up the role of pupils in the public relations program.

PORTABLE EXHIBITS

This type of exhibit is so named because it can be carried about conveniently and shown to people on short notice. An effective portable exhibit does not have to be anything more than a series of panels on which pictures, charts, small objects, and posters are fastened. The exhibit can be built around any idea which the school wishes to bring before the public. Such an exhibit is especially valuable in short, intensive campaigns because duplicates can be made and distributed widely throughout the community in bank and office building lobbies, railway stations, libraries, stores, and other locations. It can also be made available to clubs, business organizations, and civic groups upon request. Used as a platform aid to speakers, it can be most helpful in making a talk more concrete and meaningful.

FAIR EXHIBITS

The annual county fair and similar commercial fairs provide an excellent opportunity to bring the name of the school and its achievements to the attention of a representative cross-section

[4] List furnished by Dora Mary Macdonald, Director of Public Relations.

of the public. The local school system is usually invited to supply an exhibit, and enough space is assigned to permit an attractive arrangement of display items.

Because the traditional county fair takes place either shortly before or just after the opening of school in the fall, it is necessary to prepare for it at least six to eight months in advance. It is suggested frequently that plans for the next year should be drafted as soon as the fair is over. By looking this far ahead, outstanding projects and materials related to the theme can be chosen from exhibits during the year and the entire exhibit for the fair assembled with a minimum of effort. If a similar procedure is not followed, then teachers and pupils must have a six-month start to prepare their entries.

Since the school competes with many varied attractions at the fair, it must have an exhibit that appeals to and holds the attention of even the leisurely and amusement-seeking passerby. The probabilities of succeeding in this respect are good when the exhibit is skilfully designed and centered around one idea or phase of the educational program so that visitors understand and recall it clearly. At the same time, relations with the public are strengthened by having teachers and pupils answer questions and offer explanations which make the exhibit more interesting.

COMPETITIVE EXHIBITS

More is being done today than ever before to stimulate pupil interest in particular fields of learning. One of the techniques employed for this purpose is that of competitive exhibits on grade, all-school, system-wide, regional, state, and national levels. Pupils are encouraged to undertake projects in connection with their classwork. Projects having merit are then entered in competitive fairs and exhibits where they are judged and the winners are given awards and prizes. While some school systems try to avoid the incentive of prizes, others use it freely. Here is an example of how it is used by a Trenton, New Jersey, junior high school in the teaching of science:

Beginning at the opening of school in September, all 7 and 8 grade pupils, and class 9M were introduced to many topics and phases of General Science. During the first rating period eighth grade classes studied living things. As interest, participation, and individual effort became greater, the pupils were led to interpret the knowledge they had gained by placing it on a poster, making a collection, making a habital group, or explaining some feature, using knowledge gained in class or from outside reading and observation. A committee was chosen to grade and classify the projects for class room display.

The first project gave the pupils some insight into planning and executing a larger project on broader topics for the school science exhibit. This exhibit will be held during the March meeting of the P.T.A., Fathers' Night, March 17.

By December 22, class 9M and most 8th grade pupils will be required to hand in the name and working plans for the project of their choice. This will afford two months for actual work on projects.

Following the exhibit, the best 10 or 12 projects will be selected to represent Junior Two at the Greater Trenton Science Fair. These chosen ones will be exhibited in the show case of the school so all pupils may view the projects prior to their entry in the Science Fair.[5]

It is quite common for outside groups and organizations to sponsor competitive fairs and exhibits. For example, in Dayton, Ohio, a recognition banquet is held for winners of the Annual Science Fair. The sponsors of the banquet are the Dayton Board of Education, The Engineers' Club of Dayton, The Dayton Rotary Club Foundation, and the Dayton Power and Light Company. A competitive exhibit called the "Industrial Education Festival" is sponsored by the San Joaquin County Chapter of the California Industrial Education Association. Held at Stockton in the showrooms of a motor car dealer, awards are made to all students whose exhibits are judged to be outstanding. In Duluth, Minnesota, a Student Craftsmen's Fair runs under the sponsorship of the Head of the Lakes Industrial Arts Club. It is held in connection with the competition for Industrial Arts awards offered by the Ford Motor Company. The building—a downtown store—is donated, and no charge is made for lighting by the Minnesota Power and Light Company. Similar fairs

[5] Description furnished by Mary Shafer, Trenton Public Schools.

and exhibits are sponsored by state and national organizations and industrial concerns with monetary prizes and college scholarships that make them valuable.

While some educators question the educational worth of the prize motive, others point out that competitive exhibits demonstrate to the public the technical knowledges and skills being acquired by pupils in school today. They also believe that the relationships established with outside sponsors are important and that the publicity attached to these exhibits and the winners of them elevates the prestige of the school.

PLANNING THE EXHIBIT

No matter what type of exhibit is used to supply the public with information, the results are better when the exhibit is planned carefully. Careful planning means that complex ideas and materials must be reduced to simple terms and presented in ways that appeal to the eyes and to the imagination. People who attend exhibits want to see something new, something familiar in a different setting, something that to them has meaning, and possibly something which invites constructive action.

One of the first steps in planning is to appoint a general committee and make it responsible for working out the entire project in detail. The committee should be under the chairmanship of a staff member who has the knowledge, experience, and skill that must go into exhibit making. If there is no one on the staff who fits these requirements, a person with some potential for developing into this kind of chairman should be appointed. The committee should be large enough to represent the various grades and departments affected and small enough to work efficiently. The committee should make it a point to utilize the services of persons in the community whose ideas and suggestions could improve the quality of the planning.

The plan should be written out and organized under headings similar to the following; each of these points will be discussed separately although some do not apply to every type of exhibit.

DATE AND LOCATION

Several questions must be answered in arriving at the date and location of the exhibit. When will the exhibit take place? How long will it last? During what hours of the day will it be open to the public? Where will it be held? Will it be tied in with some special event like American Education Week or an open house program? Or will it be an affair by itself?

PURPOSE AND THEME

Although the chief function of an exhibit is to interest and inform the public about certain conditions, ideas, programs, and actions, the exhibit must have a well-defined purpose toward which all planning is directed. The purpose might be that of highlighting the findings of a building survey, laying the ground work for a bond campaign, or showing pupil accomplishment in a specific field of instruction—any number of things. Whatever the purpose, it should set the sights for planning and serve as a point of reference in checking the preparation of the exhibit at each step along the way.

After the purpose has been defined, the committee should then select a theme for the exhibit. The theme is nothing more than a brief statement characterizing the main idea of the exhibit. Some examples of themes used in connection with school exhibits are Teaching Arithmetic Today and Yesterday, School Health, We Continue to Grow, How Schools Serve the Community, Science on Parade, Education for Democracy, Our American Heritage, Children of Other Lands, and Music Through the Day.

AUDIENCE

To whom should the exhibit make its appeal, and how may this be done? These are important questions that must be thought through before further steps are taken in the planning process. For instance, if the purpose is to create a more intelligent understanding of the need for additional buildings, the appeal should be directed to taxpayers at large. Financial support will not be forthcoming without the approval of taxpayers who do not have children in the public schools. To reach these taxpayers, the exhibit should be a portable one that can be shown to business and civic groups, placed in store windows, and located in waiting rooms, libraries, and other public centers where many people will see it. The content of the exhibit must be selected to fit the background of community feelings on taxation and education and presented in a way that will appeal to local pride and civic improvement. On the other hand, if the purpose is to acquaint parents more fully with modern methods of teaching the 3 R's, it follows that the exhibit should be held in the school, either as a series of room displays or as an all-school affair. The subject matter should of necessity be chosen to meet the interests of parents, their viewpoints toward modern education, and to supply them with information for understanding more fully the work of the school.

EXHIBIT CONTENT

The selection of exhibit content is about as important a task as the planning committee performs. Models, charts, graphs, objects, photographs, and the like must be chosen for telling a story that is in keeping with the purpose and theme of the exhibit as well as the nature of the audience. This calls for creativeness and imagination. The committee must be able to visualize facts, ideas, and illustrations for unfolding the story to the visitor in a way that is interesting to follow, easy to understand, and vivid in the impressions it leaves.

No matter whether the exhibit is small or large, single or multiple, the chances are much greater that it will be effective if the committee outlines in writing the kind of content needed to do the job. The outline can be organized in any way that seems best to the committee and for the kind of exhibit being planned. For example, in a hobby show the outline might contain a series of classifications, such as dolls, leatherwork, ceramics, metalcraft, woodwork, and so on. Entries would have to fit these classifications and the classifications would be used in the arranging of displays. In a science fair the classifications might be general science, biology, chemistry, physics, and engineering, with further breakdowns under each of these headings. The breakdown under biology might be taxonomy of plants, taxonomy of animals, anatomy, ecology, bacteriology, medicine, and conservation. Contributors would be expected to have one or more display items for these several subheadings to illustrate classwork and home assignment projects. The outline for a science fair would be handled somewhat differently by using the same classifications and placing under them a list of the specific types of display items wanted both from individual pupils and from groups of pupils. The suggested list of individual display items might include such projects as anatomy of the head, bird identification, cotton from plant to consumer, facts about plants, grafting methods, homemade soap, and waste by fire. The suggested list of items produced by groups might include projects dealing with animal parasites, fossils, care of hands, bone structure of the cat, snake life, growth of the frog, and wheat and wheat products. It soon becomes apparent during the planning that a detailed outline of the entire undertaking plays a role similar to that of a script for a motion picture or a radio program.

Quite often the amount of material submitted by pupils, teachers, and other functionaries in the school system is so large that only a small part of it can be used. The problem of making choices presents a difficulty because much of the material looks good. However, this problem can be met by applying a series of tests to the individual items. The tests are these: Does the item fit the purpose and theme of the exhibit? How well does it agree with the nature and interests of the audience? Is it simple and concrete enough to be understood with a minimum of effort? And is it suited to the exhibit form of expression? It is surprising to find that many items which seemed acceptable at first do not pass these tests and can be eliminated. While eliminating them, remember that more can be said with a few well-chosen items than with a clutter of material.

PHYSICAL ARRANGEMENTS

Three purposes should control the physical arrangements of exhibits, and more especially those which are held in auditoriums, gymnasiums, and similar locations. First, space should be distributed fairly and wisely among the different groups of exhibits. Second, the appearance of the whole exhibit should have a pleasing effect upon the visitor. And third, the visitor should be able to move about without a sense of being crowded or hurried.

To assure an equitable distribution of space, a floor plan should be made indicating the size and location of exhibit booths or stations. Several preliminary sketches may have to be made before the final plan evolves correctly. An example of a floor plan is presented on the opposite page. This floor plan was used for a system-wide science fair sponsored by the San Antonio Independent School District, Texas. Held in the municipal auditorium, the participating schools were assigned exhibit locations according to the numbering system shown on the plan. Each had about the same amount of space for housing its exhibits. In other instances the floor plan may specify the exact dimensions of the exhibit space and also tell what exhibit has been assigned any given location.

Usually the order in which exhibits are arranged corresponds to the sequence developed in the outline of content or subject-matter. The proper sequence is most important if the visitor is directed to enter the exhibit at a stated point and to follow a route from the beginning to the end. The purpose, of course, is to give continuity to the story and to have it unfold logically as the visitor moves from one station to the next. This continuity may be broken if too much competition is created by amusements, noisy machinery, and other distractions.

The recommendation is often made by experienced and skilled planners that exhibitors be required to work out preparatory sketches indicating how floor and wall space allotments will be used. They maintain that the sketching of each booth or exhibit brings to mind many details which might other-

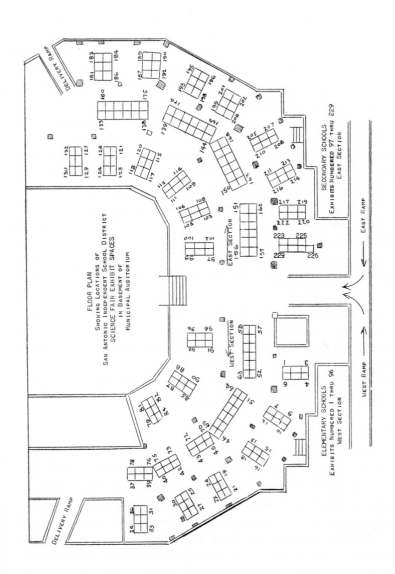

FLOOR PLAN
SHOWING LOCATIONS OF
SAN ANTONIO INDEPENDENT SCHOOL DISTRICT
SCIENCE FAIR EXHIBIT SPACES
IN BASEMENT OF
MUNICIPAL AUDITORIUM

ELEMENTARY SCHOOLS
EXHIBITS NUMBERED 1 THRU 96
WEST SECTION

SECONDARY SCHOOLS
EXHIBITS NUMBERED 97 THRU 229
EAST SECTION

WEST SECTION

EAST SECTION

DELIVERY RAMP

DELIVERY RAMP

EAST RAMP

WEST RAMP

wise be overlooked and prevents the making of serious errors. A few insist that the only way to prejudge the effectiveness of a booth or exhibit is to construct a scale model. The model should include background, panels, pedestals, tables, pillars, rails, cases, shelves, charts, pictures, cut-out figures, and objects. No doubt they are right, but it is difficult for teachers and pupils to find enough time to do this type of preparation.

The over-all appearance of the exhibit is influenced by many factors over which the school does not always have control. Too few electric outlets, for example, can reduce the effectiveness of lighting. Those about which something can be done will be treated in subsequent sections of the chapter.

Wide aisles and a one-way flow of traffic make it easy for visitors to move about the exhibit hall. In using the one-way plan, it is necessary to have directional signs posted at frequent intervals or to employ other devices for keeping people moving in the direction desired. However, the exhibits can be arranged in such a way that the visitor knows at once how to plot his route without the aid of printed placards. In any case, there should be a sign at the entrance pointing out where the visitor should begin his tour of the exhibits. If people are permitted to circulate freely in any direction, aisle space must be sufficient for them to by-pass groups gathered around booths and tables where the displays attract most attention.

VISITOR COMFORT

Visitors always think more highly of an institution that provides for their needs and comforts. This service starts when there is a parking lot with attendants present to assign stalls and protect property. It should be followed by a pleasant reception upon entering the building by student guides who assist with the checking of hats and coats and direct visitors to the exhibit location. Signs should be posted on the walls or on standards to assist the visitor further in finding his way about the building and locating rest rooms and lavatories. In connection with a classroom exhibit, the names of teachers and the grades or subjects taught should be displayed prominently outside of their rooms. For large exhibits, space should be set aside for visitors to rest and to talk with friends. It may be advisable in warm weather to have refreshment stands at convenient intervals for the purchase of cold drinks and other light refreshments. A first aid station, with a nurse in attendance, should be maintained to take care of accident and illness cases and to look after small children who wander away from parents.

DISPLAY DEVICES

The success of an exhibit depends much upon the effective use of display devices. These devices enable the exhibitor to present materials in ways that attract attention, stimulate interest, and convey a message clearly and forcefully.

Exhibit units. The materials are displayed in booths, on tables or counters, on panels, and in cases. These facilities are referred to here as exhibit units. A booth may be an enclosure walled on one, two, or three sides, a curtained enclosure, or an open space set off by rails, ropes, or counters. When a booth is enclosed on three sides, display items are more easily observed and studied if the booth is long and narrow with something across the front opening so spectators may come close to look at the displays without blocking the views of others. The visibility of objects and flat materials is also better if the booth is wider at the front than in the rear.

A panel may be described as any vertical surface that is made from wall board, heavy cardboard, or other material on which small objects and illustrative items, such as photographs, maps, charts, posters, and diagrams, can be displayed. A panel may be small or large, framed or unframed, hung on a wall, fastened to some temporary framework, or mounted on supports to stand by itself. Frequently, small panels are hinged together to form screens of two or more units or to form a zigzag pattern where display space is limited. They can be attached to a pivot display fixture as well and then turned freely by people who are looking at them. Experience suggests that no panel should be lower than twenty inches from the floor with a top height of not more than seven feet from the floor. While the size of a panel will vary with use and space, there should never be any variation from the principle of presenting a single idea on each panel and no more. For pleasing appearance, a panel should have its widest margin at the bottom, a slightly narrower margin at the top, and its narrowest margins on the two sides.

Tables are used a great deal to hold exhibit items, and particularly those which cannot be fastened to walls and panels. The exclusive use of tables, however, makes it difficult to display flat materials and small objects effectively. They do not fall within the normal vision range of a person who is walking about the exhibit center and they are lost from sight when people stand in front of the display tables. More satisfying results are attained when tables are employed in combination with walls, panels, pedestals, and cases and are set back a reasonable distance from the line of viewing.

Illuminated cases with glass fronts are excellent units for the housing of corridor exhibits. Small portable cases of one kind or another offer a fine setting for many of the items that are shown in booths, on tables, and in store windows.

Display arrangements. A display of items for any exhibit unit should be arranged so that the items "talk" to the viewer and leave him with a feeling that he has gained something worthwhile from seeing them. This effect will not be produced unless the items are presented in an orderly design which is pleasing to see and easy to understand. There must be an obvious relationship of the parts to the whole and plenty of open space between them.

The setting in which items are placed makes a difference in the dramatic impact they make on the viewer. For example, an object might be shown to best advantage if placed on a pedestal, in a shallow box, or has a spotlight trained on it. Similarly, an object might be hung from a small wall bracket, surrounded by a white picket fence, or leaned against another object. The setting in any case must be appropriate for the object displayed and the mood intended.

It is most important that display arrangements capture the attention of the spectator and interest him in the content of the

Greet the visitor with an attractive display.

exhibit. This can be done in many ways, including decorations that carry out the theme of the exhibit, a judicious use of color, contrasts in values, diagonal lines and triangles that suggest motion, broken and continuous lines pointing to a center of interest, a striking and original idea, a well-placed row of objects, a beam of light, or an object in motion.

COURTESY PUBLIC SCHOOLS, DETROIT, MICHIGAN.

Novelty of display arrangement draws and holds visitor attention.

Displays "talk" more directly to the viewer when they are built around a center of interest. A center of interest is a point to which attention is directed by the arrangement of the materials. The eyes may be guided to this point by a clever caption placed in a suitable position, a cut-out figure looking in a given direction, a limited use of converging bright-colored ribbons, or a set of objects on graduated pedestals, to mention but a few techniques adapted to this purpose. It is essential, however, that the reinforcing or related items be tied together in a balanced, unified exhibit.

The general arrangement of booths, tables, and panels in the exhibit hall should be considered in creating and sustaining visitor interest. The exhibit unit located at the entrance to the hall should attract enough attention to make the visitor want to see the rest of the display sections. From this point on he should experience a series of visual surprises that are brought about by varying the height and size of booths, the length and shape of tables, their placement in relation to one another, and by shifts from light to dark in shades of color. Key words on signs and placards can be underlined, printed in italics, or colored to encourage the visitor to look more closely at the materials displayed before him.

A wealth of practical ideas and suggestions can be obtained on good display arangements from the study of advertisements in magazines, newspapers, and billboards and from the reading of books on art and photography.

Printed matter. Although an exhibit should be as self-explanatory as possible, there are times when printed explanations are needed to interpret the subject matter to the visitor. Assume the place of the visitor and you will find it easy to discover where title cards, placards, and explanatory statements are required in order to clarify the meaning of an object or a group of objects.

A determined effort should be made to keep printed explanations accurate, brief, and appealing. They may be written in the form of statements, questions, exclamations, and even commands of merit. In some instances it might pay to have an eye-catching title in large letters followed by a fuller subtitle in smaller letters and a more detailed text after the subtitle. Titles and labels are generally more appealing when printed on colored cardboard or paper that complements the existing color arrange-

COURTESY PUBLIC SCHOOLS, LOUISVILLE, KENTUCKY.

Printed explanations should be brief, accurate, and appealing.

ment. The letters must be of a size that is easy to read from a normal viewing distance, and the placards and labels must be placed in positions that leave no misunderstanding about the objects to which they refer.

Printed matter in the form of single sheets of paper, leaflets, and small booklets are sometimes useful aids to visitors. Mimeographed sheets can be left on counters for visitors to take and read at their leisure. A printed program containing a floor plan and the titles of exhibit units is essential when there is an extensive display of materials. Information interpreting the exhibit and the work of the school can be included in the program.

Lettering. The lettering of directional signs, placards, and informative cards is an essential aspect of careful exhibit planning. Good lettering adds much to the over-all appearance of an exhibit, besides drawing attention to displays and establishing communication with the visitor.

Several media are available for doing excellent lettering. Unless letters can be drawn more or less perfectly by hand, it is better to resort to stencils and ready-made letters. Stencils come in different styles and sizes which are convenient and easy to use with pencil, ink, chalk, crayon, and paint. Stenciled letters can be cut out of the material on which they are printed and then fastened to signs and placards. Most dime stores, stationery shops, and art-supply outlets keep on hand fairly inexpensive, ready-made letters. They come in paper, cardboard, wood, and metal of varying sizes and colors. Raised letters of wood or rope create interest as do words that are underlined, colored, or enclosed occasionally in quotation marks. Printed explanations close to visitors may be typed to save time and labor.

The appeal of lettering is influenced by several other factors. One of them is uniformity in size and style of type for signs, titles, placards, and captions; not only should there be fixed standards for the size and style of type but also for the size and design of the cards that carry the printed matter. Another is the use of capital letters; capital letters are uninteresting unless restricted to titles, brief statements, and occasional emphases. Still another consideration is the fitting of letter styles to the subject matter; the subject matter may demand light or sturdy, conservative or modern, dignified or casual lettering. However, for the inexperienced exhibitor, the simplest kind of lettering, preferably plain Roman, is probably the most successful.

Oral explanations. To make an exhibit more personal and interesting, pupil and teacher attendants may be stationed at important booths and tables to give oral explanations. In acting as

hosts and hostesses, they are able in a few words to direct attention to the purpose of a display, point out significant features,
and answer questions freely. Their courtesy, knowledge of the
exhibit, and manner of presenting information combine to make
many favorable impressions. That visitors enjoy hearing oral
explanations is supported by the fact that the largest groups are
usually found, and remain longer, at booths and tables in charge
of competent attendants. Attendants may likewise conduct
groups of visitors on tours of the exhibit, or present short, interpretative talks at the entrance or in another part of the hall.

Slides and motion pictures. The showing of slides and motion
pictures is an excellent device for drawing attention and impart-
ing information. Both natural color and black and white pictures
enable the exhibitor to present graphs, charts, tables, maps, and
statistical materials in a more attractive and understandable
manner. If shown on a centrally located screen within the booth,
and surrounded by supporting materials, the story told should
take only a few minutes to view. Sometimes a shadow box with a
small screen is an effective device for projecting slides and creating curiosity as to their content. Slides as well as motion pictures
may be thrown sucessfully from the rear onto a translucent
screen in a partly darkened room. A clever exhibitor will use
many other techniques for exploiting the value of these media.

Motion-making devices. Thought should be given in the planning of an exhibit to the use of motion-making devices. Objects
in motion are certain to attract spectator attention and cause
many visitors to look much more closely at displays. Several
motion-making devices and ideas that are appropriate for school
exhibits include turntables, endless belts, vertical stop-and-start
disks, changing scenes of colors, opening and closing of doors
automatically, rotating of dioramas, concealed oscillating electric
fans for causing paper streamers to flutter and for vibrating
objects suspended on wires and springs, flasher buttons and other
flasher mechanisms that turn lights on and off at regular intervals,
forward and backward movements, miniature moving trucks and
trains, and working models showing how a process is conducted.

The devices and ideas employed to make motion should never distract seriously from a display or overshadow its informative features.

Audience participation. If physical arrangements permit, it is good business to provide a number of items that invite audience participation. Being able to do something, though it may be simple, makes an exhibit attractive and memorable. Examples of how the audience may take part in an exhibit are pushing a button to see a picture or to illuminate a series of panels; pushing a button to start some mechanism in motion; turning a knob to change from one photograph to another; looking into a box, through a microscope or a magnifying glass to view some object; guessing the weight and size of an object; pulling wires to operate a piece of equipment; listening with earphones to a brief narrative; taking a short quiz and comparing answers with the correct ones behind a sliding panel; and stepping on a treadle to cause one scene to disappear and another to replace it.

Maps and charts. Much can be done in the graphic presentation of information by means of maps and charts. Aside from the decorative qualities of maps, they are useful in depicting conditions and volume. For example, the reasons for selecting particular sites for new buildings may be revealed easily by shading commercial areas on a map of the community along with those representing the movement of population. Volume is readily understood when marked on a map with colored pins, spots, flags, cut-out figures, and lights coming through holes or mounted on the surface.

The matter of presenting material on charts, such as diagrams, graphs, and tables, poses a problem because the average person has difficulty interpreting statistical data and can only absorb a small amount of it. This problem can be handled quite conveniently by reducing figures to understandable terms, like four out of five or one in every fifteen, and by novelty of treatment. A pie graph, for example, conveys more meaning when the segments are separated and arranged in a decreasing order of size than when they are retained in a circle. A bar graph is more interesting if the bars are made up of dollar signs, figures of pupils, or other appropriate objects. The typical line graph changes its character by placing "flags" at major peaks and troughs in the form of lights, photographs, cut-out figures, and other symbols. Quantitative data mean more when represented by objects such as books, boxes, and the like piled on top of one another or placed side by side for ease of comparison; or, the same object can be shown in different sizes to bring out contrast and comparison. The use of third dimension in the handling of statistics makes the material understandable, particularly when this treatment is combined with lighting and color. The presence of brief, expanatory placards helps to clarify and drive home an important point shown on a table, graph, or diagram.

Photographs. Photographs should be employed freely because people like to look at them and they are easy to interpret. Large photographs are always attention-getters, and one that is blown up to show essential details is worth more than several small prints on the same subject. As a standard, no photograph should be smaller than 11 by 14 inches. Clear and attractive scenic photos make an excellent mural background for a display or they may be arranged in a montage of artistic character. Much can be done with pictures of faces and figures that are mounted on plywood and cut out with a jigsaw to make a display more attractive. Statements on a panel or captions above and below photographs should be used to explain the ideas and facts being illustrated. The photos may be hand colored or they may be toned with a single color to enhance their appearance. Good effects are obtained with transparent photos lighted from the rear; by combining photos with art work, objects, and models; and by using art work to show one phase and photos the other in dealing with differences between past and present and future. Framing is an aid to appearance and the sharpening of concept. Oval, Victorian frames lend a suitable touch to something of an historical nature, while glass over a photograph with no frame suggests a modern feeling. In some instances, the entire display

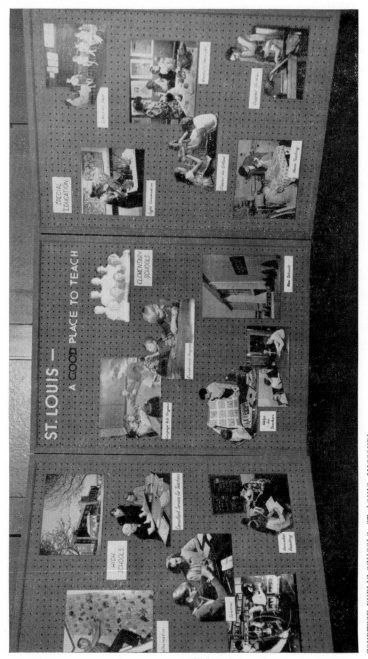

Panels with photographs draw and hold audience attention.

235

of a booth or a panel may have a strong impact on viewers when it consists exclusively of photographic materials.

Models. Models are miniature replicas of objects, both still and working. They give reality to an exhibit and always excite observer interest; this is even more true when they are

Models bring reality to an exhibit and always excite visitor interest.

accompanied by large photographs of the actual scene or process being represented. Used in the construction of dioramas, they provide excellent third-dimensional displays. They should be made especially for an exhibit—unless suitable figures and objects can be purchased at retail stores.

Demonstrations. Demonstrating how something is done is a more graphic method of explanation than words or pictures. Because people like to watch demonstrations, they should be repeated at regular intervals with a time allowance for audience questions. Care must be taken against having two demonstrations opposite one another in order to prevent traffic congestion. Demonstrations should be held on low platforms, when possible, so they can be seen by all spectators. If the demonstration requires close attention by the demonstrator, then someone else should be assigned to do the commentary and answer questions.

Backgrounds. Displays should be set against backgrounds that make them stand out to advantage. For this reason, the color of a background should bend toward the neutral. Light gray, pale yellow, some shades of green, or a color that has been grayed down will serve the purpose. Occasionally a warm color may be used, providing it does not weaken the prominence of display objects. If a background seems too monotonous, it may be broken with black borders or touches of vivid color. Colors may be placed on background materials such as Manila wrapping paper, plywood, beaver board, wallpaper, wood-grain paper, and cloth.

Color. Color application to backgrounds, lettering, trim for booths and tables, treatment of display items, floors, and ceilings may control the appearance and appeal of a whole exhibit and its parts. Floors and materials near floors should be darkest in color because dark color is heavy and tends to draw the eye, while light color on a ceiling has just the opposite effect. Light and dark colors also create illusions with regard to space, hence a small booth appears larger in light colors than in dark, and dark letters on a white ground appear narrower than letters of identical size on a dark ground.

Stimulation and attention result from a careful use of blue, orange, and red—colors that are valuable in drawing the eyes to a center of interest and for emphasizing certain points in a display. If luminosity and brightness are wanted, then use should be made of yellow, green, and orange. When common associations of ideas and colors seem pertinent, red should be used for danger, blue for sky and water, red and green for Christmas, yellow and violet for Easter, white for purity and cleanliness, green for grass, and yellow for light and sun. Generally, color use should be controlled by the thought that best results are produced by applying vivid colors to small areas and dull colors to large ones. In the treatment of panels, placards, captions, and signs, color combinations read most easily from a distance in the exhibit hall are dark blue on a white backgound, black on yellow, green on white, black on white, green on red, red on yellow, and red on white. For speed of reading, the order of legibility is black on white, green on white, blue on white, and black on yellow.

Lighting. Skilful lighting ties an exhibit together and increases its audience appeal. These results may be achieved with nothing more than ordinary light bulbs, a few spotlights and floodlights, colored gelatin sheets and filters. For example, a row of lights under a counter will bring out detail in objects located near the front of the booth. Carefully-concealed and well-placed lights increase the attractiveness of transparent and opaque objects in any part of a booth. Special sections, groups of objects, and individual display items are easily emphasized under the beam of a spotlight. Pleasing effects may be produced by wrapping colored, theatrical gelatin sheets around the bulbs and over fluorescent tubes and by attaching color clips and filters to spotlights and floodlights trained on groups of objects and larger display sections.

Sound. Music and voice recordings may be used effectively in connection with most exhibits. When music is used, high quality recordings should be placed at key positions and made an integral part of the exhibit. One minute lectures about items displayed in a booth or on a table can be made and repeated as often as necessary. They should come from a concealed tape, wire, or disk recorder.

High interest is attained when inanimate objects engage in conversation. Concealed speakers are placed to the right and left of the objects so that the voice appears to come from them. This must be done in a small area with a quiet speaker instead of a loud speaker, and with low rather than high pitched sounds. The objects can be made to describe themselves, take on a personality of their own, and supply information of value to the visitor.

ENTRY AND JUDGING RULES

School systems that sponsor competitive exhibits for pupils, with prizes to winners, or exhibits in which certificates of recognition are awarded to pupils for outstanding projects, have found it necessary to establish entry and judging rules. These rules tell teachers and pupils what kinds of projects may be entered, under what conditions, and how they will be judged. They also make administrative tasks easier by standardizing certain of the routine procedures.

Here is an example of the entry rules formulated for a science fair in the San Antonio Independent School District, Texas:

Each school has been allocated a definite number of exhibit spaces based on the school's enrollment in science classes.

Table space 4 feet long by 3 feet wide will be provided for each exhibit. There are no limitations on height other than the ceiling of the exhibit hall and the stability and safety of the exhibit. Poster space behind the exhibit may be utilized.

Each exhibit must be designed to show a scientific principle, technique, or industrial development.

To assure a variety of exhibits, each school should plan to enter not more than one exhibit from any one area of a particular field of science.

All exhibits must be constructed exclusively by students. Professional and technically trained people may give advice only.

An exhibit may be prepared either by an individual student or a group of students.

If an exhibit is prepared outside of the classroom, the work in preparing it must be accomplished under the direct supervision of the teacher of the science class.

Only displays prepared during the present school year may be entered.

Electric outlets will be provided.

All equipment must be furnished by the exhibiting school.

The exhibiting school will be responsible for transporting its exhibits to and from the exhibit hall, and for setting up, demonstrating (if necessary), and removing them.

Since it is desirable to have a comprehensive representation of the science curriculum, the science committee reserves the right to make adjustments to assure distribution of exhibits throughout the various areas in the field of science.[6]

Another example of the rules governing the conduct of the science fair at both area and final competitions in Dayton, Ohio, follows:

A. Categories
   1. Elementary Division—all entries must emphasize one or more basic general scientific principles.
   2. Senior Division—all entries must emphasize one or more general scientific principles of Physics, Chemistry, Biology, or General Science. In the area of Engineering the entry must be concerned with the *application* of such principles.
B. The entry must be something the student has constructed or developed which shows some originality of use, development, or design.
C. Each senior division exhibitor must be prepared to give a brief description and demonstration of his entry—approximately five minutes.
D. No prize-winning entry from a previous year's exhibit can be entered unless substantial additions have been made to the exhibit or it has been materially altered.
E. Judging will be based upon the following factors:
   1. Originality and ingenuity shown by the exhibitor   20%
   2. Skill in design, construction, and arrangement of exhibit   20%
   3. Clarity and thoroughness in explanation and demonstration of the exhibit   20%
   4. Interest and general knowledge of the subject   20%
   5. Practical work of the project from a scientific or engineering standpoint   20%
F. All identifying marks such as student's name, school, etc., are to be prohibited at the time of judging.
G. The entry must be so arranged that it can be displayed on a flat-top table or floor.
H. Posters and mural type exhibits, etc., must be mounted on self-supporting stands. No hanging exhibits will be accepted.
I. All projects are entered at the risk of the exhibitor. The committee can assume no responsibility for loss or damage.

[6] *General Rules for Secondary Schools, Science Fair of 1958* (San Antonio, Texas: San Antonio Independent School District).

J. All participants must be sponsored by a teacher, generally one of science, who will act as his consultant and advisor.

K. Each student must complete a prescribed entry blank, stating name, grade, teacher, division, area, category, title of project, space requirements, etc.

L. Dangerous chemicals, open flame, explosives, poisonous reptiles, and inhumane experiments must not be exhibited.

M. Only single phase, 110 volts, 60 cycle electrical current will be available at the exhibit centers. If other services are required, they must be provided by the contestant as a part of the exhibit.

N. All publicity concerning individual exhibits or any phase of the Science Fair must be released through Mr. James Harris, Chairman of Publicity Committee, BA 6-1461.[7]

The following illustration of standards for judging a science fair is taken from a mimeographed handbook published by Math and Science Departments of the Carlsbad City Schools, New Mexico.

I. Creative Ability—30 points

A. Does the work give evidence of originality in approach or handling?

B. Does the exhibit show ingenious use of raw materials rather than the use of purchased or borrowed materials?

C. Does it show new and better ways of expressing scientific ideas, principles or hypotheses?

II. Scientific Thought—30 points

A. Does the work give evidence of a probable amount of real study and thought?

B. Does the finished product give evidence of a plan carried into effect by use of the procedures followed in the scientific method?

III. Thoroughness—10 points

A. Does the exhibit tell a clear, full story about the project?

IV. Skill—10 points

A. Is the exhibit soundly and durably constructed?

B. Is good craftsmanship shown?

C. In collections, how skilled is the handling preparation, mounting, or other treatment? Are specimens correctly identified?

[7] *The Dayton Public Schools Present Their Fifth Annual Science on Parade* (Dayton, Ohio: Dayton Public Schools, Department of Curriculum and Instruction).

V. Clarity—10 points
   A. Does the exhibit illustrate facts that would be understandable to both laymen and scientists?
   B. Are guide marks, labels, descriptions, neatly yet briefly presented?
VI. Dramatic Presentation—10 points
   A. Is the principle demonstrated by the use of the most appropriate materials?
   B. Is the exhibit attractive in its presentation?

While entry and judging rules would of necessity differ somewhat with the nature and location of an exhibit, those enumerated are helpful guides in indicating points that must be taken into consideration.

ENTERTAINMENT

Entertainment by means of plays, talks, tableaux, filmstrips, music, and motion pictures can be employed to supplement and reinforce the theme of the exhibit. However, their use should be scheduled for brief periods and at regular intervals. This must be done to prevent entertainment features from absorbing a major part of the visitor's time and attention.

SAFETY MEASURES

Before final decisions are made by the planning committee with regard to construction materials, width of aisles, parking of cars, lighting and lighting equipment, demonstrations with chemicals, and other matters, conferences should be held with police, fire, and electrical inspection bureau officials. They can check tentative plans and point out the rules and regulations that must be observed for the safety and protection of teachers, pupils, and visitors. Much of this information should find its way into an exhibit manual for the guidance of sponsors and participants.

ADMINISTRATION

To make sure that the exhibit plan is carried out efficiently and on time, some form of organization is needed. Although the form of organization may differ with the nature and scope of the exhibit and with circumstances peculiar to local school systems, the entire undertaking should be headed by a person who has administrative ability and experience in exhibit management. The best plans may receive harsh treatment in the hands of a poor administrator, while those of doubtful merit may achieve unexpected success under the leadership of a skilled chairman.

Generally, work connected with fairly large exhibits is divided among individuals and committees of staff members. In the system-wide, final science fair sponsored by the Dayton, Ohio, Public Schools, there is a general chairman in charge of the project, a vice-chairman, and a set of committees for the elementary and secondary schools respectively. Headed by competent chairmen, these committees are responsible for physical arrangements and exhibits, judging, awards and invitations, hosts and guides, and publicity. Specific instructions are furnished to chairmen, describing the activities they are expected to carry out through their committees. In Trenton, New Jersey, the organization for the Public School Art Show was designed in another way.

A Planning Committee was formed to select the place, the time, the rules for submitting materials, etc. An Arrangement Committee was given the job of measuring the allotted space and arranging for the necessary tables, display boards, assignment of areas, table coverings, signs, and many other details concerned with having the display area ready. The Receiving Committee was to be on hand to receive the materials as they arrived and designate the proper placement for convenience of the Hanging Committee. The Hanging Committee selected appropriate display materials. While most of the material submitted was used for obvious reasons, some had to be rejected for reasons of duplication, inaccuracies, questionable originality or inferior workmanship.

A Hospitality Committee was formed in which teachers and pupils were assigned for specific times to greet the pupils and public, making explanations, and generally to supervise the decorum and prevent theft.

An all-important Clean-up Committee took down the exhibition materials and arranged them in piles by schools to assure care in handling and ease and accuracy in returning to the rightful owners.

Schools and individual teachers were given a suggested list of media which they might submit and asked to indicate the number and size of exhibit units and materials. Elementary schools were given a quota, depending on their size and number of teachers, of two dimensional and three dimensional art pieces they could submit. From these lists the Arrangement Committee could plan space requirements and allotments.[8]

In other systems, the organization may call for chairmen of sections into which the exhibit is divided, chairmen for different levels of the school system—elementary, junior, and senior high— or the functioning of committees under such titles as administration, finance, materials, art, maintenance, safety, and the like. No matter how the work is divided, the important point is that every committee chairman and individual know exactly what is expected of them.

Administratively, the question of cost may have to be faced when plans of the exhibit are being developed. There are practical approaches that may be adopted in meeting this problem. A reasonable cost may be estimated and then revised as the exhibit plan takes shape, or a definite sum of money may be ear-marked for exhibit purposes and spent in whatever manner seems feasible, or the cost may be absorbed in departmental budgets. An easy method to follow in determining cost is that of grouping all items needed under two headings—those available without direct cost and those that must be paid for in cash. The latter can be charged to the same account that covers expenditures for other interpretative media. In any event, precaution must be taken against the spending of money on construction and equipment and very little on ideas that are the essence of an exhibit.

After organization and cost have been determined, the planning committee should draw up a schedule of dates at which various stages of the work must be completed. Definite dates enable individuals and committees to plan their own activities within time blocks and to meet deadlines more easily.

[8] Description furnished by John T. Cunningham, Director, Industrial, Home, and Fine Arts, Trenton Public Schools.

PUBLICITY

An exhibit falls short of its goal unless it is seen by a large number of people. Good publicity is the best means available of assuring the presence of a large number of people. All too often, however, school officials tend to underestimate rather than over-estimate the amount of publicity needed. This is particularly the case with exhibits that are intended for non-parent audiences.

Besides securing a sizeable audience, good publicity brings the school to the attention of citizens and taxpayers who seldom attend an educational affair, and it acquaints them more fully with the work of the institution. Accordingly, every piece of publicity should carry repeated explanations of what the exhibit covers and the reasons for holding it. This means, further, that several different avenues of publicity should be employed in order to reach as many members as possible of selected audiences.

Local newspaper publicity should be started at least two months before the date of the exhibit. It might start with a con-ference to which representatives of the local press are invited. They could be told what the exhibit aims to accomplish, what it includes, features that are new and different, the consideration being shown for the convenience and comfort of visitors, the width of aisles for easy flow of traffic, the use of conspicuous title signs and captions, and the use of raised platforms for demonstrations. They can be given the names of pupils and teachers who are serving on exhibit committees, the names of citizens who will take part in the opening exercises, and other facts of interest to newspaper readers. These same points can be treated in a scheduled series of straight and feature stories re-leased by the school system to local papers.

In addition to newspaper publicity, radio and television spot announcements can be made just before the opening of the exhibit, announcements read at parent-teacher association meet-ings, and notices sent to clubs and civic associations in the form of invitations. School children can be instructed to write cards and letters to parents and friends telling about the exhibit and the days and hours that it will be open for their inspection. A cancellation die on metered mail is an inexpensive means of creating interest and keeping the date before the public. A rubber stamp can be used for the same purpose in imprinting the announcement on all outgoing mail and parcel-post packages. Posters can be made for placement in store windows around the community. A polite letter to a store owner ahead of time explaining the exhibit and requesting permission to display a poster is an excellent public relations practice.

Another technique that should not be overlooked is the sending of personal invitations to influential members of the community to see the exhibit at a time just before it is open to the general public. The same idea can be extended to private groups and organizations to come at specified times when there is likely to be the smallest attendance.

FOLLOW-UP ACTIVITIES

Exhibit planning should include provision for follow-up activities. Follow-up means turning to advantage the interest that has been awakened and the increased knowledge that people have acquired by seeing the exhibit, reading about it in the newspapers, or hearing others discuss it. Follow-up activities may start with visitor registration upon entering or leaving the exhibit. Visitors can be asked to fill out a card, sign a registration book, or check a special form if they wish to receive selected school publications. The names thus acquired constitute a mailing list for follow-up letters, distribution of literature, invitations to school affairs, and even requests for help in meeting pressing school problems.

Sometimes it is advisable to have a "last word" booth near the exit where visitors are invited to stop before leaving. Such a booth enables them to clear up points of interpretation, ask questions, and receive packets of printed materials. One piece in the packet might be a brief, interesting summary of the exhibit that answers questions uppermost in the minds of visitors. This piece, however, might be a more elaborate booklet with pictures and drawings. It would carry the same message as the exhibit itself and elaborate on features of outstanding displays. The supplemental pieces could give a broader picture of the school, its programs and problems.

Slides and film strips of exhibit panels and displays may be made for giving illustrated talks before parent-teacher associations and organized groups in the community. This type of follow-up activity is helpful in spreading information still farther and deepening popular understanding of the school program.

BIBLIOGRAPHY

Allen, Paul W., "Better School Exhibits," *School Board Journal,* 115:22–24, 80 (October, 1947). A detailed description of the preparation and presentation of an elementary school exhibit.

Black, Misha, ed., *Exhibition Design.* London: The Architectural Press, 1950. Intended for commercial exhibitors, and containing many photographic illustrations, this book has a wealth of suggestions that could be adapted to the preparation of school exhibits.

Boyers, R. and J. L. Goldsmith, "Exhibits Sell Shop Programs," *Industrial Arts and Vocational Education,* 47:1–5 (January, 1958). Points out the values of industrial arts exhibits and offers practical ideas for their preparation.

Gilbertson, H. W., *Educational Exhibits: How to Prepare and Use Them.* U.S. Department of Agriculture, Miscellaneous Publication No. 643. Washington: U.S. Government Printing Office, 1948. An excellent publication on the planning of exhibits.

Lane, Janet and Beatrice K. Tolleris, *Planning Your Exhibit.* New York: National Publicity Council, 1948. A practical manual dealing with several considerations that enter into the planning of exhibits.

Lohse, Richard P., *New Design in Exhibitions.* Zurich: The English Institute, 1953. A commercial handbook, well illustrated, on display arrangements for exhibits.

Museum Techniques in Fundamental Education. Paris: United Nations Educational, Scientific, and Cultural Organization, 1956.

Written in English, this booklet provides much technical information for the construction of museum exhibits.

Schwartz, F. R., "Long Island has an Art Fair," *School Arts*, 56:23–26 (September, 1956). Describes an art fair and how it contributes to community understanding of schools.

9

Now it's *your* turn! The preceding chapters have talked about telling the school story through various media—printing, publicity, radio and television, exhibits, and displays. Now we're concerned with your personal role in school public relations—talking directly with people in face-to-face audience situations.

Art Linkletter said it for us when he labeled an article, "People Are Media."[1] There isn't a more direct (and often much abused) tool of communication than personal, speaker-to-audience contact. Except for the broadcast media, printed means of communication are largely intended for absentee audiences. The message is received when it suits the readers' convenience. There is no sure way to determine if the message penetrated.

In the speech situation, the speaker's means for telling the school story are seated before him. Too many speakers feel uncomfortable and inadequate in such a situation. Perhaps because they think it's the speaker who is on the spot. He may be, but so is the audience. And what about the speech and the occasion? An understanding of these four factors is necessary if we hope to improve our speaking. This chapter will take a look at the speaker,

[1] Art Linkletter, "People Are Media," *Public Relations*, vol. 2, April, 1957.

the speech, the audience, and the occasion. We'll discuss the role and importance of speaking in school public relations.

Let's start with the man behind the rostrum.

THE SPEAKER

Some speakers say they feel like a butterfly pinned to a wall in a biology laboratory. Others report all they can see is half-a-hundred pairs of glassy eyes lined up in rows before them. This fear of the crowd conflicts with a basic desire for approval from an audience. As a result, most speakers experience varying forms of nervousness. This is natural. But, before we begin an analytical look at the speaker, we should reassure him he is only one-fourth of the total situation.

YOU'RE ONLY PART OF IT

In telling the school story, the listener is just as important as the speaker. Ralph Micken reminds us that the idea may well be more important than either.[2] In fact, the occasion for the speech may even be of greater importance than the other three factors. There wouldn't be a speech without all four elements present. Crocker underscores this point:

> . . . the speech is not what the speaker says but actually what the audience made out of what he said. To study the speech without considering the audience and the occasion is to treat the speech as an essay, words in space rather than words in time. What the audience does for the speech and what it adds to the speech situation is as important as what the speaker contributes.[3]

We're not suggesting it doesn't matter who you are as a speaker. Admittedly, the speaker's personality, appearance, reputation, mannerisms, attitude, and the choices he makes need

---

[2] Ralph A. Micken, *Speaking for Results* (Boston: Houghton Mifflin Co., 1958), p. 3. The first chapter of this book contains an excellent discussion of the speaker's attitude toward his job.

[3] Lionel Crocker, *Business and Professional Speech* (New York: The Ronald Press Co., 1951), p. 21.

to be considered. But as Micken suggests "the man who goes to work at once on what he will say and how he will say it will not have time to worry about himself. If he starts immediately to analyze his audience, he will have little time for self-torture."[4]

IT'S WHAT YOU REPRESENT

Many school public relations studies have shown that parents view their schools in terms of their child's classroom teacher. Every school day the little messengers take home with them a report of some kind about their teacher. Opinion polls have shown a parent's attitude toward the school system is directly proportionate to the attitude toward their child's teacher.

The same situation seems to apply when an educator talks to an audience. Whether you are the superintendent, business manager, public relations man, or a classroom teacher, you *represent* the Jonesville public schools. As such a representative, one of your main tasks is not to sell yourself to the audience, but to leave them with the belief that you know what you're talking about. Some school administrators feel it is not so important that they are polished, fluent speakers but that they create a feeling of confidence in the school system they represent.

Visualize the program for tonight's meeting:

> An Address by
> JOHN W. DOE
> Superintendent of Jonesville Schools

At least, this is undoubtedly what speaker John Doe imagines as the key thought in the mind of the listener. If we were properly to emphasize the element important to that listener, the same program listing might well be printed as follows:

[4] Micken, *op. cit.*, p. 3.

An Address by
John W. Doe
Superintendent of JONESVILLE SCHOOLS

The underlying purpose of all speech is to get a response. Our suggestion here is, when speaking to an audience as an educator representing a school system, that one basic response to seek is that of convincing the audience to have confidence in the people and programs of your school system. "The Schools" are not thought of as a mass of buildings, peopled by children and teachers and saturated with the fundamentals of the 3 R's! The schools, to most of our publics, are typified by individuals—by a teacher, a patrol boy, or a superintendent speaking to a noon meeting of the Lions Club.

This is not to imply that we have removed the personal element that exists in speaker-audience situations. What the audience knows about a speaker before he speaks helps shape their attitude towards him. They draw their conclusions from press reports, introductory comments by the chairman, conversations they've had with people who know the speaker, his status and prestige in the community, and his personal appearance. But there is no such thing as the "mind of the audience." An audience is a group of individuals with individual attitudes and interests. Most good speakers assume their audience will judge them fairly.

Monroe suggests, "ask yourself what will be your listeners' attitude toward you personally and toward your qualifications to address them on the chosen subject. Two things must be considered: (a) the degree of their friendliness toward you, and (b) the degree of their respect for you or your knowledge of the subject."[5]

It boils down, then, to a matter of confidence. And the best way to earn the confidence of an audience is to know what

[5] Alan H. Monroe, *Principles of Speech*, 4th brief ed. (Chicago: Scott, Foresman and Co., 1958), p. 52.

you're talking about. This is largely the result of careful speech preparation and practice. We'll talk about speech organization later in the chapter. In the meantime, how do you go about presenting your "best self" to an audience!

GLAD TO BE HERE!

This is an over-worked cliché found in too many introductory comments by speakers. But the attitude it expresses illustrates our point. By being interested in the audience and the ideas you've prepared, you've made the first step toward establishing rapport and winning the confidence of your audience. The interests of the audience are most important. If the speaker is sincerely interested, his enthusiasm is likely to be contagious.

Most basic speech textbooks offer a list of personal qualities that will help you win the confidence of an audience. McBurney and Wrage suggest the following:

The most winning quality a speaker can display [is sincerity]. [It is] a compound of genuineness, honesty, frankness, good will, and interest in the subject and the listener . . . be tolerant and fair. Prove to your listeners that you are a person who is free from pettiness and vindictiveness . . . be friendly . . . keep your sense of humor . . . be dignified . . . don't retreat into stuffiness and coldness, but behave in a way that shows you respect both your listeners and yourself.[6]

If you will subscribe to the idea of talking *with*, rather than *at*, your audience, you will find an automatic improvement in your desire to communicate. Some educators talk to audiences of citizens as though addressing a class and as if they were tired of it all! School people often find themselves on the "banquet trail," asked to give the same speech on dozens of different occasions. As Micken points out, "the smile is the best single means for conveying a feeling of good will. It is sound procedure to start every speech with a smile, and this goes for the speech in which you intend later to 'roast 'em to a crisp.' "[7]

[6] James H. McBurney and Ernest J. Wrage, *Guide to Good Speech* (Englewood Cliffs, N.J.: Prentice-Hall, Inc., 1955), pp. 29–30.

[7] Micken, *op. cit.*, p. 9.

THE RIGHTS OF LISTENERS

"This is a time of much talk."[8] The late Irving Lee prefaced his last book with this observation. He described how difficult it is to determine how good or bad this talk is. From the viewpoint of many audiences, too much talk is dull, boring, or simply a waste of time. W. Norwood Brigance, one of the deans of speech pedagogy in America, devotes an initial chapter in a recent book to the rights of listeners. It seems pertinent here to summarize his suggestions:

Although the speaker has a more difficult role, listeners are more important because speech exists to serve listeners. The typical educated listener may hear approximately one hundred speeches a year. They expect speakers to help solve problems, present information and new ideas, to stimulate thinking, or perhaps simply to entertain. Too many audiences are cheated by too many speakers who forget that audiences have the right to demand that every speaker who consumes public time should deliver the services expected.

. Brigance discusses general classifications of speakers who violate the rights of listeners: the Stratosphere Speaker who deals in the mystic realm of abstraction and glittering generalities, who, like Senator Beetlebrain, can say nothing in 300 words; the Witless Wit, who has an endless supply of funny stories—but no thought; and the Phonograph, who reproduces a magazine article and thinks it makes a good speech.[9]

Some school people need to be reminded that their job before an audience is to talk to the listener, not to themselves. Over forty years ago James A. Winans urged the concept of conversing with the audience. You can't converse with an audience by talking aloud to yourself.

Incidentally, take stock of any nervous mannerisms you may have while speaking. If you wear glasses, decide in advance whether you're going to leave them on or take them off before

---

[8] Irving J. Lee, *How to Talk with People* (New York: Harper & Brothers, 1952), p. ix.

[9] William N. Brigance, *Speech Communication* (New York: Appleton-Century-Crofts, Inc., 1955), pp. 1–10.

the speech. Don't keep putting them on and removing them during the speech. Leave the pencils, paperclips, and any other fuss-budget items in your pocket. Don't keep fussing with them while you talk. A friend of mine has a bad habit of jingling the change in his pocket throughout his speech. To avoid this distraction, he cleans out his side pockets before he talks. Most of us aren't aware of the distracting mannerisms we have while speaking. If you're in doubt, ask a friend to check you the next time you speak to an audience.

Dress conservatively for most speech occasions—unless the occasion demands a more formal attire. Men should wear a suit or sport jacket, plain shirt and a not too "wild" necktie. A neat, tailored appearance is usually recommended for women (who should beware of large, colorful earrings).

THE IDEAL REPUBLIC

Brigance has pictured an Ideal Republic where speakers would have to pass a test of competence before being allowed to appear before audiences. This may be somewhat difficult to attain, but he does suggest a hippocratic oath for public speakers:

> I swear in the name of God and my own conscience that I will never speak in public unless I have prepared myself with substance worth saying, and unless further I have put it into a form that can be understood. I further swear that when I appear before an audience I shall think of its welfare, and not of my own pride, that I shall not mumble or fidget, or otherwise evade or shirk my task, but shall present my ideas with such sincerity, earnestness, and consideration for the audience that none can fail to hear or comprehend.[10]

Utopia? Perhaps, but let's examine what the speaker can do to make such a vow possible.

THE SPEECH

I think it was Benjamin Franklin who said, " 'Tis hard for an

[10] *Ibid.*, p. 10.

empty bag to stand upright." It's not the bag's fault, but the lack of the stuff inside it. So it is with some speakers.

Our concern now is with the organization of a speech. A well organized talk helps both the speaker and the listener. If you want to do a good job before an audience you should consider such things as selection of subject, your purpose, careful analysis, structure of the speech, method of delivery, and language and style.

Every time you talk about schools to an audience you need to be confidently organized and enthused. Whether you're trying to inform them about a new policy, part of your program, or the extent of your services—or whether you are trying to convince them that the schools need more financial support, you should prepare your speech carefully. Audiences are quick to spot an off-the-cuff performance. Unorganized speech is hard to deliver. Every time you appear before any audience to speak on any school subject, make it worth their time and yours.

FIRST THINGS FIRST

A well organized speech starts with a worthwhile subject. Chances are, most of the time your topic will be selected for you. You may be asked to tell about your school district's new remedial reading program, your plan for educating the gifted student, special education for retarded children, or any of a dozen aspects of education. Your topic will be largely determined by the audience, the occasion, and your position in the school system.

Often we are asked to speak on anything. "Oh, just talk about education," the program chairman will suggest. Or you will simply be asked to talk for a certain length of time. If that's the case, start immediately with a thorough analysis of the audience and the occasion. Who are these people? How often do they meet? Why this meeting? What do they know about their school system, or what would you like to have them know? We'll talk about audience analysis in detail in a moment.

Micken makes a good suggestion when he says, "After all it's *you* they have asked to speak. Don't be afraid to talk shop. Examine the possibilities of your own field of activity."[11] A good basis for speech subjects lies in the aims, practices, and accomplishments of your school system.

Once you've determined your subject matter, decide upon a specific purpose. As we said earlier, the underlying purpose of all speech is to get a response. You speak to interest or entertain, to inform, to inquire, or to persuade. Decide upon your specific purpose. More than one purpose may be involved, for in a speech to persuade an audience of the need for more school buildings you will have to inform them of the enrolment boom, the crowded facilities, and the lack of available classrooms. But spell out *one* specific purpose for your speech before you begin organizing it. This should make clear what you intend to accomplish. If you're trying only to interest or even entertain an audience, your purpose may be, "I wish to describe the first day of kindergarten," or "I want to create appreciation for the unsung hero of the school system—the custodian." You may simply wish to inquire into or about something—"How can we best provide for the future educational needs of Jonesville?" or "What can be done to aid the gifted youngster?" When you are reporting, you remain specific and seek not to persuade or convince—"I wish to review the accomplishments of the school year," or "I want to inform the audience about our methods of teaching science in the elementary grades." When you set out to persuade an audience, your purpose indicates the need for acceptance—"I wish to convince them we need better teacher salaries," or "We must build new schools to provide for the increased number of youngsters in our community."

We're not suggesting you stand up and deliver such a topic sentence as these to your audience! But spell it out for yourself as an assist in your search for materials in preparation for the speech. Nothing is more disheartening to a listener (and to the speaker) when, after a speech, the listener turns to his neighbor and asks, "What in the world was he driving at?"

[11] Micken, *op. cit.*, p. 86.

PUT IT TOGETHER

Now that you've chosen your subject and pinned down your exact purpose, the next step is to organize this subject. Try operating under the three-up theory: Stand up, speak up, and shut up. Estimate how much time you should take in this speech, if the chairman doesn't make a suggestion. If he does not specify time, *you* decide how long this speech should be. A speaker can often accomplish his purpose more easily if he be "brief, bright, and gone."

Then make out a "grocery list."[12] Jot down the things you already know about the subject. Break this list of items up into a few main ideas. See how many key points you have. Perhaps you have too many for a twenty-minute speech so you may have to eliminate some points. No more than five main ideas in a speech is usually suggested. Now perhaps your own information on these key points is not enough or is somewhat outdated. Go ask someone in your system for facts, illustrations, statistics, evidence. Dig into your professional library, check the periodicals and take some notes. Then make a tentative outline of the speech.

Every speech can be broken down into three main parts. First you tell 'em what you're going to tell 'em, then you tell 'em, then you tell 'em what you told 'em. In other words, every speech has an introduction, a body, and a conclusion.

As Baird and Knower point out, the length, content, and general effect of the introduction of a speech depend upon the length of the speech and your specific purpose. Generally, the introduction is designed to make the initial contact with your audience—to get their attention and introduce them to your subject and to your purpose.[13] Introductions need not be formal or long. One of the easiest ways to begin a speech is through immediate disclosure: "I am going to talk about . . . because

---

[12] McBurney & Wrage, *op. cit.*, pp. 73–85. Chaps. 7 and 8 of this book give many good suggestions for exploring and organizing subject matter.
[13] Craig Baird and Franklin Knower, *General Speech* (New York: McGraw-Hill Book Co., Inc., 1957), pp. 61–88.

. . ." Here you simply state your subject and purpose. Not too motivating, perhaps, but sometimes adequate, depending upon the nature of the speech occasion and the audience. You may use the "motivated introduction" technique as a method of catching their attention. This includes starting with a rhetorical question or series of questions, an anecdote, story, illustration, quotation, startling statement, or a well-phrased proverb.[14] Whatever you do, never start a speech with an apology. If you aren't prepared, you don't need to tell them. They'll know soon enough.

There are several ways to arrange the body or discussion phase of the speech. This may be done in one of the following:

1. *Logical method.* Present the causes and results of an event, situation, or condition.
2. *Chronological method.* Divide the main points up in order of time. Simply tell what happened first, the next event, and each succeeding event in the order in which they occurred in time.
3. *Problem-solution method.* State the history, causes, and effects of a problem; suggest solutions; evaluate each solution, and accept the best one.
4. *Positional method.* Arrange your material according to space relations—from the near to the far, left to right, bottom to top, for example. This is sometimes called the space order method.

After you have selected the order of arrangement in the body of your speech, these general principles should be followed:

1. *Restrict your main points.* Based upon your purpose and time, select only those points or aspects of your subject that really need to be stressed.
2. *Give proper emphasis.* Stress your pitch, not the preliminary material leading up to it. Don't spend too much time, for example, on the problem phase in a persuasive speech. Put most of your ammunition into the solution.
3. *Arrange your points in the appropriate order.* Arrange the ideas with a weather eye on the audience acceptance as well as your own purpose.[15]

The conclusion of a speech is designed to do just that—finish it! Too many speeches sputter to a stop or speakers leave them

[14] McBurney & Wrage, *op. cit.*, pp. 89–90.
[15] Baird and Knower, *op. cit.*, pp. 72–73.

dangling in the air. A good conclusion should restate your main purpose. The easiest way to conclude a speech is to summarize what you have said in the discussion stage. This is more frequently used than any other method. How you conclude your speech will depend upon the speech, the audience, and the occasion. You may wish to use a capsule form of conclusion, such as a quotation, a brief illustration, a statement of personal intention, a plea for action or approval, or even the rhetorical question. But keep it short and to the point. As Micken says, "the audience should have a definite feeling that what you got up there to say, has been said."[16]

It is difficult to be brief in the matter of speech composition, since this is one of the most important parts of speech-making. An inexperienced speaker would do well to review a good, basic speech text. Even experienced school administrators who do a great deal of public speaking can freshen their performance by checking any of the books found in the bibliography of this chapter.

In his guide for business and professional speakers, Ralph Micken has condensed into a compact outline[17] a useful reference which we think could be well used when working on a speech:

Introduction

> Has three functions. These are not necessarily all present in every speech.
> 1. It makes contact with the audience.
>   a. By finding common ground
>   b. By giving audience a chance to get acquainted with the speaker.

Personal
appeals
go well
here

> 2. It gets attention.
>   a. By tie-in with preceding speaker, occasion, place, etc.
>   b. By story
>   c. Through paradox or other striking statement
>   d. Through rhetorical question.
> 3. It states and limits the subject of the speech. It puts the idea in a topic sentence.

[16] Micken, *op cit.*, p. 98.
[17] *Ibid.*, pp. 99–100. By special permission.

Body (sometimes called discussion)

    1. It breaks down and arranges the idea.

      a. It presents the sub-points (rarely more than five).

      b. It arranges the sub-points in most effective order.

        1. Logical order—syllogism, inductive-deductive, causal.

Logical   2. Chronological order—order of events, story.

factual

appeals   3. Conventional order—the way the topic is always treated.

fit here

        4. Positional order—left to right, top to bottom, etc.

        5. String-of-beads order—"accidental" order.

    2. It develops the idea.

      a. By exposition

      b. By narration

      c. By description

      d. By persuasion.

Conclusion

Emotional-   Has four functions.

motivational 1. Summarizes ideas.

appeals   2. Applies ideas.

belong here 3. Moves to action on the ideas.

            4. Epitomizes.

It's about at this point that the speaker has to decide upon his method of presentation. Do you memorize the speech, write it all out and read from manuscript, or use brief outline notes—or no notes at all? A word of caution about the impromptu speech. This is the situation where you are called upon to speak without any prior warning. Sometimes it is impossible to avoid such a situation, but try to! About the only way to acquire skill in impromptu speaking is through repeated practice in extemporaneous speech.

Extemporaneous speaking means unmemorized speaking that has been prepared in advance.[18] It is usually organized into outline form, and notes may or may not be used. The speaker thinks

---

[18] McBurney and Wrage, *op. cit.*, p. 114.

of how he wants to express his prepared ideas as he speaks. This type of speech should be practiced. A good extemporaneous speaker rehearses his speech to repair the first draft of its organization. Here you get a chance to hear your ideas said aloud for the first time. Practice gives you the "feel" of the speech; it allows you to check your timing and polish any part of the speech that doesn't come out just right in the practice session.

COURTESY *Times Herald,* PORT HURON, MICHIGAN.

This superintendent is discussing school organization. In answering a question from a listener, he still maintains direct audience eye-contact. Notice the brief notes, a trademark of an experienced extemporaneous speaker.

When in doubt about your ability to remember your extemporaneous outline, use notes. Keep them simple, legible, and only use them when you need to. Some speakers act as though they don't want the audience to know they're using notes. It's nothing to be ashamed of. As a matter of fact, it indicates to your listeners that you're prepared! Place your notes on the table or rostrum where you can see them easily. This leaves your hands free to help you express your ideas with gestures and bodily action.

We've been talking only about the extemporaneous speech. Other than the "panic button" impromptu speech, other methods of speech presentation include the manuscript method and the memorized speech. Sometimes you may have a special reason for using one of these latter two methods. Try to avoid either if you can since they tend to inhibit conversational directness. Each has its place in some situations.

You probably see more speakers reading from a manuscript than any other method of speech presentation. It may be necessary on formal occasions, such as dedication ceremonies, commencement addresses, or other more formal commemorative occasions. Usually, however, this forces a speaker to *read* his speech with his face buried in the rostrum. Talk about talking *at* an audience! Manuscript reading destroys audience eye contact, restricts the speaker's physical directness, inhibits bodily action, and often ends up in a recital of monotony. Written speeches are often necessary for radio or television where timing is important and the station desires a record of what was said. Before a "live" audience though, most good speakers prefer the extemporaneous method. If you have to write your speech, write it for the ear and not for the eye, practice it plenty and strive for as much audience contact as you possibly can.

A memorized speech does allow more audience contact than does the clutched manuscript, but generally it's a waste of time. If, as a child, you ever had to memorize a stanza for some school program, you can recall the painfully long time it took to stuff the selection into your head. Chances are the moment you stood up to deliver the memorized speech you forgot part of it owing to the mere presence of an audience. Delivery of the memorized speech often becomes an automatic release of "canned" sentences. Many basic speech textbooks will caution speakers that the simple fear of forgetting what you have memorized may make your mind go blank. So don't memorize, please, for the listener's sake.

SUPPORTING MATERIALS

It was Disraeli who once said, "There are three kinds of liars. Plain liars, damned liars, and statisticians." Educators often find themselves forced to accompany information or persuasive talks with statistical evidence. It helps reinforce your argument and often is an excellent persuasive device. Use figures in your speeches if you feel it is necessary, but use them sparingly. Remember the ear cannot record a factual figure as can the eye. So follow the cue of the radio newscaster. Rather than quote a figure of 8,128 students, for example, simply say, "Over eight thousand students." Give the source of your statistics and make sure your source is reliable, current, and one that is acceptable to your audience. If you are faced with the necessity of using a great deal of figures in a straight informative speech, it may be well to prepare a duplicated handout sheet for distribution to your audience. Some speakers handle only the essential statistics in their speech and pass out the information sheets after the talk rather than compete with the listener's attention while fact sheets are being examined by the audience.

Use many examples in your talks; give specific, local cases; dig up as many illustrations as you can. Try the use of rhetorical questions and answer them yourself quickly before the listener has a chance to come up with a different answer. Define new terms, and define old ones if it is essential that you be thoroughly understood (and it is!). Show similarities and differences among items to make your ideas more clearly understood.

Visual aids are important in explaining difficult or technical subjects, such as finance, taxation, or many phases of your curriculum. Psychologists proved many years ago that people are more visual minded; they tend to remember what they see better than what they hear. Although listeners usually are more moved by what they hear, they are often more permanently impressed by what they see. Too often, however, speakers rely too heavily on visual materials; combined with speech, they are more impressive than either approach used alone.

There are some important techniques to keep in mind in the use of visual illustrative materials: [19]

1. *Make charts large enough.* Don't *think* it's big enough. Test the size in advance yourself by looking at it from the back of a room. Make lines broad and heavy and use color for emphasis.

2. *Restrict the details.* Stick to the bare essentials on each chart. If you can't get everything into one visual aid, use a series of them. Forget the title; you can describe that in your speech. Remember, an audience can read only 10 to 20 words without losing the speaker's trend of thought.

3. *Talk to the audience, not the chart.* Inexperienced speakers have a tendency to address the visual aid, or graph, or even a chalkboard rather than the listener. Learn to point at the proper point on your visual aid while you're looking at the audience.

COURTESY *Times Herald,* PORT HURON, MICHIGAN.

A school administrator explains finances of the system with a simple visual aid. Notice that he is looking at his audience while pointing to the proper point on the chalkboard.

4. *Use a chart only when you need it.* Keep them out of sight until you need them and remove them when you have finished using them. They detract from what you're saying. (Erase points written on a chalkboard when you have completed that part of the speech.)

[19] Brigance, *op. cit.,* pp. 130–134.

5. *Stand beside the illustrative material.* Don't stand between the chart and the audience. If listeners are seated close to you, stand at least 3 or 4 feet to the side of the chart. Use a pointer; it simplifies the process.

6. *Visual aids should precede the oral description.* Diagrams, charts, pictures, and other materials are more effective if they are used just before you wish to make that point in your speech. This is especially true if the subject is unfamiliar to your audience. This gives the listener a chance to figure out what the chart means, and then he can make more sense from your oral exposition.

As far as pictures and slides are concerned, Brigance makes these suggestions:[20]

1. *Use a large enough screen.* Use a large screen so everyone at the rear of the room can easily see. The standard small screen, 39 x 48 inches, may be too small if anyone is seated more than 35 feet away.

2. *Have the room adequately dark.* For graphs it is not necessary. But if you plan to show films or slides, test the room for disturbing light leaks ahead of time. Test your projector or visual equipment in advance and get used to the idea of carrying a spare bulb in your pocket.

3. *Pay special attention to making yourself heard and understood.* You can only rely on your voice when the room is dark. Talk clearly and with more force than normally, especially if you are at the rear of the room operating the projector. Watch the whir of the projector. Often the pitch of this sound may make you unintelligible.

Be sure you really need to use visual aids. Too many educators, trained in audio-visual instruction, feel compelled to take along a projector or a bar graph whenever they speak to an audience. If illustrative materials will not add greatly to your talk, leave them home. If you plan on using some, survey the situation in advance. Spot the light switches, electric output, chalk, thumbtacks, or whatever else you may require. If you are using film or slides, have them focused in advance and try to take another person with you who can operate the machine and leave you free to speak.

DANGER: PEDAGUESE AHEAD

You're leading with your chin when you fail to remove educational jargon from your speeches. *Trends* reported a school

---

[20] *Ibid.,* pp. 135–136.

system which failed to consider this matter of language and vocabulary. Parents were asked to attend a forum to react to a statement of the educational goals of the school system. The statement was worded in high-sounding, fuzzy gobbledygook. Participants complained they couldn't really understand how they could react favorably or unfavorably although the words sounded very nice. A newspaper columnist observed: "There have been ambitious attempts to talk over educational problems, but they get bogged down in too many words too poorly defined."[21]

Listeners cannot agree with you or support your cause if they fail to understand you. We're not suggesting, as an extemporaneous speaker, you carefully plan every word you use in a speech. But avoid dealing in long, high-sounding, philosophical terminology. Talk with your listeners in a language they can understand. Define new words for them that you must use in your speech, and to make sure you are understood, define some of the old words, too. Analyze your language habits, start listening to yourself, review your talk immediately after you sit down. Watch your audience carefully for looks of uncertainty, puzzlement, doubt or disbelief. If you see those signs, back up and start over until you think you've made yourself understood. It's not a matter of losing your poise to talk with an audience in a simple, uncluttered style. But some school people feel it is necessary to sound like a textbook whenever they make a speech.

All this is supported by Rudolf Flesch in his rules for "plain talk."[22] He urges speakers to use plain conversational talk. This will incorporate the technical language you must use, will permit a fast pace, and allow you to follow the ordinary rules of grammar but at the same time give the listener time to understand. The secret is what Flesch calls, "in-between space." Pause more often when talking before an audience, use repetition and spread out your ideas. Use filler words, like *that is* . . . *in the first place*

[21] "Pedaguese Is a Trap," *Trends,* National School Public Relations Association, Dec. 17, 1958, p. 3.
[22] Rudolf Flesch, *The Art of Plain Talk* (New York: Harper & Brothers, 1946). Condensed summary by permission.

. . . *should we say . . . another point,* and so on. Don't pause with your mouth open, though. That's the familiar *ah, er* sound of the vocalized pause while the speaker thinks of his next idea and continues to resonate sound through an open mouth. To take the *er's* out of your speech, close your mouth between ideas.

Back to Flesch. He prefers the familiar word to the far-fetched, the concrete to the abstract, and short words to long words.

Avoid empty words such as	*instead of*
along the lines of	like
for the purpose of	for
for the reason that	since
in accordance with	by
inasmuch as	since
in the event that	if
with reference to	about

Use plenty of verbs and personal pronouns. The moment a speaker begins to tell an audience "I think" he automatically delegates to them less authority, status, and prestige. Get used to the habit of saying we, you, our, and us. It's not "their problem" as much as it is "our problem"; try saying "our idea" rather than "my idea." Talk about people; use contractions and, on some occasions, even colloquialisms. Flesch warns against using gobbledygook and cautions against a display of book learning. And he adds, "to reach an audience at a certain level [of] listening, you not only have to talk the kind of language they will be able to understand without effort, but ordinarily you will have to go one step below that level to make sure your ideas will get across."[23] He was talking about levels of language experience, not about levels of intelligence. Don't talk down to an audience if they may not have much book learning. They still have some common sense and they resent artificiality.

Here's an example of what we've been talking about. It's filled

[23] *Ibid.,* p. 137.

with jargon, abstractions, and empty words. This is from a speech by a school official to a group of parents:

An attempt has been made to offer, to a reasonable degree, subjects which will provide pupils in the junior high schools opportunities to explore their interests and, to have, to a small degree, an introduction to industrial and homemaking experiences. This is the school level where abilities, aptitudes, and interests of the pupil can best be studied with the idea of assisting the individual to look forward realistically to planning his life's work.

That could have been said:

We are offering subjects which will provide junior high pupils with the chance to explore their interests, even to industrial and homemaking experiences. This is the school level where the pupil's abilities, aptitudes, and interests can be studied to help him plan his life's work.

Obviously, the first step towards a good speech style is to have something to say. Say it simply so there can be little doubt about your meaning.

Now let's take a closer look at your listener.

THE AUDIENCE

The listener is probably the most neglected part of the speech situation. It shouldn't be necessary to point out that without an audience there is no need for a speaker. Speech is a communicative function, a desire to seek responses from other people. Before you even begin to think of a subject for your talk or how to organize it, ask first, "Who will hear this?" Monroe reminds us, "This communication of ideas to impart knowledge and to secure cooperative action is what we mean by the social function of speech."[24] Whenever you appear before an audience to tell the school story, the important factor to remember is not that you're making a speech but that something is going on between a speaker and a listener. Speech, then, becomes a social function. It is not what speech *is*, but rather, what it *does*. In

[24] Monroe, *op. cit.,* p. 24.

order to be a successful speaker before any audience, you should attempt to see things from the viewpoint of the audience. You have to keep asking yourself, "How would I feel about this if I were in their places?" To do this requires a thorough job of audience analysis. In order to get this kind of advance picture of your listeners, question a member of the audience beforehand, if possible. If not, inquire of someone who has had some dealing with the group. If you are unable to do this, you're on your own, but you can still draw a general picture of the audience based on inferences.

GENERAL INFORMATION

Audience analysis should begin with a general picture of your listeners. Basic facts you should know include:[25]

1. *Size.*
2. *Age.* About the same age level, or widely divergent ages? This will affect their ability to understand you and also indicate the degree of their experience.
3. *Sex.* Are you talking to all men, all women, or a mixed group? Men and women differ in their interests as far as the subject matter of your speech is concerned.
4. *Occupation.* This may indicate interests, background, and knowledge of the members of the audience. You can get some idea of income level.
5. *Education.* Consider both formal schooling and experience.
6. *Social membership.* Membership in special groups may indicate both special interests and prejudices. Do members of the audience belong to any particular social, professional, or religious organization? If you find a sizable portion of your audience is affiliated with some special group, you will have a valuable clue for your analysis.
7. *Knowledge of subject.* How many technical words will need to be defined for them? Should you simplify your subject or would this be too "watered down" for this group? What facts you possess are new to them? Most good speakers aim their speech at a level of knowledge aimed to hit the average member of their particular audience.

May we point out that, although you may give exactly the same speech, every time you appear before a different audience you must adapt yourself and the speech to those differences. Don't expect to be able to give the plea for support of a new building program the same way to the Business and Professional Women that you gave before the Labor Council.

[25] *Ibid.,* p. 45. Condensed by permission.

8. *Interests and desires.* Skilful, persuasive speakers know that in order to appeal to listeners you have to tie your subject in with their interests. This is the "what's in it for me?" attitude found in all listeners. Psychologists have proven that within all people are certain basic universal tendencies. These feelings are modified and directed by pressure placed on the individual by his environment. Monroe claims, in terms of the speaker, "the normal condition of the people in an audience is one of physical relaxation, mental inertia, and emotional equilibrium unless something has happened already to stir these people into motion or unless the speaker does so through the appeal which he makes."[26]

Space does not permit us to discuss in much detail the primary motives of people as they concern the speaker. We would seriously suggest that each speaker make a serious study of audience motivation in order to do a more effective job of persuasion. Monroe's *Principles of Speech* contains an excellent summary of audience analysis in the second chapter.

PSYCHOLOGY OF THE AUDIENCE

Once you know something about a particular audience, you can begin to adapt the structure and content of your speech to that group.

If your listeners are apathetic, you must begin your talk on a point of compelling interest or startling vividness; show them how your subject affects them. If they are hostile to a proposal, you must approach it more cautiously; emphasize some basic principle with which they do agree and relate your proposal to it. If they are interested already but undecided, pile on the proof. If they are favorable but not aroused, use strong motivation embodied in vivid descriptive detail.[27]

Keep in mind that one of the primary functions of an audience is to give assurance and inspiration to the speaker. Remember, too, that each listener is influenced by his fellow listener as well as by the speaker. Members of an audience are more alike emotionally than in their ability to follow logical reasoning. So if you want to convince them with logical proof, start by creating an emotional attitude toward the subject. Don't be distressed if you find audiences don't remember too much of your speech.

[26] *Ibid.*, p. 47.
[27] *Ibid.*, p. 55.

Studies have shown that a typical educated audience, fairly interested in the topic of the speech, will probably forget about two-thirds of what they heard within one week's time. (A summary at the end of the speech helps improve their memory.) Use a great deal of repetition in your speech. Repeat your main idea at least three different times. Rephrase it somewhat and distribute the repetitions, but keep hammering away to reinforce your specific objective. On this point, tell your listeners specifically, not generally, the exact purpose of your speech and repeat that purpose. Use a slogan or catch-word phrase to sum up your objective. It helps improve the memory of the speech.

Attitudes of listeners may change while you're speaking. You have to be keenly aware of the audience response during your talk. Keep your eyes on them. The manner in which they sit in their seats, their facial expressions, frowns, smiles, whispers, laughter, and applause are all important cues to a speaker. This is one of the main arguments for skill in extemporaneous speaking over the manuscript method. It enables the speaker to be relatively free of notes and be more aware and sensitive to the visible and audible responses of his listeners.

Don't expect to take the entire audience with you at once. Try to find the friendly faces in your group. Seek these susceptible people and start talking with them at the beginning of your speech. The rest may fall into line if you don't move too fast for them. In an audience seated at random, the most susceptible listeners are usually those near the center of the audience. People seated near the front are often there because they are interested and may be most easily persuaded. Don't be upset by the behavior of some members of your group, but lack of attention in the center of your audience can be a dangerous sign to the speaker. Restlessness on the sides and back of the audience need not concern you at the outset of your speech.

One note of caution about audience analysis. You have to be prepared to change your approach while you speak if it seems that your preliminary analysis was wrong. Don't expect your listeners to adapt to your pre-arranged plan; the speaker is the person who must be flexible enough to adapt to the situation.

THE PHYSICAL SETTING

Perhaps we ought to make a note here concerning the room or auditorium in which you speak. The physical arrangement, contents, and previous uses of the room all exert some influence on the listeners. The larger the audience the more formal the speech situation tends to become and the more difficult the task of speaking. A platform would help in this case. Some elevation of the speaker tends to enhance his prestige and seems to aid the speaker who is using logical persuasion. If you seek an emotional appeal, the closer you can stand to your listeners the better the rapport.

If you are asked to speak to a fairly large audience in a spacious room, ask in advance about the possibility of needing a public-address system. Don't use one unless you feel it is absolutely necessary in order to be heard at the back of the room. It is easier to move around if you are not confined by a microphone.

If a public-address microphone is necessary, test it in advance (not by blowing into it—by speaking into it). Keep in mind that the volume level which seems adequate in an empty auditorium may not be enough when the room is filled with people. As far as the use of a public-address mike is concerned, remember it isn't necessary to shout into it. Let the mike work for you. Don't move your head too abruptly and stand at least one foot away from the microphone. Keep your hands off the mike or standard and watch for sudden coughs or laughs that would be amplified by the public-address system. Even when you are confronted with a microphone talk with your audience as if they numbered only about a dozen people.

THE OCCASION

Now to the fourth vital part of the speech situation—the occasion. As a member of the staff of a school system you can expect a variety of speaking experiences. More and more school administrators are realizing that mass media are important in school finance campaigns. But on top of that lies the increasing need for more face-to-face contact, more "coffee klatsch" meetings, more small group sessions, and more doorbell ringing. You'll talk with small conference groups and large, formal audiences. Your listeners will be fellow educators, members of citizen groups, parents, youngsters, businessmen, and organized labor.

We asked several school superintendents to name some of the speech occasions in which they had appeared recently. Look at this variety: parent-teacher associations, child study clubs, church youth fellowship groups, luncheon clubs, service clubs, lodge meetings, religious groups, citizen advisory committees, general teachers' meetings, school faculties, Community Chest campaign, business and professional organizations, ladies' library club, church "circles," fund raising campaigns, labor rallies, administrative staff meetings, Board of Education sessions, and Chamber of Commerce meetings.

Why did they speak? For a host of varying reasons. Some speeches were to inform, to promote a cause, to persuade, to create good will, or to introduce another speaker. On some occasions they dedicated buildings, gave commencement addresses, served as toastmaster, presided over public meetings, or presented awards. Other numerous speech situations were involved with "sit down" speech, working with people in small discussion groups, committee meetings, and conference situations.

Let's talk briefly about some of these specific speech occasions where, as a speaker, you'll have the opportunity to tell the school story.

TO INFORM

Let's start with this speech because it is often one of the driest, dullest speeches we give. Here your purpose is simply to have your audience understand the ideas you present. Reporting to citizens about the aims, practices, and accomplishments of your school system is of vital importance. Understanding must precede acceptance and support. One of the major factors present when people do not agree with each other is that they do not understand each other. Examples of this speech would include explaining school finance, reporting on your program for the gifted child, informing citizens of the methods of reporting to parents, explaining the grading system, reporting about your testing program, and a host of other explanatory topics.

Keep in mind your role is not to demonstrate to your audience how much you know about the subject. Your objective is to have them know certain fundamental facts. Your speech should be confined to facts and expert opinions, not argumentation and persuasion.

For the informative speech, Monroe's suggestions seem most pertinent. He suggests that the speaker follow three basic steps: [28]

1. Get the listeners' attention.
2. Show why he needs to know about this subject.
3. Present the information.

Another important aspect of this speech may be the necessity to define terminology as you present the information. Monroe recommends that the body of the speech be handled in this manner:

1. Briefly state the main points first.
2. Discuss and explain the facts relative to these main points.
3. Restate the main points again in summary, plus any recommenda‧ tions or conclusions you may have.

In general, the structure of the informative speech should be clear and uncluttered. Don't have too many main points and handle these one at a time. Use specific evidence, don't generalize. Try to brighten the speech with illustrations, examples, and some humor as much as you can. Informative talks without these things can be deadly. Take your time with this speech to make sure you are understood.

TO SECURE GOOD WILL

Obviously, every time you speak you seek good will for the

[28] *Ibid.*, pp. 165–193.

school system you represent. On some specific occasions your role as a speaker will be simply to speak as a representative of your schools. This role is sometimes described as the big butter and egg speech, the ambassadorial pitch, or the straight PR job. Actually, your objective is to leave the listener feeling good about your schools! These situations pop up at civic rallies, at dinner occasions, conventions or conferences, or other public occasions.

Micken recommends a general, pleasant approach to the occasion. He suggests you stick to an informative speech and tell the audience about your schools. Tell them about those positive characteristics which will create a confident impression of the schools. Don't pour it on too heavily; don't use too much humor. Stay with facts and keep in mind one of the first points raised in this chapter: they will get their impression of your schools from how they feel toward you. Stay with the "glad to be here" approach.[29] Another good approach to this speech assignment is to give your listeners some insight into many of the newer accomplishments of your schools, rather than review all of them. And avoid matters of controversy![30]

TO PROMOTE

"In most fields the era of one-shot sales is gone, if it ever was here. Today you sell the product, continuing services, long-range advice, and permanent interest in the buyer all in one package."[31] The speech to promote has something very much in common with the speech of good will. The latter type actually attempts to lay a foundation for the speech to promote action or support.[32]

The chief characteristic of this speech is that it attempts to prove something or to influence an attitude. This is a task of persuasion and involves a relationship between belief and action.

    [29] Micken, *op. cit.*, pp. 143–153.
    [30] William P. Sandford and Willard H. Yeager, *Practical Business Speaking* (New York: McGraw-Hill Book Co., 1952), pp. 178–184.
    [31] Micken, *op. cit.*, p. 129.
    [32] Sandford and Yeager, *op. cit.*, pp. 195–223.

This speech is given before audiences who may be prospective supporters. Here is where you seek voter support for new schools, improved teacher salaries, and other needed improvements to your present school system.

First, you must make the listener *want* to do what you propose rather than feel he *has* to. The best manner we know of to approach this task is through the use of the "motivated sequence." Here's how it works: [33]

1. *Get their attention.* This can be done through the use of direct reference to the subject, by asking one or more rhetorical questions, using a startling statement (the shock technique), a quotation, anecdote, or an illustration. For example, "Where are we going to put them? How are we going to educate all of these new-born youngsters in our community when we don't have nearly enough classrooms and teachers?"

2. *Show the need.* Here's where you describe the problem. A simplified outline of this step would be:

   a) State the problem. Show what's wrong. Put it in the form of a direct statement.

   b) Illustrate this. Give one or more examples or illustrations to back up your first statement.

   c) Ramification step. Here's where you use facts, quotations, statistical evidence to make the problem impressive.

   d) Relate to your audience. You must show them why this problem is important to the members of this audience. Prove to them it is their problem.

3. *Satisfy the need.* This is the "pitch." Here is where you present your solution to the problem you've just outlined. This is where the great bulk of enthusiasm, interest, and evidence of the speaker must be directed. Now that you have started with an appeal to emotional feelings, it is time for logical reasoning:

   a) State your solution. Put in one clear, capsule sentence the attitude you wish your listeners to take. This is the topic sentence of the speech.

   b) Explain this. To make sure your solution is understood, give examples, illustrations, visual aid assistance to develop your argument.

   c) Demonstration step. Show logically how what you have proposed will solve the problem you outlined in the *need* stage of the speech.

[33] Monroe, *op. cit.*, pp. 195–223.

d) Practical experience. Do you have any actual examples of how this proposal has worked before? Any opinions of experts or factual evidence can be well used at this point.

e) Meet objections. Any good debater prepares his case with a thorough preparation of the other side's argument so he will be able to answer objections to his case. Anticipate any objections which may be raised to your proposal and answer those at this point. Sometimes this needs to be sprinkled throughout the speech, rather than concentrated at this one point.

4. *Visualize the results.* You have to paint a picture here. Show your listeners what will happen if they accept your proposal (positive). Describe conditions in the future if your suggestions are carried out. Be specific, not general. Show your listeners actually enjoying the benefits of your suggestions. Another approach is to use the negative approach. Describe what will happen if your proposals are not carried out. Again, be specific and relate your listeners to this personally. Or, use the method of contrast. Describe both the positive and negative effects and let them choose. Describe the negative approach first and contrast failure with success. This is the "what'll you have?" approach.

5. *Request action or approval.* This is the conclusion of the speech where you transfer the created desire to action. Here is where you should specifically request your audience to do something, either accept your attitude or take definite steps to achieve the goal you have outlined. This may be done through a challenge or appeal to your audience, by a quick summary of the need and solution steps, with a quotation from someone else which suggests the action you want, an illustration or anecdote, or a statement of what you personally intend to do about your suggested proposal.

This speech should contain all of the energy and enthusiasm you possess without getting overemotional. The more direct action you seek, the more dynamic must be your delivery of the speech. Don't stretch this speech out, keep it moving through the motivated sequence and finally make a *direct plea* for response from the listener.

TO INTRODUCE A SPEAKER

Chances are you'll be called upon to make many introductions of other speakers. Your job here is to present the speaker to the audience and make them want to hear him. This speech should be brief and about the speaker, not about yourself. A simple outline for the introductory speech contains these four main points:

The occasion. As an introductory mechanism, refer to the reason for the speaker appearing here. Consider the appropriateness of the speaker or his subject. Connect the speaker with this particular audience.

His qualifications. Tell your listeners why the speaker is qualified to speak on this subject. Who is he? What is his position? State his experience and background. Beware of telling what a good speaker he is; you can put him on the spot. Simply outline briefly his qualifications. Don't make an obituary rundown of everything he has ever done, select only those facts of interest to this audience on this occasion.

His topic. Don't make the speech for him—too many introductions end up this way. Mention the appropriateness of his subject but let him tell about it. If he has given his speech a title, use that. If not, a concise statement of his topic will suffice.

His name. Once a man's name has been mentioned he is introduced. Make sure you pronounce it correctly. Refer to him in the manner in which he prefers. If his name is William, and he prefers Bill, act accordingly. State his title, if he has one, before the name, not after. The only thing that follows a speaker's name is applause. For example, say, "I am pleased to present the Superintendent of the Jonesville Public Schools, John W. Doe." Not, "I am pleased to present John W. Doe, Superintendent of the Jonesville Public Schools."

Three things should happen once you've mentioned the speaker's name in the conclusion of your introduction. You should sit, he should stand, and they should applaud. It is as simple as that.

TO PRESIDE OVER ORGANIZED MEETINGS

Without going into a guide for parliamentary procedure, we should mention some of the specific functions of the chairman of an organized meeting.[34] You should first call the meeting to order. Then call for any announcements and reports which may

[34] Micken, *op. cit.*, p. 179.

be on the agenda. If you have discussion from the floor, recognize speakers fairly and clearly. See that the rules of this group are carried out but do not take part in debate or favor certain members of the group. Don't use your position to accomplish the results you seek; use your position to accomplish the wishes of the group. If you are fuzzy on parliamentary procedure, consult a good summary of the rules. Monroe's book has a simple diagram which may prove helpful to speakers in charge of large, organized meetings.

SPEECHES FOR SPECIAL OCCASIONS

You may be called upon to act as toastmaster in an after-dinner situation. Don't feel it is necessary to roll them in the aisles or to limit your stories to the off-color variety. Your main duty is to set the spirit of the occasion and keep things moving. You'll need plenty of stories and a keen sense of humor. Remember, you're the transition man, not the star performer.

When you are asked to present an award, keep a balance between that which you are feeling, and that which good taste permits. Suggest the appropriate sentiment, but don't parade it.[35] The composition of a speech of presentation is fairly simple. First, you describe the accomplishments of the person receiving the award, then you describe the gift or award.

There are other such courtesy talks—welcoming visitors or new staff members, saying farewell to members of your organization, speaking at community functions. On these or any other similar occasions, your best bet is to express genuine sentiment without going overboard in your praise. Your task, then, in a speech of introduction is to establish good relations between a guest speaker and the audience; a welcoming speech expresses greetings and hospitality while a farewell speech indicates esteem and good wishes; an after-dinner speech is usually thought of as a speech to entertain, and a presentation is used in the giving of a gift or an award.[36]

[35] McBurney and Wrage, *op. cit.*, pp. 297–298.
[36] *Ibid.*, pp. 299–300.

DISCUSSION AND CONFERENCE

Much of your activities in speaking situations will be with "sit down" speech, in the form of small discussion groups or in conferences. As the Overstreets pointed out in one of their lectures, today when two people meet on the street, you have a committee; if you can get six people you can have by-laws! More and more decision-making and problem-solving in business, industry, and school administration is being done by groups rather than by individuals.

Obviously, we can only be cursory here in a review of discussion techniques. Again we can refer you to good, basic texts in this field and heartily recommend a review of these. Sattler and Miller's *Discussion and Conference;* Franklin Haiman's *Group Leadership and Democratic Action;* and *Discussion in Human Affairs,* by McBurney and Hance are recommended references in this area of speech.

What you do and say in a group discussion situation depends upon that situation. But you will, undoubtedly, lead discussion sessions, and we should cover basic requirements of the leader. Discussion can be used to solve problems, as an information technique, or simply to create higher motivation among the participants. Regardless of the purpose of the discussion, one of the basic requirements of a conference leader is to organize the procedure to prevent it from becoming another of those time-consuming, often fruitless "committee meetings." Much time can be saved if the leader and the participants follow a critical, orderly pattern of thinking. Most used in problem-solving conferences is the *Reflective Thinking* approach. Suggested originally by John Dewey, this five-step method of thinking proves invaluable in the group process. The logical plan of organization is as follows: [37]

1. Recognition of the Problem
    A. Formulation of the problem as a question
    B. Definition of the problem

[37] William M. Sattler and N. Edd Miller, *Discussion and Conference* (Englewood Cliffs, N.J.: Prentice-Hall, Inc., 1954), pp. 32–33.

2. Description of the Problem
    A. History of the problem
    B. Causes of the problem
    C. Effects of the problem
3. Discovery of Solutions
    A. Conditions to be met by an acceptable solution
    B. Possible solutions
4. Evaluation of Possible Solutions
    A. Evaluation of possible solutions
    B. Acceptance of best solution
5. Plan of Action
    A. Methods of execution
    B. Action group to put solution into effect.

One of the chief duties as the discussion leader is to strive to have the main phases of the problem considered. On top of that, as a conference leader, you should strive to get good general participation from the group members, promote the unity of the group, encourage the giving of opinions and solutions, and check irrelevant contributions. The leader should also clarify contributions, when necessary, but be neutral himself, should try to change the behavior of troublesome participants, and should summarize the conference at its conclusion.[38]

School administrators find themselves engaged more and more with citizen advisory committees, staff conferences, policy making discussions, informational panels, and other types of group discussion activity. Here again it is important that you be well organized and prepared. Prior to any such conference, you should carefully prepare your "reflective" agenda. Plan a brief, informal social session beforehand so that members of the group have the oportunity to get acquainted. This helps promote group unity and gives you some insight into the kind of people you'll be working with. Think in advance of seating arrangements; you may want to seat people in some arrangement that will avoid having some monopolize or others withdraw from participating in the discussion. If problems arise and the group seems unable

[38] *Ibid.*, pp. 154–161.

to come to an agreement, suggest a short intermission period or even postpone the discussion to a later date.

The discussion technique is an excellent way to tell more people your school story, to work on your problems together, and to prevent misunderstandings. As Sattler and Miller point out, "Discussion emphasizes collaborative efforts rather than conflict. It is a procedural arrangement that encourages conferees to center their attention upon *what is right* rather than upon *who is right*."[39] The conference situation calls for participation in decision making; it encourages the democratic participation of many people in problem solving. It also helps participants improve their ability to think critically and to maintain better interpersonal relationships with others.

In order to accomplish your desired results through discussion, seek to create an informal group atmosphere; try to create a "we" feeling, allow participants the freedom to express themselves; stress cooperation and critical thinking, and remind your group that the responsibility for a decision rests with the group —not with the leader.

A SPEAKERS' BUREAU

More and more school systems across the country are organizing a speakers' bureau to improve school-community relationships. This is a planned means for providing staff members as speakers for various community functions. Such a public relations program increases the amount of face-to-face contact with community groups and organizations and helps citizens know more about their schools. It works two ways, since it provides a means of telling school administrators what citizens think of their schools.

A speakers' bureau is relatively simple to organize and administer. First, ask your staff if they would like to volunteer their services and would be able to appear for talks or demonstrations before community groups. Ask them to indicate the

[39] *Ibid.*, p. 11.

subject or topics they would be able to talk about. These topics do not have to relate to the operation of the schools but may be in the area of the teacher's subject field, interests, or hobbies. After you have acquired a list of speakers, prepare an attractive brochure describing the bureau, the names of the speakers, and their choice of topics. This brochure, containing instructions for contacting speakers, should be mailed annually to churches, women's clubs, businessmen's organizations, labor unions, parent-teacher associations, fraternal groups, and other civic organizations. The service should be rendered without charge, but the speakers should be permitted to accept honorariums that are offered.[40]

It isn't necessary that your speakers be polished performers, but they should be fairly capable and have a worthwhile topic. A bureau can be set up on a school system basis, or an individual school could establish its own bureau. An example of a system-wide setup is in effect at Modesto, California. There, teachers and administrators were asked whether they would like to participate in such a community service program and a total of 175 staff members responded. Available talks cover a host of subjects, book reviews, demonstrations, musical programs, and even one magician. Twenty-nine staff members are available for slide-illustrated travel talks.[41] On an individual school basis, Port Huron (Michigan) Junior College has set up a bureau as a part of its community service. Over fifteen members of the college faculty volunteered to speak before community groups. An illustrated brochure was distributed throughout the community, and staff members speak on a variety of topics. The mathematics instructor talks about telescopes and how to build them, English instructors do book reviews, while teachers who have toured Europe give slide-illustrated travel lectures. Meanwhile, administrators appear before parent groups to discuss the aims and functions of the college, the testing and counseling pro-

[40] Leslie W. Kindred, *School Public Relations* (Englewood Cliffs, N.J.: Prentice-Hall, Inc., 1957), p. 376.

[41] "Are Teachers People?" *Trends*, National School Public Relations Assn., December 17, 1958, p. 2.

gram, nursing training program, and other areas of the college's curriculum.

After you have drawn up a list of speakers, it would seem advisable to hold a short training program to equip speakers with a sense of public relations. Kindred points out that "the speakers' bureau should take a responsibility for collecting and organizing material for talks dealing with the aims, practices, and accomplishments of the local school system."[42] Your better, more capable, and more well informed people should handle these speeches. The bureau should equip them with any visual aids they may need to make such talks.

Cutlip and Center, in their second edition of *Effective Public Relations*, suggest these four points for the operation of such a bureau:

1. Select and coach the line-up of speakers with some care.
2. Select topics of broad interest which serve needs of the potential audience and carry the organization's story.
3. Provide speakers with helpful visual aids—flip charts, flannel boards, slide films, and so on.
4. Promote and publicize the availability of the speakers to get maximum mileage.[43]

Keep a central point of control over your speakers' bureau. Kindred[44] suggests making a follow-up on your staff members' appearances at community occasions. This will give you an idea of audience reaction and will help you in determining the wisdom of using some speakers or the need for more speaker training sessions. Hold periodic evaluation sessions with members of your speakers' bureau. After all, these people are your community contact team. They can bring back their impressions of the attitudes of their audiences toward schools. This two-way aspect of a speakers' bureau can pay big dividends in your continual program to understand and be understood.

[42] Kindred, *op. cit.*, pp. 376–377.
[43] Scott M. Cutlip and Allen H. Center, *Effective Public Relations*, 2nd ed. (Englewood Cliffs, N.J.: Prentice-Hall, Inc., 1958), pp. 164–165.
[44] Kindred, *op. cit.*, p. 377.

SUMMARY

We have attempted to describe the four vital parts of the speech process—the speaker, the speech, the audience, and the occasion. Although this phase of telling the school story has been rather cursory, we feel the role of speaking in school public relations is vital. Through face-to-face communication with community groups you have an unequaled opportunity to tell your school story as you know it. You have the opportunity to see the degree of acceptance, or lack of it, by your listeners. In this two-way process of speaker to audience and audience to speaker, a direct form of communication exists to guide your other methods in school public relations.

Speaking to audiences requires preparation and practice. It means a thorough analysis of each audience, each occasion, and every subject you select. You've got to do a great deal of speaking to a cross-section of your community to make this part of your communications program effective. By itself, this is only a part of your over-all public information program. If you carefully organize each speech and take special care that you are understood—if you appear confident and capable—you should find a greater understanding of, and better appreciation for, the schools you represent.

BIBLIOGRAPHY

"Are Teachers People?" *Trends,* December 17, 1958. This biweekly PR newsletter is published by the National School Public Relations Association and contains many good tips for practitioners.

Baird, A. Craig and Franklin H. Knower, *General Speech.* New York: McGraw-Hill Book Co., Inc., 1957. Chapter 5 discusses in detail the organization and outlining of a speech.

Brigance, William Norwood, *Speech Communication.* New York: Appleton-Century-Crofts, Inc., 1955. A brief textbook in speech by a noted rhetorician. Chapter 1 offers an excellent summary of the rights of listeners; Chapter 9 instructs the speaker in the use of visual aids.

Crocker, Lionel, *Business and Professional Speech*. New York: The Ronald Press Co., 1951. Chapter 3 contains a discussion of the four fundamental parts of the speech situation.

Cutlip, Scott M. and Allen H. Center, *Effective Public Relations*. Englewood Cliffs, N.J.: Prentice-Hall, Inc., 1958. Chapter 11 covers the tools of communication and includes the role of the spoken word: meetings, speakers' bureau, public-address systems, and the grapevine.

Flesch, Rudolf, *The Art of Plain Talk*. New York: Harper and Brothers, 1946. Suggested reading for any professional speaker who wants to improve his style and streamline his ability to be understood.

Kindred, Leslie W., *School Public Relations*. Englewood Cliffs, N.J.: Prentice-Hall, Inc., 1957. Chapter 18 describes special events and services in a school public relations program and includes suggestions for a staff speakers' bureau.

Lee, Irving J., *How to Talk With People*. New York: Harper and Brothers, 1952. Described as a guide for the improvement of communication in committees, this compact book is especially valuable to the conference leader.

McBurney, James H. and Ernest J. Wrage, *Guide to Good Speech*. Englewood Cliffs, N.J.: Prentice-Hall, Inc., 1955. Chapters 7 8 are a guide to speech organization and composition. This book, a basic college speech text, is a good guide for the inexperienced speaker.

Micken, Ralph A., *Speaking for Results*. Boston: Houghton-Mifflin Co., 1958. The first chapter has an excellent discussion of the speaker's attitude toward his job. Chapter 4 contains a good summary of the role of the speaker in typical speech situations.

Monroe, Alan H., *Principles of Speech*, 4th brief ed. Chicago: Scott, Foresman and Co., 1958. Chapter 2 emphasizes the author's belief in the relationship between a speaker and his audience; Chapter 7 on persuasion should be required reading for all speakers.

"Pedaguese is a Trap," *Trends*, December 17, 1958. Another good tip from the NSPRA newsletter.

Sandford, William P. and Willard H. Yeager, *Practical Business Speaking*. New York: McGraw-Hill Book Co., 1952. Chapter 12 offers suggestions on speeches to create good will while the entire book discusses various types of business talks.

Sattler, William M. and N. Edd Miller, *Discussion and Conference.* Englewood Cliffs, N.J.: Prentice-Hall, Inc., 1954. Chapters 9, 10, and 11 are devoted to conference leadership, its functions and stages. The entire book is recommended for group discussion participants and leaders.

10

KEEPING PARENTS INFORMED

"As the child thinks of the school, so does the home," has been aptly said, and we should add, so also think the child's relatives, friends, and neighbors. School public relations began when the first teacher met the first pupil, and today the attitudes of parents toward the school, teachers, and education in general are the by-products of teaching.

Schools belong to the parents who provide the children and finance the educational program. Every school must accept the challenge of developing a continuing program of keeping parents correctly informed about its program, as well as stimulating and utilizing parental interests and talents. Contacts may be direct or indirect, but the more personal the contacts, the more rewarding.

1. Schools should be alert as to the scope of information parents want.
2. Schools should study and plan successful ways of relaying or taking information to parents.
3. Schools should see that information travels on a two-way street both to and from parents.
4. Schools should help all persons connected with a school system feel that they are public relations interpreters and keep them informed on school policies and procedures.

Parents need to know what the members of the board of education think about the schools and their children. The schools need to know what the parents think about them and their teaching methods; and the parents need to know what the schools think about pupils and their abilities to learn. Exchanging and sharing knowledge about a child builds mutual understanding and cooperation between parents and teachers—and only through this mutual understanding and cooperation can a child find the security which forms the basis for his best learning. Sometimes school personnel are blissfully unaware of or complacent about parental opinion until some explosive incident reveals an accumulation of intense feeling. Increasing interest in education makes the schools a timely topic of conversation, and parental interest needs to be directed into positive channels.

Continuous, truthful information is more valuable in interpreting the schools than periodic publicity, regardless of high pressure methods. This information should include all grade levels and every activity of the school; it should be properly balanced and in the proper amount; too much at one time becomes overpowering. Only three per cent of the people can be relied upon to read any one article, so repetition is one of the keys to successful interpretation.

TECHNIQUES FOR INFORMING PARENTS

The most effective way of keeping parents informed is to involve them in the planning activities and problems of the school. Lack of understanding on the part of the parents between *what* and *how* we teach and what we are actually accomplishing is usually due to the schools' failure to include the parents in the planning periods. We know that schools do a much better job of teaching than they do of telling the public how they teach. Principals hold in their hands the reins which guide cooperative planning between parents and teachers. An astute principal soon learns to what extent to use the parents' suggestions and still maintain control of the situation.

Before successful planning can be accomplished, the head of the school must understand the needs of his students; be aware of the potential of his community and know if the parents are ready for group planning; know how to organize group planning; and be skilled in using authority wisely. From such cooperative planning can come increased confidence on the part of the parents in the leadership of the school; the acceptance by parents of the responsibility to contribute something of value to the schools, and a bond of understanding and appreciation between parents and teachers.

SERVICE ON SCHOOL COMMITTEES

Cooperative educational planning can only be begun after an atmosphere conducive to sharing ideas and feelings has been established. A channel of communication between the school and parents must constantly flow freely; parents appreciate direct information and must be informed if they are to assist the schools.

The principal, teachers, and homeroom mothers make an effective group for planning building policies and regulations. When possible, student representatives should be included. Members of the group should be divided into grade levels or subject areas to meet parents' interest, especially if the size of the group is unwieldy.

Some rules of procedure for cooperative planning are:

1. Establish the purpose of the planning meeting.
2. Set up objectives and work toward genuine results.
3. Keep all plans child-centered.
4. Avoid all personality conflicts if possible.
5. Be generous with sincere appreciation.
6. Enlist the interest of all parents and utilize parent talent.
7. When conducive to improving understanding, use parents on committees as channels of interpretation to all patrons.

Parent participation in curriculum planning may be beneficial. The value is largely in the understanding and insight which par-

ents develop and their ability to interpret the curriculum correctly to the community. On the negative side, it is possible that
a limited knowledge of the needs of children could result in a
curriculum curtailed by personal prejudices.

ADVISORY COUNCILS

Advisory councils are valuable in some areas of fact-finding
and curriculum planning. They differ from citizens committees,
which may be organized to perform a specific assignment. Carefully selected parents contribute new ideas, stimulate interest,
and often change potential critics into boosters for the school's
program.

Rapidly expanded school population in suburban areas may
produce community frictions. An advisory council could help
absorb and direct the parents' interest. In one city an advisory
council, selected by the board of education to advise on new
building sites and the construction and equipment of new
buildings, served as a means of conveying information to the
community and prevented hard feelings because of delayed
completion dates.

The lay membership of this council included a broad
representation of interested patrons selected economically, geo-
graphically, occupationally, and socially. Sometimes these lay
committees are not confined to parents. However, it should be a
group that can work together, although not necessarily only
those who agree with established trends, but also some who are
known to be critics.

Parents seldom criticize a school when they have helped to
plan the programs. However, parents need and respect strong
leadership. The principal is the head of the school, not the parents or the students. He must always maintain his position and
skilfully channel parental interest.

BRIDGING THE GAP

School systems which do not have kindergartens need a
program for bridging the gap between the home and school.

From the annual school census and from the children who attend school, the names of the prospective pupils can be obtained. In the spring the parents and children can be invited to the school on a special date. While the parents attend a meeting, children visit the first grade and see the wonders of school life. In May, the pre-school children may be invited back, a few at a time, to visit and participate in class activities, such as simple rhythms and nursery rhymes with the other children.

Of course, a visit in the home by the teacher the following fall (during the first week of school) gives the teacher an opportunity to obtain helpful information. After observing the home environment and the child's place in the family, a teacher can usually discern the child's maturity development; obtain pertinent facts about his health habits; see the parent-child relationship, and establish a friendly teacher-parent relationship and set up common goals for the child. This exchange plan of visitation of the parent and child in the school and the teacher in the home is accepted as one of the most successful of school public relations practices for orienting kindergarten children.

HOME VISITS ON ALL GRADE LEVELS

Parents always like the teacher and the school when they see a sincere interest in their children. Parental interest in the school may be developed through many techniques, but a visit to the home is most effective on every grade level. A visit to the home during the first week of school may help explain the attitudes and behavior of the eighth grade student as well as the preschool child. What sort of people are the parents? What financial class are they in? Do they listen to music? Read books? Fish? Travel? Are they hostile toward the school? All these things have an influence on the activities of the child—and should determine, in part, your approach to school-parent relations.

As part of the new teachers' orientation, they should be given help as to planning visits in the home and suggestions on how to organize these visits to save time. New teachers—as well as experienced ones—should also be shown how to avoid such common mistakes as speaking in pedagogical clichés instead of simple, everyday language; complaining about the child in his home; talking too much or being insincere; discussing other children or parents; repeating or discussing neighborhood gossip; or becoming involved in argumentative subjects or situations.

In some cities the lower grade children are dismissed at noon the first two weeks of school and the upper grade children for one week, so that teachers can make brief calls in each home. The visits are grouped by neighborhoods to save time. Notes are sent to parents in advance to prevent surprise calls and make parents feel more at ease with teachers. When the parents realize that each child now has three people genuinely interested in him, a relaxed wholesome relationship is usually established. However, time and distance do not always permit visitation. It may be necessary to establish communication through other media.

GETTING PARENTS TO VISIT SCHOOL

Parents who visit actual classrooms usually have a better understanding of what the school is teaching and the methods of instruction used. Actual observation can dispel many rumors and build confidence and appreciation between the parent and teacher. A teacher can capitalize on everyday classroom activities as a basis for inviting parents.

Some fathers can be encouraged to talk about hobbies or travels, and, while contributing to the education of the children, can come to a better, more appreciative understanding of the activities of the schools. Mothers are more free to work on extended projects with the students and teachers and can usually be counted on to take part in organized activities—such as singing groups—which involve them intimately in the everyday functions of the school.

TELEPHONE CALLS

The way the telephone is answered and the tone of voice of the speaker may set the opinions of patrons in regard to their school. A pleasant voice is a valuable asset and, fortunately, can be developed. A voice can reflect poise, joy, pleasure, sadness, annoyance, or perhaps just dull indifference—which is most disturbing to the one who initiated the call. Let the person who called replace the receiver first, lest a too hurried-to-be-polite attitude is detected.

Everyone who answers the telephone should identify himself whenever a question may be in the mind of the caller as to the one responding. When students answer the telephone at school, teach them to state their school and name in a polite manner and record or relay any message accurately and speedily. Writing the message, time received, name of the caller, and name of receiving party is always advisable. The telephone company will usually send one of their expert trainers out to give instruction, free of charge, in telephone etiquette. This serves a double purpose by also getting a working patron into the school periodically.

PERSONAL LETTERS TO PARENTS

Letters to parents may serve many purposes. At the opening of school, a warm friendly letter from the pupil's teacher stating her educational background and philosophy helps parents to know and respect the teacher. The letters should close with a desire to know the parents and an invitation to visit the school.

A note to parents in recognition for some contribution their children made to classwork, or a progress report on a child's development in reading, helps parents to know the school's program—a *parent's* picture in the paper is also an oportunity for a congratulatory note. Recognizing the achievements of former pupils always pleases parents. The stork furnishes opportunities for a friendly contact—a note to a new baby, congratulating it upon its choice of parents and inviting it to be the room's "mascot" will bring the mother and baby into the school at the first possible chance. Often this attention helps the older child to accept a younger brother or sister when they see the enthusiasm of their classmates.

Some form of recognition and appreciation for the years of

service from the Board of Education at the death of an adult employee is greatly appreciated by the nearest of kin. Several large cities have prepared a tribute of appreciation which cited the employees' various places of service and contributions to children and co-workers, when a personal visit from the administration office was not feasible. The tribute was signed by both the president of the Board of Education and the Superintendent of Schools. A personal letter accompanied this certificate of appreciation.

Helping a child who is ill to keep in touch with his classroom builds the morale of the child and his parents. The home-bound child needs psychological help from the school as part of his convalescing therapy. The Junior Red Cross program has a well-organized plan which includes advice on procedure from the physician, nurse and mother.

Letters from a school should always be on letterhead stationery with correct spelling, punctuation, and properly signed. Avoid technical terminology, pedagogical phrases, and negative terms. Always answer letters promptly and courteously.

Every organization or business receives a certain number of complaints and schools are no exception. Misconceptions and misunderstandings are usually the root of dissatisfactions, but a minority group of disgruntled parents can influence a community adversely. These complaints can be used advantageously as a barometer of the public relations program. When communication by letter is the advisable method, the utmost care should be taken to present the complete truth substantiated by facts and figures in such a concise manner that the information could not be misunderstood.

It is well to establish a series of communications over a period of time that will serve to build complete understanding and confidence in the school.

PARENT NEWSLETTERS

Another avenue of communication with parents and community leaders is the newsletter. Published weekly or monthly, it has the following uses and advantages:

Weekly bulletins from the principal keep the patrons up-to-date on all school activities.

Newsletters relay important and interesting information.

It may include mothers' and dads' club and PTA news.

A progress report of any building redecorating and the purchase of new equipment are newsworthy.

Notices of appreciation to patrons who contributed special assistance and to cafeteria and custodial staff for extra services are important. Recognition of successful classroom projects stimulates both teachers and pupils.

School newspapers furnish an excellent medium for informing parents since they are usually read with avid interest. A few complimentary copies can be strategically placed in the hands of citizens who do not have children in school.

Use slogans or catchy words in titles to attract reader's interest.

Radio and television schedules assist parents in selecting worthwhile programs. How the schools follow up these programs helps parents to appreciate the learning value of the telecast and also the teacher's skill in utilizing them as teaching aids. Much needs to be done in the area of proper utilization of television on both educational and commercial stations. Fortunately, the potential of teaching by television is unfolding.

REPORT CARD COMMENTS

The merits and demerits of reporting to parents by means of a printed form have stimulated much research and many conferences. The inadequacy of a printed or written report has been established. Frequently a variety of teacher's reports are shuffled back and forth between schools and parents because the figures, letters, symbols, and check marks tell parents very little.

The importance of involving parents in planning the method of reporting should not be underestimated, although it may take many months of actual work. In some schools the children are invited to help the teacher establish the grade or record. Some teachers invite the parents to help them evaluate the pupils and record the grades. In some communities the parents and teachers work out the "Report to Parents" after a series of studies and evaluations has been made. Temporary reports are sometimes used in pilot schools.

Some parents work out a check sheet or report on how they work with the child at home. This gives the teacher useful information. However, parents should instigate and enjoy such an activity and not have it thrust upon them by the school. The parents' comments to the teacher are equally successful in establishing good will when a parent has reacted with either appreciation or understanding.

Honest, complimentary comments by a teacher on a pupil's report card may soften the reaction to poor marks. When a conference follows, it establishes an understanding which is impossible to form on paper.

PARENT-TEACHER CONFERENCES

Parent-teacher conferences have become an accepted practice in many school systems. By working together, parents and teachers have discovered there is no one technique of making them successful since different types of conferences have different values. In some instances, they have replaced the report card and, in others, they have served as a supplementary or correlated report since a couple of thousand words may be exchanged in a 20-minute conference.

Careful preparation should precede all conferences. The teacher needs pertinent information about the child, including family background, academic ability, quality of work, test results, health and attendance records, and samples of his school work. A brief outline of what the teacher wishes to accomplish by the conference and suggested helps for the parents should be prepared.

Appointments should be scheduled for personal conferences with parents. The get-acquainted conference differs from the problem-solving and joint-planning conference.

There is a desire by both parents and teachers for better communications. Recently at the request of a group of city-wide PTA council officers, a committee of parents, selected by the city PTA council president, met with the public relations director and made suggestions as to how to establish better timing of various types of communications between parents and schools. These suggestions were given to a committee of principals who in turn presented them as recommendations to their entire group. A committee of principals held the same type of meeting and gave their suggestions to the PTA officers to be submitted to their members. Most of the suggestions were the same, which indicated the parents and the schools had the same desire for better communications.

SUGGESTED APPROACH FOR PERSONAL CONFERENCES

Here are some directions that represent the tested products of experience in handling conferences with parents:

a) Arrange a choice of meeting times to make it possible for working parents to be present.
b) Give parents some idea of the nature of the conference.
c) Let the student make suggestions for the conference.
d) Meet and cordially greet the parents at the door.
e) Arrange a comfortable place for waiting, should the parents arrive early.
f) Allow time to make notes between conferences, not during the conference, if possible.
g) Put the parents at ease by a pleasant opening of the conversation. Guide it adroitly to the desired points for discussion. Encourage parents to make suggestions and volunteer information. Adjust conference time for working mothers, before or after school, or during noon hours. Invite some for lunch.
h) Be honest and include necessary negative situations.
i) End on a positive plane by suggesting how they can help, but limit suggestions in order to prevent overwhelming the parents.

A series of simplified bulletins, explaining the purpose, preparation, and value of conferences may be sent to parents who are unable to attend conferences.

Cooperative planning with parents makes rules and regulations more acceptable and may include arrival and dismissal time for pupils on different grade levels; traffic regulations around the buildings to prevent congested one-way drives; explanation of supervised street crossings; pre-school and after-school activities that affect home routines (for example, regulation of the time for chorus and band practice before school, and athletics and dramatic activities after school save many phone calls); and attendance rules relative to exceptions, types of excuses, and excused absences.

During the summer, junior high school counselors in some cities invite every student and his parents in for a conference. Aptitude tests are discussed, schedules arranged, and both parents and students have some idea of what is expected. Parents are interested in the requirements for honor societies and scholarships in secondary schools and colleges as goals toward which students may work (conferences on the senior high school level may include counseling for a vocation or for college entrance requirements). A simple folder containing date, time, place, purpose of the conference, and discussion areas is useful. A handbook for parent-teacher conferences which has been jointly planned by teachers and parents, stating the objectives to be obtained from the conferences, and the preparation each should make before the conference, will improve the results. Parent conferences from 7:30 to 8:00 a.m., or late afternoon or evening, may be necessary.

In one school system, the board of education approved 18 scheduled conference days on which the pupils were dismissed at 2:30 p.m. Although most of the visiting parents were mothers, some of the fathers attended. The findings of these conferences were compiled and publicized in the community with satisfying results.

JOINT PLANNING CONFERENCES

The same concept governing personal conferences between parents and teachers should be carried over into group situations. Problems may arise concerning the lunchroom, transportation, social affairs, and a host of other matters in which parents have a strong interest. By calling them together to discuss these problems and by making them parties to decisions reached, real bonds of friendship and appreciation can be cemented.

A few basic suggestions for making joint planning conferences successful are:

1. An atmosphere of willingness to share ideas and suggestions
2. An understanding of the problem and its ramifications
3. Reaching a consensus before a decision is made
4. Having parents share in carrying out the decision whenever this is feasible
5. Using enthusiastic members to help influence those who are less interested
6. Rotating honors and privileges among members of the group
7. Sensing the needs and temperaments of parents and trying to avoid a feeling on the part of some that they are being excluded
8. Keeping communication simple so that parents are not confused by too many facts at one time.

STUDY GROUPS, WORKSHOPS, AND CLASSES

Parents can become involved even more extensively in the life of the school through participation in study groups, workshops, and classes that are related to institutional needs, problems, and practices.

PARENT-TEACHER STUDY GROUPS

Parent-teacher study groups have become an integral part of school systems in many communities throughout the country. Organized by administrators and teachers—and now and then at the request of parents—these groups make it their business to analyze and discuss report cards, child growth, discipline, health habits, and the like. The primary purpose is to know more about a given subject and to act more constructively with regard to it. Not infrequently, problems will be studied and solutions recommended to proper school officials. Leadership in directing the work of study groups is generally assumed by the school.

There are two valuable contributions that come from the activities of parent-teacher study groups. First, the thinking of the group finds expression in the practices of the school, and second, the parents take it upon themselves to interpret the school to the community. These groups also tend to develop in *both* parents *and* teachers unsuspected leadership ability and an increasing awareness of and desire to solve school problems.

Certain typical problems do arise in these groups, however; lack of coordination that leads to poor communication is an ever-present threat. Assumption of too much authority by the group can lead to trouble and can cause the group to dissipate its energy in too many fruitless projects.

Materials for PTA study groups are being presented on television, most frequently on educational channels. The parents meet in homes, discuss the topics and telephone in questions during the latter part of the program. This procedure meets the requirements for study credit as specified by the National PTA Council. Individual viewing is encouraged when group participation is not possible. A monthly questionnaire helps to keep the evaluation of the program current and permits the parents to suggest topics for study. In forming study groups, it is well to have a planning committee take over responsibility at the beginning and to work out the details of how the group will function. Meetings of the groups may be held at school, but a private home lends a greater feeling of freedom. The ratio of at least three lay people to one educator should be maintained as a minimum. Present trends indicate that successful study groups far exceed those that fail and that careful planning and proper supervisory leadership nearly always result in improvement of the schools and a better school-community atmosphere.

PARENT-TEACHER WORKSHOPS

The workshop method of "growing while learning" gives parents and teachers an opportunity to really exchange ideas and work together. Like any organized effort, the purposes and procedures should be formulated in advance and then explained fully to chairmen, discussion leaders, and recorders. The presentation of this information and the general plan of the workshop should precede any division of the members into working groups. The groups should be small enough to permit full participation by all members, yet large enough to stimulate interest.

A group of eight to ten people is considered as a good working unit.

There does not appear to be any one pattern of organization or established time for holding workshops with parents. Some may be single evening meetings or a series of evening meetings. Others may be all-day affairs, including luncheon or a covered dish meal. Occasionally, panel discussions will be held with pupils taking part, or the workshop may be a closed meeting followed by a social hour. One mid-western city held a one day, joint-areas workshop for parents of a secondary school and of the elementary "feeder schools." Parents of children from kindergarten through the twelfth grade participated.

Some topics for workshop discussion are:

1. Guidance at home and school
2. Discipline at home and school
3. Home work and recreation
4. Mental health and emotional problems
5. Testing and reporting to parents.

Orientation programs for parents of high school students may include a series of lectures. Topics pertinent to the needs of the specific school precipitate discussion, and reports on professional reading stimulate thinking.

PARENTS' CLASSES

Supplementary to the regular, monthly, PTA meetings, mothers' clubs, and study groups, many schools hold classes for parents. Instructional classes for parents, such as upholstering, bring them into the school and provide a setting for developing friendship and understanding. Parents often discuss many mutual problems while working together.

Night school and the G. I. educational programs give older people a second chance to improve their education and give teachers an opportunity to interpret what the schools are doing for children. Adult education institutes and classes are organized in some communities to give those over sixteen years of age, of all walks of life, some of the opportunities that are available to students. In one mid-western city, duplicate programs for adults are offered in two schools in different areas of the city.

Adult education is assuming greater proportions as cultural classes are being added. Education never ceases. This philosophy is being incorporated into services for adults by the public schools.

MOTHERS' AND FATHERS' GROUPS

Much more is being done now than in the past with mothers' and fathers' groups. As adjuncts to the parent-teacher association, though they may be independent of it, they are formed in both elementary and secondary schools.

ROOM MOTHERS

Room mothers are parents of children attending a particular school. They are either elected to their posts by parents of children in a given grade or room or else they are appointed by officers of the parent-teacher association. Their function is to represent the parents of children in the grade or room, work with the teacher, and serve as a link between the home and the school. In setting up a room mothers' organization, it is necessary to have the place and responsibility of the parents clearly understood. Moreover, the period of service should always have a specific time limit.

The responsibilities of the room mother may be:

Helping to develop friendliness among parents of children in the room
Encouraging parents to attend PTA meetings
Helping to develop fathers' interest and attendance at school meetings
Assisting as hostess at open house and other school functions
Handling the room's money for Saving Stamps
Assisting in the cafeteria and on school grounds on special occasions
Providing transportation for special excursions, refreshments for parties, and procuring clothing for the needy
Helping new parents and their children to be accepted in the community.

The room mother is the special liaison between the room and community for that particular year. She can render valuable services to the schools and interpret the work of the teacher better than any other one person at that particular time. The terms *room mother* and *grade mother* are being replaced by *room chairman* in order to include more fathers. Sometimes *room parents* is used so that a couple serves as sponsors for a certain period of time.

MOTHERS' CLUBS

Mothers' clubs function on many levels and fathers' clubs are growing in popularity. The mothers of pre-school children are eager to learn child psychology which will help them to help their children adjust to school and to other children.

A club that meets regularly with a well-planned study program is ideal. Where it is not practical for an organization to function regularly, meetings may be held periodically for specific reasons.

Pre-school parents need early indoctrination as to school entrance health rules, medical and dental attention for school children, and facilities available locally for obtaining attention and help for under-privileged children. A knowledge of the kindergarten program will dispel the "baby sitting" evaluation and the mothers will become ambassadors for the program.

Techniques for preparing children for learning may be sent in bulletin form to prospective patrons, encouraging them to read to their children and to take them to places of interest in the city, such as zoos and art galleries.

In a few isolated communities, where English is not spoken, parents and children are taught school terminology in English so they may help their children follow the directions given by the teacher.

Mothers of special groups, such as "band parents" or "music club mothers," become valuable liaisons between the school and the home. If each child's activities influence an estimated five persons, these groups enlist many boosters for the school and

are well worth the time the school's staff devotes to these organizations.

FATHERS' CLUBS

Fathers' clubs are effective as a means of bringing the fathers
into the school. The schools should keep activities wholesome
and avoid exploitation of children to promote community
projects. In a southern city, the fathers' groups sponsored and
financed after-school activities and recreation—midget baseball,
Scout groups for both boys and girls, Camp Fire groups, and
track meets. Playground equipment, landscaping, redecorating,
stage craft, and building furnishings may be procured at a nominal price through joint efforts of interested fathers.

One city organized the "Big Brother" program for fatherless
boys, 8 to 15 years of age. This plan gave a boy an opportunity
to have a man as a friend, to visit in his home and to be associated
with a man.

Some schools now hold all their PTA meetings at night so
that fathers may attend and take their turn as officers and leaders
—and gain new insight into the problems of the schools.

Student hobby clubs may use parent sponsors, but the school
staff always works closely with the parents to see that the parents selected are informed about the objects that are collected
and the activities undertaken. Parents frequently need assistance
in maintaining discipline and stimulating interest in children.
Teachers also need to prevent a sponsor's personal interest from
superseding and replacing the students' interest to such a degree
that the hobby club program is endangered.

OTHER OPPORTUNITIES FOR PARTICIPATION

Besides the means that have been described thus far for keeping parents informed and for involving them in the life of the
school, there are other opportunities to strengthen the partnership that has been formed.

PARTICIPATION IN CLASS ACTIVITIES

Every community offers opportunities for using parents in the school. Usually members of the local newspaper staff are glad to help with school news coverage. Radio and TV personnel are happy to advise, assist, and serve as consultants. Parents who are professional writers often help with school papers and teach courses in creative writing. Other parents teach arts and crafts, music, literature, and aviation. Parents enjoy teaching dancing, posture and good grooming, and talking about hobbies, They give travelogues and discuss career opportunities. This sharing builds good will toward the school by helping the parents feel a part of the school. In one school, a parent with a Ph.D. in chemistry helped the students learn to make chemical analysis of their food. Parents connected with special occupations, such as electronics, are invaluable in communities where the teachers may have limited backgrounds. Parents frequently chaperon train and plane trips, furnish transportation for field trips, visits to industry, the zoo, and so on. They sponsor youth activities, loan properties for science classes and electronic equipment for shops and laboratories.

The legal aspects of gifts, grants, and parent participation should be understood before acceptance or commitments are made to donors, well-wishers, or "do-gooders." Parents should never be permitted to assume functions which are legally functions of the board of education.

Parent participation in school activities gives the child a greater feeling of security and the parent a better understanding of the true philosophy of American education.

TELEVISION

Both commercial and educational stations furnish opportunities for parents to see and hear about their schools. Sometimes parents study the television lessons with their children in order to help them with their studies. Creative art and craft programs have wide viewing interest. Actual instruction in languages, science, and math have been successful and are being expanded in many communities.

Instructional programs on television should be educationally sound. Good teaching should not be sacrificed for dramatic techniques. Educational television cannot compete with entertainment for the child's interest. Parents must work with teachers in helping the child develop a sense of values which will make learning, studying, and the acquiring of knowledge desirable. The potential of educational television is unknown but its value, both as a teaching aid and as a public relations medium, is indisputable.

SPECIAL AFFAIRS

Each school has its own social needs which should be met adequately by enlisting as much of the community's cooperation as desirable. Sometimes family night activities vary from banquets to picnics, plays, or night carnivals. Care should be taken to avoid exploiting the true purpose of the school by dissipating the learning time of the pupils and the energy of the teachers. However, some joint school activities often weld a group of parents into an harmonious group through a common interest and the schools' program of activities affords many opportunities to do this by enlisting parents as sponsors and chaperons: a springtime tea is an ideal time to show color slides of the work done during the year. Parent and teacher hobby shows at which types of hobbies are explained or demonstrated develop mutual admiration and provide an exchange of ideas (the students are impressed and proud of both parents and teachers). Invite half a dozen parents on a rotation basis to sit in on the monthly board of education meeting (they will appreciate the invitation and are effective in interpreting the work of the board of education). Tours of the school system's administrative office, with explanations of funds and other administrative facts, give parents information for wide dissemination; they also combat erroneous reports.

SPECIAL LUNCHEONS AND DINNERS

Special breakfasts, luncheons, and dinners help to bring the community into the schools. Some of the opportunities for special meals fall into the following categories:

1. Superintendent and board of education entertain the press and representatives from local television stations each year
2. Father and Son, Father and Daughter, and Mother and Daughter functions
3. Education-Business Day luncheons
4. Parent entertainment of school staffs
5. School staffs honoring PTA members
6. Simple farewell refreshments for the leaving class
7. Family night dinners for all patrons
8. Staff-family night dinners
9. Youth club dinners as Scouts, Cubs, Camp Fire Girls
10. Community civic clubs and PTA groups
11. A culminating activity luncheon honoring the parents of a class which has completed a type of work justifying a meal such as a Forum Luncheon, French Breakfast, or Mexican Dinner. Children as young as the primary grades can be at least nominal hosts and hostesses.

STUDENTS TELL PARENTS

Students are the "Number One" public relations persons and the most potent medium of communication. When a generation of children from the kindergarten through the twelfth grade are taught to understand and appreciate the importance of the public schools, we will have a generation of parents who will finance all necessary educational services.

This is a long range but infallible program and it is receiving national endorsement. Children should be taught about the contributions of teachers to their lives just as they learn about the milkman, postman, and policeman. Children should know that schools are not free but are provided at everybody's expense. They should be eager to learn, proud of their school, and appreciate the opportunity that has been provided for them.

Teachers on all grade levels can help boys and girls crystallize in their minds what they have learned during the day. "What have you learned today and why" is a simple way to prepare each child for dinner table discussion, as desks are cleared in preparation for going home. One teacher arranged for the students to compile a *Friday Fan Fare* bulletin in which each child stated in three to four sentences the most interesting experience at school during the week. Each was signed by the child's name. The statements were mimeographed and every child took home a copy. A first grade teacher sent home a daily paper containing a three-sentence reading lesson, which the child could proudly read to his parents. Second grade teachers took apart old text books and made single story booklets to show parents how their children could read. One teacher aroused the children's interest on Friday by suggesting a special activity on Monday and had the parents sharing the pupils' anticipation. Each class can contribute to a building-wide plan for Parents' Visitation Day by preparing their classwork to reveal actual learning situations. School newspapers on all levels give parents a view of the general activities in the building and help to keep the parents interested in the school.

WORKING MOTHERS

The working mother, with her limited time and energy, places another responsibility upon the schools. The number of working mothers with small children has increased 66 per cent in the last eight years. Nearly 60 per cent of all women who work are married and about a third have children under eighteen years of age. Schools are adjusting their schedules so the working mothers can take part. During American Education Week, the Education Committee of the Chamber of Commerce recommended, in some communities, that employers permit working parents to visit their children's schools without loss of salary.

One school even furnished dry socks for children who came with wet feet on a rainy day. The only requirement was to launder the socks and return them. Parents of kindergarten pupils were asked to teach their children the size of their socks, along with their street address and phone number.

PTA meetings at night enable working parents to attend. Parents may wish to transport their child's teacher and use this occasion as an opportunity to visit with her enroute.

Newsletters and bulletins to parents are especially important to working mothers. Send them as often as needed and make them informative and explicit. "Know Your Schools" is the desire of all parents and many have to rely upon the written word. Cartoons and pictures may effectively interpret to parents, in an enjoyable manner, just what they need to know.

PARENTS' NIGHT PROGRAMS

Parents' night programs can pay big dividends if parents are shown actual classroom instructional results and not a padded program. Programs for parents' night vary, but should always build understanding between home and schools. Tell parents what the school is doing for their children and why. Sometimes only parents are invited and the evening is educational or explanatory. Parents may follow their children's schedules for a brief view of work in each classroom. A social period follows, and dates are set for additional interviews, if desired.

If children are accompanying their parents, teach them to make proper introductions in advance. Give every child a chance to show his parents what he had learned in many areas. The school is just as successful as the individual child's work.

Include everybody from grandparents to kindergarteners on "Family Night." Poll parents and grandparents well in advance and learn what type of social and recreational activities they want. They frequently like table games, shuffle board, square dancing, but also include some "mixers" for adults.

Junior and senior high school students, as well as PTA members, can take the lead in keeping both the older people and preschool children entertained, with special attention to "mixers" for adults. Both teachers and parents share in the limelight as hosts and hostesses. This enables parents to learn the teachers' names and gives teachers time to circulate and talk with many parents.

Every day is "Open House" in some schools and students serve as office helpers to conduct parents about the building. The students' pride in the building is reflected in the clean halls and litter-free rooms. The student escorts on the secondary level should learn a great deal of information about their schools—such as dates, costs, uses, over-all opportunities—and function as public relations people as they conduct the parents through the building.

GRANDPARENTS AS PARENTS

Grandparents frequently serve as parents today and have time to "beat the drums" for the schools. However, surveys show that older people are less informed and, therefore, less approving of our schools than parents.

One city held a special visitation day to which the boys and girls invited their grandparents to visit and observe regular class-work. The students welcomed them and escorted them to the classrooms. During coffee in the cafeteria, the grandparents visited with each other and later commented to all their friends upon the changes in education, and how easily and happily the children were learning today.

In one community, where moving from an old school to a new school aroused nostalgic emotions, the removal parade was led by city officials and old settlers who had graduated from the old building. The school band helped to establish the prestige of the new school and emphasized the happy memories which the new building had to offer incoming students.

TEACHER AIDS

Some schools use parents as teacher aids, depending upon the qualifications and availability of the parents. Qualified patrons and former teachers frequently substitute for teachers while they attend professional meetings and conferences. Some schools use parents as activity sponsors, both in and out of school, and also in planning and carrying out room and building social functions. Parents frequently assist in the lunch room at noon time and with playground activities, sponsor clubs, and substitute in case of sudden illness of a teacher.

Often parents with specific talents, experience, and skills are overlooked. In an elementary school a mother edited the newspaper, cut the stencils, and operated the mimeograph machine. Foreign service, travel, hobbies, collections, and unique skills or experiences may be capitalized upon for both instructional purposes and establishing parent-school relations. In a large city school, mothers operated the clinic on a five-day schedule each week, even mending torn skirts and replacing lost buttons. Another group kept the library and catalogued and mended the books. The pupils learned to use the library facilities and after that parents transported them to and from the main city library to obtain books for leisure reading at home.

CONTACTS IN THE COMMUNITY

Teachers, retired teachers, and parent alumni are powerful agents in keeping the community informed through the everyday contacts they have with people on the street, in the neighborhood, and through participation in the life of the community.

THE TEACHER IN THE COMMUNITY

Teachers should know a great deal about the systems in which they are employed. People ask them many questions that touch deeply on matters of educational policies and the programs, and they expect to receive satisfactory answers. This is important public relations. Teachers cannot do justice to themselves or to the school system when they plead ignorance or give incomplete replies. The school system should see that they have the information that is needed for this purpose. It can be furnished by means of a small manual, revised annually, that contains the more common questions people ask and the answers they should receive. Such a manual ought to be reviewed at the opening of school each year by the principal and all members of the building staff. They should be instructed to report questions asked of them that are not found in the manual and which they are unable to answer. If the name and address of the person seeking the information is known, then a polite letter from a school official containing the information wanted should be sent soon afterwards. This procedure does much to develop respect for the system and an appreciation of the public service that it renders.

When teachers become identified with the life of the community, they take on a new importance in the eyes of fellow citizens. No longer are they considered as individuals apart from the rank and file of people. Not only are they presented with numerous opportunities for leadership but their special talents soon win respect and open acknowledgement. Furthermore, they are in a position to talk informally about educational questions and to straighten out misconceptions they encounter. Frequently they are asked to talk before groups and to lead discussions on educational and social issues that are far reaching in their effects upon the men and women of the community.

RETIRED TEACHERS AS INTERPRETERS

Retired teachers continue to have many contributions to make to their community. They are accepted authorities on education by all who knew and admired them. Most schools have failed to utilize the interest and ability of these co-workers who are no longer on the staff. Seldom are they kept informed on changing methods. Why not invite retired teachers to hear visiting lecturers? Why not send them bulletins of information, copies of personnel directories, brochures and superintendent's bulletins? Why not invite them to social functions both city-wide and at neighboring schools?

Retired teachers can serve as substitute teachers, cafeteria assistants, club sponsors, and playground supervisors. The new teacher could use a retired teacher as an assistant in learning classroom routine and disciplinary techniques. Some teachers in this group are sensitive of the age stigma, but many are capable and would be eager to contribute to the well-being of boys and girls.

ALUMNI AS PARENTS

School alumni members who become patrons have a special bond of affection for a school; they can be instrumental in helping newcomers, or negative patrons, to understand methods and problems.

Many junior and senior high schools keep former students interested in their schools through alumni associations or alumni back-to-school functions. Programs are built around family groups, three or more generation groups, parent and child teams, farthest distance traveled to attend, largest family, children all one sex, musical families, and unusual experiences. As further attractions, former students participate in men and women competitive sports against students in attendance, in musical groups such as bands and choral clubs, and reunite for a special number on a program. Everyone shares in the fun and the students develop an increased pride as they see parents and grandparents interested in their school.

POINTS TO REMEMBER

1. Being "firstest with the mostest" helps to prevent erroneous rumors. Establishing good relations before negative situations can develop is certainly expedient but not always possible.

2. Give honest appraisals of situations, regardless of the schools' position; the true situation will be discovered anyway.

3. Explain money needs in understandable terms, e.g., cost per day or per pupil, not total of millions of dollars for a specific need, which is usually incomprehensible to the average parent.

4. When medical and dental appointments may not be obtainable during school hours, how do parents adjust to school rules and doctors' office hours?

5. Music lessons and special appearances should be clarified for parents at the opening of school.

6. Classification of students and rules for promotion from grade to grade are always important to parents.

7. Disciplinary methods help parents to exercise more control at home, while neighborly thinking and planning give parents and pupils a feeling of security.

8. Teachers and parents should at all times try to conceal from pupils any incompatible feeling toward each other. The insecurity which a child feels when parents and teachers have strained relations creates an atmosphere which greatly hinders the child's learning.

9. When parents complain about teachers, the principal has a difficult job trying to effect a reconciliatory attitude.

   a) After talking with the parent, invite the teacher to sit in on a 3-way conference.

   b) Let the parent tell the story through as she sees it, perhaps even take notes on the important facts.

   c) See the parent's side of the picture but skilfully build in the teacher's position as a constructive measure to meet the needs of the situation.

   d) Always maintain and build confidence in the teacher unless a serious infraction of ethics demands the removal of the teacher.

   e) Be appreciative that the parent came and be cordial upon her departure.

10. Parent participation in the schools should be preplanned, guided, and as much success as possible insured. No one can guarantee that all teachers, principals, and parents will profit from certain experiences, but care should be taken to prevent unfavorable situations from developing.

   a) Parent groups sometimes develop pressure groups.

   b) Parent groups sometimes defeat their purpose by absorbing too much of the staff's time away from the classroom and pupils.

   c) Impractical ideas may be promoted by some.

   d) A committee may try to perpetuate its position after its usefulness has expired.

11. In some instances, parents have legal rights to file complaints against teachers. Tenure laws protect teachers and the National Education Association Defense Commission has successfully defended, in a dignified manner, educators on all levels.

Although parents and teachers have worked together for many years, the changes that are taking place in education make it necessary that they be kept informed. They should know what is taking place and how new methods, materials, and content are affecting the nature and the quality of the learning process. As pointed out in the chapter, there are many ways that this can be done. Keeping them informed is the key to the effectiveness of any school program.

BIBLIOGRAPHY

Fitzwater, Gertrude H., "Parent Contributions Enrich Classroom Programs," *Citizen Cooperation for Better Public Schools,* Fifty-third Yearbook of the National Society for the Study of Education, Part I. Chicago: University of Chicago Press, 1954. Chapter 5 contains many examples of how parents are able to take part in the improvement of classroom activities.

Grimes, Leslie K., "A Fact a Day," *Nations' Schools,* 46:52 (December, 1955). Tells how one school system presents a fact a day to the public by means of a cartoon in the daily newspaper.

Hines, Vynce A. and Hulda Graham, "What Parents Think of Their Schools and 'What They Know About them,' " *Bulletin of the National Association of Secondary School Principals,* 41:15–25 (February, 1957). Reports findings on parental attitudes toward schools and how their attitudes are affected by the nature of the administrative leadership.

Langdon, Grace and Irving W. Stout, *Parent-Teacher Interviews.* Englewood Cliffs, N.J.: Prentice-Hall, Inc., 1954. A detailed treatment of techniques for conducting successful interviews with parents.

Laycock, S. R., "Partnership with Parents," *Education Digest,* 22: 24–26 (November, 1956). Points out that the quality of teaching is determined by the public.

Nixon, Richard M., "A Searching Look at Our Schools," *The Nation's Schools,* 60:47 (February, 1958). Maintains that American education will be no better or no worse than the individual American parents want it to be.

11

Pupils are among the best agents of the school in interpreting its work to the public. Through newspaper stories of their activities and accomplishments, through entertainments they present to parents and interested patrons, through demonstrations they take part in, and through their own behavior in school and community, they furnish striking evidence of what they have learned in regular class and extraclass programs and the methods by which the products of their learning have been acquired.

In many ways, pupils do more to keep the school in the public eye and win support for it than many of the other things that are done to bring about good public relations. For example, parents will go out of their way to attend a play, read a newspaper account, see an athletic contest, or listen to a concert in which their children have a part. Even people in the community without children in school attendance feel a certain sense of loyalty and pride when individual pupils win academic contests and scholarships or one of the athletic teams enjoys a successful season. Psychologically, some of these people identify themselves with the institution and, as a result, take more interest in the total instructional program.

Whenever parents and patrons witness a demonstration, read a student publication, or watch a skilled performance by pupils, they generally express surprise that youngsters can do so well. Their impressions are conveyed by word-of-mouth to friends and acquaintances in the community. The cumulative effect of favorable reactions in the course of a year may influence, more than is realized, the attitudes and opinions of citizens toward the school and how they vote on financial proposals.

The pupils themselves tend to judge the school in the light of their activities and to make these judgments known at home and in the community. They consider their activities the real basis for developing spirit in the school. According to a publication of the United States Office of Education:

When school spirit is high, pupils are more likely to consider the school a dynamic organization and are proud to be a member of it. Follow-up studies of high-school graduates and drop-outs have shown that boys and girls attach importance to the total extraclass activity program regardless of membership in an activity group. Adults, graduated from high school many years ago, in response to questioning . . . , declared that their most vivid recollection of high school was the extraclass activities in which they and their schoolmates participated.[1]

There is not much doubt about the value of pupil activities and accomplishments in cultivating and strengthening relations with the community. It happens, however, that some schools overlook the public relations opportunities connected with routine events, such as commencement, plays, musicals, and service projects, while others emphasize the publicity side of these events and lose sight of their educational worth to pupils.

PUPIL CONDUCT

Most adults are sensitive to the behavior of pupils both inside and outside of the school. They assume that principals and teachers are doing a good job of teaching common rules of courtesy

[1] Ellsworth Tompkins, *Extraclass Activities for All Pupils* (Washington, D.C.: United States Government Printing Office), pp. 4–5.

when pupils conduct themselves properly. They are inclined, however, to be critical of the school when the opposite is the case and to form low opinions of the instructional program. This is natural because they want and expect the school to develop responsible self-discipline in pupils and obedience to common standards of social behavior.

Situations are numerous in which adults observe the behavior of pupils and render judgments of the school. Seldom do they fail to note the attitudes and actions of youngsters who ride public transportation on their way to and from the school. Home owners are even more alert to the behavior of those who go by their property in the morning and afternoon. While they seldom praise pupils for good conduct, they are quick to offer criticism and file complaint against the few who engage in noisy conversation, cut across property, throw paper on the sidewalk, or crowd pedestrians into the street. This is equally true with pupils who drive automobiles to school and are forced to park them in the neighborhood. Any boisterousness, improper parking, blockage of driveways, or creation of traffic hazards inevitably results in a condemnation of the entire student body and loss of respect for the school.

The presence of safety-patrol members at street crossings represents another type of situation with possibilities for good or poor public relations. The same possibilities extend to the work of ushers at school-sponsored, public events, the service of guides who direct or escort visitors in the building, pupil participants in public meetings, and members of activity groups in their soliciting of advertising, ordering of supplies, and doing of business with merchants in the community.

Interscholastic athletic contests offer, perhaps, the most dramatic opportunities for bringing out the best and worst in pupils. No matter whether they are players or spectators, they earn the respect of the public through examples of good sportsmanship, fair play, courage, courtesy to visitors and opponents, and the graceful acceptance of losses. They lose this respect whenever they engage in sideline coaching, employ abusive language, persist in a win or else attitude, resort to the usual alibis, and refuse to abide by the rules of good sportsmanship. It only takes a short while for negative criticism to grow when pupils fail to conduct themselves properly.

Every school should develop a constructive program for shaping attitudes and conduct along socially acceptable lines of behavior. It should start with each new group and continue through to graduation. Moreover, each pupil should be taught to recognize and accept the fact that he represents the school and is expected to maintain its standards of conduct in the community.

ENTERTAINMENT

While public entertainment by pupils is hardly a function of the school, nevertheless there are sound educational reasons for having them present enjoyable and entertaining programs. The mere knowledge that they will appear before the public adds incentive and zest to the work they are doing in school.

At the same time, the institution has an excellent means at its disposal for acquainting adults with different phases of instruction and for demonstrating the nature and quality of the result.

MUSICAL PROGRAMS

Aside from athletics, no activity has caught the fancy of the public more than music. Taxpayers are perfectly willing in most communities to have their boards of education start music instruction in the elementary grades and to loan instruments to pupils during these early years. Parents likewise have expressed their approval by buying expensive instruments for children who show promise and by paying for supplemental instruction after school hours. As a result, school systems do a great deal to further musical understanding and appreciation through band, orchestra, glee club, and chorus. Although these activities are carried on usually before and after school or during a club period, the tendency is growing to include them in the regular program of studies on a credit basis.

Opportunities to present the musical accomplishments of pupils are numerous. Musical groups can be scheduled in connection with other events like assemblies, commencement exercises, and dramatic productions. The band can play at athletic contests and take part in civic celebrations. Invitations can be accepted by all musical organizations to appear before interested clubs and societies in the community and to put on radio and television programs when there is no conflict with regular studies.

It is difficult to estimate how many people will come into contact with school musical groups during the year, but the number is significant even in districts where not too much is done in this field of instruction.

DRAMATIC PRODUCTIONS

Dramatic productions in the form of plays, puppet shows, pageants, and operettas rank high on the list of entertainments that bring people into the school and which are sought by groups in the community. Here again spectators are usually amazed at the versatility and skill displayed by pupils. Not only do they derive satisfaction and pleasure from seeing young people perform, but they also recognize the fine direction by teacher-coaches and the work that is done in handling costuming, lights, scenery, and properties. It is customary to have a "sell out" for a dramatic production even in the elementary grades.

Dramatic productions make it possible to involve parents and interested citizens. They can help with the making of costumes, properties, and stage sets. In some instances, they can take part in programs. An example of such a joint undertaking is described by the assistant superintendent of the Wyandotte, Michigan, Public Schools:

Two years ago during Michigan Week, Washington Elementary School . . . produced a pageant entitled "I'm Goin' to Leave Ol' Texas." Children from 4th, 5th, and 6th grades and from one kindergarten class participated. During the pageant several representatives of

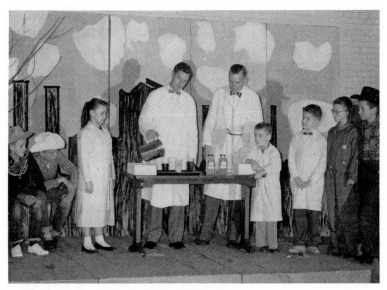

A "magic show" put on by adults and pupils always draws an audience.

the research staff of Wyandotte Chemicals, Inc., the largest industrial organization in our community, gave a chemical "magic show." During the production of this pageant many representatives of the above-mentioned research staff visited our school, observed classes and children in an effort to determine the type of chemical demonstration that would be most effective for an elementary school audience. During these visits and during the rehearsals, which the performing chemists faithfully attended, there was a fine interchange of ideas and a spirit of cooperation between research staff and teaching staff. Not only were parents interested in the final production, but a large number of Wyndotte Chemicals, Inc., employees attended the performance as well. A feeling of mutual benefit that has persisted grew out of this close contact.[2]

FORENSIC ACTIVITIES

Although forensic activities of pupils lack the appeal of dramatic productions, yet they do much to place the school in a

[2] Furnished by Fred P. Davenport, Assistant Superintendent, Public Schools, Wyandotte, Michigan.

favorable light before parents and citizens. Debates, declamations, dialogues, and addresses demonstrate the ability of pupils to think on their feet, organize material, and express their thoughts in a clear and convincing manner. More good is often done in "selling" the school through the forensic activities of pupils, and especially before civic groups, than any number of speeches by members of the professional staff.

OTHER TYPES OF PROGRAMS

Besides musical programs, dramatic productions, and forensic activities, other types of entertaining programs, rich in educational and public relations values, can be devised in most school systems. As examples, radio broadcasts are produced in the Wellesley, Massachusetts, Public Schools by pupils and teachers that cover a wide range of subjects. In York, Pennsylvania, pupils from the William Penn Senior High School take over complete control of a radio station one evening a week. They write all the scripts, commercials, and schedules and operate the equipment, tape machines, mikes, and master controls. A Safety Week is held annually in Cecil County, Maryland, that features special programs and parades, each dealing with different phases of safety in home, school, and community. A cooperative venture, this undertaking brings many leading citizens and representatives of civic groups and governmental agencies in contact with pupils and school officials. Spelling matches between children and business men never fail to attract sizeable audiences in districts where they are held.

ASSEMBLY PROGRAMS

Regular and special assembly programs are another avenue for presenting the pupils and educating the public to the affairs of the school. They may be built around everyday happenings in class and extraclass activities or around the observance of special days, weeks, and anniversaries. Significant dates in state and local history—Armistice Day, Flag Day, birthdays of national heroes, Fire Prevention Week, and Book Week—are observances calling for special assemblies. The programs for these assemblies may be developed by pupils or undertaken jointly with outside groups and organizations. There are always a number of groups and organizations in the community that welcome the chance to share in programs of this character.

Regular assembly programs have appeal for parents and invited guests, particularly when their own children are participants and programs deal with topics related to their interests. In one junior high school, an A9 Pin Day Ceremony is looked upon with much favor by parents. Homeroom teachers present pins to A9 pupils who have qualified for graduation.[3] In the Senior High School, New Britain, Connecticut, an Honors Day Program is held annually. Its purpose is:

the induction of newly elected members to the National Honor Society —along with the awarding of scholarships to prospective graduates. All civic organizations who are contributors of scholarships are present to make the awards. . . . This represents about 45 people on the stage and represents Rotary, Kiwanis, Quota, etc., clubs. The press is present and a tremendous amount of goodwill is engendered.[4]

Similar programs can be held for winners of athletic and activity awards and for pupils whose services to the school have been outstanding.

The opportunity should never be overlooked of asking prominent citizens to take part in programs. They might administer oaths to incoming officers of the student council, chair a discussion, or speak on a vital subject. Like parents, they hold the school in higher esteem after experiencing well organized and presented assembly programs.

CONTESTS

Presenting pupils through contests is a major source of publicity and a strong factor in the building of local pride in the

[3] Reported by Marcella E. Ashley, Girls' Vice Principal, Charles Evans Hughes Junior High School, Woodland Hills, California.
[4] Report prepared by Vincent Sala, Principal.

schools. As determined by the measurement of column inches of print, contests receive more space than all other school-news stories combined. The local pride factor is evident in the mass attendance at games and other types of contests, the organization of adult boosters clubs, and the praise heaped upon the members of winning teams.

A sizeable percentage of contests, and more especially those in academic fields, are sponsored by local, state, and national organizations. Held in essay writing, play writing, poetry writing, and practically every subject of study in the curriculum, they often carry valuable awards and prizes. Winners may receive outright sums of money, college scholarships, promises of employment following graduation, jewelry, trips, and clothing. Most of these contests are conducted on an individualized basis without the presence of an audience. They receive considerable attention, however, in the press. Winners are feted by parent-teacher associations, at school assemblies, and by interested community groups. This type of contest now commands more respect and has a larger following than it did in the past.

Contests that enjoy mass audience attention are mostly in athletic sports, though more and more people are turning to those in music, dramatics, and public speaking. Adults who view athletic contests, for example, often admire the fine precision with which a team makes a play and the resourcefulness shown by its members in the face of stiff competition. They observe the physical stamina of players and the products of character building experiences, such as cooperation, good sportsmanship, modesty, courage, strategic judgment, and fair play. They go away from these contests with many impressions that are passed on to others—and out of which opinions are formed of the school and the contributions it makes to pupils.

Unfortunately, attention is sometimes diverted away from the educational side of participation in contests by the premium attached to having winning teams. Adults seem more interested in enhancing the reputation of the school and community than in the welfare of pupils. Pressure is brought on boards of education and school officials to replace unsuccessful coaches and to over-look eligibility requirements. No expense is spared to support contestants at regional, state, and national championships. The winners are accorded community-wide recognition and treated like heroes returning from the wars. Under these circumstances, the public conception of the worth of the educational program is determined by the outcomes of contests.

PUBLICATIONS

Pupil publications are standard practice in many elementary and most secondary schools. They take the form of newssheets, newspapers, school news pages, magazines, handbooks, and annuals or yearbooks. Parents and taxpayers are able to learn from these publications a great deal about the instructional activities of pupils and the nature of the educational program.

NEWSSHEETS AND NEWSPAPERS

Thousands of elementary teachers and pupils prepare simple, one to three-page newssheets at intervals during the year that are sent home to parents. Usually dittoed or mimeographed, they contain samples of work done in class and describe and explain some of the learning activities carried on with a particular group of pupils.

Greatly underestimated for their value in communicating with parents, checks on readership show that they are read thoroughly and are genuinely interesting to most mothers and fathers. They find these papers to be clear and convincing evidence of pupil achievement. Quite often these newssheets are passed around to neighbors and friends when something related to their own children is reported.

Practically all junior and senior high schools publish a student newspaper either weekly, bi-monthly, or monthly. Most of them are printed rather than mimeographed. Aside from the educational experiences received by pupils on the newspaper staff, a well-organized and carefully prepared paper gives an accurate reflection of the daily life of the school. Its stories deal with courses of study, methods of teaching, extraclass programs, special services, special opportunities, accomplishments, and shortcomings of the institution.

An excellent statement of what a school newspaper should be like and what it should do is described by Koppenhoefer as follows:

1. It covers the school news adequately in acceptable news style, is properly headlined, and is printed on reasonably good stock, with carefully planned layout. News includes school programs, classroom and laboratory projects, scholastic honors, faculty achievements, student activities, sports, entertainment, school personalities from principal to custodian in action, and alumni enterprises. Stories also report a host of events outside the school which affect the school's life or prepare the students for citizenship. . . .

2. It pursues an editorial policy designed to give students a voice. Students are encouraged to express opinions on any topic which interests them even if their limited knowledge is unequal to the issue, on the theory that it is helpful to adults to know what young people are thinking. . . . These ideas may appear under editorials, student forum, student polls, letters to the editor, or signed columns.

3. It strives for an interpretation of the school to the community. Articles on procedure in curriculum and instruction will clarify objectives for students and remove parental doubts.

4. It breaks down the barriers between generations. Faculty interviews reveal the human side of teachers. Discussion of student problems in dating, boy-girl relations, use of family car, hours for parties, clothing styles, parent-child complications, occupational objectives, and current hobbies bring parent, teacher, and child to a level of understanding.

5. It supports causes: the building of a stadium; the painting of the school; revamping of school regulations outmoded in student minds; better interschool athletic relations; health examinations; civic campaigns; local, national, and international projects such as Community Chest, Red Cross, Anti-Tuberculosis League, Conference of Christians and Jews, . . .

6. It introduces students to opportunities: contests, scholarships, vocations, community service, good government, international good will, philanthropy, interracial and religious amity.

7. It substitutes good clean fun and wholesome humor based upon genuine incidents of school living for the innuendo of gossip and sug-

gestiveness of radio and screen comedy. It sets itself against vulgarity and chicanery.[5]

All members of the administrative and instructional staff should recognize the fact that parents, merchants, professional persons, and other classes of workers in the community read the school newspaper as well as students. Copies are taken home by pupils and mailed, in some school systems, to selected adults, including the editors of local, commercial newspapers. Surveys indicate that from 45 to 75 per cent of the parents read the school newspaper when it is brough home by their children and that it is reviewed with interest by others who receive it.

A successful student newspaper is always under the close supervision of a capable teacher, and it has the loyalty and endorsement of the principal and faculty.

SCHOOL NEWS PAGE

Schools sometimes publish their newspaper as a special page or section of a commercially operated journal in the community. The material is gathered and prepared by pupils under teacher guidance before being sent to the local editor. A wide variety of news items are included, with most emphasis on activities, social affairs, and athletics. While much can be said in favor of using the medium of a commercial paper for reaching parents and citizens who have no children in school, it is doubtful if this page or section enjoys as strong a readership following as a student newspaper. For one thing, it is not considered to be the same as a pupil publication, and for another the coverage of news is more limited. Commercially-operated papers cannot afford to release space for the types of features and editorials that appear in a school newspaper and which help to interpret the total educational program. However, in the absence of a school newspaper, this page or section should be utilized.

[5] Hazel L. Koppenhoefer, "The Junior Fourth Estate," *The Bulletin* of the National Association of Secondary School Principals, 32:130–31 (February, 1948).

MAGAZINES

Magazines are published by a number of the larger secondary schools of the country. They are designed to stimulate pupil interest in writing and to illustrate the literary work that is done in school. Although their circulation is generally limited, still there are instances where they reach a good many people. In Wellesley, Massachusetts, the school magazine, the *Phillipian*, for example, goes into over eight hundred homes four times a year.[6] The importance of this type of publication in telling the school story should be considered.

HANDBOOKS

Handbooks have been issued annually by junior and senior high schools for many years. They serve as a source of information for pupils and parents with regard to school organizations, traditions, objectives, curricular arrangements, courses of study, schedules, marking periods, graduation standards, special services, and rules and regulations. Generally small in size, they carry a cover embodying the school seal and colors, a title page, and a faculty directory. The format is good as a rule but the print is too small for ease of reading. Despite this limitation, they are perused with care by pupils and their parents.

The practice is growing of publishing handbooks in elementary schools. At the Ferguson School, York, Pennsylvania, student council members gather and edit information for *A Handbook for Parents* which is distributed shortly after the opening of school in the fall.[7] Where the principal purpose of handbooks at the secondary level is the orientation and educational guidance of pupils, the purpose at this level of the educational ladder is that of acquainting parents with the policies and practices of the individual school.

[6] Reported by Roger W. Woodbury, Assistant Superintendent, Wellesley, Massachusetts, Public Schools.

[7] Reported by Anna Mary Melhorn, Student Council Faculty Sponsor, Ferguson School, York, Pennsylvania.

ANNUALS AND YEARBOOKS

It has been a long-standing tradition in senior and some junior high schools for members of the graduating class to publish an annual or yearbook. A ready source of memories in the years that follow, the annual contains pictures of class members, teachers, administrators, activity groups, and events that took place during the period of attendance. A history of the class is usually included along with a statement of what the school has meant to the prospective graduates. It can well serve as a foundation of good will toward the school and a reason for continuing interest in the affairs of the institution. Most annuals would be worth more in school-community relations if they devoted space to a discussion of educational objectives and the academic accomplishments of past and present graduates.

DEMONSTRATIONS

Demonstrations make it possible to dramatize for parents and interested citizens the materials, methods, and outcomes of instruction. By observing pupils in action, they are able to see for themselves how the school operates from day to day in a variety of learning situations. Few activities are more informative and enlightening than actual events in the instructional program.

Demonstrations can take place in regular classrooms, on playfields, and in the auditorium and gymnasium of the school building. They can also be presented in store windows, over television, and before groups in the community.

While some instructional fields lend themselves better than others to demonstrations, all may use this medium of communication with good results. A few examples will illustrate the range of opportunities. Since 1949, the Somerville, New Jersey, Public Schools have carried on a program in French and Spanish beginning in the third grade. According to the elementary supervisor in Somerville:

Parents take much pride in the program and the distinction it has

COURTESY PUBLIC SCHOOLS, SOMERVILLE, NEW JERSEY.

Pupils enjoy showing parents how they learn to read.

brought to the school. At intervals, during the years, our teachers have given demonstrations before parent and citizen groups. One teacher took children to several service groups, others have worked on T.V. and Radio programs. The local demonstrations have drawn large and appreciative audiences.[8]

In Hingham, Massachusetts, the music department holds demonstrations for parents of elementary pupils who are studying instrumental music. "Each parent is sent a letter inviting [him] to the demonstration. This has resulted in a parent being able to see clearly just where his or her child stands in relation to others taking the same instrument."[9]

At the Charles Evans Hughes Junior High School, Wood-

[8] Report prepared by Margaret C. McCormack, Elementary Supervisor.
[9] Report prepared by Daniel W. Gibbs, Jr., Principal, William L. Foster School.

COURTESY PUBLIC SCHOOLS, INDIANAPOLIS, INDIANA. PHOTO BY GEORGE TILFORD.

Store window demonstrations dramatize modern education.

lands, California, a Spring Cotton Festival is put on by the Physical Education Department. Every girl takes part in a dance activity that is covered in the regular curriculum. About four hundred parents attend this festival.[10] A somewhat similar but more extensive demonstration is given annually at the Conestoga High School, Berwyn, Pennsylvania. A student narrator explains the work done in health and physical education while students are demonstrating different physical activities, including gymnastics, modern dance, sports fundamentals, and so on.[11]

In Peoria, Illinois, "one type of demonstration used before school communities has been clinical-type classrooms. Another type . . . has been through television. These programs range from minor demonstrations of art, science, and music up to total

[10] Reported by Marcella E. Ashley, Girls' Vice Principal.
[11] Reported by B. Anton Hess, Coordinator of Secondary Education, Paoli Area Joint School Systems, Berwyn, Pennsylvania.

classroom programs taught on half-hour television presentations."[12] During American Education Week, the Indianapolis Public Schools conducted a demonstration classroom in the display windows of a downtown department store. It was estimated that at least 20,000 persons saw the classes in action over a four-day period. They were classes ranging from the third to the sixth grade from eight schools in different parts of the city. Regular work was followed so that spectators could get a clear picture of what they would see in visiting an actual classroom.[13] In New Britain, Connecticut, demonstrations of classwork in biology and chemistry have been held at the request of the parent-teacher association. The attendance has been well over a thousand parents and interested visitors.[14] Many more illustrations could be cited concerning the nature and value of demonstrations, but these are sufficient to indicate what may be done to reach the public through this avenue.

COMMUNITY PROJECTS

When the classroom is extended beyond the walls of the building, the community becomes a laboratory for learning. Pupils now have opportunities to brush against reality, develop sensitivities to social needs and problems, and to acquire a deeper sense of civic responsibility. The by-products of their study and involvement in the community are increased public confidence in the abilities of young people, better understanding of the educational program, and a willingness to support the school system more adequately.

SOCIAL SERVICE PROJECTS

There are any number of projects which pupils can undertake to assist with the work of social agencies and philanthropic or-

[12] Report prepared by Robert O. Burt, Director of Pupil Services.

[13] Jack T. Parker, *Progress Through Public Relations* (Indianapolis, Indiana: The Board of Education, 1958), p. 22. A mimeographed annual report by the director of school-community relations.

[14] Reported by Vincent Sala, Principal, Senior High School.

ganizations, such as the Red Cross, Community Chest, March of Dimes, Goodwill Industries, and Workshop for the Blind. They may take part in fund drives, make articles, prepare food baskets, sort clothing, and do clerical work. As examples, pupils in the Brighton Avenue School, Atlantic City, New Jersey, "have filled Junior Red Cross boxes to be shipped to children overseas, have stuffed envelopes for use of workers in the Cancer Drive, folded letters for Christmas Seal Sale Drive, etc."[15] Members of the Oxon Hill Senior High School Student Council, Upper Marlboro, Maryland, raised a considerable sum of money which they donated to the Southeast Hospital Fund. The money was raised by washing automobiles.[16] It might be well to have students observe the programs of different agencies and organizations and then work with a half-dozen or more on some sort of a rotating plan. In this way they would come into a broad pattern of experiences and promote a wider range of interest in themselves and the school.

COMMUNITY IMPROVEMENT PROJECTS

Generally speaking, pupils develop a real sense of membership in the community when they take part in projects related to its improvement. Examples are legion of how they have made surveys of social conditions and have stirred communities to action. In some instances their findings have caused them to perform services that have led to the establishment of local advisory councils containing both student and adult members or to the absorption and continuation of their work by qualified individuals and agencies. For example, they have organized and supervised playground activities for young children which the city eventually took over; have started a series of recreation programs for youths and adults which became a joint undertaking; and have begun a community band and chorus for all who cared to take part in these activities.

Not infrequently their services are performed in connection

---

[15] Report prepared by Emily H. Surtees, Principal.
[16] Reported by Eugenia Balsley.

with projects sponsored by community agencies and groups of citizens. The projects may pertain to tree planting, clean streets, safety, traffic control, beautification of homes and unsightly lots, eradication of ragweed, and the development of recreational facilities. A good illustration of their part in a community-wide improvement project is the annual clean-up, fix-up, and paint-up campaign in Dearborn, Michigan.

Working cooperatively with the City Beautiful Commission, parents, and teachers, the students have charted a plan aimed at helping maintain the "A grades" Dearborn has earned in the past for cleanliness, health, and safety.

Student activities are being directed by the 88-member Junior City Beautiful Commission composed of representatives from each school. Through this Commission clean-up activities have been a year-round project in the schools with special emphasis in the Spring.

A tally of last year's Clean-Up Report Sheets showed that 23,015 were completed by residents and returned to the schools via the students. Individual clean-up tasks reported totaled 789,352 or a 108 per cent improvement over the previous year.[17]

By cooperating in a campaign like this one, schools take their services right into the homes of pupils besides winning the good will of sponsoring groups and agencies.

CITIZENSHIP PROJECTS

Citizenship projects may be described as those related to the political life of the community. They furnish another base on which adults are likely to judge the school by its pupils. A few of the more common citizenship projects engaged in by pupils are occupancy of civic offices for a day, campaigns to have parents and neighbors go to the polls to vote, interviews with government officials for the purpose of learning about their work and applying the information received to problems under study; preparing a community history necessitating the use of public records, citizenship forums and panel discussion with adult par-

[17] *Dearborn Schools Report Card to the Community*, March, 1959.

COURTESY PUBLIC SCHOOLS, OKLAHOMA CITY, OKLAHOMA.

The school is judged favorably when capable students take over government offices for a day.

ticipants, and projects to reduce and eliminate, if possible, vandalism on Hallowe'en.

BEHAVIOR CODES

Behavior codes for parents and teenagers have grown in popularity throughout the country. Their purpose is that of trying to establish some sense of uniformity in the pattern of conduct enforced by parents and accepted by their children. One code entitled *Socially Speaking* was prepared by students and parents of the Alexis I du Pont Special School District, Wilmington, Delaware. The topics dealt with in this guide were social activities, hours for parties, appropriate dress, rules of etiquette, smoking, driving, responsibilities of parents, and responsibility to the community. In Springfield, Missouri, a more extensive booklet entitled *Living Around the Clock* was produced by a city-wide committee made up of students, teachers, parents, and leaders of youth organizations. Published by the Springfield Public Schools, it treats of personal interests and problems, personal appearance, health and physical fitness, homework, reading, television and radio, telephone, dating, parties and other social events, allowances, movies, athletic events, and travel in cars, by bicycle and motorcycle, on busses, and as a pedestrian— an exhaustive list!

In every known instance where behavior codes have been written cooperatively, parents and other adult members of the community taking part in the project develop respect for the thinking and judgment of students and loyalty to the system responsible for their education.

FIELD TRIPS

Field trips to places of interest in the community are an excellent device for bringing notice to the school and for explaining some aspects of the educational program. A merchant, for example, who takes pupils on a guided tour of his store shares an important learning experience with teachers and pupils. When boys and girls ask questions which indicate their grasp of a subject, their hosts recognize the fine work the school is doing.

In planning field trips with pupils, the convenience of the agency, institution, industry, or business must be taken into account. The trip must be conducted so that pupils will not disturb the operation of the business or interfere with its scheduled program. Too many visits to one place should be avoided. Follow-up letters expressing gratitude and appreciation are likewise necessary to leave a good feeling toward pupils and the school.

At the same time the full cooperation of parents should be secured. They like to know when a trip will take place, how pupils will be transported, and the measures adopted for supervising conduct and protecting the safety of pupils. In Wellesley, Massachusetts, parents are often invited to go along on trips with the children and to share in their learning experiences. The reactions are always favorable.[18]

Field trips may be taken from the kindergarten through the senior high school. There is a wealth of resources in the community and surrounding areas that fits into the curriculum. Among the places visited by pupils of the Edgar Fahs Junior High School, York, Pennsylvania, are the city council, county commissioners, United States Congress, United States Supreme Court, Pennsylvania General Assembly, and the local county court.[19] In Somerville, New Jersey, elementary pupils go on trips to art museums, historical sites, science exhibits, fire stations, public libraries, and other nearby places of interest.[20]

Some public relations outcomes of field trips are pointed out by the principal of a junior high school who says:

Our 8th grade mathematics class, while studying "Banks and Banking" sent a committee of six (2 from each of 3 sections) to the bank for visitation. This committee had met and was prepared to take notes and ask questions regarding the operation of the bank. Upon their return they reported to each section as a group after which a period was allowed for questions. The project was so successful that we asked them to make the same report to the PTA. This proved to be most valuable, in that the bank was pleased and parents became aware of what was being done at school.[21]

EDUCATIONAL PLANNING

Experience has proven that cooperative educational planning by pupils, parents, teachers, and resource persons drawn from the community promotes better public relations. Besides acquiring a more detailed understanding of the instructional program, adult laymen come to recognize and admire the accuracy and value of judgments made by pupils in appraising current needs and practices and in suggesting desirable changes for the future.

[18] Reported by Roger M. Woodbury, Assistant Superintendent.
[19] Reported by J. A. Hertzog, Principal.
[20] Reported by Ruth B. Mayers, Principal, Van Derveer School.
[21] Report prepared by Lyle B. Hunkins, Principal, Columbus Junior High School, Columbus, Nebraska.

Pupils have a contribution to make in several different aspects of educational planning. A rather simple but effective one is that of orientating entering pupils and their parents in junior and senior high schools. As upper classmen, they can explain the curriculum and the general organization and operation of the school as well as answer questions. Often they perform this service with excellent results and they are usually requested to repeat it with the next incoming group of youngsters.

Pupil opinion may be obtained at any time regarding the strengths and weaknesses of the school program. They see the institution from an entirely different point of view than the principal and the teachers. Generally they can put their fingers on important problems and bring up matters that escape the notice of the faculty.

Some school systems have made them members of adult survey teams for the study of instructional needs and conditions. In keeping with their maturity, they are asked to help with the construction of inventories, fill out questionnaires, gather information, and take part in the discussion of findings.

They are also asked to meet with adult groups and to contribute their ideas and suggestions for dealing with particular problems. The problems may concern facilities for a new building, the design of the curriculum, policy on social events, improvement of citizenship practices, report card revisions, and control of interscholastic athletic contests. Some surprisingly good ideas frequently turn up.

The practice is growing of inviting pupils to be represented on curriculum committees along with parents and other members of the community. In this capacity they work on the revision of old courses of study and the construction of new ones. Here their contributions are esteemed because they are fully acquainted with the units of study and are able to point out needed improvements. They may even take part in the selection of instructional materials. It is a reasonable assumption that the curriculum is better because of their participation in its study and revision.

ACCOMPLISHMENTS

The reported achievements and successes of pupils and alumni have a receptive audience in any community. People are interested and naturally curious to learn what pupils are accomplishing and how well their preparation fits them for life. If the school wants citizens to value its program and acknowledge the competencies of staff, it must show them continuously what pupils are achieving and acquaint them with the recognition, awards, and honors that have come to its graduates.

Services performed by members of the student council are a form of achievement in citizenship training that deserves public recognition. Citizens should know, for example, that these youngsters publish a handbook, arrange and conduct commencement programs, act in an advisory capacity to the principal, operate an after-school employment bureau, and do many worthwhile things for the benefit of all pupils in the school. While these activities in themselves may seem to lack news appeal, actually they make excellent stories when treated properly.

When athletic banquets are held to honor members of teams, the true purposes and outcomes of the health and physical education program may be emphasized and its contribution to attendance, scholarship, and character delineated sharply.

Ratings received on school publications from journalistic associations, like the Columbia Scholastic Press Association and the National Scholastic Press Association, open the door to public honors for individual student writers, editors, and helpers. Attention may well be directed at this time to the educational purposes of student publications and the extent of their realization.

Whenever standardized achievement tests are administered in basic subjects, the results should be published and interpreted against the background of the pupil population. Significant comparisons can be made with the norms of previous groups in the system and with state and national averages. Sometimes it is advisable to treat the data by individual schools, grades, and curricular divisions.

Pupils can be featured who receive college scholarships and win awards for outstanding accomplishments. People are more interested than ever before in high-level attainment and the recognition it brings to school and community. Newspaper editors are aware of this interest and assign a prominent place to stories of outstanding pupil achievement. This publicity can be supplemented by honoring winners at special assemblies, presenting them over radio and television, introducing them at service club and civic organization meetings, and by issuing citations to parents for their contributions to the success of these children.

In addition to scholarship and award winners, there are always a number of pupils in every school who have unusual talent and ability. They may be skilled photographers, collectors of rare coins, talented vocalists, fancy figure skaters, dramatic artists, wood carvers, fine pastry cooks, fashion designers, or very rapid typists. The school should make sure that the unusual talents and abilities of such pupils are made known to the public.

Nor should it overlook the accomplishments and honors bestowed upon former students. When an alumnus receives a scholarship, wins election to public office, heads an organization, establishes his own business, receives a merit award for distinguished service, or attains recognition in some other way, the fact should be told to the public and a relationship shown, whenever possible, between his success and his school experience.

COMMENCEMENT

Activities that mark the close of a school year and the educational achievements of a particular class of pupils are known as commencement, graduation, or promotion exercises. As one of the oldest activities of the school, they make it possible for pupils to highlight for themselves and their parents the meaning and value of public education.

Traditionally, commencement programs follow a rather simple pattern of organization. A few remarks are made by class officers and the principal of the school on some suitable theme or subject adopted for the occasion. The main feature is an address by an outside person chosen because of his prestige and oratorical ability. The solidity of this arrangement may be broken with musical presentations by the school orchestra and chorus.

In the newer types of graduation exercises, members of the class being honored take over responsibility for most of the program. They may give short talks explaining what they have studied and accomplished in school, introduce honor students, present awards to outstanding classmates, or dramatize in play and pageant form some of their school experiences. During the week of commencement, demonstrations and exhibits of classwork may be arranged for public inspection and open house held for tours of the building. The newer types of exercises are not only more interesting to parents and visitors but they also enable them to get a better insight into the school and its products.

Commencement is an appropriate time to invite leading citizens and distinguished alumni to the school. Their names can be printed in the program and they can be honored from the stage.

EMPLOYMENT

Too many employers are inclined to judge the school and the quality of its instruction by the work performance of early school leavers and recent graduates who enter their employment. They do this without any real knowledge of their intellectual capacities, academic records, and personality characteristics. The fact that a recent graduate, for example, takes a secretarial position without an adequate background of preparation and a fairly high level of native ability is scarcely a justifiable reason for indicting the institution when she fails to transcribe, type, and spell correctly or follow directions in filing correspondence and handling purchase orders. Actually the fault lies with the employer in hiring a young person for such a position without first calling the school and finding out what she is like and capable of doing.

Greater service would be rendered to former students and employers if a more cooperative approach was taken to the whole problem of employment. There is no reason why employers could not be circularized periodically with the request that they check with the school on the preparation and achievement of young people before they are hired. This relationship could be strengthened by holding periodic conferences for the discussion of job standards and methods of using pupil personnel information. It might be advisable as well to establish a placement service in the school where employers could list available positions and receive the names of qualified pupils.

SOME PRECAUTIONS

Activities through which pupils are presented to the public should be a logical part of the instructional program and should fit in with its educational objectives. Unless this principle is respected, there is always a danger of exploiting pupils for publicity purposes.

This is especially true in districts where an exaggerated sense of importance is attached to the winning of athletic, forensic, dramatic, music, and journalistic contests. Backed by sentiment in the community, coaches and sponsors adjust their aims to the training of those pupils who can bring recognition to themselves and the institution.

Too often the routines of the school are disrupted when an activity is being prepared for public presentation. Pupils are taken out of regular classes for rehearsals, or practice is held nights so that participants are unable to do their homework assignments. The prospect of a forthcoming event may likewise create enough excitement and tension in the school to distract attention from studies, making it difficult for teachers to accomplish much until the event is over.

The normal running of the school can also be disrupted by the acceptance of too many invitations from community groups and organizations wanting entertainment by pupils. This may mean releasing them from classes and other responsibilities in the school several times during the year, or it may mean a series of evening engagements that take them away from home and prevent them from doing much preparation on outside assignments. While it must be acknowledged that pupils derive educational benefits from taking part in public performances and that the school receives favorable publicity, still the welfare of pupils must take precedence over all other considerations. The school can meet this problem by limiting the number of engagements and selecting only those that seem most appropriate. Relations with community groups will not suffer if the reasons are understood and a policy is formulated.

A somewhat similar issue is raised by the large number of essay and individual prize-winning contests that are sponsored by industries, business firms, and civic organizations. In the interest of furthering their own special purposes, they would like the school to make their contests a part of the classwork done by pupils. This is an impossibility in view of their numbers, let alone the time they would take away from other instructional matters. Perhaps the best way of dealing with this issue is to post all legitimate contests for the notice of pupils. If they cared to enter them, it would be with the understanding that preparation must be done after school hours—and that *class* preparation will still take precedence.

Finally, the school has a moral obligation to see that pupils maintain a desirable balance between participation in public activities and preparation for scheduled studies. Instances are common of how talented pupils have been encouraged to undertake a variety of activities at the expense of their own health and educational progress. This is a form of exploitation when the school is anxious to put the best foot forward and to paint a bright picture of itself in the eyes of the community.

BIBLIOGRAPHY

Blanding, D. C., "Public Relations Via Speech Contest," *School Activities,* 28:147–50 (January, 1957). The author shows how speech contests help to interpret the work of the school.

Brier, H. M., "School Paper is a Public Relations Medium," *School Executive,* 73:84–85 (March, 1954). A useful article for sponsors of school newspapers.

Fitzwater, Gertrude H., "Cooperation Helps Individual Class-rooms," *Citizen Cooperation for Better Public Schools,* Fifty-third Yearbook, National Society for the Study of Education, Part I, Chicago: University of Chicago Press, 1954, Chap. V. Many excellent examples are presented here of how pupils can work with adults and help to interpret the school.

Frost, N. F., *Pupil Participation in Community Affairs.* Washington, D.C.: American Institute of Cooperation, 1954. Both a theoretical and practical discussion of the role students can play in the life of the community.

Hart, L. J., "School's Responsibility for its Students in Public Places," *The Bulletin* of the National Association of Secondary School Principals, 42:101–03 (September, 1958). Emphasizes the need for good conduct on the part of pupils who represent the school.

Kindred, Leslie W. and W. Paul Allen, "Cooperation Improves Individual Schools," *Citizen Cooperation for Better Public Schools,* Fifty-third Yearbook, National Society for the Study of Education, Part I, Chicago: University of Chicago Press, 1954, Chap. VI. The illustrations here reinforce the concept of pupil activities as an interpretative medium of the school.

Merrifield, N., "Our Music Department Promotes School-Community Relations," *School Musician,* 24:8–9 (April, 1953). The values that come from music programs in school public relations are emphasized in this article.

Moehlman, Arthur B. and James A. van Zwoll, *School Public Relations.* New York: Appleton-Century-Crofts, Inc., 1957, Chap. 17. This deals with the place and importance of student activities in the interpretative program.

Public Relations for America's Schools. Twenty-eighth Yearbook, American Association of School Administrators. Washington, D.C.: The Association, 1950, Chap. III. Much of this chapter is given over to a consideration of the roles pupils play in building good will and understanding of the school.

12

CONDUCTING CAMPAIGNS

The nation's public schools have experienced an unprecedented growth during the past several years. Enrolments in hundreds of school districts throughout the country have more than doubled since the end of World War II. Such districts, therefore, have been faced with the problem of providing more and more classrooms to house new pupils. Few such districts can provide sufficient funds in their annual budgets to finance the building of additional classrooms. Consequently, most districts must present school bond proposals periodically to their voters.

Current operating expenses also have been increasing, in many cases more rapidly than the assessed valuations of communities. Many school districts, then, must win voter approval to increase the amount of millage levied against taxable property if they are to maintain the quality of their educational programs. The discussion in this chapter will be limited to the planning and conducting of school bond elections. However, the principles of good campaigning are the same whether applied to bond campaigns for new buildings or campaigns to increase tax levies for current operating expenses.

No two communities are exactly alike. Their populations will differ when such factors as occupations, educational backgrounds, ages, and economic status are considered. Many communities have long histories of voting favorably for school bonds and other proposals for civic improvement. In other communities it is extremely difficult to win elections for such purposes. The kind of community served by the school district, therefore, will determine in some measure the type of campaign planned. However, "a school system which is about to undertake a bond election cannot be content with just informing the voters of the need for the bonds. It must present its case so vividly and energetically that the public will agree that the situation is serious enough to warrant favorable action."[1]

NEED FOR EARLY PLANNING

In a rapidly growing school district the administration has the responsibility for continuously assessing school housing conditions and anticipating future needs. Only in this way can steps be taken in time to provide enough classrooms for all the children. The administration must keep informed of developments which may affect school enrolment. By working closely with the other governmental agencies in the area, with the local chamber of commerce, and with public utilities companies, school administrators will be in a position to learn of any plans for locating new industries in the district which will bring more people into the community. This knowledge will make it possible to purchase school sites at reasonable cost and to provide new schools when and where they are needed.

Long before all funds for school construction have been expended, school administrators should begin making plans to secure additional finances for this purpose. Many months pass from the time a new school or addition to an existing school is authorized until the facilities are completed and ready for use. Much time is also required to plan and conduct a campaign

[1] John A. Smith, *An Appraisal of School Bond Campaign Techniques* (Los Angeles: University of Southern California Press, 1953), p. 3.

leading to an election which will determine whether or not the voters of the district approve the plans for financing new school construction.

PRELIMINARY STEPS

From several months to more than a year may be required to survey the building needs of a school district and to make preparations for a campaign. Although such surveys are usually made by school administrators, some districts employ the services of college or university consultants or local architects for this purpose. Citizens, too, are often invited to examine the housing conditions existing in school districts and to make recommendations for additions or improvements.

Besides surveying building needs, the administration will want to begin assembling all data pertinent to the problem. These preliminary steps should be taken before any public announcement of an election is made. Included among such useful data will be the following:

1. A complete report on how funds from the most recent bond issue have been or are being spent, including lists of completed projects, current projects, and proposed projects. The report also should include such facts as square foot costs of buildings and the number of children for whom the projects have provided housing.

2. An analysis of enrolment trends over the past several years.

3. An analysis of current enrolments by grades to determine future classroom requirements in the upper grades.

4. A census of preschool-age children by attendance areas. Members of parent-teacher associations are usually willing to conduct the surveys needed to supply this information.

5. An enrolment projection for approximately five years, basing the projection upon steps 2, 3, and 4 above and upon other known factors which may tend to increase or decrease enrolment.

Most of these facts are newsworthy, and the superintendent will want to take advantage of every opportunity to inform parents and the general public. Newspapers and radio stations are usually happy to use stories about enrolment, school building programs, and community surveys. Many administrators publish regular reports on the schools and mail these to parents and other citizens in the district. A continuous public information program will inevitably result in a greater understanding of the school district's problems and a more ready acceptance of the need for a bond issue when the proposal is finally announced.

DETERMINING THE PROPOSAL

As soon as these preliminary steps have been taken, the superintendent and his staff may begin developing the specific proposal for meeting the future building needs of the district. The board of education should be kept informed at all times. In fact, members of the board should be encouraged to assist in formulating the plans. Local architects and contractors may be invited to furnish assistance in estimating costs of the various building projects. The proposal should be acceptable to the administration and to the individual members of the board of education. Every aspect of it should be defensible.

TIMING OF CAMPAIGN

Timing is an important ingredient of successful school bond campaigns. Well-planned campaigns will have three distinct phases. The first, beginning several months to more than a year before election, will include a careful survey of building needs and detailed planning of the campaign proper.

The second phase will be a period of community education concerning the needs of the school district. Activities during this period will include newspaper stories, talks to community organizations, public meetings, and the distribution of informational materials to parents and other citizens. Most experienced campaigners agree that this informational program must be started far enough in advance of an election in order to clear up questions, distribute informational materials, and furnish opportunity for personal contact with as many people in the community as possible.

Phase number three of every school bond campaign is usually from two weeks to one month in length. It is during these last few days before election that posters are displayed, bumper strips distributed, house-to-house canvasses conducted, brochures mailed, and advertisements placed in newspapers and on radio and television. Campaign efforts should reach a climax just before the vote.

A good summary statement on the importance of timing in campaigns is to be found in *Campaigns Triumphant:*

> Of utmost importance is the timing of the campaign. Of course, preparation will date back as much as a year, but actual group partici-pation in the campaign proper will be confined to from two to three weeks. Many elections have been lost through a long, drawn-out cam-paign in which the public and the workers lost interest before election day.[2]

REGISTRATION OF VOTERS

One technique often overlooked by school districts in their efforts to secure "yes" votes for school bond or tax measures is the registration campaign. It is especially important to make certain that parents of school-age and preschool-age children are registered, for these young parents are most likely to support school bond issues. An appraisal of election results in a large California district revealed that the greater the ratio of school-age and preschool-age children to adults in a census tract, the greater were the chances that the percentage of favorable vote in that tract would be relatively high.[3]

Schools are used not only for polling places in many elections; they are sometimes used for the registration of voters. The school clerk or secretary may be deputized to perform this function. When she enrolls new children in school, she may register the parents at the same time. She may attend parent-teacher asso-

---

[2] *Campaigns Triumphant* (Chicago: The National School Service Institute, 1951), p. 13.
[3] John A. Smith, *op. cit.*, p. 45.

ciation meetings and meetings of other community groups at the school for the purpose of registering voters.

School administrators may obtain up-to-date registration lists which may then be checked against school rolls to determine which parents are registered. Every effort should be made to encourage them to register. A letter from the chairman of the parent-teacher association's citizenship committee might be the first step taken. If necessary, this could be followed by a telephone call or a home visit by a member of the committee. Parent-teacher association members may also be asked to conduct a survey of the district to discover parents of preschool-age children. These parents, too, should be contacted and urged to register. By following this procedure, the administration will have a list of potential "yes" voters to be used during the actual bond election campaign.

FINANCING THE CAMPAIGN

School bond campaigns cost money. Funds must be provided to pay for newspaper advertising, posters, billboards, radio and television time, brochures, and the many other things used in a campaign. The amount required will vary according to the size or type of the school district. Voters in some districts consistently support their schools at the polls; in other districts of the same type and size, long and arduous campaigns must be waged to win even grudging support. School administrators and members of the citizens' committee, therefore, must decide on how much money will be needed to conduct a successful campaign in their district.

A study made in 1957 of 156 school bond campaigns in California disclosed that the amounts of money spent on these campaigns ranged from nothing to $20,000, the median amount in all types of districts being $300. However, the amount expended varied according to the type of the district. For example, the median cost of campaigns in elementary school districts was only $100, while high school districts spent an average of $200, unified districts spent $500, and city school districts as much as $800.[4]

In most states school districts are prohibited by law from spending public funds on campaigns. It is necessary, therefore, to solicit money from individuals, organizations, and businessmen who will be most likely to support such an activity. The California study revealed that school districts solicited campaign funds from businessmen, architects, parent-teacher associations, contractors, teacher organizations, bankers, chambers of commerce, unions, and subdividers. Solicitation of funds is usually made by Citizens' committees, although in many districts requests for campaign funds were made by boards of education or the superintendents.

CITIZENS' ADVISORY COMMITTEE

Generally speaking, the more people involved in a school bond campaign the greater the chances for success at the polls. It is extremely important, therefore, to make certain that any citizens' advisory committee invited to participate in a campaign is more than a "front"; it should be a working committee. Some task, great or small, should be found for every volunteer. This involvement technique was used successfully in a campaign in Long Beach, California, where approximately 10,000 persons formed a Good Schools Committee and actively worked for the passage of school bonds.[5]

Most citizens' advisory committees, of course, are not as large as the one in Long Beach. The number of active members will usually range from 25 to 100. An effort should be made to include representatives from as many "interest groups" in the district as possible. Parent-teacher associations, labor unions, the American Association of University Women, the League of

---

[4] John W. Adamson, *A Survey of Bond Campaign Procedures Followed by a Selected Number of California Districts*, an unpublished master's thesis (Stockton, Calif.: College of the Pacific, 1957), p. 50.

[5] Harry Karns, "Long Beach Defeats the School Shortage," *American School Board Journal*, 134:45-6 (February, 1957).

Women Voters, veterans' organizations, service clubs, junior and senior chambers of commerce, religious leaders, taxpayers' associations, bankers, realtors, leaders in agriculture, newspaper, radio, and television people, fraternal orders, medical associations, and racial groups probably should be represented on the committee.

The school superintendent or the board of education, independently or together, usually invite citizens to serve on the advisory committee. The group should be organized before final decisions are made concerning the amount of the bond issue and the date of the election. The organization should take place from three to six months before the election. Any proposal submitted to the citizens' committee should be tentative, subject to change upon the recommendation of its members.

Presented below are suggested steps on organizing and working with a citizens' advisory committee. These suggestions represent a synthesis of the opinions expressed by many school administrators in literature dealing with this subject.

1. As soon as a definite proposal for a school bond election is announced, preferably at a meeting of the board of education, an open invitation should be extended to all citizens who may be interested in serving on a citizens' advisory committee.

2. The school administration should then prepare a letter, signed by the president of the board of education or the superintendent of schools, to be sent to every known organization in the district, inviting each one to send a representative to the organizational meeting of the citizens' advisory committee.

3. Letters of invitation also should be sent to other persons who may have influence in the community or who would be able to make worthwhile contributions to the work of the committee.

4. At the first meeting, members of the board of education and the administrative staff should present the current and anticipated building needs of the district, the proposal for meeting these needs, and the estimated cost of such projects. A detailed report covering these points should be distributed to everyone in attendance. This report should also be mailed to groups not represented at this first meeting.

5. At least two subcommittees should be chosen at this meeting—the first to make an intensive study of the proposal and to prepare a report for presentation at the next meeting, and the second to prepare a report on committee organization. This second subcommittee could nominate

a general chairman and suggest other needed subcommittees and their chairmen at the next meeting. The administration should offer all help necessary for these subcommittees to carry out their assignments.

6. After allowing enough time for a thorough study of the proposal, a second meeting of the citizens' advisory committee should be called. In the meantime, follow-up letters will have been sent to all groups not represented at the first meeting. These organizations will be urged to be represented at the second meeting.

7. First order of business at the second meeting should be the presentation of the report from the first subcommittee. This should be in considerable detail and any modifications in the original proposal should be thoroughly explained. Following discussion, the citizens' committee should vote on the proposal. If the vote is overwhelmingly favorable, the committee can proceed to organize as a working committee to assist in planning and conducting the campaign. If any appreciable number of people oppose the issue, the committee should be asked to continue their study of the problem. Anyone unwilling to accept the recommendation of the subcommittee should be asked to serve on this study group.

Other subcommittees of the citizens' advisory committee usually named to assist in carrying out specific tasks of a bond campaign are those on finance, endorsements, speakers, printed materials, newspaper publicity, and radio and television publicity. Ordinarily, a steering committee is also selected to coordinate campaign activities.

OTHER CAMPAIGN PARTICIPANTS

Roles played in school bond and tax elections by certain individuals and groups are so important that they deserve special attention in this chapter. Among these are members of boards of education, school district administrators, teachers, students, and parent-teacher associations.

MEMBERS OF BOARD OF EDUCATION

The board of education, of course, is responsible for officially determining the amount of the school bond issue and for authorizing the holding of an election. Its responsibility does not end at this point, however. Board members are also responsible for doing everything in their power to assure that a vigorous campaign is waged. They should be involved at every step. They should assist the superintendent and his staff and the citizens' advisory committee in planning the campaign; they should volunteer their services to the speakers' bureau and to the other sub-committees responsible for specific aspects of the campaign; they should as individuals and as the official policy-making body of the school district set the pace and the tone of the school bond campaign.

A few educators are still of the opinion that board members should stay in the background and avoid publicity during school bond campaigns. The overwhelming majority (nine out of ten in the California study), on the other hand, believe that school trustees should take active parts in all phases of the campaign. As one superintendent expressed it, "If board members don't believe enough in the bond issue to work for its passage, how can they expect others to do so?"

SCHOOL ADMINISTRATORS

Administrators, too, should be in the forefront of any school bond campaign. The superintendent and his staff have the primary responsibility for developing the statement of needs, for developing the initial proposal for meeting these needs, and for presenting this information to the board of education. Working cooperatively with the board of education and the citizens' advisory committee, they will plan and direct the campaign, and they will have a major role in developing campaign materials and in conducting the publicity campaign.

Principals of individual schools within the district should be involved in bond campaigns. Their assistance is needed especially in large districts, for in these districts campaign techniques will probably vary from one part of the district to another. Principals are in positions to know their neighborhoods better than most other people. They will know what campaign techniques will probably be most effective in their own attendance areas, and they should be made responsible for coordinating the campaigns in these areas.

TEACHERS

Opinions differ with respect to the role teachers should play in school bond campaigns. Certain points should be perfectly clear, however. In the first place, teachers should be kept informed at all times. Administrators should meet with individual school faculties or with the entire teaching staff of the district to discuss thoroughly the bond proposal. Administrators should also place in each teacher's hands a rather detailed informational brochure which will include answers to questions likely to be raised during a campaign. Secondly, teachers should feel free to volunteer to assist in one or more of the many campaign activities. They should not be requested to serve, however. Finally, teachers may be asked through their own organizations or through the citizens' advisory committee to contribute to the campaign fund. Absolutely no pressure should be brought to bear on them for contributions.

Teachers, especially in social studies classes in the secondary schools, may be encouraged to discuss with their students the responsibility citizens have to register and to vote in elections. They may also wish to discuss the school bond proposal; however, they should not attempt to influence parents through their children. Furthermore, they may be expected to cooperate with the parent-teacher association in the task of registering as many parents as possible for any election. This task is a legitimate part of teaching good citizenship and should not be considered as part of any campaign.

STUDENTS

Many writers describe school bond campaigns in which pupils were used in various ways. One, for example, in listing 14 steps by which Marion, Ohio, "sold" a school building program to the community, reported students made posters in art classes, took home drawings shortly before the election urging their parents to vote for the bonds, wrote letters to neighbors, and took part in a parade on the night before election day.[6] Others have told of campaigns in which students distributed brochures, partici-

---

[6] L. L. Dickey, "Marion Sells School Building Program to Community," *American School Board Journal*, 126:61–3 (January, 1953).

pated in house-to-house canvasses, made posters and window cards, and spoke before community organizations.

Nevertheless, a strong and widespread feeling of opposition toward the use of students in bond campaigns was shown in the California survey by the fact that 94 districts, or about 60 per cent of those reporting campaigns, did not use students in any way. This feeling was also indicated by some of the comments made by superintendents. One wrote, "Students should not be used at all!" Another said, "Student activities may be effective means of winning elections, but I am 100 per cent against using students!" Still another administrator wrote, "This is a matter of principle; students should not participate." One superintendent typed "NO!" on every question concerning the role of students in bond campaigns to emphasize his opposition.[7]

Certainly the evidence seems quite clear that most school administrators oppose the use of students in school bond campaigns except in a very limited way. Before the campaign has actually begun, students may be asked to take home information explaining to parents the needs of the district. Older students may wish to discuss the merits of the school bond proposal in social studies classes. This, as has been mentioned previously, seems to be a legitimate classroom activity.

On the other hand, the great majority of school people apparently believe that students should not be used to influence parents; they should not be used to distribute campaign materials, either to their own homes or to homes of other people; they should not be used in parades; they should not be asked to make campaign materials in classrooms; they should not be used as campaign speakers.

PARENT-TEACHER ASSOCIATIONS

Strongest support for school bond proposals, especially in elementary school districts, is likely to come from parent-teacher association members. For this reason, school administrators are

---

[7] John W. Adamson, *op. cit.*, p. 43.

advised to enlist their help early and to make full use of them at every stage of the campaign. Following is a list of suggested ways for employing parent-teacher association members:

1. Invite every parent-teacher association unit within the district to be represented on the citizens' advisory committee.

COURTESY STOCKTON UNIFIED SCHOOL DISTRICT, STOCKTON, CALIFORNIA.

Strongest support for school bond proposals often comes from parent-teacher associations.

2. Arrange through the district council to have meetings of all units. Administrators, board of education members, and district council officers should plan the programs for these meetings.

3. Invite the parent-teacher association to assist in carrying on the registration campaign.

4. Invite the parent-teacher association to make periodic surveys in all attendance areas of the school district to determine the number of preschool-age children in each area.

5. Ask the parent-teacher association to help in preparing campaign materials, assembling speakers' kits, addressing postcards and letters, taking notes at meetings, and duplicating and distributing minutes.

6. Ask the parent-teacher association to organize and conduct the house-to-house canvass, if this technique is employed in the campaign.

7. Ask the parent-teacher association to organize and man election day machinery.

OPPOSITION TO BOND PROPOSALS

Some degree of opposition may be expected in almost every school bond campaign. Scattered and unorganized opposition is not likely to have an appreciable effect upon the outcome of the election. Opposition that is organized and that is willing to spend a considerable amount of money against the school bond proposal has a better than even chance of defeating the bond issue.

It is important, therefore, in the early stages of the campaign, to contact potential opponents and attempt to obtain their support. In most communities this opposition is likely to come from taxpayers' associations, large industries, or elderly citizens. Invite them to become members of the citizens' advisory committee and to assist in studying the needs of the district and in arriving at a reasonable proposal for meeting these needs.

This plan of action will usually succeed. However, in those communities where the opposition refuses to cooperate and subsequently wages a campaign against the bond proposal, there is only one course open—answer every point made by the opposition, vigorously and often.

ENDORSEMENTS

The practice of obtaining endorsements from community organizations and individual citizens is a common campaign technique. Among the 156 campaigns studied in California, 109 districts obtained endorsements from individuals and 119 districts, or 76 per cent of those reporting, obtained endorsements from organizations. Even more important, 98 per cent of the superintendents who used this technique considered it to be an effective means of influencing voters.[8]

In most campaigns, school administrators or members of the

[8] *Ibid.,* p. 53.

citizens' committee write letters to all known organizations in the community asking for time on their programs to present the proposal for school bonds. Following the presentation, the speaker asks for an endorsement from the organization. At the same time, he can distribute individual endorsement cards to the members and ask for their support of the bond measure. In Eyria, Ohio, for example, endorsements were secured from practically every club and organization in the city. Campaign leaders expressed the opinion that this support from groups was vital in the success of the campaign.[9]

Endorsement cards, approximately eight by five inches in size, should be used for ease in alphabetizing and filing. They should contain a brief statement of the proposal, followed by a statement indicating that the person or organization signing the card endorses the proposal and is willing to support it. The card should also indicate that the signer authorizes the use of his name or the name of his organization in the publicity campaign. These endorsements should be publicized in newspaper advertisements

---

ORGANIZATION ENDORSEMENT

The Board of Education of the .... School District has called for a School Bond Election to be held on .... The amount of the issue is $............................ .

We agree that additional funds are needed by the school district to provide adequate housing for the children and youth of this community. For this reason, we endorse the proposed bond issue, we shall work toward its passage, and the name of this organization may be used in publicity during the campaign.

Name of Organization ....

Address ....

Signed by ....

Office in Organization ....

---

[9] L. N. Nicholas and F. J. Gottfried, "Citizens Voted Yes Because They Knew the Facts," *School Executive*, 72:50–2 (June, 1953).

shortly before election, if finances permit. In one campaign, a full-page advertisement in which were listed more than 1,000 names was run in a local newspaper during the week before election. Smaller advertisements were run on other days, one listing all organizations which had voted endorsements, a second listing the labor groups which had endorsed the bond proposal, and a third reporting the endorsements of leaders of major religious groups.

HOUSE-TO-HOUSE CANVASS

A house-to-house canvass of the school district, if properly organized and carried out, is an effective means of gaining support for a school bond issue. Below are listed suggestions for planning and conducting the canvass.

1. In districts with several schools, organize by school attendance areas, with the school principal and the parent-teacher association president serving as co-chairmen for the canvass in this area.

2. Divide each attendance area to be covered into several sub-districts and appoint a lieutenant to be in charge of the canvass in each sub-district.

3. Secure enough workers to have at least one canvasser for each city block. Block workers should be assigned to the neighborhoods in which they reside if possible, thus giving them the advantage of approaching the voters as neighbors and friends. If workers know the voters' names, better impressions are gained.

4. Arrange for an indoctrination meeting in each area for all those who will be taking part in the house-to-house canvass. At this meeting explain how the block plan works, provide a booklet of factual information to each worker, give instructions on how to make home calls, and answer all questions which may be asked.

5. Have a sufficient number of reserve workers for each sub-district. These people may be called upon to make home calls in case of emergency.

6. Home calls should be made no earlier than two weeks before the election. Probably the best time of day to make calls in most districts will be between 6:30 and 8:45 p.m.

7. Block workers should not spend too much time on any one call, approximately 10 minutes should be adequate. If questions are asked which cannot be answered by the worker, he should refer such questions to someone who can supply such people with answers to their questions.

8. Plan to make all calls in the district on the same evening; publicity can thus be given the house-to-house canvass.

9. If some people are not at home, workers should make follow-up calls on the next evening. If no one is home at this time, the canvasser should leave the campaign materials and a prepared note stating that a parent-teacher association member had called to discuss the school bond issue.

10. A second home call on the evening before election day is often made to remind voters of the election and to urge them to vote.

SPEAKERS' BUREAU

A speakers' bureau should be organized as soon as the school bond election has been announced. The person designated to coordinate the activities of campaign speakers should be certain that anyone who is used is thoroughly familiar with all aspects of the proposal. Informational kits for speakers, therefore, should be carefully prepared. Briefing sessions should be scheduled. Visual materials, such as film strips, slides, charts, and pictures, should be furnished speakers. Don't ask for volunteers; select only those board members, administrators, and laymen who will speak effectively.

As has been mentioned before, contact every local organization as early in the campaign as possible and endeavor to schedule a speaker for one of their meetings. Request each unit of the parent-teacher association to arrange for a meeting during the campaign when a speaker or a panel of speakers may discuss the school bond proposal. Arrange for talks over radio and television stations for your speakers. Prepare special letters to all ministers of the community inviting their support as "speakers" for the bond proposal.

COMMUNICATIONS MEDIA

The number of communications media employed to promote a bond proposal in any particular district will depend upon many factors. For example, the media must be available. A few districts may not have newspapers of general circulation, radio stations, or television stations. The support of the public for schools may be so great in a few districts as to make widespread use of communications media in a bond campaign for new schools unnecessary. Lack of campaign funds in other districts may be a limiting factor. Furthermore, the character of certain communities may make it unwise to inundate citizens with publicity. The superintendent of schools, working with members of his board of education and the citizens' advisory committee, must consider these factors and then determine the kinds of communications media to employ and the extent of their employment.

It should be understood that communications media may be used for different purposes. A brochure, for example, is used mainly to inform. A carefully prepared and cleverly designed brochure may also convince. Bumper strips or billboards, on the other hand, are used mainly to remind citizens to vote in the school bond election. They certainly won't convince anyone that he should vote yes.

NEWSPAPERS

The most widely used of the media for communicating with the public is the daily or weekly newspaper. The superintendent should contact all newspapers in the district as soon as it is determined that a bond issue is to be proposed. He should endeavor to win the support of the newspapers and to obtain definite commitments concerning what they will do in their news columns and on their editorial pages. He should seek their advice on planning the publicity program.

Stories concerning the needs of the school district should begin appearing many months before election; in fact, they should appear before the election is even announced. A survey of preschool-age children which would indicate future increases in enrolment is the subject for one or several stories. Reports by the superintendent of schools to the board of education on enrolment trends, overcrowded classrooms, and dangerous or outmoded physical conditions in the schools should be publicized.

Planned, continuous newspaper publicity will furnish voters with an adequate background of the school district's needs and will thus make the proposal to meet these needs more acceptable.

The appointment of the citizens' committee and its discussions and actions are newsworthy. If the newspapers have no representation on the committee, appoint someone capable of covering meetings of the committee and writing stories for the press. Develop a story on every talk made before service clubs and other community groups. Report each endorsement voted by an organization. Submit architects' sketches of proposed buildings, charts, graphs, and pictures for use by newspapers. Plan to have something in the local newspapers every day during the final 10 days or two weeks of the campaign.

If campaign funds permit, develop a reasonable number of advertisements for placement in newspapers during the final days of the campaign. Ask the citizens' committee to solicit businessmen for space in their advertisements for slogans or brief statements concerning the bond proposal. Advertisements listing individual and organizational endorsements are also effective.

RADIO AND TELEVISION

Radio and television stations should also be contacted early in the campaign and their support solicited. In most cases, provided the issue does not become political because of organized opposition, radio and television stations will assist school administrators in planning programs, spot announcements, and other types of publicity. Stations may be willing to donate this time on the air as a public service.

INFORMATIONAL BROCHURES

In most campaigns informational brochures are developed which are distributed to all registered voters of the district by mail or by means of a house-to-house canvass. Brochures should be attractive but should not appear to be expensive. They should briefly explain the needs, the proposal for meeting these needs, and the estimated cost to the average taxpayer. They should be written in terse, easily understandable language and should include some pictorial features, such as graphs, cartoons, or photographs. They should be distributed to voters about two to three weeks before the election. A reminder of the election in the form

MONTAGE BY JOHN W. ADAMSON.

Informative brochures are essential to the success of a bond campaign.

of a postcard or simple pamphlet should be sent to voters just before election day.

The importance of the informational brochure or pamphlet in educating the public about the building needs of a school district was recognized in a Denver, Colorado, campaign. Here the campaigners developed and distributed four pamphlets to parents and community groups.

Copy was written by school personnel, and the layouts were made by a local advertising agency. The first three pamphlets reduced the story of school needs to three basic points: (1) the effect of increasing birth rates on enrolments, (2) the needs in newly-developed residential areas where there were no schools at all, (3) the need for replacement of at least some of the obsolete buildings in the school plant. The fourth pamphlet summarized the problem.[10]

LETTERS AND POSTCARDS

Special letters to parents of preschool-age and school-age children, signed by the superintendent, the president of the board of education, or the chairman of the citizens' committee, have proved to be an effective campaign technique in many districts. In large districts, school principals or parent-teacher association presidents often send letters to parents in their attendance areas. This is especially effective when the bond issue will provide a new school or an addition or improvement to the existing school in their neighborhood. Another technique often employed is the distribution of postcards to teachers, administrators, and members of the citizens' committee and an accompanying invitation to write personal notes to friends.

OTHER COMMUNICATIONS MEDIA

It is incumbent upon school administrators to use every possible means to inform the citizens of the community concerning the bond election. Among the other media often used to announce school bond elections are posters, billboards, banners, window displays, bumper strips, and sound trucks. As was noted earlier in this chapter, the use of these media probably will not win "yes" votes. They are useful, however, in keeping the bond election before the public during the final days of the campaign. Their use may, in addition, bring out a heavier vote on election day.

[10] K. E. Oberholtzer and A. H. Anderson, "Denver Votes Bonds for School Buildings," *N.E.A. Journal*, 38:178–9 (March, 1949).

An excellent window display keeps the bond election before the public.

ELECTION DAY PLANS

Plans for election day should be developed carefully and carried out, even though the bond campaign apparently has been successful and no organized opposition has developed. These plans should include at least the use of telephone committees, transportation pools, and baby sitting service. Some districts may wish to use poll checkers on election day. Parents should be used to perform these tasks. Only if they volunteer should teachers or other school district employees be used. Any work performed by school employees should be done after school hours.

Each attendance area should be organized. Telephone committees should be thoroughly instructed on how and when to make calls. They should begin their calls late in the morning of election day and should continue calling until they have reached everyone on their lists or until the polls have closed. They should call only potential "yes" voters.

The purpose in calling on election day is to remind citizens of the election and to offer transportation or baby sitting service. No attempt should be made to influence voters at this late date.

CAMPAIGN TIME SCHEDULE

The following suggested time schedule for school bond campaigns may be helpful to school administrators when they begin making plans for conducting a campaign in their district.

Six months to year before election. Determine future needs by studying current enrolments by grades, recent enrolment trends, adequacy of present facilities, and results of a survey of preschool-age children residing in the district.

Four to six months before election.
1. Develop specific proposal and present it to the board of education.
2. Publicize the proposal and the reasons for making it.
3. Organize a citizens' advisory committee to review the studies leading to the proposal and to assist in organizing and conducting a campaign.

4. Meet with the parent-teacher association to determine cooperatively what roles members will play in the campaign.
5. Begin campaign to register all parents of preschool-age and school-age children.
6. Attempt to discover any possible opposition to the bond issue and to win it over or to neutralize it.

Three to four months before election.
1. The board of education should officially set the date of the election and announce the amount of the bond issue.
2. Contact all organizations in the community and endeavor to arrange for programs concerning the school bond proposal.
3. Organize speakers' bureau.
4. Prepare information kits for speakers and for house-to-house canvassers.
5. Take advantage of every opportunity to publicize the bond issue in newspapers and over radio and television. Continue until election day.
6. Have sub-committees of the citizens' committee begin work on all phases of the campaign.
7. Prepare information for teachers and arrange for meetings with them to discuss the proposal and to invite their support.
8. Begin soliciting endorsements from individuals and organizations, publicizing the fact each time an organization endorses the bond issue. Continue until election day.
9. Begin preparation of campaign materials, such as brochures, posters, bumper strips, billboards, letters, postcards, film strips, banners, slides, window displays, and newspaper advertising.

One to three months before election.
1. Organize workers for house-to-house canvass.
2. Organize workers for election day. Prepare specific directions for every type of worker who will be employed on election day.
3. Arrange advertising schedules with newspapers, radio stations, and television stations.
4. Begin using motion pictures, film strips, and other audio-visual materials before meetings of community organizations.

Three to four weeks before election.
1. Put up window displays.
2. Distribute posters for placement in store windows.
3. Distribute bumper strips.
4. Put up billboard advertising.
5. Send letters to all ministers in the school district asking for their support of the bond proposal.

Two to three weeks before election.
1. Mail general brochure to all registered voters of the school district or distribute them through a house-to-house canvass.

2. Schedule informational type programs, such as panel discussions, for radio and television. Continue until election day.

Final two weeks before election.

1. Mail special letters to all parents inviting their support on election day.
2. Space newspaper, radio, and television advertising throughout this period.
3. Mail postcards or pamphlets to all potential "yes" voters to arrive the day before election reminding them to vote.
4. Attack vigorously any opposition that may develop.

Election day.

1. Telephone committees should begin calling all parents and other potential "yes" voters.
2. Check polls periodically to make certain that "yes" voters are voting.
3. Provide transportation and baby sitting service to "yes" voters if these are needed.
4. Remind teachers and other school district employees to vote.

Follow-up.

1. Analyze the campaign and endeavor to determine points of strength and weakness. Interview members of the citizens committee, the parent-teacher association, and school district administrators who actively participated in the campaign to determine the most effective aspects of the campaign.
2. Analyze election results in various areas of the school district. Attempt to discover why people in these areas voted as they did. Record results and conclusions for use in future campaigns.
3. Write letters thanking everyone who took active parts in the campaign. Also write to newspapers, radio stations, television stations, and businesses or organizations which assisted in promoting the bond issue.

RECOMMENDATIONS TO ASSURE SUCCESS

The following recommendations are offered for the consideration of school administrators and members of boards of education as measures which have proved to be successful in other school bond elections.

It is recommended

1. That the organization of a bond campaign be started not less than six months to one year before election day.
2. That a complete survey of needs be made and publicized before announcing the possibility of a bond election.

3. That a citizens' committee be chosen with representatives from as many diverse groups in the community as may exist.

4. That this citizens' committee be permitted to study thoroughly the statement of needs and the tentative proposal to meet these needs.

5. That everyone who volunteers to serve on the citizens' committee be given something specific to do.

6. That a voter registration campaign be conducted and efforts be made to register parents of all preschool-age and school-age children.

7. That schools be utilized as places for registration and that school secretaries be deputized for this purpose.

8. That every known community organization be contacted and asked to schedule a program concerning the school bond proposal.

9. That an effort be made to obtain endorsements of the bond proposal from all community organizations.

10. That individual citizens be asked to endorse the bond proposal.

11. That endorsements from organizations be publicized in newspaper stories or in advertisements.

12. That newspaper editors or publishers and radio and television station managers be contacted before the campaign begins for the purpose of asking for their advice and support.

13. That an effort be made to locate potential opposition and to win their support for the proposal.

14. That a complete handbook of facts be developed for use by teachers and other school employees, speakers, and members of the citizens' advisory committee.

15. That teachers and other school district employees not be directed to participate in the campaign but that they be encouraged to volunteer their services.

16. That religious leaders in the community be contacted and their support solicited.

17. That all union groups in the community be contacted and their support solicited.

18. That pupils *not* be used in school bond campaigns.

19. That the final publicity campaign be no longer than two to three weeks.

20. That house-to-house canvasses be conducted in those attendance areas where principals and parent-teacher association members believe they will be effective.

21. That at least one carefully prepared brochure or pamphlet be developed and mailed to every registered voter or distributed to voters by means of the house-to-house canvass.

22. That election day machinery be planned which will get probable supporters to the polls.

23. That the cooperation of the parent-teacher association be solicited; that members be invited to conduct a survey of the district to discover preschool-age children; that they man the election day machinery; and that they conduct the house-to-house canvass.

24. That administrators and members of the board of education play active roles in planning and conducting the school bond campaign.

25. That all potential "yes" voters be reminded of the election by a letter, postcard, or telephone call.

26. That carefully selected media of communications be employed to keep the election before the citizens of the community.

27. That opposition be vigorously attacked, if any develops, up to election day.

28. That the bond campaign be financed by contributions and that no pressure be brought to bear on any individual or group for funds.

29. That everything done in the campaign be in good taste and that nothing be done which might discredit the school district.

30. That letters thanking everyone who participates in the campaign be prepared and mailed immediately after the election, regardless of its outcome.

BIBLIOGRAPHY

Adamson, John W., *A Survey of Bond Campaign Procedures Followed by a Selected Number of California School Districts*, an unpublished master's thesis. Stockton, Calif.: College of the Pacific, 1957. Describes results of a survey of 156 school bond campaigns. Seventeen important aspects of campaigns were studied.

Campaigns Triumphant. Chicago: The National School Service Institute, 1951. Has practical suggestions on how to plan and promote school bond campaigns, including some excellent ideas for informational brochures.

Karns, Harry, "Long Beach Defeats the School Shortage," *American School Board Journal*, 134:45–6 (February, 1957). Builds a most convincing case for the use of as many citizens as possible in a campaign.

Kindred, Leslie W., *School Public Relations.* Englewood Cliffs, N.J.: Prentice-Hall, Inc., 1957, Chap. 18. Includes excellent summaries of "Elements of Success" and "Causes of Failure" in bond issue and millage campaigns.

Miller, I. T., "Seattle Schools Vote Bonds," *American School Board Journal*, 112:62–3 (May, 1946). Describes how a large city can be organized effectively for a bond campaign through the efforts of parent-teacher association members.

Nicholas, L. N. and F. J. Gottfried, "Citizens Vote Yes Because They Knew the Facts," *School Executive*, 72:50–2 (June, 1953). Especially fine description of how a citizens' committee can be organized and of the work done by the various sub-committees of this group.

Oberholtzer, K. E. and A. H. Anderson, "Denver Votes Bonds for School Buildings," *N.E.A. Journal*, 38:178–9 (March, 1949). A fairly complete description of how a successful school bond campaign was planned and carried out. Includes descriptions of use of informational pamphlets, endorsements, and parent-teacher association cooperation.

Sayles, Donald and J. J. Moran, "Our School Bond Referendum," *American School Board Journal*, 130:62–4 (January, 1955). Valuable for its suggestions on how the school board can be used in a campaign. The article also includes a discussion of two schools of thought on the matter of answering any opposition to a school bond proposal.

Smith, John A., *An Appraisal of School Bond Campaign Techniques*. Los Angeles: University of Southern California Press, 1953. One of the best studies available showing the relationships between favorable votes in a school bond election and such selected factors as socioeconomic status of the populations, publicity media, techniques, and conditions.

13

Our complex society has produced a multiplicity of groups for promoting almost every phase of "similar interest" among people. These groups are part of the school's public and they offer numerous opportunities for interpreting the needs, program, and problems of the institution. Their concern and cooperation should be enlisted to such an extent that they assume a responsibility to work for the support and advancement of education in the community.

POLICY ON COOPERATION

Good public relations means that the community is pleased with the educational services which the tax dollar has purchased for young people. Though this statement is simple, the procedure for bringing about this result is complicated; it is complicated because the school must deal with many publics and satisfy a wide diversity of opinion on education.

As a matter of policy, the local board of education must recognize that the school has an obligation to promote intelligent understanding of what it is doing and win good will from as many groups as possible regardless of the size of the group or the sex or age of its members. People who belong to community groups are paying the school bill and they are entitled to know what services the schools offer and why, as well as the problems confronting them. This policy is vital to the survival of the public school system in an economy where competition for the taxpayer's dollar is increasing rapidly.

The local policy on cooperation with groups should likewise provide that every person connected with the school system gets into the act, from the president of the board of education to the worker in the cafeteria. They should get into it by joining organized groups and sharing in their activities; by being invited to assist in the program of the school whenever possible; and by taking full advantage of opportunities for cooperative action related to school and community welfare.

To work successfully with groups, school personnel must know, for example, something of the fears, ambitions, and frustrations of parents in their relationships to the school. They must recognize that childless couples and career women may be heavy taxpayers who represent a sizable segment of the population and that these men and women should not be neglected in enlisting support for the school.

They must be aware of the fact that older members of the community can interpret the school only in the light of their own experiences unless they are informed differently. This group seldom understands the impact on schools made by the increased birthrate, child labor laws, and compulsory school attendance regulations. They cannot fathom the demands of a curriculum expanded to meet individual needs of children, nor the tremendous cost of education that has accompanied these changes.

The policy must be one of interpreting the school program to all groups in the community and inviting their cooperation in the tremendous task of advancing the cause and quality of public education in our democratic society.

SURVEYING GROUPS IN YOUR OWN COMMUNITY

Before an effective public relations program can be organized, a survey of the community should be made to accumulate pertinent facts and eliminate guesswork. The survey should concern the historical background of the community; customs, and traditions of the people; social and economic levels; organized groups with names of leaders and channels for communications.

The administration directs the survey but school personnel assist by obtaining information from the school records of former students, school census, questionnaires, chamber of commerce records, school board minutes, personal interviews, and church records. Needless to say, all information of a confidential nature is respected as such.

The public should be informed in advance of the purpose and procedure of this survey in order to prevent arousing distrust in the community.

Through a survey of the organized groups in the school district, a list of community leaders may be obtained. Usually, the Chamber of Commerce keeps a complete roster of civic and welfare clubs and youth organizations. Community Council and church alliances may furnish additional names of groups and give the chairman of each.

A card file should be set up, listing the name of each organization and its officers, type and number of members, dates of meetings, purpose of organization, how it can work with the schools, special interest in education, and a record of each cooperative activity.

A list should be compiled of school personnel who are members of different groups and who can serve as a liaison between the system and the organizations with which they are affiliated. The superintendent can best interpret the educational program to some groups, while other members of the staff may work just as effectively with members of their own organization. In this respect, it never pays to underestimate the value of a carpenter or a custodian in furnishing information to his friends and acquaintances.

Moreover, the schools need to know what people in the community think of the schools and what they expect of them. Everyone has opinions about schools. Being asked to express them is a compliment. The schools can gain much information useful in their relations with the public. It takes only a bit of stimulation and direction to make school personnel fine reporters of thoughts and feelings expressed by members of groups to which they belong.

Otis Crosby, Assistant Director of Information Service, Detroit Public Schools, has compiled the following procedure for obtaining the cooperation of various groups:

1. The public relations director, or someone in administration should survey the community for organizational resources. Besides PTA, organizations may be classed as fraternal, welfare, religious, luncheon, political, governmental, educational, professional, scientific, cultural, veterans, unions, patriotic, commercial, industrial, business, civic, recreational, tax-husbanding, statutory, youth sponsoring, alumni, and community councils.

2. These groups should be studied as to their relation to schools. Always assume that all groups are honestly interested in schools. Even the negatives pose as interested.

3. Decide what interaction would be best with each organization and what each can do to help the schools.

4. Make a survey of personnel contacts with the organizations and develop friendly relations.

5. Make actual contacts with the groups and set up machinery for working together.

6. If possible, attend meetings with the officers and general membership and develop friendships.

7. Publicize the favorable actions and successes of the schools. Did the local schools produce the local, successful businessmen? Help them to realize that the economy of the community is in direct ratio to the educational services provided the youth of the community.

8. Use the organizations' communications services, i.e., their bulletins and brochures.

9. Avoid controversial issues irrelevant to schools.

10. Handle smoldering reactions before they become brush fires.

OPPORTUNITIES FOR SCHOOLS TO COOPERATE

The opportunities for schools to cooperate with outside groups and organizations are large in number. Some of these opportunities are pointed out in the paragraphs below and others will be cited in subsequent sections of the chapter.

USE OF PHYSICAL FACILITIES

School facilities in many communities receive year-round use by citizens and taxpayers. Workshops and summer-school classes are held for their children. Civic groups use the recreational areas for square dancing, baseball, swimming, football, and other sports. Clubs, committees, and youth groups hold meetings in the school during the day and at night. The school library serves the community and works closely with the city library. Opportunities of this kind are limited only by the size and needs of the community in expressing a policy of cooperation.

STUDENT TEACHERS

Student teachers serve as media for cooperation between school systems and educational departments of institutions of higher learning. Both organizational and evaluation meetings give student teachers and their instructors a chance to discuss the school program with the principal and teachers in individual buildings. By working together, the training program for student teachers can be improved as well, and the school system will have future teachers coming into it who are partially oriented in the methods, policies, and practices it follows.

SCHOOL BOARD MEETING

School board meetings present opportunities to build top interpretation of the schools. An intelligent, sincere, interested school board, dedicated to serving all the children in the community, inspires confidence—the foundation of a successful school system and a public relations program.

School board meetings offer an opportunity to build community relations by inviting representatives of business, industry, and all organizations and clubs to attend meetings and hear discussions of educational problems and routine business. Of course, professional groups and PTA members should feel they have standing invitations, but a special invitation for a specific date is always appreciated. Different PTA unit members may be introduced as special guests at each meeting. Agendas of the proceedings of the meeting, reserved seats, and a welcoming committee promote a warm response from the guests.

Press and television have an open door, but they should be sent reminders or announcements before each meeting. Every effort should be made to include representatives of all mass media.

Special installations for new school board officers, conducted by a local person of authority, provides an occasion for inviting representation from all interested groups and also provides a good news story.

Don't forget staff members! Principals and teachers can obtain valuable information at board meetings for dissemination to all community groups, especially on policy planning and finance. Teachers can save the board members many telephone calls if they are sufficiently informed to answer questions because parents usually approach the local school staff first when they want answers to their questions.

PARENT-TEACHER ASSOCIATION

An informed parent-teacher association is most effective in interpreting the school and gaining support for it in the community. No other social or civic organization takes quite as direct an interest in the instructional program nor assumes as much responsibility for promoting the cause of education.

Opportunities for keeping members informed and for involving them in the life of the school are plentiful. Through regular monthly meetings, speakers, motion pictures, tape recordings, slides, filmstrips, demonstrations, and open discussions can be employed to acquaint them with instructional practices and problems.

A tape recording, for example, of the actual teaching of reading in a classroom illustrates one of the possibilities of educating parents; such a recording could be accompanied by teacher commentary and followed up with a round table discussion of reading by teachers and parents. Another example might be the use of small discussion groups after a filmstrip had been shown on health needs and habits of children; here parents and teachers could arrive at a common meeting ground on what each should stress with children in building sound health habits and in meeting health problems.

A parent-teacher association can likewise undertake many special projects and services related to the existing needs of the children and the institution. As examples, committees might be formed to look at report cards, summer recreation, success of high school graduates in college, medical services, adult education, and the adequacy of instructional materials.

Furthermore, the parents might offer their services in assisting with such things as health examinations, field trips, library, scout troops, cafeteria, assemblies, plays, and safety patrol. They could take on the job of preparing a monthly news letter for distribution to their own membership, the supplying of glasses and hearing aids to needy children, or the welcoming of new families with children into the community.

There is no reason why every parent-teacher association should not engage in direct study of school practices and problems. Under competent direction, representatives of the association could engage in a study of child growth and development, symptoms of maladjustment, methods of assisting children with homework, conference procedure in discussing children with teachers, or regulations pertaining to social affairs for teenagers.

Moreover, they could take part in curriculum-study committees engaged in the revision of old courses and the preparation of new ones. Many parents have a rich contribution to make to curriculum improvement, and they welcome the chance to be of service.

When efforts are made to keep parents informed and to involve them in the life of the school, they feel that they are partners in the great task of education and that they have a responsibility for the nature and quality of the instruction. This is reflected clearly in what they say about the school to friends and neighbors and how they respond when support is needed for a bond or millage proposal.

TEACHERS WORK WITH GROUPS

Although the superintendent of schools sets the public relations policies for the school system, the principal is the top liaison officer in each school building, and the person in charge of public relations in each school must take direction from him.

When the teaching staff is kept informed on public relations policies and practices, the principal's influence is multiplied. If the school district is too large for the superintendent to establish personal relations with teachers, area groups are logical divisions. For example, the feeder elementary schools can meet with the neighborhood secondary schools to plan public relations procedures in the community.

Informal meetings, where teachers feel free to ask questions and have problems and criticisms explained, are invaluable to the morale of the staff members in relaying information to the public.

Schools of similar size, or with similar problems, may form other groupings for the interpretation of educational philosophy and practices.

Teacher representatives to all school-oriented groups, including PTA City Councils, are important.

Commercial radio and TV stations often like a member of the schools' administrative staff as an educational consultant.

An administrator usually serves as county chairman of the Junior Red Cross since that organization functions only in the schools.

The PTA or room mothers honor the teaching staff with a "Teacher Appreciation" function before the close of school in many communities. These affairs may be held in a home, the school, or appropriate eating place, and range through outings, coffees, brunches, luncheons, teas, parties, dinners, and formal banquets. Sometimes the cafeteria, clerical, and custodial personnel are included—as well as part time or traveling teachers, nurses, and counselors.

Symphony orchestras, bands, and choruses composed entirely or partially of educators serve their communities by furnishing enjoyable cultural entertainment. Some music groups have won professional recognition, as in Cleveland, Ohio, and Wichita, Kansas.

In one community, a committee of teachers in the business-education department met each year with a group of local businessmen from manufacturing and industrial firms, retail merchants, bankers, and insurance companies. These meetings created a closer relationship between the schools and business and established the need for joint research and planning to determine the specific goals which vocational classes should set in order that students would receive the proper training for employment. The teachers received practical help from the group of businessmen, who, in turn, helped the schools to know what business expected. The businessmen also felt they had a part in planning the schools' business-education course of study in their community. From this cooperative work, the schools were able to obtain many part-time jobs for students and a friendly attitude of interest was maintained.

Both students and adult personnel interpret the school and build good public relations when they serve as speakers.

COMMUNITY RESOURCES

Rich resources for instructional purposes are available in all communities. The school needs merely to know what these resources are and where to ask for them. Several examples of their availability and application to the improvement of instruction will be described in the paragraphs that follow.

INTEREST OF GROUPS

Some school systems furnish their instructional staffs with a current guide to community resources. They describe the type of business or activity useful at each grade level, including addresses, telephone numbers, and names of contact persons. The days and hours for visitation are recorded. Printed materials are sent to school personnel before they make visits so they may have background information.

Interpretative pamphlets indicating the purposes and services of community groups may be obtained from the national headquarters of civic, service, and welfare organizations. However, local organizations usually have brochures explaining their work and their purpose. Fortified with these materials, teachers take pupils on trips to the neighborhood fire station, water department, police department, bank, shopping center, library, bakery, dairy, capitol and historical buildings, art gallery, airports, and zoo. More extensive trips are made to military bases, docks, mines, lumber mills, refineries, and state and national shrines.

Besides utilizing these resources, language classes serenade hospitals and rest homes with songs sung in foreign languages, and, consequently, the visit becomes more of a two-way exchange of values.

Some men and women's civic clubs sponsor junior organizations in high schools, and the Kiwanis International organized the Junior Police movement. The National Council for Economic Education is one of the strongest contributing groups; it furnishes scholarships for teachers from all over our nation to attend area workshops. Outstanding speakers in many areas of economics are brought in to these workshops from neighboring colleges, national firms, and industry—they are often financed, or partially financed, by local businessmen who want to help the schools improve the teaching of economics in their community.

DEVELOPMENT OF SCHOOL INTEREST WITHIN GROUPS

All groups are interested in schools, but the degree of interest may have a wide range and may need to be stimulated into action or directed into useful channels. In approaching an organization, give it an opportunity to share in or feel that it is contributing to the promotion of education. For example, business and industry often have visual aid instructional materials to contribute and their contribution can lead into extensive sponsorship of some area of school activity. Utilities and insurance companies, banks, industry, and state departments have valuable films, filmstrips, and transparencies which they will lend or give to the schools.

Safety activities in the schools enlist the interest of state, county, and local departments of safety. Local women's and men's business and professional clubs and the police and fire departments sponsor safety programs. In one city, the Junior Chamber of Commerce sponsored "The Teenage Road-E-O" and the Association of Insurance Agents furnished the "Drive-O-Trainers" in four of the secondary schools. Certificates of award were presented by the Chamber of Commerce.

The City Park Department and the public schools of one city jointly finance and sponsor a year-round recreational program for children. Scrap materials from local merchants and war surplus materials are used in the arts and crafts classes.

Women's clubs are valuable allies of the schools and members often become interested as individuals through contributing to or participating in school activities. Study clubs sponsor such educational projects as exhibits, fairs, symphonies, plays, programs, broadcasts, telecasts, and workshops. They also serve with church groups and welfare agencies by providing health services, character building organizations, recreational facilities, and home and family guidance.

Students need to learn that every adult has an obligation to the community in which he lives. In one system a packet of brochures and pamphlets, outlining briefly the services and expenditures of each of the 35 agencies included in the United Fund

Association were sent to all secondary teachers of social studies to be used in their unit study on the community. This educational program was planned to develop an understanding of community responsibility. A share in the United Fund monies for the Free Lunch Program of the schools gave teachers and students a greater interest in the annual campaign for funds.

COURTESY PUBLIC SCHOOLS, OKLAHOMA CITY, OKLAHOMA.

Teachers take a lesson in merchandizing at local department store.

Local chambers of commerce, in cooperation with the schools in many communities, help sponsor Education-Business Days so that the businessmen may look in on the schools and learn some of the schools' problems. In turn, the teachers spend Business-Education Day visiting firms and taking a lesson in the operation of business and industry. Usually one visit occurs during American Education Week in November, and the other in the spring.

Last year in Oklahoma City, Oklahoma, the Education Committee of the Chamber of Commerce, in cooperation with the U.S. Air Force, sponsored a one-day Space-Age Workshop in the Municipal Auditorium. Five thousand science students from over the state were invited to attend. The Chamber of Commerce has also sponsored national state and local secondary school science fairs for several years in this city. It has furnished sponsorship and provided finances for rocket clubs where high school students may receive technical advice and observe the safe launching of their rockets by professional military personnel on military bases.

The chambers of commerce in many cities entertain teachers new to the school system and frequently provide dinners, luncheons, and other social functions, as well as tours of the city, in larger communities. In one city, the downtown banks gave a luncheon for all new teachers and the administrative staff. Following the luncheon the teachers were taken on a tour of the city in air-conditioned buses, as guests of the Chamber of Commerce.

In one state an annual state Teacher Recognition Day honoring one teacher selected by each county has been sponsored jointly by the State Fair Board, The Hotel Association, The State Educational Association, and the Chamber of Commerce. A noon luncheon and an afternoon at the State Fair are climaxed with an Awards Dinner where each teacher receives a bronze trophy and an evening at the grandstand spectacular. The hotels provide a night's lodging as a courtesy to each teacher and her guest who has been her companion during the day.

Business, industry, civic, and welfare groups are pleased to receive requests for materials and organize tours for pupils and teachers.

Some communities hold Oilman for a Day or Career Day where a student from each secondary school is invited to be the guest of an oil company or business firm. These are examples of tying the interest of local industry to the schools.

The local Secretaries Association sponsored a Career Day for girls which included a day as guests of women executives, secretaries, welfare agencies, and head nurses in hospitals.

Judges, county and city officials, presidents of civic organizations, and government department heads are valuable as speakers and are always enthusiastic in planning many aspects of citizenship training with social studies instructors.

Through cooperative activities, community leaders become better informed as to successes of the schools and the scope of educational responsibilities.

ADVISORY COMMITTEES

Two kinds of advisory committees of citizens and the services they can render to the local system will be discussed here. Both have excellent potential as well for letting the community know what is being done for pupils and for reporting how people think and feel about the schools they are supporting.

COURTESY PUBLIC SCHOOLS, OKLAHOMA CITY, OKLAHOMA.

Invite community leaders to the school.

CITIZEN ADVISORY COMMITTEES

A dedicated group of citizens can furnish the leavening which inspires an entire community and brings about educational services otherwise impossible for the schools to establish. Parents will always pay for whatever kind of schools they want for their children, and the schools always reflect the interest of the adults in the community. Citizens' committees have been successfully organized in communities of all sizes.

The board of education and administrative staff should first determine the purpose for organizing a citizens' committee and set up the objectives to be obtained. Successful citizens' committees are almost always school initiated. The authorization of the committee and the policy under which it will work should be the responsibility of the board of education along with the superintendent of schools. The board members may wish to have consulting services from some outside experienced source.

The board of education policy should outline the number of members of the committee, the manner in which members are selected, the term of office, and the method of replacement. The relationships of the committee to the school personnel and the community at large, including the procedure for communicating with the board of education and the schools, should be determined.

A nominating committtte may be used in selecting the committee members. Young men and women will bring enthusiasm and fresh viewpoints while older members can contribute from their experiences.

The size of the group should be large enough to bring a good cross-section of the community's opinions, yet small enough to be a good work group. Fifteen to thirty-five members have been found to be efficient groups which still allow for unavoidable absenteeism. Many groups adopt the ruling that three consecutive, unexcused absences terminate membership. Vacancies are filled by the group and approved by the board of education and superintendent.

The rules governing the activities of the committee should be understood by all members.

1. The committee serves only in an advisory capacity to the board of education, as the board is a legally empowered group.
2. The committee should work only as a whole on the assigned task. It should advise and report findings as a group and not as individual members.
3. Any dissension should not be made public and dissenting members should withdraw and then act as individuals.
4. Members should obtain suggestions from as wide a source as possible.
5. Since large gatherings stymie progress, the public should know who the members are but should attend meetings only upon invitation.
6. The committee should keep the board of education and the public informed of its progress.
7. A small steering committee from various interest groups should be carefully selected (approximately 8–10 members).
8. The steering committee should understand thoroughly the purpose of organizing the group.
9. The cooperating administrative personnel should be genuinely interested in assisting and should also be well informed.
10. A work plan should be outlined.
11. The steering committee may now be enlarged to a working committee.
12. Carefully selected men and women should represent interest group; geographic area; religious, political, and civic groups; labor and capital; economic and educational levels; and all racial and minority groups.
13. All members should know the purpose, plans, and goals, before dividing into working groups.
14. Arrange for resource material and consultant personnel.
15. Allow ample time but terminate the study when the time is right. Avoid clashes of personalities and long delays that destroy interest.
16. Disband the committee when the work is completed, unless a standing committee is needed. If a standing committee is retained, assign definite duties.

The story of how Winnetka, Illinois, improved the welfare of their teachers has attracted national attention. A committee of thirteen citizens, mostly business executives, appointed by the board of education, made an eight month study of the schools. As a result of this study, the Winnetka teachers were given a higher salary scale, fringe benefits, including medical, hospital, and life insurance, and an annuity income above the state retirement program. The businessmen of Winnetka have assumed the lead in putting teaching on a professional basis with regard to salaries and prestige.

Some school systems have maintained citizens' committees for many years and have found them highly successful as public relations personnel. Other schools have found that standing citizens committees become frustrated because they have not had specific duties and prefer the formation of a new citizens' committee to meet each specific need.

VOCATIONAL ADVISORY COMMITTEES

Because of insufficient funds for universal higher education, European schools for many years have been forced to limit their educational services to the best academic students who want to become the leaders. This neglect of vocational education has helped to keep down production, both of foodstuff and manufactured goods.

Today America is helping feed a world which needs vocational education. Many organizations are trying to help people in undeveloped countries to help themselves. Both private industry and private contributions are being used to provide education and reduce illiteracy.

The vocational departments of American schools work with many lay groups. Some schools make a direct approach to community groups and ask carpenters, printers, and mechanics to volunteer to assist the school. Still other systems have advisory committees with representations from all lay vocational groups.

Vocational teachers may obtain assistance from such groups as architects, carpenters, plumbers (usually all labor unions), printers, newspapermen, vocational agriculturists, nurserymen, greenhouse operators, soil conservationists, mechanic and auto body workers, electronics technicians, and adult education groups. The recent demands on vocational education in America have increased the program. Businessmen are eager to cooperate.

An advisory committee of businessmen can evaluate the vocational program, see that it is adapted to the demands of the community, stimulate interest in students, and interpret the program to the community.

Vocational teachers serve as liaison persons between the schools and the skill unions. The trade and labor unions will work with vocational classes which furnish them apprentice workmen. In one city the printers' union sponsored a National Printing Week poster contest for art students. Since it tied in with art classes, many schools endorsed this program. The printers' union awarded prizes and co-sponsored a luncheon for the students and teachers. They advised the printing classes and helped the students find jobs upon graduation. With the assistance of the printers' union, one large high school has placed every student for years who wanted a printing job upon graduation.

The mechanics and auto-body workers have helped the teachers and students in these classes; part-time work after school and full-time jobs upon graduation have resulted. The radio and electronics classes have also affiliated with organizations which absorb student workers. High school radio and television studios which train student cameramen find their students working in commercial studios as soon as they graduate.

The Distributive Education and Diversified Occupations teachers meet the work-a-day world and are valuable public relations liaisons. Principals should help these teachers to keep informed on all levels and departments of educational services and administration. They are asked many questions and hear many criticisms. These staff members are especially helpful in planning the interpretation of the schools to civic and business groups.

A vocational supervisor arranged for the vocational students from one high school to build a complete house, including air-conditioning. Men from the different unions assisted the students and inspected their work. The completed home was landscaped by the vocational agriculture classes that operated a greenhouse and nursery. An open house was held for the public and the home was sold. The money became a revolving fund for the next class.

A vocational director arranged for the schools to obtain military surplus materials. The personnel from the military installation extended many courtesies to the schools. They sponsored tours for both teachers and students, picked up toys collected by the schools at Christmas time, furnished flag and bugle ceremonies for programs during educational conventions and other meetings.

Since the federal government has become acutely aware of the importance of vocational education in America, and foreign countries are making ever-increasing demands upon American production, the vocational program in the high schools should have careful and wise supervision. The more the local groups can be of service the greater will be the interchange of information and understanding.

EXAMPLES OF COOPERATIVE PROJECTS

Many demands are made upon the schools which would exploit the instructional program and dissipate the teacher's time and energy. However, with care and diplomatic discernment, noneducational innovations can be avoided since most thinking people are sincerely interested in protecting class time so children may learn.

One superintendent holds a monthly open press meeting in the evening. The entire community is invited to come and present questions for one hour. The director of public relations acts as chairman. The superintendent tries to answer every question, but maintains the privilege of refraining from answering inappropriate queries. Rumors and misunderstandings can be cleared away through such meetings.

The "Know Your Schools" type of meeting has been sponsored by various community groups. The PTA, citizens committees, or other lay groups, have organized the meetings, invited the public, and presented school personnel, who have explained each phase of the school organization. Students have participated on panels, giving their views on parent-school-student problems; many of these programs have been broadcast or telecast to the entire community.

Women's auxiliaries to men's civic clubs have provided medical and dental attention for needy children. Children with defective eyesight have received free eye-glasses. School children have collected and sent to the American Society for the Blind old eyeglasses and scrap silver and gold. In turn, a local hospital received a check which was used for buying children's glasses.

A superintendent of schools was asked by the State Turnpike Authority to prepare and administer a two-weeks training course for the men who were to operate the exchange stations on a newly completed turnpike highway. A speech teacher, a social studies teacher, and an English teacher developed the course. The social studies teacher taught state history, location of historical markers, museums, parks, recreation and sports facilities. The English and speech teachers worked on diction, pronunciation, human relations and efficiency. The Turnpike Authority and the trainees were impressed by both the instructional program and the school personnel.

The schools, PTA, and Goodwill Industries in a large city worked out a plan for improving the quality of clothing and the method of distribution to needy children. Goodwill Industries is a self-supporting organization that is operated by handicapped people who turn discards into usable articles. The articles are sold for a very small price. Cleaning and repairing used clothing is the main activity of the industry, which has expanded to include three outlet stores. The annual solicitation through the schools produced tons of used clothing. Since the schools and PTA are limited by space and time for distributing clothing, most of the clothing needs attention. The manager of the Goodwill Industries agreed to allow the PTA the estimated amount of clothing annually distributed free of charge in return for the clothing collected by the PTA. The sale price on the clothing and shoes was usually less than the cost of repair and cleaning.

The students were given credit slips by the principals, and accompanied by a parent or teacher, were permitted to select their own clothing. The students have better clothing, the feeling of charity was removed, and the PTA members were freed from the daily routine of keeping shop.

The local American Red Cross chapter furnished staff members to teach water safety, home nursing, and baby care in each high school. Classes in disaster training attracted many boys.

The Theatre Owners Guild, the PTA, and the schools compiled a teenage code of ethics for movie attendance and had identification cards made for each teenage student. These cards admitted students to any theatre at a reduced rate.

The postmaster arranged for a specially designed cancellation stamp to be used on mail during American Education Week, reading "Visit Your Schools." Mail trucks also carried American Education Week posters inviting everyone to visit the schools. Three of the local bakeries used American Education Week seals on their bread wrappers. Art students made American Education Week cards which the transportation company posted in its buses.

STUDENTS AND COMMUNITY GROUPS

All boys and girls want to be part of a group and to be accepted by their peers. While still in school, students receive personal satisfaction from working with adults. The opportunities for students to work with community groups are limited only by the size and interest of the community. The following are some examples:

Boys, especially from broken homes, need association with men. The Big Brother and Big Sister organizations have sponsored students, furnishing companionship, counseling and guidance, as well as material assistance. The Policemen's Boys Club has furnished and supervised recreation centers for students in many underprivileged areas. The Lions, Rotary and Kiwanis Club have furnished recreational centers, play areas, and nursery schools. The Kiwanians' Junior Police organization in the elementary schools has spread throughout the nation.

One midwestern city held a city-wide Beautification of School Grounds Campaign in the schools, with assistance and consulting services from the City Park Department, Association of Nursery Men, Council of Junior Flower Clubs, local seed stores, and the Parent-Teacher Association. The Chamber of Commerce presented special Certificates of Award to each school which participated in a creditable manner. The Junior Chamber of Commerce presented a Certificate of Merit to each school that passed the inspection made by businessmen on the clean-up phase of the campaign. (This type of campaign is effective in building civic pride in the schools and reduces student vandalism.) One school used the certificates as an incentive for stimulating pride in the school to such a degree that the last day of school became a "dress-up day" which had been planned to be a "hobo-day."

Students on all grade levels and in many study areas have worked with community groups through the Junior Red Cross program. Vocational classes have produced, from wood and war surplus metal, carts, tables, trays, and so on for use in local hospitals. The electronic classes maintained year-round radio and television repair service for the County Home for the Aged. In addition, students worked with local hospitals and rest homes in providing regularly scheduled entertainment and escort and shopping services, during the entire year.

The Junior Red Cross serves as a valuable liaison organization as students on all social, economic, and academic levels may belong. A PTA chairman of Junior Red Cross for each unit, whose duty is to assist the teacher-sponsor, will establish an effective channel of interpretation for the homes.

The mothers who serve in this capacity discover that the Junior Red Cross program makes learning more meaningful as the program is integrated into the school's curriculum. Through the chairman's interpretation the other patrons learn to understand more clearly the school's program.

Students assisted Veterans groups, religious groups, and civic organizations in charity drives, welfare activities, and promotional parades.

Students from each secondary school served as paid "string reporters" for the weekly "Teen Page" in the local newspaper.

During "Father and Son Week," the Y.M.C.A. and the schools jointly sponsored a secondary student as an understudy for one day of every top official in school, city, county, and state offices.

A third grade class toured the city, visiting the City Hall, Chamber of Commerce, publishing companies, newspapers, and a military installation. They wrote thank-you notes to the top officials of each organization they had visited, inviting them to a forum they had planned. They also invited their parents, representatives from the two television stations, and the newspapers. The Mayor, Manager of the Chamber of Commerce, the City Manager, and the other top officials accepted as also did the parents.

After other pupils had finished their lunches, tables were rearranged and the guests went through the cafeteria line. The class had decorated the tables and made the place cards. The pupils presided, made introductions, and presented the program, "Know Your City." At the close of the program, each official was given a "Certificate of Good Citizenship" designed by the children and individually signed by each of the 36 third-graders. This excellent piece of public relations was covered by both television stations and newspapers.

Secondary students frequently present panel programs for PTA meetings on parent-student-teacher relations.

One city class in social studies won state recognition for a soil conservation project. A group of farmers assisted the students in reclaiming eroded land located several miles from the school. The students who lived in a city learned to appreciate rural living and the contributions of farmers to our economy.

The Y.W.C.A. and Y.M.C.A. permitted the children from an elementary school in a low economic area to take weekly shower baths at their buildings. The principal transported the pupils in his station wagon, the school furnished the towels, and a nearby laundry contributed laundry service.

At the same school, the Kiwanis ladies taught the older girls in a Saturday morning "Charm Class," which included personal grooming, table manners, the proper setting of a table, hand laundry and pressing, vocabulary-building, party planning, and simple arts and crafts.

In one area a civic club built shelters at the bus stops so the children would be protected from the weather while waiting for transportation.

A group of students in a social studies class and their teacher became aware of the need for a branch library in their new suburban school district. They studied the situation, visited the library board, the city council and the community builders association. The contagious enthusiasm of the students spread to the parents and community leaders, and the branch library was built and equipped.

In a mining area the children were taken to the pit and shown the adjoining manufacturing plant as guests of the industry. A private bus company furnished the transportation.

During the state fair a transportation company picked up children at the schools to attend the afternoon "Folk Dance Festival," returning them before dark.

The high schools in a large city opened sub-post offices during the Christmas rush. Patrons in each neighborhood appreciated the service, and the students working in the post office received excellent training.

One history class enlisted community interest when each student interviewed 10 men and wrote a theme on "How 10 Men I Know Happened to Have the Jobs They Now Hold." Four hundred men were made to feel the schools needed them.

The National Council of Christians and Jews have held annual workshops in many communities. Social studies teachers have used these group meetings as an opportunity for developing interracial understanding. Student representatives from all secondary schools spent the day together. They faced problems, analyzed situations, exchanged ideas, and came away with an appreciation of each other.

The pep clubs earned funds while enlisting the good will of the "senior citizens" by running errands, chauffeuring, and doing odd jobs after school, on Saturday, and during the summer.

An assignment for avowed history haters was turned into the study of the history of automobiles, airplanes, and clothing. The students visited the manufacturing plants to collect data. Two boys studied the history of baseball and enthusiastically correlated their favorite sport with significant dates in history through the help of a professional ball club.

Students of government rang neighborhood door bells and reminded adults that the next day was the last chance to register to vote. They attended precinct meetings and studied the background and platforms of both the Republican and Democratic parties.

Following the National Presidential Nomination Convention, the secondary students, under the financial sponsorship of the Chamber of Commerce, held both Republican and Democratic mock-presidential nominating conventions. Over 1500 students and their teachers participated in this two day activity. Enthusiasm ran high. The general decorum was much better than the authentic conventions.

When students and adults work together both groups gain a better understanding of each other. Students develop poise, learn new skills, and a respect for adult leadership. Adults see students develop at different rates, observe individual differences, and better appreciate the schools' program of educating for citizenship, as well as continuous learning.

RESOLVING CONFLICTS WITH GROUPS

Schools are constantly approached by organizations that wish to use them as a means of communication with the home or for the advertising of their products and services. Some of these contacts are educationally worthwhile and some exploit children. A policy for meeting such requests should be adopted by the local system. With regard to the use of free materials supplied by outside organizations, the Philadelphia Public Schools established the following policy:

> It is generally understood that the school cannot be used as an agency for the distribution of advertising materials. No materials from outside of school sources should be distributed to homes through pupils without the approval of the Department of Superintendence.
>
> Materials of a sectarian nature should not be accepted.
>
> Other free materials may, however, be accepted for classroom and school purposes under conditions that meet the following criteria:
>
> 1. The initiative for securing the material should come from the school. In other words, the materials should be of the type that teachers seek, not materials that are thrust upon them to promote the interests of an outside agency.
>
> 2. The materials should fulfill a legitimate purpose of the school curriculum.
>
> 3. The selfish private purposes of the sponsor should not be prominent or dominant in the material.
>
> 4. The advertising features of the material should not be blatant.
>
> 5. No material should be used that violates the attitudes which are recognized as ideals of the school system or of our society.
>
> 6. No books, bulletins, pamphlets, or papers that are clearly in the nature of propaganda for any form of totalitarian government are to be kept on open shelves in any classroom or library.
>
> Such materials may be used, at the discretion of the principal, and under careful teacher supervision, in classes that are studying propaganda analysis, or that are learning to refute the arguments of groups antagonistic to American ideals.

On the matter of contests sponsored by outside groups and organizations, the Richmond, Virginia, Public Schools formulated this set of regulations:

> 1. The central office will screen contests in terms of sponsoring organization and general suitability for school use. Each principal will decide whether the contest is suitable for that particular school, and school participation will be voluntary.
>
> 2. Contests will generally not be considered a part of the school

curriculum, but may be used by teachers in the school program if the teacher feels that the contest is appropriate to the work of the class.

3. The contest should not seek to assume any teaching function or infer [*sic*] a deficency in school instruction on the subject presented. The purpose of the contest should be to provide pupils with an interesting occasion to apply the school instruction they get.

4. Teachers will not be asked to supervise the contest.

5. The principal responsibility of the school is to provide means of announcing the contest to pupils.

6. Pupils will participate in contests on an entirely voluntary basis.

When an organization is led to understand the philosophy of the school and how its request might infringe upon the students' learning, an improper request is usually withdrawn.

Occasionally, a civic or service club may become a pressure group. If possible, anticipate the situation and forestall its development. Diversion of the activity may save the situation.

Religious differences prevail in every community, and the state laws governing religious practices should be well understood by the administration. If board of education policies are established, the principal and teachers will feel more secure when religious problems arise. The principal has the position of leadership in both philosophy and practices in regard to religious differences. He sets the pattern for the community by his attitudes of tolerance and understanding. Local customs and observances present opportunities for teaching spiritual values, brotherhood and cooperation. Conflicts, pressures, or intolerances should never be permitted to invade the schools or to cause embarrassment to children on any occasion. If the school property serves as a community center, its use by religious sects should be carefully arranged so that the promotion of religious doctrine will not occur. Children are tolerant of religious practices and schools can promote an understanding and appreciation of all cultures and philosophies.

Sometimes scholarships tamper with the curriculum. Occasionally, someone wishes to establish a scholarship to promote the addition of a pet subject to the course of study. Occasionally, this situation may be introduced to promote personal or individual aggrandizement.

In some localities, politics or business development is promoted through the schools. At times the board of education can handle the situation best, sometimes the superintendent of schools or a citizens' committee may be needed to make the decision, suggest a policy, or interpret this adverse situation to the public.

The school board should determine and support a definite policy concerning the use of school buildings and also the replacement of school property damaged by vandalism.

Keeping the channels of communication open with a two-way flow of information between the schools and community groups is the best way to prevent misunderstandings and to develop wholesome public relations. Constant vigilance on the part of the schools is necessary because the membership of most community groups changes frequently. However, the rewards are great whenever the schools meet this challenge with well organized information and planning.

BIBLIOGRAPHY

Brodinsky, B. P., "New Patterns in Citizen-School Relations," *Education Digest*, 21:18–19 (March, 1956). Tells how the school executive may develop channels of communication with the community which will prevent a crisis from developing.

Drieman, David B., *How to Get Better Schools*. New York: Harper and Brothers, 1956. A tested program showing how lay citizens can and should exercise a public voice on behalf of the schools.

Grinnell, J. E. and Raymond J. Young, *The School and the Community*. New York: The Ronald Press, 1955, Chap. 11. The second section of this chapter enumerates the principles of public relations that should underlie good practices.

Kindred, Leslie W., *School Public Relations*. Englewood Cliffs, N.J.: Prentice-Hall, Inc., 1957, Chaps. 9, 10, 12. These chapters deal specifically with relationships with community groups and point out many opportunities for cooperation.

Muller, Leo C., "The Role of the Administrator in Winning the Voice of the People," *School Board Journal*, 135:27–28 (December, 1957). Explains the role of the administrator as a leader in the professional and community relations programs.

Stearns, Harry L., *Community Relations and the Public Schools.* Englewood Cliffs, N.J.: Prentice-Hall, Inc., 1955. Develops and illustrates the theme that the school must recognize the importance of and the methods of using community relations.

Stoddard, Alexander J., "The Schools Just Keep Rolling Along," *The School Executive*, 77:57 (January, 1958). A view of relationship problems and how administrators came to grips with them.

14

The physical facilities available for working with the various community groups mentioned in the previous chapter are a form of community service. Comfortable and attractive conference rooms indicate friendly administrative leadership and inspire creative group thinking and increase public interest in a school system. In addition to physical facilities for working with groups, a number of less tangible community services are discussed in this chapter. The proper emphasis on these various services provides a sound foundation on which to build an effective program of community-school relations.

To be effective any public relations program must be all inclusive, both from the point of view of involving the entire staff and every phase of the school program and from the point of view of utilizing every conceivable medium of communication and contact with the community. The good will of school personnel is also required as well as the proper application of the various techniques of public relations (which have been discussed in previous chapters). Reference will be made to the need for utilizing all types of services that schools are equipped to render a community. The emphasis can be either very direct or so indirect that it is almost unnoticed, except for the impression on the subconscious mind, as in the case of an attractive reception room.

The purpose of this chapter is to help teachers, principals, and central office personnel recognize the inherent public relations values in the many everyday functions and services performed by a school or a school system; it brings into clearer focus the influences these services have on the development of effective relationships among the people, their board of education, and the teachers.

IMPORTANCE OF EFFICIENT SERVICE

The importance of efficient school services cannot be overstated, but it is often overlooked. Efficient services have an immediate public relations value, but often their good influence extends into the unknown future. The true measure of this influence is the support, both in spirit and money, a community gives its schools.

In the article "Who Runs Our Schools?" in *Look*[1] magazine the author states:

This is a year of satellites and soul-searching; national interest in school elections is especially high. But citizens long have used the school boards to make the schools what they wanted. They have done this by individual grievances and gripes, by pressure of special interest groups and by silent acquiescence when change was not desired.

In short, there is but one answer to the question, "Who runs and will continue to run our schools?" The answer: "You."

The evolution of the American public schools can be characterized as an effort on the part of an enlightened people to assure a future society in which their children would enjoy a way of life better than their own. In one sense the people developed a Frankenstein's monster—a system of education which has become so complex that they no longer understand it in all of its ramifica-

[1] George B. Leonard, "Who Runs Our Schools?" *Look*, 22:79–82 (June 10, 1958).

tions; nor can they direct its further growth and development. The complexities of a modern education system, growing in part out of the numerous services offered, confound not only the lay public, but experienced board members as well.

In the process of developing the American public school system, the superintendent evolved as the key professional leader. To be successful he must recognize that the schools belong to the people and that the people must be given opportunities to have their thoughts and ideas reflected in the foundations of the educational program.

The change from an educational system which the people comprehended to one which requires that the people have confidence in the professional educators who administer it has brought about a need for new techniques of public relations with greater emphasis on services to the community.

The historical development of our schools suggests three major reasons why professional educators should be concerned that the public has confidence in its schools. In the first place, the people have voluntarily turned over to the educators a school system which they themselves created and nurtured through its early and difficult years. The least teachers can do to merit the confidence placed in them is to provide the best possible community relations program involving efficient services.

Secondly, school services become an important aspect of successful administration, for they do much to create a feeling that the schools belong to the people and stand ready to serve them. The proper emphasis on services often helps win adequate financial support for the schools.

The third reason is related to self-preservation. Constitutions, laws, and court decisions have established a pattern of public control of education. No public institution in our free society can long endure without the approval and support of the people. A change in the administrative pattern of a school system by the people is a complex process often requiring considerable time. The change of a board of education—and, through the board, an administrator—is not uncommon, however.

A dynamic public relations program is complex and time consuming and demands great professional skill on the part of teachers, principals, and administrative personnel. One of the most important ingredients of such a program is a positive emphasis on efficient services to the community.

THE SCHOOL PLANT AND PUBLIC RELATIONS

Because the concept of service is relatively new in school administration, until recent years little effort was made to provide for the community service function in the design of school facilities. The development of the school office, for example, parallels in many respects the development of a public relations consciousness on the part of school officials.

The introduction of the school office in architectural plans occurred just before the turn of the 20th century with many of the first offices appearing on stair landings. This location made them readily accessible to teachers and children, but little or no thought was given to accessibility for the public. School service facilities such as storerooms also were built on stair landings, often at a considerable distance from the office.

Modern school architecture places greater emphasis on school offices, and a well-designed school is practically built around the office and its adjoining service facilities such as conference rooms, guidance centers, and clinics. These facilities serve not only as the center of the school's education program but also as the center of the public relations program.

The evolution of central administrative offices for a school system also bears a striking similarity to the recognition of the importance of the service function of schools. The early practice of using a small suite of rooms in the city hall or county court house persisted for many years and is not completely out of vogue even today.

The use of school buildings abandoned as a result of population shifts from downtown areas was the next step. There is no evidence that this development was in the interest of emphasizing services to the community, for, unfortunately, many downtown buildings have inadequate playgrounds for conversion to parking facilities. From the decor of the offices to the rest room facilities, the public generally was overlooked in converting old school buildings to central offices.

Consider the effect on community relations of a central office reception room in which visitors sit in public view on old-fashioned straight-back chairs standing stiffly in a row. Not only does this have a negative influence on the public, but it also fails to create a sensitivity to public relations on the part of many teachers for whom the service function of education is a new, untried, and often unacceptable idea. Talks, newsletters, and other efforts to encourage a public relations approach are difficult to reconcile with such facilities.

THE TELEPHONE

A mother, concerned because her daughter telephoned her teacher almost daily during summer vacation, called to apologize. The teacher explained in complete sincerity that calls from the children were appreciated for they were the best possible contact with school life during the summer months. The teacher's reply was not motivated by a desire to be a good public relations agent, but rather it was a true expression of her feeling. A teacher who treats all persons in a friendly, courteous manner and is concerned about the welfare of children naturally wins support for the schools.

Each time an employee of the board of education picks up the telephone to answer a call from a parent, to talk with someone in the community, or to inquire about the price of instructional materials, he is a public relations agent. This little electronic gadget which we take so much for granted is a powerful influence for good or for poor community relations. The tone of the voice and the inflections used in casual comments which bespeak confidence and appreciation for teachers, principals, the superintendent, or the board, leave the impression that all is well.

To attempt to leave an impression other than that parents are always welcome to talk with school personnel is simply to be naive. Parents are naturally interested in their children and should feel that it is proper to pick up the telephone and inquire of an understanding teacher when a question arises about Johnny's reading, writing, arithmetic, or about what was said at school. Any hesitancy to call the teacher first for fear of a discourteous reply usually will result in a call to a neighbor or friend followed by another and on and on. The final outcome seldom is what school personnel would desire.

The handling of telephone calls to or from the home which involve children at school requires tact and good judgment. Messages from parents usually can be delivered to the child rather than to call the child to the telephone. Knowing that the child can be contacted if necessary leaves parents satisfied that the school is doing its part and the child is in good hands.

The telephone is the most personal contact some lay citizens have with the superintendent and central office staff. Impressions of the type of people in the office begin with the switchboard operator. It is easy to conclude that a school system is well run or poorly run by the "Hello, City Schools" and the conversation during the next few seconds. In a business, this voice can mean a satisfied customer or the loss of a sale. In a school system it can mean a vote for the schools at the polls or the loss of a friend of education.

The telephone manners of the switchboard operator and other personnel should receive careful consideration at all times. It behooves a superintendent to put the best voice forward. A frequent busy signal or long wait can play havoc with a school system's public relations. School systems should call upon the telephone company for assistance in developing the best telephone techniques.

Citizens calling the superintendent or other administrative personnel soon learn that the next voice they will hear after the switchboard operator is that of a secretary. The use of a secretary to screen calls is accepted in business. Since this practice often adds to the long wait, however, it should be as pleasant as possible.

The efficient secretary is one who recognizes the voices of the people who call frequently and greets them in an appropriate, cheerful manner. She knows that certain calls are transferred to the administrator, some are handled by "Can I help you?" and in other cases the number is requested. "May I tell Mr. Jones who is calling?" is a more acceptable greeting for a strange voice than "Who is calling?" or "Who is this?"

In originating calls, courtesy is equally important. A secretary placing a call for her supervisor should begin the conversation with "Hello, Mr. R. P. Jones is calling Mr. Smith." Mr. Jones then should be on the line when Mr. Smith says "Hello." The secretary also should be informed on what to say if Mr. Smith is not available.

All school personnel can prevent undue embarrassment and win friends by beginning each telephone conversation with "Good morning, this is R. P. Jones of the city schools," or some similar identifying statement.

Another consideration in telephone relations is the chance remark which may spark a chain of gossip or criticism. Although the voice on the modern telephone is faithfully reproduced, this means of communication sometimes leads to misinterpretation because personal contact is not possible. A smile or other facial expression so important in direct communication cannot be reproduced to tell the other person that a casual remark was made in jesting, or perhaps a statement made in complete earnestness and emphasized by a facial expression in a personal contact is missed because only the voice can be heard.

This discussion is not intended as a complete guide to good telephone relations. Rather it was written to challenge all school personnel to give careful consideration to the major public relations potential of the telephone.

SCHOOL CORRESPONDENCE

Community undestanding and acceptance of schools are often products of personalized messages in school correspondence. A teacher, a school, or a school system may have a distinctive personality in the eyes and minds of the public as a result of the written word which leads parents to view school personnel as cheerful and helpful, courteous and friendly, or perhaps dull and forbidding.

Robert Louis Stevenson identified the problem when he said, "The difficulty is not to write, but to write what you mean, not to affect a reader, but to affect him precisely as you wish."

Words and ideas used in letters to the public should be simple. To tell an effective story, however, the educator must consider not only the simplicity but also the emotional content of words. Some words, for example, affect people agreeably while others are disliked. There also are words which have no effect and can be considered neutral. Note the different reactions to the following words:

cost	helpful	death
investment	right	home
mother	blame	child
wrong	fault	play

Most people react favorably to investment, mother, helpful, right, home, child, and play. However, a severe loss through an investment or an unhappy home life may produce an unfavorable reaction to these words. The reaction is due to the connotative power of words, many of which have a personal or emotional significance apart from and beyond accepted definitions. Teachers who are responsible for written documents need to consider carefully this emotional content of words, for advance knowledge of the readers' reactions gives a tremendous advantage.

NEGATIVE AND POSITIVE LETTERS

The emotional impact of the following letter is decidedly negative, and Mr. Myers probably would assume that the writer is offensive, abrupt, and discourteous. The letter also may raise questions in his mind about the board policy and its application.

Mr. John W. Myers
60 Church Street
Chattanooga, Tennessee

Dear Mr. Myers:

We *cannot* comply with your request of June 10 to assign your child to the Barger School next year. In *rejecting* your request may we call your attention to the fact that children *never* are allowed to attend a school in another school zone since the Board of Education's policy *prohibits unjustifiable* assignments outside a school zone.

Very truly yours,

To improve the letter, the writer should substitute positive or neutral words for the negative words. The result may, at best, be a neutral letter.

Mr. John W. Myers
60 Church Street
Chattanooga, Tennessee

Dear Mr. Myers:

I always welcome an opportunity to correspond with patrons who are sincerely interested in the education of their children. It is with regret, however, that I explain that Mary will not be able to attend the Barger School as requested.

School zones have been established for all elementary and junior high schools in the city to help assure that one school is not crowded while other nearby schools have vacant rooms. Although attendance at the school in the zone in which a child resides is required under Board of Education policy, our Board has provided means of adjusting class loads between zones. However, in your case the Woodmore School which Mary will attend has small class loads, whereas the class loads at the Barger School are among the heaviest in the city.

I believe Mary will enjoy going to school at Woodmore as much as she did at Barger for it also has a fine school spirit and a principal and faculty devoted to children. I hope there will be an opportunity to meet you personally and to discuss this and other matters of interest at a later date.

Sincerely yours,

The ability to say "no" or to write a "turned-down" letter is an art and the person who can do it and win a friend for the school system is a valuable staff member. A simple rule to follow is: If you can say yes, be very brief; if you must say no, take a little longer.

The "you" approach often is important in letters since the interest many people have in the school system begins and ends where it affects them. Appeal to each person on his own terms in a way that will convince him you have his interest at heart. For example, compare these two sentences which have about the same meaning but convey that meaning in different ways:

1. We give every request fair consideration.
2. You may be sure that we have given your request every consideration.

Words should be used which mean essentially the same to most people. A sentence intended for one of Roosevelt's famous fireside chats read in its original form, "We are planning an all-inclusive society." In the talk the sentence had been rewritten to read, "We are building a society in which no one will be left out." Simple words transformed this sentence to one which practically everyone could understand.

RECEPTION OF VISITORS AND GUESTS

If educators are sincere in saying that the schools belong to the people, every effort should be made to leave the impression that the people are welcome when they visit a school or the superintendent's office. The implications of this statement are many and varied. It is necessary, for example, to consider the effects of frequent visitors on the instructional program as well as on the public relations program.

Teachers in schools which have frequent visitors have worked out procedures which encourage visitation and prevent interruption of classroom activities. In one school visitors, after going by the office, enter classrooms without knocking. They are greeted by a student host or hostess sitting near the door who escorts them about the room explaining the various types of projects on display and the activities in which pupils are engaged. Questions are answered and the person is invited to observe the class discussion or other activities. The host or hostess writes the name and the purpose of the visit on a piece of paper and unobtrusively places it on the teacher's desk. At an appropriate time the teacher greets the visitor.

Since all persons visiting schools should first go to the office, the importance of having an attractive office near the main entrance is obvious. The reception of visitors and guests generally is the responsibility of the secretary or a student host or hostess. After a cordial greeting, the name, reason for the visit, and room or rooms to be visited should be ascertained and filed in the office. This information may be needed to contact the person while in the building.

The receptionist should know which visitors to introduce to the principal and which visitors to take directly to the rooms. The public relations value of a gracious reception of visitors by the prinicipal far outweighs the small investment of time. In some cases he should escort them through the building explaining art work, student projects, displays, and school activities of particular interest. Special features in the building and their contribution to the educational program also should be interpreted if an interest is demonstrated. The extent of the tour will depend on a number of factors known to the principal who is alert to public relations as a tool of administration. The same considerations should be shown by the secretary or student host.

The importance of proper preparations for committee meetings, PTA board meetings, or other special meetings cannot be overemphasized. Rooms should be ready with sufficient comfortable chairs, and the principal should have his work scheduled so that interruptions will be held to a minimum during the time the guests are arriving as well as during the meeting.

In the Board of Education office, the reception of visitors and guests is equally important. Large school systems frequently have a full-time receptionist who sometimes serves as the switchboard operator or assists in other ways with office details. In addition to a pleasant smile and disposition, this person needs to understand the office organization so she can refer visitors to the staff members who are best qualifed to take care of their needs.

With proper encouragement, visitation by appointment will become the pattern. Staff members must realize, however, that only negative public relations values obtain if persons with appointments are required to sit in the waiting room ten, fifteen, or perhaps thirty minutes. Regardless of the efficiency of the school personnel, however, there will be times when appointments cannot be maintained on schedule. An attractive and gracious secretary can do much under these circumstances to make the visitor feel that he has not been forgotten.

There always will be those who call without having made an appointment. The school administrator concerned about the public relations aspects of his day-by-day activities will take time out of a busy schedule to talk with such persons for a few minutes. If necessary, an appointment then can be made by the secretary.

In the reception of visitors and guests, as in other services emphasized, the "Golden Rule" properly applied will produce the type of public relations about which people talk approvingly.

REQUESTS FOR INFORMATION

Expressions such as "Do they think we are supposed to know everything?" have been used by teachers following telephone calls requesting information. Instead of being critical, school personnel should consider this a challenge and an opportunity to provide the public with the type of school system it desires.

For those school systems which accept the supplying of information as a normal service function, there are certain techniques of public relations to be observed and implemented. Since many requests will be made by telephone, the basic principles of telephone courtesy discussed previously need to be observed. Procedures also should be established to insure that such requests do not violate the basic principle that schools operate primarily for the education of children.

Important documents which assist teachers in answering requests for information are a handbook, directory, and school calendar. As a part of their programs the local professional organizations should provide teachers with information on all activities affecting schools on the local and state levels.

Lay citizens do not expect teachers to be walking encyclopedias, but they do have a right to expect that they will have readily available certain basic information about the school system. If a teacher is unable to supply information requested, he should give the name and telephone number of the person who can supply it.

A common dodge used by teachers is to explain that the question does not pertain to the work they are doing. But this cannot be considered an adequate reply for those who really are concerned about public relations. The high school teacher asked about the entrance age for first graders should bridle the impulse to say "That doesn't concern me," if for no other reason than that his personal prestige may be at stake.

Here are a few of the questions patrons ask. If teachers cannot answer them, both the teachers and the administration should be challenged to take steps to correct the situation. The questions follow:

> What guidance services are available at Hardy?
> In what grade does the teaching of science begin?
> Who is the principal of the Trotter School?
> What are the dates of the Christmas vacation?
> What is the compulsory attendance age?
> How does a child secure a work permit?

The principal in the office and at home also must consider the supplying of information a normal function of his position. Questions will range from the type asked teachers to others about the operation of the school or the school system. Citizens in communities in which the principal graciously accepts this opportunity for service have confidence in the school and appreciation for teachers.

Junior and senior high schools may serve in a somewhat different role. In a community without a public library the school library can fill an important need. Student librarians are used effectively to answer the phone and look up the information requested.

The main information center for a school system is the board of education offices. Requests for information should be directed to the person who is best qualified to supply it with a minimum of delay. Public information most frequently requested about school employees such as the telephone number, address, school, salary, and so on, should be maintained in a personnel file at the switchboard.

Superintendents and administrative officers have an opportunity to serve a broad segment of the community. The Chamber of Commerce, civic clubs, city, or county government officials, industries, businesses, and many other types of organizations should feel that the information needed can be secured quickly and easily by calling the office of the superintendent of schools.

School systems dedicated to the philosophy that the maintaining of effective public relations is a *sine qua non* of success generally follow the practice of maintaining open files except for confidential personnel records. Certain basic principles need to be considered, however, in the handling of requests for information involving board policy. In the first place policies adopted by a board of education and administrative regulations should represent the thinking of the staff. Confusion results, for example, if parents are told by uninformed teachers that their children should be allowed to enter school before the official entrance age.

In the second place time should be taken to explain fully the policy or regulation and its purpose.

No matter how adequate its equipment, modern its buildings, or complete its instructional program, a school system cannot be more effective than its public relations program and its services to the community. Teachers who accept the supplying of information as a normal service to the community win respect for the schools and the profession. Through a gracious acceptance of this responsibility they help the community understand that teaching is not an eight hour a day job.

HANDLING COMPLAINTS

School personnel who are called upon to handle complaints need to learn the gentle art of listening while people purge themselves of the problems which weigh upon them. Anger, fear, or resentment growing out of a feeling that a child has been mistreated builds up within the individual until finally release must be provided. An understanding of the effectiveness of a sympathetic and attentive listener under these circumstances is most important.

Complaints and criticisms usually should be allowed to flow freely. Experience has taught many superintendents and principals the effectiveness of listening without comment. When the relaxation which follows severe tension under such circumstances is attained, it often is advisable to explain that the matter will be investigated and that the person will be called upon for assistance if necessary.

When handled in this manner, most complaints seem to lose their seriousness and quite frequently the parent, lay citizen, or teacher who came to see that justice is done will request that an investigation not be made if it will embarrass the wrong person. The reason for bringing the matter to the attention of the school official, it is pointed out, was not to get the person in trouble, but rather to be sure that the official had all the facts.

To argue or to defend unnecessarily the person who has

caused the trouble during the early stages of emotional outbreak or even after the catharsis is completed often will only increase the irritation. Such defense may precipitate a letter to the paper, a letter to the board of education, or a public complaint. To defend the person, other than in a strictly professional manner, also can have the effect of alienating the listener thus making further discussion more difficult. After an interval of a few days, a telephone call to the person who registered the complaint often will result in a request that the whole affair be forgotten.

The educator who is sensitive to the power of good public relations will not forget the matter, but will try to determine the cause of the complaint. Perhaps a teacher has made a mistake and needs help or guidance. Or it may be a child needs the assistance of a school social worker. In either case the complaint should not be handled simply by using the effective art of sympathetic listening since there is the possibility of a recurrence of the problem. This could result in public opinion that the administrator or teacher is a person who cannot be trusted or perhaps is a person who only listens but never acts.

It is important that the art of listening not be considered the panacea for all criticisms. Some complaints signal the need for medical or psychiatric consultation which the administrator should not attempt to provide under any circumstance.

School systems throughout the nation are beginning to employ trained school social workers. Superintendents, principals, and teachers who have this resource available for handling certain types of complaints are most fortunate indeed. It is a comforting feeling to be able to say to a disturbed patron, "We will have Mr. Jones, the school social worker, look into this matter," knowing that Mr. Jones will use approved techniques and also that he has the resources of the community at his disposal.

School personnel and especially those in administrative positions must learn to analyze criticisms and complaints on a strictly objective basis. Better public relations and an improved educational program usually are noted when appropriate steps are taken to adjust a bad situation identified by public criticism. Unjustified criticisms and complaints should be handled in a dignified and professional manner. A sincere belief that the schools belong to the people leaves no other course of action.

The best safeguard against criticisms and complaints is a dynamic program of instruction emphasizing services to the community administered by educators who treat the people as members of the team and keep them informed through attractive and understandable publications.

COMMUNITY USE OF SCHOOL PLANT, FACILITIES, AND EQUIPMENT

One of the most tangible methods of emphasizing services is through community use of the school plant, facilities, and equipment. There are many ramifications of this service, and there are many different practices in the country. The superintendent and professional staff must be guided in the handling of requests for the use of school facilities by a carefully thought-out board policy supplemented by detailed and easily understood written administrative regulations. The policy and regulations should be under continuous study to assure that they reflect the thinking of the community and the staff.

At first glance this may appear to be a simple matter, but such is not usually the case. In some communities, school buildings and facilities are available to all groups without charge. If this is the policy, care should be exercised in its administration to create appreciation for the schools and an acceptance of them as an important part of the community which the people naturally expect to support financially.

Some communities have found it easier to administer a policy which provides a set fee for the use of each building or part thereof. Sometimes the fee covers all costs plus an additional amount for upkeep, and in other cases it is a token amount. The practice of charging for the use of school buildings usually discourages their use by individuals or groups to which otherwise it may be necessary to refuse permission.

Community use of school plants frequently is limited to non-profit organizations or activities such as symphonies, Audubon Societies, and so on. The administration of such a policy requires that the schools pass judgment on the various organizations, which sometimes leads to misunderstandings and criticisms. This type of policy is required in communities with municipal auditoriums or other buildings which are supported mainly by the income from their use. School facilities usually are more in demand because of the lower rental charge. Under these circumstances good relations with those responsible for administering the municipal facilities are important.

The use of instructional materials, such as audio-visual, school shop, and homemaking equipment by the public also can become an important service to the community. Citizens generally approve of the increased emphasis on audio-visual aids and also recognize the need for instruction in the fields of industrial arts and homemaking. However, the expensive equipment required sometimes results in references to these items as fads and frills. The public soon learns of the importance of these materials to the learning experience of children when first-hand experiences are provided.

The board's policy and the administrative regulations on the community use of schools, therefore, should include a section on the use of instructional materials. Generally a teacher is in charge of such equipment and is on hand whenever a particular item is used by the community.

Although this discussion is not intended to serve as a guide for writing policies and administrative regulations on the community use of school facilities and equipment, it does suggest that these policies be written to emphasize positive public relations. Such policies often are helpful in setting the stage for an effective school-community relations program.

ADULT EDUCATION PROGRAMS

Adult education as a function of the public schools is a relatively new concept. Outstanding exceptions may be noted, however, in Los Angeles, San Francisco, New York, Philadelphia, Baltimore, and Miami where adult schools rival the regular schools in size and enrolment.

There are three interpretations of the purpose of adult education which are generally accepted by lay citizens and educators. In its broadest sense it includes all the experiences that help the adult who is no longer engaged in a formal school program acquire new attitudes, interests, knowledge, skills, understandings, and values. In this sense it encompasses those experiences in the life of the adult which represent learning.

Other people interpret adult education as embracing only organized self-improvement activities. This includes great book study groups, lecture series, evening courses in schools and universities, and so on.

Another meaning which has taken form during this generation considers adult education as a popular movement encompassing both concepts mentioned above. Its purpose is the improvement of the learning process, the expansion of learning opportunities, and the provision of cultural advancement.

To the reader who is alert to the many opportunities for improving public relations through services to the community, the possibilities of adult education should offer one of the greatest challenges. This popular movement has a great and promising future in the expanding role of education in our culture.

Adult education takes on added significance in view of the developing emphasis on universal education which moves schooling out in all directions to include both the younger or preschool children and the older or post-school groups. In place of the generally accepted three levels of public education—elementary, secondary, and college—universal education involves five levels beginning with the nursery program and ending with adult education.

The challenging feature of this evolving broader concept of education is the realization that the adult program will reach almost twice as many persons as the present three levels. Numbers alone are significant, but more significant is the fact that many of these are the people who are directly responsible for our government. The public relations possibilities of this development beggar description.

From the point of view of the curriculum, it is thought that vocational and recreational training activities should be a part of an over-all adult education program, but they will become less important by comparison than more formal programs of learning.

COURTESY PUBLIC SCHOOLS, CHATTANOOGA, TENNESSEE.

To have its fullest public relations impact, education for adults must be functional.

To have its fullest public relations impact, education for adults must be functional. This, of necessity, requires a philosophy of administration that recognizes the need for closer school-community cooperation in planning, goal setting, and evaluating. With liberal education and education for better citizenship taking on added importance in the adult education field, it is only natural to assume the adult citizens who benefit directly from this program will become deeply concerned with the welfare of the schools at all levels. Their influence will be strongly felt in the areas of financing and policy making.

The need for new concepts of administrative philosophy to meet the challenge of providing functional adult education opportunities is obvious. Not only do these concepts represent a challenge as a new area of education, but they also will have a far-reaching influence on the conventional school program. It will be necessary to re-study objectives and methods at all levels when adult education adds the ingredients to the school program that make formal education a life-long process. A number of new concepts will evolve, one of which conceivably could be the early planning of a life-long program of formal learning activities. The designing of school buildings and facilities for these activities will offer many new challenges.

A better, more comprehensive, and more sensitive public relations program to achieve the goal of universal education is one of the greatest needs facing education today.

SPECIAL PROGRAMS FOR ELDERLY PEOPLE

Sixty plus is no longer a signal for adult citizens to be taken off the school rolls. At ninety-eight Grandma Moses continues to paint pictures and hob-nob with presidents. Frequently older adults are not enthusiastic supporters of public education because they have not been inside a classroom for twenty or more years. If schools lose touch with these citizens, they often become suspicious of the modern curriculum which, according to them, neglects the three R's.

Administrators who are sensitive to the importance of public relations cannot overlook the need for establishing special programs catering to the hobbies and secret ambitions of senior citizens. Many persons after living for years with an unrealized ambition to work with tools, to master the fundamentals of radio and TV repairing, or to discover the fascination that Grandma Moses finds in art finally have the time to indulge.

Programs must not be restricted to the evening school, for many senior citizens prefer to pursue their hobbies or more formal educational activities during the day. Such programs have the added advantage of placing the adult in close contact with the regular school programs, particularly if carried out in the same or an adjoining building. Alarm over what modern schools are doing to children often changes to public statements of support as these citizens become personally involved in a special program for elderly people. Such programs are valuable also because they provide opportunities for these citizens to learn to know teachers and administrators as people and to see first hand that they are devoted to the education of our youth.

Programs for older adults can be initiated on the proverbial shoestring. The school system furnishes the buildings, facilities, and coordinating personnel and the program is under way. Instructors are available in the ranks of the adults. School buildings become an investment producing increased dividends when they serve all age groups, and bond issues are more meaningful and better supported.

As the miracles of modern medicine continue, the senior citizen will become an increasingly important political and economic force in the community. It is estimated that adults over sixty-five will represent ten percent of the total population within the next twenty-five years. Since children under voting age constitute a large portion of the population, the voting potential of the older adult group takes on added significance.

The trend in the future undoubtedly will be toward day-time programs for older citizens who, although retired from business and industy, are active in mind and body. The wise school leader recognizes that grandpa and grandma have wisdom to be tapped, skill to pass on, prestige to offer, and time on their hands.

GRANDMA AND GRANDPA AND THE REGULAR SCHOOL PROGRAM

Here are several ideas, some of which are adapted from *Public*

Relations Gold Mine,[2] for making grandma and grandpa feel they are a part of the regular school community through friendly gestures, personal invitations, and opportunities for service.

In one community, student clubs meet after school hours in the homes of the older folks who have well-equipped shops or kitchens or interesting hobbies. Some of the citizens go to schools to help out.

The Lake Charles (Louisiana) Teachers Association recognized that grandparents were being overlooked and planned "Horace Mann Day" for older folks. Children sent written invitations, and the grandparents were greeted by students who escorted them to classrooms and then invited them to a friendly cup of coffee. Pleased as punch, grandparents soon were buzzing among themselves about the many changes since the Golden Rule days. They noted approvingly the relaxed manner of the teachers and the fine modern teaching aids.

In one school an old matron never before connected with or interested in school doings became one of the most popular acts on the Halloween carnival night midway. Her palm reading and fortune telling won a new friend for the school.

The Chattanooga High School (Tennessee) graduating exercise features all the living members of the class which graduated *fifty* years previously. The honored guests are introduced during the commencement activities, but the most thrilling experience is that of being asked by the members of the graduating class for their autographs.

School systems should not forget the retired teachers and former school board members. One city superintendent received a number of heart-warming letters when he sent a copy of the annual report to 750 retired teachers with this note: "With your many years of service to the children of our schools, I thought you would be exceptionally interested in this report."

One board of education presents publicly a certificate of ap-

---

[2] *Public Relations Gold Mine* (Washington, D.C.: The National School Public Relations Association, N.E.A., 1957), pp. 25–28.

preciation to all retiring teachers. This is done at a regular board meeting which is open to the public and the press.

Opportunities to recognize senior citizens and to provide school experiences for them are limitless as are the public relations values that result therefrom. Not to be overlooked are the possibilities inherent in taking adult programs to the community via television.

TWELVE-MONTHS SCHOOL

Good school-community relations result from many kinds of activities, varying widely in scope, complexity, intensity, and timing. Research has shown that the quality of a school program can be judged from the number of contacts the school has with the community as well as from the effectiveness of the staff or other similar factors. The twelve-months school is another service which increases these contacts. Reference is made to the year-round use of buildings for school-related activities rather than to the four-quarter plan of school organization.

Before Russia placed its Sputnik in orbit, a superintendent in a large midwestern city conceived of a simple technique for enriching the teaching of high school science. Announcement that the science laboratories would be open each Saturday brought out a profusion of complimentary newspaper editorials as well as many potential scientists. Not to be overlooked is the deterrent effect such programs have on delinquency and the importance of the extra pay for teachers who often are tempted to move into more lucrative fields.

A school building, except for minor replacement items, will last as long when used fifty-two weeks a year as under the conventional nine- or ten-months school term. School facilities are easily adapted to continuous use and many teachers welcome year-round employment. The twelve-months use of school facilities has public relations value because it appears to the taxpaying public as a much better return on an investment.

Teachers have special assignments during the summer months

such as recreation directors, instructors of special summer classes, college or university attendance, local curriculum work shops, and approved travel. The last three activities will not be expanded upon other than to suggest that their public relations value lies largely in the fact that they contribute to the general improvement of instruction.

The need for a summer recreation program has long been recognized. In many large communities a separate recreation department in the city government administers the summer program as well as a year-round evening program for youths and adults—and frequently employing teachers during summer months.

Since child growth is an integrated process, instructional and recreational services cannot easily be separated with responsibilities divided between two agencies. This is particularly confusing because a portion of each school day involves instruction in physical education including recreation activities. It, therefore, generally is considered advisable to include community recreational activities as a part of the over-all school program. The twelve-months school is a convenient vehicle for making the transition in communities without organized summer recreation activities.

One of the important outcomes is the contribution such a program can make to an understanding of the importance of physical education on the part of the teachers and a desire to provide more adequate physical education programs during the school year.

Special summer classes can be held for a number of reasons, all of which have public appeal. These include enrichment, advanced classes for gifted children, make-up classes, special subjects which students cannot take during the school year, and classes for extra credit either for college entrance or in some cases just because children enjoy school and want to continue during the summer months.

Consideration also should be given the use of art, homemaking, general shop, and science facilities in the summer. This is an ideal time, for example, for boys to do some work in the homemaking laboratory and for girls to spend a few weeks in the general shop.

In the elementary grades, alert teachers provide enrichment activities during the summer months, making it possible for children to do things which they have no opportunity to do during regular school months. The program is carefully planned with the teacher using the permanent records of the children to find areas of interest, hobbies, and abilities around which to build the summer program. Summer classes carried on to help children better prepare for the next year also become an effective service to the community as long as advanced skills are not taught.

The twelve-months school program designed to meet the needs of the community is a service which will win the plaudits of concerned parents. Even those who criticize the schools as being too costly or as having too many frills often realize that a school can meet the needs of all the children better on a twelve-months basis than in nine or ten months. This idea thus has its own built-in public relations value.

LIBRARY SERVICES

In communities with public libraries, superintendents of schools or other staff members often are invited to serve on the library board. Such membership should be encouraged. The needs for effective liaison between the schools and the library are many and varied.

Opportunities for public libraries to serve the community and the schools are numerous. These include special story hours on radio, TV, or in the library; bookmobiles; special film showings; and special book displays. Sometimes authors of children's books visit the town library to talk with the children.

A public library with a well-qualified librarian in charge of the children's section is a valuable resource for the schools. It is an ideal place for teachers to browse when they are compiling lists of classroom library books. Suggestions from the librarian are a real service to the teacher.

The schools also have certain responsibilities, the performance of which has important public relations implications. Children can be taught in school to use the public library in a way that will win community respect both for the library and for the schools. Library staff members can be invited to the schools to discuss the library services with faculty and student groups and to explain the method of signing out books. Special assignments requiring the use of the public library can be made in any class, particularly on the high school level. Schools which do not take advantage of the public library as an extension of the school library are overlooking a vital resource.

Not to be overlooked is the possibility of setting up regional public libraries in school buildings to reduce transportation problems. Library personnel in one city were invited to participate in the planning of a large new school some distance from the public library. A branch public library in the same building as the school library now serves the school as well as the community.

Cooperation between schools and the public library during Book Week and on other special occasions usually is mutually advantageous. Book displays and other appropriate exhibits are more complete and are available for viewing by more people as a result of cooperative planning.

But the picture is not always rosy and bright. Professional jealousies sometimes arise over difference in salaries. Occasionally friction develops as a result of the behavior of school children in the city library. The demand for books or services the public library is not equipped to provide sometimes leads to misunderstandings. These and other problems represent another area of public relations which calls for alert leadership on the part of the schools. The best defense against criticism is an active program involving cooperative planning, mutual understanding, realistic working agreements, and established limits of services. The formula evolved will be different for each community.

In communities which do not have public libraries, the school libraries can take on added significance for parents, community leaders, and citizens who feel the need for this type of service.

A school library can be opened in the evenings and on Saturdays and also during the summer to serve the community. Carefully thought-out rules and regulations are important to the success of this combined service function.

A special section of a school library might be set aside for use by parents. It would, naturally, contain books; pamphlets; and magazines on child growth and development, education, and family living.

Cooperation between a public library and the schools generates the type of services a community has a right to expect and when proper relationships exist, the schools and the library benefit from the increased community acceptance and support.

HAVING FUN TOGETHER

When people have fun together, many strange and wonderful things happen—tensions are released, formality becomes informality, titles become unnecessary, stuffed shirts lose their stuffiness, strangers become friends, and sometimes those who criticize see the schools in a different and more favorable light. The various types of activities in which lay people and teachers engage during the school year become more meaningful and easier to accomplish for those who have joined hands together in fun and recreation.

The methods by which lay citizens and teachers have fun together are so diverse that it is possible to bring practically everyone into the act. This section contains examples of activities which schools can sponsor as part of a program to emphasize services. Some of these have been adapted from *Contact Plus*[3] which is a handbook of ideas for improving school-community relations.

ICE BREAKERS

For new teachers the first contact often is the most important meeting of the year. Many school systems have found ways of

[3] *Contact Plus* (Washington, D.C.: The National School Public Relations Association, N.E.A., 1954), pp. 29–34.

letting new staff members know they are appreciated from the start by bringing the public into the picture. Here are two sample ice breakers to get new teachers into the swim by helping them see their colleagues, parents, and pupils in a different and very favorable light.

An Apple for the New Teacher and a rhythmic ditty entitled *PTA Welcomes You* were presented by a PTA Council president who greeted each new teacher at the September board meeting in one city. The teachers received a personal invitation from the superintendent to attend the meeting.

A Royal Welcome is given new staff members of the Tulsa, Oklahoma, schools during a four-day Welcome Teacher program. Highlighting the numerous events is a luncheon at which the teachers are guests of the Chamber of Commerce.

FAMILY FUN

Few buildings are better designed and equipped to accommodate a family fun night than are schools which have facilities for sports, dances, dinners, clubs, dramatics, and other forms of recreation. The investment of time on the part of the faculty and the investment for electricity, heat, and other building expenses are among the finest that can be made. Family fun nights generate interest and appreciation for schools, teachers, and the educational program.

Recreation Night in a small town was held weekly in the school gymnasium-auditorium. Community leaders, the principal, and the physical education teacher worked out the plans which included volleyball, kickball, and table tennis for the vigorously inclined and shuffleboard, cards, and checkers for the quiet ones. Square dancing brought each evening's activities to a close.

The Hobby Approach was used by one school system which provided a series of family night classes for the children and their parents. Under the direction of regular teachers both fathers and sons learned how to make and repair furniture.

Working together they built a ping-pong table for the school's recreation room. Mothers and daughters had classes in ceramics, dressmaking, knitting, and flower making. At the end of the semester the community was invited to see an exhibit of the completed projects.

COURTESY PUBLIC SCHOOLS, CHATTANOOGA, TENNESSEE.

Hobby night programs for adults generate interest in and appreciation of the school.

Arts, crafts, and hobby programs in schools occasionally are referred to as frills. Adults often change their minds after placing their hands in the clay, glue, tempera, shavings, or around a volleyball. One community alternates courses in cake decorating and hat making and has a full complement of parents all year long. Any such program which brings parents into the school either during the day or at night has inestimable public relations value.

THE SHOW IS THE THING

In their play-time activities, children give a large amount of time to make believe or acting. This interest continues into adulthood, and the school that capitalizes on it will benefit by an enriched public relations program. Usually it doesn't make any difference if the acting is good, fair, or poor as long as everyone has a good time. The show is important because it generates a feeling of good will, understanding, and appreciation.

Role Playing in the spirit of fun can build deeper appreciations among parents and teachers. In a rural community the parents and teachers got the idea that they could learn a great deal about each other and from each other by role playing. At a PTA meeting groups of parents and teachers put on skits to give impressions of each other. It proved to be an hilarious experience in which the rehearsals were almost as much fun as the final skit. This can be chaotic, however, if personal hostility colors the proceedings with ill will.

All the World's a Stage in one metropolitan community in which school auditoriums have become the little theaters for amateur theatrical groups. Rehearsals are scheduled during the day when the schools are not using the facilities and at night. Citizen groups with a full range of interest in the Thespian arts, including scenery making, assure well-equipped stages and stand ready to assist the schools in their productions.

There are dozens of ways school facilities can be used to bring teachers and the public together in relationships that are mutually advantageous. Even those who prefer to do the serious thinking often find it can be done better after a period of relaxation and recreation.

The ideas listed in this section on Having Fun Together are intended only to act as a catalytic agent. A school faculty which catches the spark and understands the importance of good public relations will generate all kinds of ideas to enrich this fellowship. In the end the children will benefit as well as the community from this emphasis on service.

ACCIDENTS AND ILLNESS

School personnel who desire to emphasize services must ever be alert to the concern of parents for the health and safety of their children. Criticisms sometimes are heard even where the best relations exist between the school and the community over colds children catch at school, accidents they have on the playground, and other misfortunes which occur during the day.

The first and foremost consideration of a school should be to prevent accidents and illness. Sympathetic assurance that a particular accident is covered by insurance does little to ease the first shock experienced by the mother or father of a child who has been injured at school. Prevention involves the construction of modern, easily cleaned and maintained buildings; the purchase of safe and dependable equipment; and the constant inspection and careful maintenance of buildings, sites, and equipment.

The responsibilities assumed by school personnel for the education of five or six hundred children almost stagger the imagination. Rules and regulations are necessary to control the movement of children inside and outside the building and also to control the movement of vehicles around the building. School personnel should use every opportunity—PTA meetings, bulletins, and conferences—to interpret the rules and regulations.

The planning of school facilities, including first-aid rooms, exits, drives, and parking lots, provides opportunities for the administrator to utilize the know-how and practical experience of parents, health department personnel, police, fire department personnel, and traffic engineers where available. The cooperation of the representatives of these agencies also should be sought when the building is placed in operation to help work out the ground rules to guard the health and safety of the children. The utilization of these individuals as speakers for PTA meetings and school assembly programs is another feather in the public relations cap.

But where there are thousands of school children there will

be accidents. Therefore, not only is it important to work out cooperatively the rules and regulations to protect the health and safety of children, but it is also necessary to involve the community in the development of procedures for dealing with illnesses and accidents.

At the top of the list of procedures in any school should be that of calling the parent in the case of a serious injury immediately after the nature of the injury has been ascertained and first aid has been rendered. It is important to take cognizance of the fact that some parents prefer a certain doctor and some even refuse to have a doctor. If a child must be taken to a hospital, it is best to do it with the consent of a parent who should take the child to the hospital himself, if possible, or at least should meet the child at the hospital.

The handling of illnesses, such as an upset stomach, at school also calls for established procedures. Although a child often needs only a short rest, it is necessary sometimes to take a child home. There are many homes, however, in which both the mother and father work, creating additional problems for the school. Information assembled at the beginning of the year on each child is valuable for guiding school personnel in such matters.

A basic knowledge of first aid also is important for school personnel. It is advisable to use only those first-aid supplies approved by the local medical association or the department of health, and teachers should be trained in their proper use.

The knowledge that school personnel are attempting to provide safe and healthful buildings and facilities and are taking every precaution to guard the health and safety of the children earns a rewarding community reaction and helps prevent widespread criticism when accidents happen.

Proper emphasis on health and safety as a service to the community has a two-pronged public relations value. Not only do people respond favorably to a school with a good safety record, which uses proper care in case of illness or accident, but public participation in the development of the rules and regulations responsible for this success wins additional friends for the school system.

SPECIAL SERVICES

The basic design of an educational program that provides meaningful learning experiences tailored to the needs of all the children is far broader than a textbook-centered course of study. Children with physical, mental, emotional, and social problems or handicaps, education leaders contend, should be treated first of all as children and secondly as children with a problem. The term used to define the various activities having to do with the education of those children who differ sufficiently from what is considered normal behavior to require specialized attention is *special education.*

Specialists in the special services field have evolved a philosophy which enhances the powerful public relations appeal inherent in any program for the handicapped. They point out that even the so-called normal children differ from one another to a large degree, and that handicapped boys and girls do not differ from normal as much as people previously thought. The outcome of this observation is an educational program which emphasizes the importance of training the child to use those capacities he possesses rather than to expect little of him.

A handicapped child's greatest need is happy parents who seek ways of helping him instead of blaming themselves and feeling resentful of the way fate has treated them. The educational process of working directly with parents to achieve an understanding and acceptance of the child is potentially one of the most popular services the schools can render.

It has been said that there is nothing as unequal as the equal treatment of unequals. A school system dedicated to a complete educational program will understand the full meaning of this statement. Special classes such as those for children with serious visual difficulties necessitate a per pupil expenditure two or three times the investment required for normal classes. The possibility of misunderstandings growing out of this disparity in operational costs challenges school personnel to interpret these specialized programs in a way that wins support not only for these classes, but for the total program as well. Civic clubs and other community groups are quick to recognize the value of a project in-

Special instruction for homebound children wins public approval.

volving assistance to some special education program such as a cerebral palsy class. Parents of boys and girls who benefit directly through home or hospital instruction, for example, are enthusiastic in their support of a school system which provides these special services.

One of the services impinges on many community organizations and agencies to a considerable extent. This is the work of the school social worker or visiting teacher who deals with children with serious emotional, social, or psychological problems and who also works directly with their parents. The investigation of the cause of such maladjustments calls for special abilities, skill in human relations, training, and understanding of home-school relations.

Children who are emotionally upset over a home situation, such as an impending separation, cannot be expected to live normal lives at school. Often a satisfactory solution to such problems requires a case conference involving the church, welfare agency, guidance clinic, if available, as well as school personnel. Increased respect and appreciation for the total school program is a by-product of such conferences out of which evolve effective solutions to serious problems.

In some cases school social workers find that a pair of shoes or a coat means a difference between a happy child in school and an embarrassed and unhappy child absent from school. Lay citizens who contribute items of clothing for such children gain a better understanding of the schools and a deeper appreciation for teachers.

Perhaps it is the characteristic of Americans to sympathize with the underdog—which gives rise to a quick understanding of the need for special educational facilities and classes. Schools which fail to meet the needs of boys and girls with unusual problems not only are neglecting their obligation to society, but also are failing to realize a large measure of public support which is readily available.

OTHER OPPORTUNITIES FOR SERVICE

Some additional services, the performance of which results in an enriched public relations program, are included in this section.

OBSERVANCE OF COMMUNITY EVENTS

The concept that the schools belong to the community sometimes results in school participation in community activities which have little or no educational value. Many people think of the school first in planning a parade, fair, or historical celebration because this represents a source of free entertainment which can be tapped with a minimum amount of individual or group effort.

Requests for the cooperation of the schools in the observation of community events should be carefully evaluated in terms of the contribution to the learning experiences of the children. Activities which have little or no educational value should not be permitted unless, of course, there are extenuating circumstances. People generally will understand and accept the school's position if a request cannot be granted—provided proper explanations are given. Do not forget, however, that there are teachers who can make almost any activity a learning experience.

It is advisable to have a policy statement on school participation in community events and a central clearinghouse for handling such requests. When participation has an educational value, everyone benefits and the schools move closer to the heart of the community.

CORRECT TELEPHONE LISTING

People are inclined to become irritated when they cannot locate a telephone number needed in a hurry or in an emergency. The absence of an alphabetized listing of schools in a telephone directory, though a small matter, can become a source of public concern and the basis for criticism. Schools should be listed separately by name and also listed as a group under the name of the school system.

AIDING PARENTS OF NEW CHILDREN

Children and parents who move from city to city usually learn the technique of making proper contacts and arrangements with respect to assignments to schools. In some cases, however, a change of residence becomes an almost insurmountable problem. The situation often is made more difficult if the previous school experience was a very pleasant one for the family.

Schools which have pupils freely moving in and out develop effective techniques for handling these details. This is advisable, though in no case should the parent feel that his child's enrolment in a school is just a routine matter. The parent and child should be escorted through the building and introduced to the teacher and the new classmates in a way that will leave the impression the school is glad to have them.

Some school systems have developed special materials designed to give newcomers a warm and friendly welcome. These include school directories, maps showing locations of schools and school zone lines, brief descriptions of the school philosophy and program, and other pertinent information. Realtor organizations and chambers of commerce often will give financial assistance for this type of project.

Many parents of new children have been members of the community for a number of years. The placing of a child in kindergarten or first grade, however, may be the first direct school contact, and, as such, it is of major importance for the parent and the school. A pleasant and effective relationship on this occasion usually creates a firm supporter of the public schools.

Distributing handbooks for parents of pre-school children is an excellent practice. Carefully planned meetings of these parents to discuss the school program, methods of conducting classes, and the philosophy of the school also are very important.

Opportunities for service are limited only by the vision of the school personnel and the imagination with which they are undertaken. The benefits derived therefrom are improved educational opportunities for the boys and girls, and more satisfying and profitable experiences for teachers.

BIBLIOGRAPHY

Contact Plus. Washington, D.C.: National School Public Relations Association, 1954. Describes the "extra something" that comes when school staffs and lay citizens think, play, discuss, study, and act together in behalf of better schools and better communities.

Effective Letters. New York: New York Life Insurance Company. An excellent portfolio of suggestions for making ourselves understood which are easy to adapt to school correspondence and publications.

Fine, Benjamin, "Better Public Relations With School Publications," *The Clearing House*, 31:515–517 (May, 1957). The basic discussion in this article concerns methods used to make school publications effective.

Kindred, Leslie W., *School Public Relations*. Englewood Cliffs, N.J.: Prentice-Hall, Inc., 1957, Parts III and V. Chapters 8 and 9 contain a number of references to services performed by schools. Part V deals effectively with the various media of communication which schools use in emphasizing services.

Knowles, Malcom S., "What Should You Know About Adult Education?" *The School Executive*, 77:19–21 (August, 1958). This article reviews the best current thinking on adult education and includes a challenging look into the future.

Public Relations for America's Schools. Washington, D.C.: The American Association of School Administrators. This book ". . . deals primarily with purposes, principles, relationships, and values" of public relations. However, Chapter 9 contains some practical suggestions on services in the areas of school plant, materials of instruction, pupil safety, the telephone, handling complaints, and special services.

Public Relations Gold Mine. Washington, D.C.: National School Public Relations Association, 1957. A collection of descriptions of actual public relations practices drawn from school systems throughout the country.

Stearns, Harry L., *Community Relations and the Public Schools*. Englewood Cliffs, N.J.: Prentice-Hall, Inc., 1955. Chapters 5, 6, and 12 contain valuable suggestions relative to services schools can perform as part of a public relations program.

15

As long as we have school systems, we will have critics
and criticism. Strange as it may seem, the content of
criticism seems to repeat itself every generation, and the
critics seem to follow general patterns which can be
identified over and over again. Variations are most likely
to be found in terms of intensity and number. Today
education in America faces the challenge of intense,
widespread criticism.

The purpose of this chapter is to offer insights into
and procedures for handling criticism. The aim is not
to eliminate it but to increase the effectiveness of the
persons designated to handle this aspect of public relations. Although stress is placed on techniques, it needs
to be emphasized that the personality of the school official in the situation is a crucial factor in determining
what will happen. The manner in which he works is as
important as what he does. It is fallacious to assume that
anyone can handle critics and that "common sense" is
all that is needed.

ROLE OF CRITICISM IN PUBLIC EDUCATION

Since the nature of criticism is usually unfavorable

or fault-finding, there is a tendency to overlook, discount, or suppress it. This is a mistake. Neglected criticism grows and becomes exaggerated. Criticism is inevitable and when used wisely, can be valuable to a school.

First of all, it can be used to measure unrest in the community. A sudden increase or decrease in phone calls and letters about school problems may be significant. This crude index usually measures community climate rather than the efficiency and effectiveness of the schools. A community with low morale will pick on its schools. Communities suffering from disorganizing influences such as unemployment, political upheaval, religious bickering or other negative factors often involve the schools in their problems. Periods of unrest are a poor time to sponsor bond elections or introduce innovations into the curriculum.

Criticism can also measure interest. When people want to help, they are often interested in the neglected and inadequate aspects of the school system. This type of criticism is well intentioned, though often unenlightened and vague. The critic in this type of situation is also different from other critics.

Critics sometimes tell us things that other people hesitate to mention. Constant involvement in a situation sometimes produces "blind spots" and educators are as subject to this difficulty as other people. Punctuality, for example, may become very important to a principal if he continually has troubles with it. He may have in mind other things that need attention but actually not be aware that they are being neglected. Sometimes only the frankness of a critic can motivate further evaluation and action. Instead of avoiding the critic, we should realize that his barbs and frankness can add perspective to the management of a school.

As long as there are human beings working in our school systems, there is a need for criticism and evaluation. The possibility that our mistakes will be subject to public discussion should keep schools dynamic, flexible, and subject to change. *However, to build school programs on the basis of anticipated criticism leads to frustration and very little positive action.* The role of criticism in education is to prompt and cue its leaders in doing their jobs. In no way should it be the dominant factor in determining policies and practices. Some criticism calls for change, while other criticism is a certain sign that the school program is sound and effective.

TYPES OF CRITICS

The art of meeting critics hinges on the capacity to identify the different types. The nature of the critic usually determines the nature of the criticism. Following are some general categories into which most critics can be classified. It must be remembered that these categories are general and that they do overlap. It should also be remembered that a particular critic may be reclassified as times and situations change.

One of the most bothersome of all critics is the *hostile* critic. This person is suffering from uncontrolled feelings of hostility. Instead of becoming upset or angry with the real cause of his feelings, he "takes it out" on the schools. Psychologists call such attacks misplaced hostility. Earmarks of the hostile critic are fairly uniform but vary in degree. Mrs. X may be temporarily upset with her neighbor and therefore call the school about the poor supervision at recess time. Mr. Y may have a five year old grudge against his boss. He probably feels that all principals are wasting the taxpayer's money.

The *hostile* critics can be identified by the following characteristics:

1. They are unduly emotional. These critics are not only angry, they are full of other emotions as well. They are irate, highly incensed, and easily insulted.
2. They are personal in their complaints. Complaints from this type are almost always in terms of personal happenings. They or their children have usually been insulted or neglected. They demand immediate action and punishment of the alleged offender. They and theirs, from their point of view, do nothing to cause problems.
3. They classify people by status. These people appeal to personal privileges. Because they live in a certain neighborhood, know the mayor or the board member, they feel they should have deferential treatment.

4. They have a deep sense of right and wrong. For these people there is only one *right* answer. They usually have the "right" answer before contacting the schools. Their thoughts and actions are rigid and allow for few exceptions.

5. They are suspicious by nature. Extremists of this type demand investigations. They suspect that the nation is going to the dogs and that there are subversives around every corner. The most radical of them pester police stations and the Federal Bureau of Investigation.

Less dramatic are the *uninformed* critics. However, in terms of numbers and influence, they are the most important. They, too, have identifiable characteristics.

1. They are indifferent. These people are usually uninterested in school programs and activities. Their visits to the schools are few. Unless someone talks about schools when they are around, they are not bothered by what is going on in the classroom.

2. They repeat criticism, don't create it. After they hear or read about the schools, they willingly repeat what they have heard or read—it is seldom that this type of critic has first-hand information.

3. They tend to be negative. Because other interests are more important to them, they are willing to believe criticism. If this criticism justifies their apathy or their position about taxes, they are likely to pay attention to what they hear or read.

4. They accept explanations and facts. Since they are not emotionally or intellectually committed to a point of view, they are responsive to facts and explanations that make sense to them.

Few, in number, are the *professional* critics. They are self-appointed, or work for particular organizations interested in low taxes or some particular brand of education. They are motivated by income from the organization, notoriety, and feelings of self-righteousness for saving education from "professional" educators. This type of person has some of the following characteristics:

1. They are intelligent and clever. These people could be of great help to education. It is unwise to underestimate their influence. Their supporters are usually few in number although their actual strength is difficult to determine because many of them are hidden behind some front organization.

2. They profess friendship and support of education. This group mingles with school people. Sometimes they are people who left the

teaching profession because of various dissatisfactions. They study education and can speak highly of it when it serves their personal purposes.

3. They sponsor organizations and resolutions. They seek strength and recognition through organized fronts. They have impressive letterheads and do considerable corresponding with newspapers and other groups.

Finally, there are a group who can be considered *enlightened* critics. They are friends of the school but avoid or reject any suggestion that they are rubber stamps for school officials. These critics can be identified as:

1. Friendly. These people have no axes to grind. They know many school people. They are proud of their associations in education.

2. Educated on school subjects. Facts and information are important to them. They criticize after studying a situation.

3. Specific. Criticism from this group is usually spelled out in detail. They ask questions more than they give answers. They know what they are talking about and expect to receive specific replies.

PRINCIPAL CRITICISMS

Criticism, too, needs to be classified. On one hand is the usual type of criticism to which any democratic institution is regularly subjected. Its purpose is to develop and improve. On the other hand, there are some generalized criticisms which have become nationwide. The validity of these criticisms has no relationship to their frequency.

Most broad in its allegation is the opinion that the whole American system of education is a mistake. Instead of accepting education as the right of every individual, critics are suggesting that the European system should be instituted in our educational philosophies and practices. These critics would be more selective in educating children. The brilliant groups would receive extra time, attention, and money. Whatever is left over would be distributed among the rest of the children.

Other critics charge that the quality of American education has been gradually deteriorating during the past thirty or forty years. Particular students are chosen as typical examples of our schools to show they can't read, write, spell or do arithmetic with any degree of proficiency. The conscientious, well-trained student seen every day by teachers is classified as an exception by these critics. When asked to be more specific in their criticism, one of their common rebuttals is that American schools are neglecting the intellectual side of education. In other words, education is producing too few intellectual competents. The much publicized courses in fishing or social dancing are cited as typical courses, rather than as the exceptions they are. In this same category is the contention that high schools are failing to train specialists to live in this specialized world.

At the same time, another group is demanding that more time be given to "practical living." There is pressure on schools to give student driver education, more physical education, marriage education, and more vocational education.

Criticism is not always directed toward the curriculum or the school graduates. A constant series of complaints is being registered against the professional educators. They are accused of being concerned only with the methodology of teaching. According to some, professional educators depreciate mastery of a subject or the emphasis on liberal arts education. Charges are made that they are an idealistic group of people who know how to talk but are not very practical.

There are other criticisms, but the above are current and are being voiced nationwide. The stresses of another crisis or the interests of another influential writer may vary the emphasis in the future, but variations will probably be based on the above basic charges.

WHERE DO YOU FIND CRITICISM?

Don't wait for criticism to find its way to the school office. Seek it out by having constant contact with its sources. Responsible staff members of the school or the school district should be assigned to check criticism that stems from different sources.

The criticism most difficult to reach and to handle is the gossip that takes place during face-to-face contacts at the bridge club, over the backyard fence, and other similar settings. This is hard to handle because it is difficult to pin down. Its form and content vary with each telling. Nevertheless, organized effort to know what is being said should be made.

Speakers are another source of criticism. Convention speakers, after dinner speakers, club panels, and impromptu remarks are popular means of carrying messages about the schools. As opinion molders, these sources of information and influence rank high. Most of what is spoken becomes hearsay and gossip, and some of it makes newspaper headlines.

Most educators pay attention to what the newspapers are saying. Headlines and news stories, editorials and special features are often the topic of conversation when they meet. Special attention needs to be given headlines. Often the average reader does not read beyond them. Misleading headlines may not give the same information as the story which follows.

Although a part of the newspaper, letters-to-the-editor deserve special consideration as a source of criticism. They represent a broad section of a community. At one extreme are letters by professional cranks who write to see their own opinions in print. At the other extreme are conscientious writers who wish to further useful programs and ideas. These letters help give a crude measure of the atmosphere within the community.

Although newspapers are not likely to be overlooked as a source of criticism, a lack of regular and constant attention to them may lead to biased evaluations of what they are reporting. Methodical attention to newspapers is a part of a sound public relations program.

Less important, but not to be neglected, are the articles in magazines and pamphlets. Most of this material will be national in nature, but the contents can be and will be used by local critics. Familiarity with the contents of these publications is essential. Subscriptions to them should represent a wide variety of opinion. When the budget limits the number of subscriptions, teachers and other interested people may be willing to donate their magazines for perusal. There are many opportunities to be included on mailing lists where no cost is involved. These should never be neglected. The temptation to read and peruse only favorable materials must be resisted if all sources of criticism are to be used.

Personal criticisms take the forms of letters, personal notes to teachers and principals, phone calls and visits. These criticisms are usually thrust upon the school. However, a hostile reaction to them may limit their number. Whenever this is the case, criticism can become intense and determined, which in turn increases the difficulties in dealing with it. Also, the stifling of criticism might create the illusion of well-being when serious problems are in the making.

Whatever the source of criticism, it should be consistently recognized, tabulated, and evaluated. Sensitivity to criticism does not imply that there should be a general invitation to the public to seek out practices and procedures of which they do not approve in the schools. Only under special circumstances, such as at times of evaluation, does a public relations program encourage people to view schools critically. This can be done through advisory groups or school-community relations councils. The name is not too important as long as it designates its nature. Membership should consist of both educators and lay people. When such groups are organized and their purposes clearly stated, much potential criticism can be converted into constructive suggestions. Whether a group is temporary or permanent will depend on the nature of the goals desired. If it is permanent, a rotating membership is usually best. Another safeguard for the successful functioning of such groups is a wide representation of the different segments within the community.

An example of a successful solicitation of criticism took place in one district during the Johnny-can't-read period. A few vocal citizens had aroused the community about phonics. To meet the criticism, a citizen-educator group of fifty people was organized.

This group was informed in detail about the reading program. They also studied all the educational purposes of the district.

The second phase of the project was to have the committee inform the community of the actual school program and seek critical reaction to it. The committee constructed a questionnaire to measure the reaction. Ten copies were taken by each committee member to distribute to friends. A scientific polling was also conducted by the school officials. The results of the two polls were similar.

The conclusion of the study indicated that over eighty per cent of the community approved of the school program when they understood it. The results made the headlines and editorial pages of the newspapers. Parents and patrons were pleased to know what the schools were doing. They were pleased to make suggestions. The schools followed through on the suggestions. The projects dissipated severe criticism, won friends for the schools, and spurred the schools in their efforts to improve a few neglected areas.

WHAT CAN BE ACCOMPLISHED?

An opportunity to meet the critic should seldom be refused. Before each meeting, however, we need to have some general idea of what broad goals might be achieved. Ideally, we would hope that he will listen to our explanation and agree with us. Actually, it is unlikely that he will agree or listen very long.

Conversion to our point of view seems to be a worthwhile goal in public relations, but practically speaking, it is too often an impossible one. As long as a person has an opinion, it will be different from the next person's. Conversion implies very often that the other point of view is wrong or valueless. Such an implication is not likely to win friends or influence the critics. This is particularly true with the hostile critic whose very criticism develops out of insecurity and confusion. The more he is attacked, directly or indirectly, the more he will defend his position.

The school representative will find the creation of understanding a goal with many more possibilities. Understanding is based upon facts and explanations. This type of approach should bring favorable responses from many, particularly the uninformed critic. It can also make the professional critic use care in what he has to say. Critics who comprehend will usually support a well organized, purposeful program. They may say that if they were responsible for a program, it would be somewhat different. However, these critics do not want such responsibility and would rather just accept the school's programs, providing they understand what is happening in the classroom.

Many of the hostile critics lack the emotional stability or capacity to understand, whereas special interests of some professional critics color their understanding. Goals in such instances must be more limited. In contacts with such critics, we have opportunity for developing a sense of respect for educators and educational programs. No matter how prejudiced or upset emotionally a person may be, he is capable of recognizing understanding, consideration, and capacity to study a situation. He can also realize when an educator is well informed on the situation and has facts to justify his conclusions. All this should be accomplished without the hope or expectation of being deferred to. This attitude is an impediment to successful communication.

The greatest gain from facing critics is the development of understanding—not necessarily conversion. A more limited but sometimes the only practical goal is that of developing respect. If understanding and respect are achieved, there is every reason to believe that better support of the schools will follow.

FACING A CRITIC

All critics should have at least one interview with a designated school representative. There will be two general types of interviews. One will be with people who seek out a school representative. The other will be with people who are asked for a conference because of their statements or articles about the school.

When someone asks to speak with a school representative, the representative's main task during the first interview is to listen and to ask questions. He should get a detailed description of the complaints and find out what happened as understood by the complainant. When did it happen? Who was involved?

If criticism centers around policy and practices, find out what the person knows about school policies. Seek the source of his information. While this questioning is taking place, try to get some insights into his motivation. A word of caution is in order: don't assume the role of district attorney. Remember this person is not on trial. Questions which ask for further enlightenment and specific examples are least likely to offend.

It is helpful to know if the critic is speaking for himself, his family, his neighborhood, an organized group, or if he is there to repeat random comments he picked up in the barber shop. It also helps to know if the criticism is local or part of a national reaction. Is it chronic or the result of a particular situation? Is it hearsay or factual? Getting details about the critic and the criticism in the first interview is more important than giving answers.

Whether or not explanations should be given during the first interview is a matter of judgment. There is considerable satisfaction in receiving immediate answers, and time may be saved. On the other hand, some people call just to complain and are satisfied after doing so. Explanations only upset them further. An advantage of a second interview is that it allows time for feelings to settle and new perspectives to develop. The situation might correct itself in the meantime.

The temptation to defend the schools or their representative should be avoided while one is listening to complaints. This may be difficult, particularly when the attack seems unjustified. It should be remembered that defense often implies some degree of guilt and that there is no reason to assume such a position. Furthermore, defensiveness sometimes handicaps a person in his efforts to develop understanding, respect, and support.

The stronger the disagreement, the more important it is that the communication be honest and effective. Don't assume that the other person is understanding what you say or write. Ask him occasionally to check his understanding against yours. Likewise, be sure you understand what *he* is trying to communicate. Listen to everything he says before you begin to formulate your answer or question.

Preparation should be made for the second interview, which may be a public meeting or some other means of communication. Tentative goals should be outlined, then the appropriate techniques should be chosen. Facts, explanations, and clarifications organized around the criticism should be assembled.

If the meeting is a personal interview, the critic should be invited to the school office. Home visits are to be discouraged because of the potential distractions in the home. The visitor should first be given an opportunity to revise his story or to state his new conclusion. Time, as indicated, may have erased his complaint or he may have been satisfied after telling his story. If such is the case, the school representative can thank the complainant for his interest in the school and tell him that his interests and services will be useful to the schools in the future.

If the critic is not satisfied, the conference should proceed. The essence of the conference should be communication, so that some form of understanding may be reached. The school representative need no longer assume a passive role.

When the critic is sought out for purposes of clarification or rebuttal, the conference should be conducted differently. A policy of friendly and constant contact with critics will make such approaches easy. Informality and friendliness can be positive factors in the situation. On the other hand, if the critic is a stranger, adequate introductions should be made. Don't assume that because of your position you are known. After meeting, state the case as you understand it. Then ask the critic if your understanding is correct. Discussions are useless unless both parties are discussing the same thing. Accept what modifications he may offer.

In presenting the school story, be mindful of the time involved. Long interviews may defeat your purpose. Emphasize your points but avoid repeating them. Assume that the critic is capable of asking for clarification if he doesn't understand what you are presenting. Remember that, in any interview, it is necessary to extend to the person what you are seeking from him. That is, if you want understanding from him, show understanding of his ideas. If you disagree, either at the beginning or at the end, you should still show respect for his point of view. The more you disagree, the more important it is to maintain further contact.

FOCUSING THE ANSWER

Personal attention to a critic calls for answers tailored to his particular needs. Clichés and generalized explanations repeated over and over again may temporarily satisfy many critics but they do very little to build genuine understanding and support for the schools. To help focus answers, the following suggestions are offered:

1. Measure the cultural and intellectual background of your critic. It is better to overestimate his intelligence and training than to underestimate them. However, errors in either direction should be avoided. We need to remember that a growing percentage of school patrons are college graduates. Although they may not know too much about the professional aspects of education, they are well read and motivated to learn. This is particularly true of both the uninformed and enlightened critics.

2. Evaluate the emotional climate when the complaint is made. Hostile critics are not seeking answers—they want to release tensions. Appeals to reason are not likely to succeed—at least in the beginning. Understanding through listening and patience are usually good antidotes to emotion. You can give them reasonable answers later.

3. Make use of personal interests and needs. People will try to understand what concerns them. Application of this truism will do much to focus your answers. Members of the Chamber of Commerce, for example, will be more interested in comparative costs, vocational education, and productivity. Members of the League of Women Voters will be more interested in classroom activities, school supplies, and philosophies.

There is no reason to believe, however, that other interests cannot be developed in people or that such interests do not already exist. Eventually, the public can learn to think in terms of school needs.

4. Include illustrations and examples in your answers. People tend to think in concrete terms. A person is not likely to think philosophically when playing the role of critic.

5. Avoid side issues and exceptions. Admittedly, education is complex and interrelated. However, we are faced with the challenge of giving simple answers. Side issues and exceptions only complicate matters when we are trying to create understanding.

6. Don't give the history and background of problems unless requested. As interesting as the total story is to you, it can't be assumed that other people will want to listen to the details. Keep your focus on the problems or criticisms expressed by the critic.

7. Avoid long answers; they can create hostility and destroy interest. The fact that educators have been accused of being "long winded" should invoke cautiousness.

8. Avoid professional jargon. Even if it is understood its effectiveness is limited.

The attempt to use the other person's language should never lead to distortion of the facts. The stronger the disagreement, the more important it is that the communication be honest and effective. Don't assume the other person is understanding what you say or write. Likewise, be sure you understand what he is trying to communicate. Listen to everything he says before you begin to formulate your answer or question.

CREATING RESPONSIBILITY

Responsibility is often an antidote to criticism. People should be held accountable for what they say or write. When possible, they should also be involved in responsible action when it is taken. Anonymous phone calls or documents are useful as clues of thinking and feeling, but they should not be recognized as cause for action and judgment. Publicly stated school policy which requires personal identification of a critic will eliminate a considerable amount of petty and malicious annoyance. However, a policy of identification does not eliminate receiving confidential information. There are reasons why a particular statement shouldn't be identified at a particular time, but one should be cautious in promising to keep a confidence. A school official should not have his hands tied before he knows the nature of the commitment. He is the one to decide when the confidence is to be given.

Another means of creating responsibilty is to offer a person an opportunity to find some of the answers himself. This can be done through individual research or observation, or as a member of a committee.

WINNING OVER THE CRITICS

Your answer to a critic may satisfy him and the case be considered closed. However, a dynamic public relations program does not stop at this point. Many critics can become friends and supporters of the schools. Criticism should be the beginning of the relationship, not the end. This is particularly true for the uninformed critic and the friendly critic.

After the final interview, there is need for follow-up work— a phone call, a letter or a personal visit to ask if everything is still in order. There might also be opportunity to tell him how the school has offered time and effort to resolve his complaint. Let him know his interest in the schools is important.

A file of critics' names should be kept. These people can be used on committees. They can be called upon to answer questionnaires. Send them invitations to dedications and other special events. And remember that they can serve as barometers of opinion in their particular segment of the community.

PUBLIC MEETINGS

Using public meetings to face and answer criticism is full of dangers. The emotional impact of mass psychology is constantly present. To be sure, the group might stampede the meeting in favor of the school but even if this happens, such support is temporary and not substantial.

The attraction that public meetings hold for crackpots always opens up the possibility of useless talk and wasted time. Unless meetings are carefully organized, there is no way to control these purposeless speakers. If they are controlled, you run the danger of being accused of "railroading" the meeting.

Prestige and vanity also become involved in public meetings. Sometimes useless and undesirable commitments are made in public. Because they are made publicly, it becomes more difficult to persuade people to change their evaluations and opinions.

Such meetings should seldom be decision-making, and therefore are likely to be disappointing to some of the audience. They can also be very dull.

This does not mean they are not useful. Public meetings can be constructive if they are called and designed for specific purposes. A meeting organized to clarify issues and impart information can be productive. The basic requirements are good speakers, effective visual aids, and prepared speeches. People can also be brought together for purposes of debate. In such instances, respected and reasonable leaders should be invited to present the issues. Questions from the floor should be written.

Another technique is the small group discussion method. Issues can be presented in a general meeting and then discussed in small groups by trained leaders. After discussion, summaries are prepared to be given to the whole group and to interested citizens.

In rare instances, where feelings are particularly intense and widespread, meetings can be called just to "blow off steam." When this is done, there should be little attempt to develop understanding or make decisions. About all that can be hoped for is order. This type of meeting may clear the air, but there is also the risk that feelings will become more intense.

MINIMIZING CRITICISM

Although criticism cannot be avoided, it can be minimized. Because schools are handy targets for misplaced hostility, a part of a public relations program should be devoted to the development of skills and policies that prevent such attacks. Following are some suggestions for avoiding criticism.

Never ask for advice unless you are able to use it. There are a number of reasons for this policy. First of all, people usually guard their own opinions. They want approval of them. To be invited to offer an opinion and have it completely rejected creates a defensiveness in a person that often is expressed negatively toward the person who requested it. In the second place, if it is really approval you want, instead of advice, the intelligent person can distinguish the difference. It is an insult to him for you to use subterfuge to gain his approval. In one situation, for example, it was necessary to transport students by bus to a distant school because of overcrowding. To ask the parents' opinion as to how this problem should be solved would only have invited trouble because there was only one answer, and school officials could best organize and execute it. Parents should be and were told what would happen and why it was necessary.

On the other hand, when advice is needed and can be used, there is no more effective way of gaining support than to ask for it. In this way, a program or an idea becomes community property and will be accepted and promoted. Such an instance took place when a school district found it necessary either to transport students by bus or organize schools on double sessions. Although the school people preferred double sessions, the use of another school requiring bus transportation was a reasonable possibility. The parents were invited to make the choice and their wishes were carried out. The good will and support thus created carried over into many other activities.

Avoid telling "half truths." Even though the complete story is not always favorable, it is better to give all the facts. By doing so, you show the school position is one of strength—a strong program can afford to expose its weaknesses. This policy also avoids the danger of a hostile critic "revealing" something to the community. Such "exposés" are embarrassing and sometimes even damaging. The public should never be led to feel that the school officials don't trust them. Usually it is better to let all the facts of a situation be available and risk criticism than to try to conceal unfavorable facts—only to have them become known later on. As long as the schools are public, the public will want to know the entire story.

Seek support in advance. People criticize for not being told as well as for not understanding. The critic's sting can sometimes be blunted or dispelled by having the school supporter prepared to face him.

Be consistent. It is usually best to have one person make all important policy announcements. Other statements and clarifications should refer back to the official announcement. Written releases always serve as a record in case of misquotations or misunderstandings. A briefing of the employees will help avoid conflicting reports. Besides their public relations value, staff briefings also contribute to good morale.

TEAMWORK NEEDED

Although the responsibility of meeting the critic is delegated to particular individuals, the ultimate success of any program depends upon the entire personnel of a school or a school district.

Complaints will be made to everyone. The best thing on this level is for the person who receives the complaint to evaluate and then to deal with those that can be settled immediately. The others should be referred to the central office. The same principles of understanding and listening are applicable whether you resolve the complaint or refer it. Criticism resolved on the spot should be summarized periodically and reported to the responsible department. Only if this is done, can a systematic study of the community be made.

In return, the central office staff should report back to the teacher or person making the referral. If the criticism is received by someone in the central office, it is important for morale and teamwork that any individuals involved be informed. When advisable, the critic should be referred to the individual involved. Occasionally, a summary of this aspect of public relations should be given to the entire staff.

Public relations leaders within the school should constantly advise the staff of positive ways of working with critics and alert them to effective public relations techniques. In other words, effective communication on all levels is the key to teamwork in facing criticism.

BIBLIOGRAPHY

Berrien, F. K., *Comments and Cases on Human Relations*. New York: Harper & Brothers, 1951, Chap. 4. Cases and discussion on human motivation.

Caswell, Hollis L., *The Attack on American Schools*. New York: Teachers College, Columbia University, 1958. A good summary of the criticism of the American schools. Also answers to the criticism.

Cornell, Francis G., "Socially Perceptive Administration," *Phi Delta Kappan*, 46:219–223 (March, 1953).

"Earmarks of a 'Front' Organization," *Nations Schools*, 47:29–30 (April, 1951). Useful in identifying the silent critics.

Griffith, Daniel E., *Human Relations in School Administration*. New York: Appleton-Century-Crofts, Inc., 1956. This book is concerned with behavior of people in the social institution known as the public school. Part 1 is particularly useful in meeting critics.

Johnson, Wendell, "Do You Know How to Listen?" *A Review of General Semantics*, 7:3–9 (Fall, 1949). Comments on the techniques of listening.

Kindred, Leslie W., *School Public Relations*. Englewood Cliffs, N.J.: Prentice-Hall, Inc., 1957. This book charts a course of action in public relations that is both practical and consistent with the role of the school as a social institution in a democracy. Chapter 9 deals specifically with handling complaints.

Public Relations For America's Schools, Twenty-eighth Yearbook, American Association of School Administrators, 1950. A basic pioneering book in the field of public relations. Chapter 9 deals specifically with the public.

16

Checking the results means trying to determine as accurately as possible just how well the school has realized the stated objectives of its public relations program. Estimates can be made from casual observations, and quantitative measures of activity may prove helpful in arriving at judgments as to outcomes. As useful as these procedures are at times, they fail to yield the kind of data which indicate changes that have taken place in public attitudes, feelings, and opinions.

As will be discussed in this chapter, opinion polling and surveys of citizen demands are the only reliable means available for checking the nature of outcomes. From the information procured by polls and surveys, changes can be noted from one period of time to another, issues defined, and a redirection of effort plotted that is in line with the findings.

THE FIREMEN'S CAMPAIGN

Because opinion polls and surveys of citizen demands apply just as much to measurement in business and other types of public relations as they do to educational public relations, a recent campaign, conducted by the Fire Department of Jersey City, New Jersey, will be used to illustrate some of the techniques involved and the value of the information that was obtained.

The Jersey City firemen sought to reduce their work week from fifty-six hours to forty-two. They decided to bring their request to the people in the form of a referendum at the polls. Since a reduction of fourteen hours for nearly four hundred firemen would necessitate the hiring of more men and, of course, raise the tax rate, the firemen had to establish a close relationship with the taxpayers and gain the sympathy of the community.

The firemen realized that they would have to raise a large war chest to support their public relations program. Like most groups of this kind, the fire department had had little or no organized public relations. Although firemen had served the community well not only in the line of duty but also in their off-duty hours by playing benefit ball games, donating blood, and participating in many other civic and charitable activities, the public was not generally aware of the firemen's important role in society. Hence a job had to be done in a few months that should have been done over the course of several years. The firemen were in the position of the small boy who is good just before Christmas. The public is always somewhat nettled when it hears of the wonderful work an organization is doing a few months before the organization seeks its approval and support. To attempt to overcome this attitude, the firemen had to be especially careful in guiding the course of their public relations program.

They planned an extensive campaign covering some areas thoroughly, some moderately, and others not at all. Much money and time were spent on this campaign, which if successful, was to be a milestone in the careers of all the city's firemen. But how did the firemen know they were approaching their problem in the best way? Should the area they were covering extensively be covered only lightly or not at all? How were the people reacting? Was their campaign winning them a good percentage of potential votes? Or was it actually losing votes? They would not know until after the votes were counted. Then, however, it would be too late to do anything. There would not be the opportunity to correct mistakes.

It is very important to know the effect of the public relations program while a campaign is still in progress. For one thing, this information enables an organization to change its policies, if necessary; for another, a knowledge of the thinking of the public can give a group new ideas on how to present its case.

The firemen conducted a postcard poll. The results of it gave them an indication of the effect of the first two months of their campaign. It produced a fairly sharp picture of public attitudes which enabled the firemen to pinpoint the issues with which the public was most concerned. These issues became the core of the campaign. The manner in which this public relations test was made and utilized will be referred to later in the chapter.[1]

THE PUBLIC AND THE MEDIA

No matter what media of communication are used to disseminate information to people in the community, school stories that are told can be broken down into three general classes: stories that appear to bring credit to the system and create interest in its problems; stories that may espouse the cause of education but, because of some factors in them, may at the same time be detrimental to the public relations program; and stories that appear destined to undo months of hard work in establishing better understanding between the school and the public they serve.

On the other hand, it is not always safe to place a story in one of these categories. Many times a story is estimated as being favorable to education, yet the public reacts differently. For example, a story telling of work begun on long-needed repairs to an old school would seem to be the kind of a story that would place the school system in the favorable eye of the public. If

[1] For a comprehensive study of the Jersey City firemen's campaign see *International Fire Fighter*, Vol. XLII (June 1959), pp. 2–4.

the cost of the work is reasonable, if the need is great, if the potential lift to the morale of students, parents, and faculty is obvious, then there should be no reason to suspect that the overall effect of the story would not be positive. It seems reasonable to assume the public, in reading about this reasonably-priced improvement, should feel that school administrators are doing their job well, are conscious of the taxpayer's pocketbook, and are meeting the nationwide demand for improving schools.

Even a positive step such as this could boomerang, as far as public opinion is concerned. If you are in a community that has many schools, it is quite possible that teachers and parents of children in one or several others will become infuriated that similar work is not being undertaken in their buildings. Even if the school being replaced is in more urgent need of improvements, the possibility of ill feeling still exists. It is natural for parents to want the best for their children. This and the pride that teachers have for their own school bring about a self-inflicted myopia to the problems of the entire system.

Unfortunately, conditions may exist that cause a board of education to repair one school that is not in as bad a condition as another. Perhaps the latter building requires extensive work and there is not enough money on hand to go into a complete rehabilitation program. Therefore the board may decide to clean up a few minor repairs with the money that is available. This, of course, causes a furor among parents and teachers of the school needing the repairs most. And on the surface it would seem to be a just complaint.

Sometimes stories appear destined for the third category, namely, those which seem severely critical of the school system but actually are not. For example, suppose a newspaper takes the school system to task for refusing to adopt a more forward-looking view in its educational philosophy. Despite its position, it may in time become increasingly apparent that many parents prefer stricter adherence to the fundamentals and a more rigorous type of mental discipline. Accordingly, they represent a bloc of public opinion that is favorable to the school in spite of the attack by the newspaper and the readers who believe that the paper is right.

THE INTANGIBLES

It is evident that in evaluating the effect of newspaper and magazine stories, radio broadcasts, and television shows, measures of space and time received are not enough. They help in getting an idea of exposure to the public, and they are worth keeping if for no other reason than to show the Doubting Thomases that school stories make news and that there is an important place for this news in the media field. The real point, however, is that there are too many intangibles that make judgments difficult. The reader may not see the story. He may react to it differently than expected. The language of the story may not leave the message intended. The reader may sympathize with the school problem but dismiss it from his mind seconds after reading it and forget it for good the next day. Newspaper analysts say that some people pay more attention to three-paragraph "brights" than they do to stories that extend for five and six columns across the top of a page. The way a story is played, i.e., the headline used, the type of print, the borders to decorate it, and the photographs to illustrate it, have a bearing on the number of people who at least glance at it. It cannot be said that because X number of people saw a story in the paper that X number of people will be moved to think more favorably of the school system.

There is only one way to get any reliable and valid information on how people are reacting to the public relations program and that is to go to the people themselves. The question, then, is how does a school system tap this source of information in order to find out what it wants to know?

PROBLEMS OF INTERVIEWING

If the source involved is small, such as a college faculty of thirty or more, for example, it is not too difficult to deal with this public directly. Group discussions, private interviews, requests for suggestions from the staff, and even questionnaires may be used as means of gauging the effect of a public relations program. There would seem to be less chance of error in working with a small group than in spot-checking a large one. In the former case all members of the faculty can be checked, whereas only a sample can be taken when a group runs into the thousands. And yet this is not necessarily the case. When the group is small there is a closer relationship between the members and their superiors, hence when they are asked questions, geared to determine the progress of public relations, they are apt to drape their answers in optimism, or they may find it more difficult to speak frankly.

Vance Packard in *The Hidden Persuaders* points out that people are often not willing to give a candid reply to a question because it may reveal too much of their personal habits to the interviewer. He writes:

The Advertising Research Foundation took magazines to task for asking people what magazines they read frequently, and naively accepting the answers given as valid. The people, it contended, are likely to admit reading only magazines of prestige value. One investigator suggests that if you seriously accepted people's answers you might assume that *Atlantic Monthly* is America's most read: whereas actually the confession magazines in question may have twenty times the readership of *Atlantic Monthly*. . . .[2]

In another case the institute asked a group of people if they borrowed money from personal-loan companies. Every person said no. Some of them virtually shouted their answer. The truth was that all those selected for interviewing were people who were listed in the records of a local loan company as borrowers.[3]

On the other hand, testing the reaction of a large audience is not as difficult as it seems. It is true that only a fraction of the public can be polled. It is likewise true that many safeguards must be taken to insure a reasonable degree of accuracy. Never-

[2] Vance Packard, *The Hidden Persuaders* (New York: David McKay Company, Inc., 1957), p. 14.
[3] *Ibid.*, p. 15.

theless, a poll of a large audience has the advantage of achieving responses that are much more candid than could be obtained from polling close associates.

A study of all the known methods of checking results in public relations soon reveals that the public opinion poll is one of the most effective methods, especially in cases where the audience is large. Staff conferences, the amount of newspaper space, frequency of radio and television announcements, public response in the form of letters or increased attendance at school functions, the increase in volunteers for programs, the growth of citizens' committees, and the increased ease by which problems are solved are all indications of the progress of a public relations program. The poll, though, is the best device available for judging the public's reaction. It is not foolproof, to be sure. It cannot always be undertaken because of the cost and time involved or because of reasons peculiar to a given situation. The *Voice of America*, for example, sends thousands of feet of film overseas to the nations of the free world with the hope of giving them a better understanding of the American people. The films are sent to television stations, whose directors use them according to their own discretion. Some films are used several times, some not at all. As a result, there is little opportunity to ascertain which features are received most favorably by the many foreign audiences. To attempt to develop an accurate miniature of the vast audiences of millions of people of many races, creeds, educational backgrounds, political philosophies, and ethnic differences for the purpose of conducting polls would be too costly a task for the *Voice of America's* tight budget. Its staff must select subjects according to factors other than the reaction of their audiences. Past experiences, stories that shed new light on American democracy, and subjects that seem to have universal appeal are among the *Voice's* guideposts.

Since public opinion polls may well be the best means available of exploring that undiscovered country—the area of checking public relations results—it might be well to explain the process of conducting a poll and evaluating the results.

THE PUBLIC OPINION POLL

Although polls have not yet achieved the complete confidence of the American public, like almost everything else in our democracy, they are constantly being improved upon. Researchers have learned from the errors of the past. One of the best examples of this is the *Literary Digest* poll of the Landon-Roosevelt election of 1936. Although Roosevelt won by a landslide, capturing every state except two, the *Digest* predicted that Landon would win. The mistakes made then would not be made in a modern poll. For one thing, the sampling was poorly conceived. Many of the names selected were taken from telephone directories or lists of automobile owners. Since this was the depression era, a time when a great many people could not afford the luxuries now considered as commonplace as television sets today, the people polled were, in the main, in the upper half of the economic stratum of the nation. Because of the depression, there was a division of votes along financial lines, with the Republicans gaining more support among the upper half than the lower half. A great percentage of those polled were Republican voters. Naturally the poll could not be expected to reveal an accurate cross-section of the thinking of the people. The survey also did not take into consideration as well a substantial increase in voters since the 1932 election. Most of the new voters were in the lower income bracket, potential Democratic votes, and not reached by the questionnaires. The fact that the ballots were mailed might have had some effect on the returns. Survey experts feel that persons of high income or educational levels are more likely to return questionnaires than others. In the case of the Jersey City firemen's poll, post cards mailed to residents of low rent housing were coded. When the returns came in it was noted that the percentage of coded cards returned compared to ones sent to families of average income was about one to ten. If the experts are right, it is possible that a majority of the ballots mailed back came from high-income Republican voters in 1936.

HAZARDS IN POLLING

Another poll that caused the skeptics to shake their heads was the 1948 presidential survey by Gallop which indicated that Dewey would receive 49.5 per cent of the vote and Truman 44.5 per cent.

In a booklet published by the American Institute of Public Opinion these four factors were attributed to the results of the poll:[4]

1. Polling was terminated too early. Final interviews were completed almost a month before the election. On October 18, three days after the poll was completed, there was a drop in farm prices which probably contributed to the shift to Truman. The candidate from Missouri also had the advantage of being generally considered as the underdog, even by his own party. When Americans began to think seriously of the election in late October many followed the old American tradition of casting their weight behind the "little fellow." This, of course, was not reflected in the poll. Interviewers now work up to the Saturday before the election, telegraphing their final reports to Princeton headquarters.

2. The proportion of "undecided" voters was unusually high. The institute declares that fourteen per cent of those questioned had not made up their minds. It had been assumed that this group would vote in small numbers and could probably be eliminated from the sample. Results proved they did vote and, according to post-election tests, in favor of Truman by a three to one margin. Present pollsters question the "undecided" much more thoroughly to try to determine how they would vote if they do.

3. Wallace, who had been expected to poll 4 per cent of the total vote, actually received only 2.4 per cent with most of the difference being picked up by Truman.

4. The total vote was smaller than expected. Only 48,794,009—about 50 per cent of the potential voting population—went to the polls. Since many of these people were included in the voting sample, either directly or by representation, it necessarily followed that the results were going to be affected. Under modern methods, careful questioning is used to determine the likelihood of a citizen going to the polls, regardless of how he feels about the candidates. It is important to note that although this poll gave Dewey the largest percentage of the national vote, its margin of error was not as enormous as might be imagined, despite the four errors mentioned. Instead of receiving 44.5 per cent of the total vote, as the survey had indicated, Truman had 49.9 per cent of the vote.

[4] *The Story Behind The Gallup Poll* (Princeton, N.J.: American Institute of Public Opinion).

The margin of error was thus 5.4 per cent. In the case of Dewey, estimated to take 49.5 per cent but receiving 45.3 per cent, the margin of error was 4.2 per cent. Although the outcome was not as the poll would indicate, the margin of error was not too drastic, considering the mistakes made. Under present conditions the margin of error is usually between one and two per cent. Gallup declares that if one hundred persons, who had been carefully selected, were interviewed in a national survey, the margin of error would be 15 per cent;[5] if nine hundred were interviewed, the margin of error would drop to 5 per cent; if ten thousand were interviewed, he adds, the error potential would drop to 1.5 per cent. As the number interviewed increases the error range would continue to drop, but the actual reduction of error becomes smaller and smaller while the number interviewed becomes larger and larger, making it extremely costly to seek a margin of error much lower than 1.5 per cent.

ORGANIZING A POLL

Let us fashion a polling situation. You have spent considerable time and money on a public relations program, one of the most important facets of which is the construction of a new high school. You wonder how the public is receiving the news that local newspapers and radio and television stations have generously circulated. You are aware that the location of the proposed high school has caused a great deal of comment. Since you have several possible sites, all of which have similar advantages and disadvantages, you wonder if there is a strong feeling among residents of the community in favor of or opposed to one location. Since you seek public approval, and the construction of a high school *per se* should be a plus reaction, it would be ironic if the selection of an unpopular site negated all the good will the building of the school was expected to generate. It is necessary to ask yourself how people *really* feel about the proposed school. Have you properly prepared them for it, or do they consider it a waste which will add to their tax burden? If this is the case, what can be done to turn the public's antagonism, or apathy as may be the situation, into sympathy and enthusiasm? Are there any objections besides the cost?

[5] George Gallup, *A Guide To Public Opinion Polls* (Princeton, N.J.: Princeton University, 1944).

You decide to conduct a poll and use the information gathered to evaluate your public relations program. You have two choices: will you do it yourself or will you hire an outside agency? Cost may influence your decision. Although it is usually more expensive to have an outside concern conduct your poll, you must weigh the cost against the importance of having as accurate and successful a poll as possible. You alone know your own facilities. If you feel you have aides who are competent to carry on the task and have the time to do so, and the information sought is not too complex to break down, you will probably decide to conduct your own poll.

MANNER OF COMMUNICATION

The next decision to make is the manner of communication —by cards, letters, or by interview. If you select the former method you have the choice of mailing the ballots. Mailing is more expensive, not only because of the postage involved but also because of the time required for addressing. If interviewers are utilized, they should be selected with care since a good deal of the success of the poll depends upon the relationship between the poll-takers and the public. Courtesy and common sense on the part of the interviewer go a long way in guaranteeing the maximum number of accurate answers.

FRAMING THE QUESTIONNAIRE

The method of polling determined, you can go about defining your problem and asking yourself what information you are seeking. Questions should be worded with care. Remember many people answer queries by saying what they are expected to say, not what they actually feel. Others may not understand the question and, rather than appear ignorant, will guess at its meaning, giving an inaccurate reply. Many times the public is confused by the categories offered to them. For example, if a person is in favor of the construction of the new high school, but is not certain of the degree of his interest, he may be perplexed by a question like this:

Do you think the proposed high school is
- *a*) Essential to our community?
- *b*) Important to our community?
- *c*) Fairly important?
- *d*) Needed, but not at this time?
- *e*) Needed, but too costly?
- *f*) Unnecessary?
- *g*) An utter waste?

The nature of the alternatives seems certain to cause the interviewee to respond erroneously, despite himself. He is in favor of the school, but doubts that he feels that it is essential. He may answer "Needed, but not at this time" because in his haste to complete the questionnaire he responds to whatever category sticks in his mind. And yet he may really be in favor of immediate construction. If there had been a question, "Do you think delay in construction of the high school would impair the education of our youth?" he might very well answer in the affirmative despite his previous response.

THE DANGER OF "LEADING"

Questions should be worded to yield the information being sought. Sometimes the questions are slanted to give a favorable reaction. For example, many people opposed to a new high school, might not reveal their true attitude when asked: "Do you think our youth deserve better facilities in this scientific age?" By answering "no" a citizen might feel that he becomes a combination of Ebenezer Scrooge, Iago, and Simon Legree. Although this query is an exaggerated version of some of the questions asked in polls, it serves to give an idea of the temptation to lead your public to tell you what you want to hear, not necessarily what is true. Of course, a number of queries like this would invalidate the entire poll.

If possible, the language should be framed in such a way that the person interviewed is unaware of the purpose of the answer. When he does not know what is expected of him, he may merely write what he feels, which is the information you are seeking.

PRE-TESTING

Since post card or letter surveys, and interview polls involve printing and other costs, it is well to test the poll by sampling a small group of people before sending the final draft to the printers. These pre-poll tests often reveal faults in wording, the double-meaning of questions, or the slim possibilities of obtaining comprehensive replies to certain types of questions. When these instances are noted before the poll is distributed to the public, a more accurate survey is assured and the extra expense of re-printing is eliminated. Sometimes a single ambiguous phrase, which may pass undetected by the authors of the poll, may seriously harm the effectiveness of the survey. A pre-poll brings most of these errors to light. It is important to remember that many people are confused by any type of questionnaire. The vast number of people who still fill in the blank after "Race" by writing "Human" is proof of the importance of simplicity and preciseness in wording. In their poll the Jersey City firemen sent out two attached post cards. Each bore a government-engraved stamp. All an addressee had to do was fill out his answers and drop the card in the mailbox. Yet a few went to the trouble of pasting stamps over the perfectly good stamp engraved on the card. The firemen had been advised by a postal employee not to use a permit with return postage guaranteed if they wanted to have the maximum number of cards returned. The postal clerk declared that many people still did not understand this process and felt it was necessary to place a stamp on the card. The inconvenience of hunting up a stamp would deter many from mailing the card back. Errors in filling out forms and confusion about postal privileges do not necessarily imply ignorance on the part of some of the public. Bank presidents and ditch-diggers, college professors and dish-washers have made the same simple errors in filling out questionnaires.

SELECTING THE PUBLIC

The next question to ask yourself is, "whom do I want to

poll?" Usually it is not necessary to consider the entire population. Generally, the opinion of children is not required. If a vote is involved, you may eliminate all those under 21 unless you wish the sentiment of those who will be eligible to vote in the next few years. In some school issues the opinion of parents may be the only pertinent ones. Sometimes the information sought may be of such a limited nature that only parents of public school children need be queried. In more specific instances only parents who reside in a certain section of the community or whose children attend a certain school constitute the public. Environment, financial status, education, and many other factors may determine the nature of the public to be polled. Each time a poll is taken, the opinions of a different public may be sought. Once the limitations on the population have been decided, a sample may be selected.

SAMPLING

A sample is to a public as an architect's model of a skyscraper is to the finished structure. Just as the model building contains every detail in miniature, so too must the sample have the exact characteristics of the population that is being polled. If 40 per cent of the public is Democratic, 40 per cent Republican and 20 per cent independent, the sample should be broken down accordingly, unless political persuasion is not pertinent to the poll. Cross-sections generally include a proportionate breakdown in age, sex, color, race, financial status, environment, educational background, religion, occupation, and other areas which affect man's thinking. A good sample will have the exact percentage of doctors, lawyers or whatever the case may be in its miniature as is present in the community. It is important to realize that every one does not have an opinion on an issue, although relatively few care to admit it. Even many of those who have opinions, or claim to have them, do not really possess opinions of their own. They are easily influenced by their articulate friends, by what they read in the papers, by their clergyman, by the advice of an esteemed member of the community, by a glib-speaking politician, by their wives, or by their barbers. In Jersey City, a prominent politician gave a spirited address that was thunderously received by his constituents, one of whom remarked afterwards to a friend, "You missed a wonderful speech. It was marvelous." "What did he speak on?" his friend asked. "Oh, I don't know," came the reply, "but it was wonderful." The reaction of the crowd had caused this hero-worshipper to accept the talk without listening to it or understanding what was said.

There are certain men and women who affect opinions—I mentioned clergymen, respected civic leaders, wives, politicians and barbers. Teachers, doctors, lawyers, gossips, newspaper editors, bartenders, and men and women who are quick to express their feelings on a subject are leaders, informing and passing on opinions. The number of people who do not explore subjects for themselves but prefer to borrow the ideas of others is beyond estimation. Because of this, the opinions of those who think for themselves or who are quick to adopt and pass on the ideas of others should be the aim of poll-takers, if possible. Each of these opinions should be worth many passive views. Of course, the number of these people interviewed should be in direct proportion to the number of men and women of these walks of life in the community.

SIZE OF THE SAMPLE

Although many people feel that one of the most important elements in polling is the size of the sample, experts contend that the size is relatively unimportant providing the sample itself represents an accurate cross-section of the community.

Gallup cites a poll on the nation's attitude on prohibition, taken by the American Institute of Public Opinion in 1944, as an example of the minute changes in the results of a poll despite enlargement.[6] He declares that this particular poll was selected

[6] George Gallup, *op. cit.*, pp. 13–14.

entirely at random from the many others that might have been chosen.

In the first national sample on the prohibition question 1,327 carefully selected persons were interviewed. This sum was divided into three areas of approximately the same number. Of this first group of 442, 31 per cent declared they favored the return of prohibition, 62 per cent opposed its return, and 7 per cent stated they had no opinion or were undecided. The totals of the first group were added to the totals of the other two and it was found that 30 per cent (1 per cent more) opposed its return and 7 per cent (the same amount) had no opinion. Subsequently a total of 12,494 persons were interviewed with 32 per cent (one more than the original) favoring prohibition; 61 per cent (one less than the original) opposing it, and 7 per cent still with no opinion. Gallup's point is that while the number interviewed contributes to the accuracy of the poll, this same number reaches a saturation point after a time, bringing on unnecessary costs. He also points to a question concerning the National Recovery Act, "Would you like to see the N.R.A. revived?" which was conducted by the American Institute of Public Opinion in 1936. After the first 500 ballots were cast, 54.9 per cent indicated they were opposed to revival of the National Recovery Act. When 30,000 ballots were examined, the number against return of the National Recovery Act was estimated at 55.5 per cent.[7] Once again the addition of more interviews did not change the results of the poll to any great extent. Thus a few hundred carefully selected interviews should provide more accurate results than thousands of interviews taken at random.

THE 1944 GALLUP PROHIBITION POLL[8]

Persons favoring the return of prohibition	137 or 31%
Persons opposing the return of prohibition	276 or 62%
Those without opinions or undecided	29 or 7%
Total	442

[7] *Ibid.*, p. 15.
[8] *Ibid.*, p. 14.

When results of the second and third samples are added to the figures given above, the following totals emerge:

	Favor prohibition	Oppose prohibition	No opinion
First sample of 442	31%	62%	7%
First and second samples totaling 884	29%	63%	8%
First, second and third samples totaling 1,327	30%	63%	7%

Additional surveys were conducted on this issue until a total of 12,494 persons had been interviewed, with results as follows:

	Favor prohibition	Oppose prohibition	No opinion
When 2,585 persons had been interviewed	31%	61%	8%
When 5,255 persons had been interviewed	33%	59%	8%
When 8,253 persons had been interviewed	32%	60%	8%
When 12,494 persons had been interviewed	32%	61%	7%

INTERPRETING THE RESULTS

Let us suppose that one of the questions you asked was, "Do you favor the proposed new high school?" If the response showed 80 per cent in favor, 14 per cent opposed, and 6 per cent without opinion, you can be reasonably sure that at least the plan to build a new school meets with the approval of the majority. The wider the range, and 80–14 is a very wide range, the more certain you can be of the "pro" and "con" aspect of the question. If, for example, 48 per cent had favored the proposed school, 46 per cent opposed it, and 6 per cent had lacked opinions, it would be difficult to assume that, generally speaking, the majority of the community was in favor of the new school because the poll had indicated that not even half of those interviewed wanted it to be constructed. Since the difference between the "pros" and the "cons" was only 2 per cent, even the chance of a small margin of error was enough to reverse the results of the poll.

Questions such as this give a general idea on the subject but do not tell how seriously the public regards it. These types of queries also fail to tell the reasons behind the opinions of the citizens. It is one thing to have a general idea of the attitude of the public; it is another to discover the motivations of people and ways to supply reasons to change thinking that may be detrimental to your school system. To do this, it is necessary to ask a series of specific, detailed questions, concentrating on the "whys."

LIMITATIONS

In evaluating the results of the poll you should always keep in mind its limitations. Even if the participants of the survey answered the questions candidly they may not represent a clear-cut cross section of the thinking of the community. Many factors are involved. Maybe the issue at stake is not a real problem to those who are interviewed. In this case, you could expect answers that are not carefully thought out. When people are in a hurry, when they do not fully understand the question, or when they have a difficult time selecting the proper alternative in the poll, the results will suffer.

ANALYZING THE RESULTS

Once aware of the possible limitations of your poll, you can check it against the original plans of your public relations campaign. You may find that some of the projects you began in order to inspire public interest in your schools were the cause of many people staying away from parent-teacher and citizen meetings. You may find that some programs which you had regarded lightly are, in effect, the core of your public relations. You may receive the reassurance that projects upon which you spent a great deal of time have brought many parents closer to their children's teachers and schools. The results will tell you in what areas to concentrate and in what areas to lessen your activities.

Polls have been used to determine whether the school story is reaching the citizens of your community. It would be futile to expect public support and cooperation if parents and civic leaders have not been reading your school story in the local press or hearing about it on radio and television.

HOW THE SCHOOL STORY IS RECEIVED

A survey conducted by the Montclair, New Jersey, school system gave a good indication of the way the citizens learned about their schools. Asked what was their main source of information on their schools, 449 persons answered this way:

Children	136
Neighbors	95
School People	63
Newspapers	122
Other Sources	33

Thus, by learning that children and newspapers were the best means of bringing the school story home, the public relations director was able to point out to teachers the importance of the little public relations ambassador with the curly hair and freckles and also to put more time into newspaper releases and suggestions for feature articles.

The same poll listed 12 newspapers in the Montclair area. Citizens were asked to check the papers which brought them the news of school activities in their community. This was another aid in evaluating the influence of various newspapers to a school system. As is almost always the case, the greatest percentage of people read the Montclair school story in the local paper. However, a considerable number declared that the New York City papers had been their source for school news in Montclair.

INTEREST IN SCHOOL STORIES

Another question sought to determine the regularity with which residents read school stories in the press. The answers were:

Usually	147 or 58.3%
Sometimes	67 or 26.6%
Seldom	19 or 7.5%
Never	12 or 4.7%
No Answer	7 or 2.7%

With 58.3 per cent reading school stories on a regular basis, the Montclair school system was in a good position to ask the press for even more extensive coverage. Editors know that their best stories are rarely read *in toto* by half of their readers. Advertising managers often receive premium rates for pages that have better than 50 per cent readership. At the same time the poll indicates the value of a possible campaign by the school system to have more citizens read about their school in the press. A newsletter to the parents and announcements by the teachers to their students often help in this regard.

Another question, the responses to which must have been particularly gratifying to the public relations department, involved the school system's task of supplying citizens with enough news about their schools. To this 159 or 63 per cent answered "yes"; 42 or 16.6 per cent said "no"; and 51 or 20.4 per cent did not answer. Even the fact that 16.6 per cent said no is encouraging because it might indicate that some of the citizens were so interested in their schools they wanted more information on them than they were then receiving.

THE DENVER STUDIES

The Denver, Colorado, school system conducts a survey of their schools every three years. After asking the broad question, "In general, would you say the Denver Public Schools are doing a good job, just a fair job, or a poor job of educating children these days?" the poll tries to pinpoint the areas of criticism. A decrease in complaints in certain areas indicates that the survey has been useful in letting educators know what phases of their program require special attention. Answers to the general questions in 1950, 1953, and 1956 are as follows:[9]

[9] *Denver Looks At Its Schools* (Denver, Colorado, 1956), p. 2.

	1950	1953	1956
Good job	49%	59%	53%
Fair job	35%	31%	35%
Poor job	5%	4%	4%
No Opinion	11%	6%	8%

An increase in "Good Job" from 49 per cent in 1950 to 59 per cent in 1953 seems to be due in part to improvements in the teaching of English and the teaching of fundamentals. In 1950 English was criticized by twenty-eight parents of each hundred as compared to five per hundred in 1953; fundamentals in general by twelve in 1950 as compared to five in 1953.[10]

In 1956 Denver showed less good ratings, more fair ratings, and the same percentage of poor ratings as it had in 1953. Detailed questioning indicated that one of the main reasons for the decline in good ratings was a dislike for growing crowded schools.[11]

Other areas covered in the polls included instruction techniques, discipline, teacher qualifications, grading and promotion practices, extracurricular activities, teacher-pupil relations, teacher-parent relations, personality development, the health program, the curriculum, and athletics. The comments citizens made in these areas helped to determine why they had given the school a good, fair, or poor rating.

POLLS REVEAL STRANGE THINGS

In University City, Missouri, one thousand carefully sampled residents were asked about what percentage of their property tax went to schools. Almost 79 per cent declared they did not know. The 21 per cent that answered made a wide span of estimates, ranging from five per cent or less to more than 50 per cent.

Asked how much a year was spent per child in the University City public schools, 64.9 per cent of one thousand respondents said they didn't know; 4.5 per cent said $100 or less; 5.7 per

[10] *Ibid.* (1953), p. 4.
[11] *Ibid.* (1956), p. 3.

cent said $101 to $200; 6.8 per cent said $201 to $300; 4.8 per cent said $301 to $400; 6 per cent said $401 to $500 and 7.3 per cent said over $500. Only 6 per cent knew; the average was $450.[12]

This is a solid indication that many people do not know what is going on in their schools. When 82 per cent of one thousand respondents admitted they had never attended a University City school board meeting, this finding gave some idea of the amount of interest in school affairs. This, of course, is not an accurate barometer because many parents who do not attend board meetings do attend parent-teachers conferences and similar school activities. There seems to be a general aversion on the part of the public to attending board of education meetings. Over the past eight years in Jersey City, which has a population of 300,000 of which 170,000 are adults, an average of one hundred attend the monthly board meetings or about .0006 per cent of the adult population. The largest attendance in the past ten years was about six hundred or about .0035 per cent of the population. Since the same people do not attend every meeting, the percentage of the adult population that has ever attended a session would be higher, but probably not as high as the 17.1 per cent figure the University City poll produced. Extensive public relations are needed to increase attendance at board meetings in most parts of the nation.

THE UNDISCOVERED COUNTRY

Despite the more extended use of public opinion polls in school systems, the increasing number of staff questionnaires, the sympathetic attitude of the press in publishing and interpreting school news, the process of checking the results in school public relations is still almost unexplored. Although much material has been published on public relations since its infancy in the 1930's, when only a handful of names were listed under the heading of

[12] *University City Schools*, University City, Missouri, Vol. XV, No. 5 (January 1959), p. 2.

"Public Relations" in the Yellow Pages of the New York telephone book, little research has been devoted to testing public relations programs while they are being carried on. Public Relations specialists are always eager to study successful procedures with the hope of utilizing them in their own communities. However, it is for the public relations men and women of the future to venture deeper into that undiscovered country of testing devices, wherein may lie the secrets that will insure the successful public relations programs of tomorrow.

BIBLIOGRAPHY

Cantril, Hadley, *Gauging Public Opinion*. Princeton, N.J.: Princeton University Press, 1944. Chap. 12. Cantril explains in detail how small samples may be used effectively.

Denver Looks At Its Schools. Denver, Colorado, 1953, 1956, 1959. Three booklets featuring highlights from opinion studies of the Denver Public Schools. The 1953 and 1956 pamphlets make comparisons with previous surveys.

Feel Their Pulse: A Guide To School Opinion Polling. Washington, D.C.: National School Public Relations Association, 1956. A concise and clear explanation of how to organize and administer an opinion poll.

Gallup, George, *A Guide To Public Opinion Polls*. Princeton, N.J.: Princeton University Press, 1944. A list of 80 pertinent questions and answers on public opinion polls, covering such vital areas as the size of the sample, the cross-section, and polling accuracy.

Parten, Mildred, *Surveys, Polls and Samples: Practical Procedures*. New York: Harper & Brothers, 1950. A detailed and technical discussion of survey and poll procedures that is easy to read and follow.

Stein, Herman, *Measuring Your Public Relations*. New York: National Publicity Council, 1952. Although this pamphlet deals with Public Relations in fund-raising campaigns, it is also a valuable aid in setting up a public opinion poll for schools.

Stephen, Frederick F. and Philip J. McCarthy, *Sampling Opinions*. New York: John Wiley & Sons, Inc., 1958. A technical volume of polling procedures that brings together research findings and their application.

The Story Behind The Gallup Poll. Princeton, N.J.: The American Institute of Public Opinion. A brochure explaining the operation of the Gallup Poll. Although much of this text is devoted to political polls, the booklet sheds some interesting light on the thinking of the "common man."

West Virginia Appraises Schools and School Taxes. Princeton, N.J.: Princeton Research Service, January 13, 1958. An opinion study for the West Virginia Education Association. A survey to determine how the people of West Virginia felt their tax dollar was being spent on education.